D0560391

MADELEINE ALBRIGHT

and the

*New American
Diplomacy*

MADELEINE ALBRIGHT

and the

New American

Diplomacy

~

THOMAS W. LIPPMAN

Westview Press
A Member of the Perseus Books Group

All rights reserved. Printed in the United States of America. No part of this publication may be reproduced or transmitted in any form or by any means, electronic or mechanical, including photocopy, recording, or any information storage and retrieval system, without permission in writing from the publisher.

Copyright © 2000 by Thomas W. Lippman

Published in 2000 in the United States of America by Westview Press, 5500 Central Avenue, Boulder, Colorado 80301-2877, and in the United Kingdom by Westview Press, 12 Hid's Copse Road, Cumnor Hill, Oxford OX2 9JJ

Find us on the World Wide Web at www.westviewpress.com

Text design by Cynthia Young
Set in 11-point New Baskerville by the Perseus Books Group

A CIP record for this book is available from the Library of Congress.
ISBN 0-8133-9767-7

The paper used in this publication meets the requirements of the American National Standard for Permanence of Paper for Printed Library Materials Z39.48-1984.

10   9   8   7   6   5   4   3   2   1

For Jessica, Elizabeth, and Steven

CONTENTS

PREFACE

DIPLOMACY, THE ART and practice of negotiation between nations, is by its nature conducted mostly through private conversations and the exchange of confidential documents. The same is true for the formulation of foreign policy within the United States government, where the announcement of a new position on any issue is usually preceded by weeks or months of undisclosed meetings and negotiations among the officials involved.

There is, of course, a substantial public component to the conduct of international affairs. Foreign ministers and ambassadors use public statements and news conferences to explain their policies, seek support for them, and put pressure on other countries in the negotiations of the moment. But the actual give and take of bargaining—if you let us keep troops here, we will make more water available there—is carried out behind closed doors. Most of the time, the press and public learn of some negotiated agreement or policy initiative only when this secret work has been completed and the outcome is announced. The conversations and documents containing proposals and counterproposals are not made public until years afterward.

Sometimes, the cloak of secrecy extends even to the fact that negotiations are taking place at all, the best known recent example being the breakthrough negotiations between Israel and the Palestinians in Norway, which began as clandestine, unofficial meetings of self-appointed emissaries.

For journalists assigned to write about national security and foreign policy matters, the challenge is to find out about such events and initiatives as they are happening, rather than wait for official announcements, and to obtain confidential appraisals from the officials involved to help us explain them. To the extent that we are able to do so, we are indebted to people with access to nonpublic information. The source may be a member of Congress or a congressional staff member who has been briefed on a policy initiative and for whatever reason doesn't like it; disclosing the initiative might head it off. Or the source could be a foreign diplomat who feels that his or her country is getting the short end of some negotiation. It could be a well-placed person within the State Department with whom the journalist has been friendly for many years and who is willing to exceed his or her authority to help the reporter. Or it could be the secretary of state herself or someone authorized by her to disseminate nonpublic information in an effort to advance some argument or policy decision while retaining the ability to deny it if the reception is unfavorable.

In the nine years I wrote about security and foreign policy issues for the *Washington Post,* from the Iraqi invasion of Kuwait in 1990 to the war against Yugoslavia, I received many such "background" briefings and unauthorized disclosures. This was a tribute less to my journalistic skill than to the prominence of my newspaper, which along with the *New York Times* is the preferred conduit for many officials and diplomats who wish to influence or promote American foreign policy.

Such disclosures and unofficial conversations are essential to journalists trying to understand and explain the evolution and conduct of American foreign policy. Information from such contacts often appears in print attributed to anonymous "officials" or unidentified diplomats. In this book, however, I have tried to minimize the use of unattributed quotations and disembodied information. Experience has taught us that such material, however essential to the practice of daily journalism, irritates readers and arouses their suspicions.

Madeleine K. Albright has made this book easier to write without the benefit of anonymous information because she has been an extraordinarily visible and outspoken secretary of state. Most of the time, her own words are the best guide to what she is thinking and what she is trying to accomplish, and I have cited them extensively.

A nearly complete record of her speeches, news conferences, television appearances, and question-and-answer sessions with audiences is posted, in chronological order, on the State Department's World Wide Web site at [www.state.gov]. The site also contains an extensive archive of public statements by other senior State Department officials, arranged by subject matter. The Internet has become the U.S. government's principal tool for communicating with the public about the activities of its peripatetic chief diplomat and about the evolving relations between this country and the rest of the world.

Opening the State Department's public files to instant worldwide access is just one small indicator of the ways in which American diplomacy is changing at the advent of a new century. Madeleine Albright, a secretary of state like no other, has tried to renovate diplomacy in theory and practice to reflect—and to promote—the inevitable evolution of her adopted country's global role. This is the story of that effort, to which she has brought boundless enthusiasm, an immense capacity for work, and an absolute confidence in the special talents of women.

Thomas W. Lippman

Chapter 1

I LOOK PRETTY GOOD IN A STETSON

THE GOSPEL-ROCK voices of the Knights for Christ Singers swelled through the hall. The audience clapped and swayed. And then the Reverend Lewis M. Anthony, smartly turned out in a cherry-red suit with matching derby hat, stepped forward to present the guest of honor, "the baddest thing this side of heaven"— Madeleine K. Albright, the secretary of state, emissary to the world of the United States of America.

The setting was not some inner-city church but the Dean Acheson auditorium in the stuffy State Department headquarters building in Washington. Albright, just back from a grueling round-the-world trip, was celebrating Black History Month with rank-and-file employees.

Welcomed by a standing ovation from the mostly black crowd, Albright joined them and the beaming Anthony in belting out "Lift Every Voice in Song," the harmonies spilling out into the normally hushed corridors. At its conclusion, Albright took the microphone to make a promise: She would not sing solo. "I've been called many names since I was named secretary of state," she said. "To my regret, Aretha was not one of them."

This allusion to the popular African-American singer Aretha Franklin, delivered as an inside joke between cultural soulmates, drew laughter and more applause from the delighted workers. Career employees of the State Department, they had never heard any secretary of state speak to them this way. And that was the idea. Madeleine Albright wanted it known that she was as different from her predecessors as a pink skirt is from a pinstriped suit. Hurricane Madeleine was blowing through the decorous halls of diplomacy, which would never be the same.

~

Madeleine Korbel Albright was in the right place at the right time.

When President Bill Clinton selected her in December 1996 to be secretary of state in his second term, political Washington and the American media were hungry for a new star. The United States was prosperous and secure, but inside the Beltway there was a celebrity vacuum. In the capital's fickle culture of transient acclaim, the novelty of Bill and Hillary Clinton and their Arkansas cronies had long since worn off. Newt Gingrich, the hot ticket of the Republican takeover of the House of Representatives two years earlier, had been diminished by miscalculation and scandal. Colin Powell had taken himself off the screen. General Norman Schwarzkopf was history; so was Ross Perot. Bob Dole, thrashed by Clinton in the 1996 election, was making television commercials. Vice President Al Gore was boring. Ron Brown was dead. Monica Lewinsky had not yet surfaced. Who was there to get excited about?

Then Clinton nominated Albright, who was permanent representative, or ambassador, to the United Nations in his first term. She would be the first female secretary of state in the nation's history and the highest-ranking woman ever to serve in the executive branch of government. It was the perfect moment for the tough-talking, wisecracking former Georgetown University professor to command the stage, and she was ready. She sought the job and accepted it eagerly, making no pretense of reluctance and offering no sham modesty about her credentials. She loves being a celebrity, and she understood from the start that personal fame and popularity could be effective levers in negotiations with Congress and with foreign leaders. Unlike the monochromatic Sandra Day O'Connor, the first woman to serve on the Supreme Court, Albright appeared all over town—and all over the television screen—in bright suits and eye-catching jewelry. She craved acclaim and embraced it without embarrassment. Instantly, she became a magazine-cover celebrity and a household name; the afternoon after Clinton announced her appointment, passengers on an Amtrak train taking her back to her job at the United Nations in New York cheered and applauded, asking for autographs as she worked her way through the cars.

Political Washington, including Republicans in Congress who invited her to visit their districts, embraced her. *Newsweek* and *Vogue* published admiring profiles. She appeared on *60 Minutes* and *Larry King Live*. Dignitaries from overseas praised her and sought her attention. The *Wall Street Journal*'s Al Hunt gushed over her "abundance of smarts, charm, toughness, and political prowess."[1] Schoolgirls wrote her touching letters.

Albright was recognized everywhere she went and was ogled as though she were a show-business celebrity.

When she went to the ladies' room at the Washington Hilton Hotel during the annual White House correspondents' dinner, other women inside—tourists and hotel guests—pulled cameras out of their purses and snapped her picture. In Milwaukee, she got a standing ovation from workers at a Harley-Davidson motorcycle engine factory, whom she buttered up with remarks about the "land of the cheeseheads," in reference to Green Bay Packers fans who wear hats shaped like wedges of cheese. *Vanity Fair* put her at the top of its list of the 200 most influential women in America, ahead of Hillary Rodham Clinton, Tipper Gore, the women on the U.S. Supreme Court, Janet Reno, Martha Stewart, and Katie Couric. "Albright battles superbly in velvet gloves," the magazine burbled.[2] Even after she had been in office two years and the early raves were inevitably being soured by criticism as troubles mounted overseas, she rated an admiring cover profile in the Gannett newspaper chain's Sunday supplement, which saluted her as "The Most Powerful Woman in the World."[3]

Guests at the Laromme Hotel in Jerusalem found in their rooms a photograph of Albright with the hotel's public relations manager, Anat-Adi Atis, with this comment: "It's wonderful to experience the promotion of women in the hotel industry. It always makes me proud to welcome those women who really make a difference in world, like Madeleine Albright."

The owner of an art gallery in Philadelphia, struck by Albright's habit of wearing pins and brooches appropriate to the diplomatic theme of the day—such as the dove of peace she wore in Israel—invited jewelry designers around the word to create pins in tribute to Albright. (One of them, by the American designer Daniel Jocz, depicted a fist striking a distorted face, celebrating Albright as "a person able to deliver the ultimate punch in negotiations." Another, by designer Merrily Tompkins, was presented as "a brooch for Madeleine Albright to wear when she visits people who condone the practice of female genital mutilation.") The collection, assembled in a show called "Brooching It Diplomatically: A Tribute to Madeleine K. Albright," toured museums in Belgium, Estonia, and Finland as well as the United States.

In Vancouver, Washington, 5,000 people, half of them students, packed a high school gym to hear her speak, and gave her a foot-pounding welcome worthy of a rock star. They cheered enthusiastically when Mayor Royce Pollard introduced her as "a wonderful example of the very best in public service." Teenagers scrambled across rows of seats to get in position to snap her picture.

When six girls there interviewed Albright for the high school newspaper, she wowed them with what she called the most important advice she could give to young women trying to make their way in a competitive world: "Interrupt!"—that is, don't wait for men to solicit your input. She said she learned that lesson while teaching at Georgetown, where she instituted a no-handraising rule. If students were told to raise their hands before speaking, she said, the women tended to do so, politely waiting to be recognized, whereas the men would speak right up.

Albright had been telling that story for years, but the young interviewers had no way of knowing that; it was all new to them. Their breathless account of the encounter ended with these words: "The Albright interview was an event which will always be remembered by those who participated. The group's opinion was summed up by [Liz] Harper in just four words: 'What an amazing woman!'" The headline called it "The Interview of a Lifetime."[4]

Albright was elected to the National Women's Hall of Fame in Seneca Falls, New York, even though, as she said at her induction ceremony, she could not "sing like Ella Fitzgerald, write like Emily Dickinson, act like Helen Hayes, or shoot like Annie Oakley." Surrounded by admiring women, she hailed the "courage, vision, and brilliance of our foremothers" in building the nation. It was Albright in her favorite role as woman and real person, showing the folks out there in America that she was not one of those self-important Washington policy wonks.[5]

Unlike her reserved predecessor, Warren Christopher, Albright is often seen at social and theatrical events and is happy to make small talk—about gardening, children, fashion, journalism, food, whatever comes up. (I once found myself seated next to her at a dinner in Cape Town, South Africa, engaged with her and one of her assistant secretaries of state, who had just had a baby, in a discussion of whether fathers should be present in hospital delivery rooms. Albright naturally agreed that they should. On another occasion, at a trendy Asian restaurant in Seattle, she treated me to delicious, nasty gossip about a prominent hostess whom we both dislike.)

On her worldwide travels, Albright was a star and was treated like one. The only time I saw her come in second in the crowd-appeal sweepstakes was while shopping in a mall in Cape Town. She was up-staged by two other shoppers, Andre Agassi, the tennis star who was playing in a tournament there, and the actress Brooke Shields, who was then his wife.

The acclaim couldn't last, of course. Washington's fascination with celebrities is balanced by a culture of cynicism that turns on everyone sooner or later. The more adulation accorded a new star in the beginning, it seems, the more intense the disillusionment and criticism that follow; the higher the profile, the more visible and inviting the target, and nobody in Washington other than the president had a higher profile than Albright.

Albright's modern predecessors were all white men in suits, and except for Henry Kissinger their personal styles and idiosyncrasies varied only within a predictable range. Christopher, William Rogers, Cyrus Vance, Dean Rusk, Christian Herter, all spoke guardedly and played by well-known, if unwritten, rules. Albright's relative openness and flamboyance set her apart from them as much as her gender did. At first these traits were an asset, boosting her popularity with Congress and the public. But as time passed and the novelty wore off, they would become liabilities, too. Kissinger was one of the few public figures in Washington who could be voluble and still appear profound, but that was because he was duplicitous as well as brilliant. Albright is neither. She is smart and relatively straightforward, but in Washington, the more an official talks, the harder it is for that official to be perceived as deep. As time went on and trouble erupted around the world, Albright would increasingly find the currency of her word devalued by overuse and the novelty of her style diminished to some extent by its irrelevance. Her determination to be up front with the public resulted in overexposure, fostering the impression that the real foreign policy director in the administration was the much less visible, much more circumspect White House national security adviser, Samuel R. Berger, known as Sandy.

There is no specific list of qualifications required to become secretary of state. Albright's predecessors included lawyers, generals, professional diplomats, bankers, scholars, senators, and political intriguers. Other than the fact that they were all white men, they had little in common. Still, to those who knew Albright only from her résumé, she might have seemed an unlikely choice as the nation's chief diplomat and foreign policy steward. At the age of fifty-nine, she had never held or even run for elective office, never managed a major organization, never as an adult worked for a profit-making enterprise, and, like the vast majority of American women her age, never served in the military. She had never been in the diplomatic service. She was thirty-nine years old before she secured her first full-time paying job. She had good but not brilliant scholarly credentials. As a refugee from communism and an immigrant from Czechoslovakia, she was well versed in European issues but knew relatively little about Asia or Latin America, or about international economic matters. She lacked the personal relationship with the president that James A. Baker III had had with George Bush. Her greatest assets were a commitment to hard work, a worldwide network of connections, and a deep affection for what she often called "this amazing country," the United States.

On another level Albright was the obvious choice. As permanent representative to the United Nations in Clinton's first term, she held cabinet rank, keeping an office at the State Department and participating in the administration's highest-level foreign policy deliberations. She built a reputation as a vigorous advocate of American global interests, blunt to the point of rudeness in her argumentation, effective and politically well tuned in her public appearances.

She had the support of women's groups and of the most influential American woman of all, the president's wife, Hillary Rodham

Clinton, who had enjoyed Albright's company on a trip to the Czech Republic earlier in 1996. Albright spoke five languages. And she knew Washington inside and out; unlike election-campaign insiders who are rewarded with prominent jobs only to founder in Washington's peculiar culture, Albright understood that culture and would use it to her advantage. Nor was she one of those aggressive status seekers who arrive in Washington with every administration hoping to use a prominent position in government to advance their political or business careers. To be secretary of state was itself the summit of Albright's aspirations.

"Let me say I'm very proud to have had the opportunity to appoint the first woman secretary of state in the history of America," Clinton said as he announced her selection. "I'm proud of that. But it had nothing to do with her getting the job, one way or the other. She got the job because I believe, amid a list of truly outstanding people, she had the best combination of qualities to succeed and to serve our country at this moment in history."

That was not the whole truth; it sounded a bit like George Bush insisting that he had selected Clarence Thomas for the Supreme Court because he was the best person in the country for the job. There had in fact been a vigorous campaign by women's groups to support Albright for the post over high-profile male rivals. Nevertheless, it was true that Albright had legitimate credentials.

Before her prominence at the United Nations made her a public figure, Albright was the classic Washington insider, well connected on Capitol Hill, in academic circles, and in the Democratic party. Washington is like a big company town in which the product is not steel or chemicals but ideas and influence; the assembly lines run through congressional offices, trade associations, law firms, classrooms, political caucuses, and the news media, and the producers all know each other. Albright had been at home in that environment for two decades.

As director of the Women in Foreign Service program at Georgetown University's School of Foreign Service, she had developed a network of women in diplomacy and academia who supported her candidacy for the job of secretary of state.

Even while serving at the United Nations in New York, she kept her home in the capital's tony Georgetown neighborhood and an office in the gloomy State Department building near the Lincoln

Memorial. For years she had presided over dinners at her home at which foreign policy specialists met for conversation and connections. People tend to like her; she is an engaging dinner companion and a witty observer of life's peculiarities. Her credentials as an insider were part of the reason Clinton found her interesting when they first met during the ill-fated 1988 presidential campaign of Michael Dukakis.

Most people who achieve prominence within this Washington culture remain virtually unknown to the rest of the country. They become assistant secretaries of state, or directors of study programs at organizations such as the Center for Strategic and International Studies, or staff directors for influential congressional committees, or partners in well-regarded law firms. If their field of interest is foreign policy, they are probably members of the Council on Foreign Relations, which Clinton joined after the Dukakis campaign with Albright as his sponsor for membership. They may work for famous bosses, but outside the Beltway they are usually as anonymous as the colonels who carried out the orders of Powell and Schwarzkopf during the Persian Gulf War.

With her appointment as secretary of state, Albright was immediately propelled to an international prominence that most of her peers in this inner circle could never imagine attaining, a prominence enhanced by the fact that she was a woman, a single mother, a refugee, and an immigrant with a dramatic personal history that was politically irresistible.

By the time Albright was appointed, women had already served in cabinets; Franklin D. Roosevelt had selected the first one, Frances Perkins, more than half a century earlier. But Albright seemed to capture the public's imagination more than any of her female predecessors for two reasons: The story of her life epitomized many of the things Americans like best about their country, including the opportunity to rise to power from immigrant penury; and she so conspicuously relished being a woman, flaunting colorful outfits, big jewelry, audacious hats, and jokes about motherhood.

"It used to be that the only way a woman could truly make her foreign policy views felt was by marrying a diplomat and then pouring tea on an offending ambassador's lap," Albright said in an address to the Women's Foreign Policy Group in Washington shortly after Clinton's reelection, when she was conducting an undeclared campaign to be named secretary of state. "Today women are engaged in every facet of global affairs, from policymaking to dealmaking, from arms control to trade, from the courtroom of the War Crimes Tribunal to the far-flung operations of the U.N. High Commissioner for Refugees. Even in the U.N. Security Council, there is, thanks to President Clinton, one skirt to balance the fourteen suits. I like to think that is just about even odds."[6]

At the time of that speech, Albright was competing for the top State job against several prominent men, including George Mitchell, the former majority leader of the Senate, and Richard Holbrooke, a former assistant secretary of state who had presided over the negotiations in Dayton, Ohio, that had ended the war in Bosnia. Clinton liked Albright and admired her performance at the United Nations, but Vice President Gore and others in the president's inner circle favored Holbrooke. What put Albright over the top was the energetic support of influential women, including Hillary Rodham Clinton, Senator Barbara Mikulski of Maryland, and Geraldine Ferraro, the first woman nominated for vice president by a major political party.[7]

When the Senate Foreign Relations Committee met on January 8, 1997, to consider whether to confirm Albright's nomination, the members heard first from her predecessor, Warren Christopher. Evoking her past as a refugee, he told the committee that "Ambassador Albright's entire life has prepared her to be our chief diplomat" because it reflected the history and ideals of the nation she would represent.

"Her family twice took refuge from totalitarianism," Christopher said, "first from Hitler and later from Stalin. Her childhood taught her that freedom can never be taken for granted and that American leadership is always critical to the defense of liberty. Throughout her career, she has applied those lessons to the benefit of the United States and of the world as a whole."[8]

The life Christopher was talking about began on May 15, 1937, in Czechoslovakia, where her father, Josef Korbel, was a member of his country's diplomatic corps. The family fled to London when the Germans invaded Czechoslovakia in 1938, an event that began a decade of fear and turbulence for the family. After World War II, during a brief interlude of democratic government in Czechoslovakia, Josef Korbel was posted to Belgrade, Yugoslavia, as ambassador, while Albright was sent to a boarding school in Switzerland, where she learned French to go with the Czech and English she already spoke.

The communist coup of 1948 dragged Czechoslovakia behind the Iron Curtain and put an end to Korbel's career as a representative of its government. He, his wife, and their three children made their way to the United States the following year and were granted asylum as displaced persons. Eventually they settled in Colorado, where Ambassador Korbel became dean of the School of International Affairs at the University of Denver.

"I arrived in America when I was eleven years old," Albright told the Senate Foreign Relations Committee at her confirmation hearing. "My family came here to escape communism and to find freedom. We did both. My ambition at that time was only to speak English well, please my parents, study hard, and grow up to be an American."

Madeleine Korbel's life as a young adult was typical of bright, well-bred women of that era. She attended Wellesley College, just outside Boston, as did Hillary Rodham a few years later. In the 1950s, many exceptionally talented young women went to Wellesley and other all-female schools such at Mount Holyoke and Smith because they had far fewer choices than today's female students. In that era, most Ivy League schools and other elite undergraduate colleges did not admit women, nor did the military service academies.

Right after college, the young Madeleine Korbel made two life-defining decisions that were standard for women in those days: She married, and she put aside her aspirations for a career in journalism in deference to her husband.

The man she married was Joseph Medill Patterson Albright, heir to a newspaper empire that included the *Chicago Tribune.* An executive of that paper took the young couple to dinner to explain to them the facts of professional life: It would not be proper for the two to work together at the *Tribune,* nor would it be understood if Madeleine went to work for a competing paper. Such a conversation would hardly seem credible to ambitious young women today and might provoke a lawsuit, but Albright did what was expected of her generation and put her own career aside.

Albright recounts this story often, more with wonder than regret. Shortly after she took office, she recalled during a television appearance on *60 Minutes:* "One of my husband's editors actually said to me, 'Honey, you may want to be a reporter, but you can't be on a competing paper and you can't be on the paper that your husband works on. So why don't you find another career?' And I did. And I didn't fight it."[9] She says that it was "weird" and "strange" that she put up no resistance, but she also says that she had little choice. Joe Albright was not in a position to shelve his career plans to enhance hers, and she had three daughters by the time she was in her mid-twenties.

The Albrights were living on Long Island at that time, as Joe was preparing to take over another family-owned publication, *Newsday.* The restless Madeleine threw her intellectual energy into academic work, first taking an intensive course in Russian, then enrolling in graduate school at Columbia University to study Eastern European politics and history.

It seemed that her future life was clearly laid out: She would raise her children, carry out her social responsibilities as the wife of "a man with four names" who would be prominent in the community, and perhaps take up college-level teaching as her daughters grew older. But Joe Albright's expectations for his own future were dashed on the rocks of family politics in the late 1960s. Passed over for a top management job at *Newsday,* he moved the family to Washington, D.C., where he became *Newsday*'s deputy bureau chief. Joe Albright's aunt, Alicia Patterson, sold the paper in 1971, ending his expectations of becoming publisher. He took a job with Cox newspapers.

The young Albrights weren't exactly struggling. Joe Albright took out millions in his settlement with *Newsday.* He and Madeleine already had "a wide circle of well-heeled friends," as biographer Ann Blackman put it, and quickly began inviting big names such as Senators Edward M. Kennedy and J. William Fulbright to parties and dinners at their home in Georgetown.[10]

In the capital, the Albrights enrolled their children at Beauvoir, a private school for kindergarten through third grade. Many of Washington's most powerful people send their children to Beauvoir because it is a feeder school for the elite National Cathedral School for girls and St. Albans School for boys. The family directories of those and a handful of other exclusive private schools in the Washington area amount to A-list guides to the power elite—into which Madeleine Albright would soon find herself welcomed.[11]

Through her volunteer work at Beauvoir, she met another parent, who worked for Edmund S. Muskie, a Democratic senator from Maine. This parent asked Albright to cochair a fund-raising event for the senator. Albright and Muskie hit it off, and when she finally received her doctorate from Columbia in 1976 she went to work in his Senate office as his chief legislative assistant. Her career in politics and public service was just beginning; she was thirty-nine years old.

Muskie would later serve eight months as secretary of state in the final year of Jimmy Carter's presidency; his deputy was Warren Christopher. The White House national security adviser in the Carter administration was Zbigniew Brzezinski, an immigrant from Poland. He had taught Albright at Columbia and hired her onto his White House staff after she had worked two years for Muskie. Links such as these are the lubricant of Washington's policy engine.

On a snowy day in Washington in 1982, Joe Albright abruptly announced to Madeleine that their marriage was over; he was in love with someone else and he was leaving. In private conversations, Albright still talks about this event as the biggest shock and disappointment of her life. She has never remarried, although she is often accompanied to social events by interesting men, such as *Star Trek* actor Patrick Stewart and metals tycoon Maurice Templesman. She loves parties, dancing, and the company of men but has told many interviewers that she has no steady romantic interest and does not intend to remarry.

As devastating as it may have been emotionally, Albright's divorce opened possibilities as well. In the settlement, Albright got a lot of money, a farm in Virginia that she uses as a weekend gardening retreat, and the townhouse in Georgetown that she turned into a foreign policy salon for the important people in Washington who became part of her network. Free from responsibility for her husband's career, she could pursue her own.

Following the divorce, her opportunities for public service were limited, with Muskie out of the Senate and Republicans in control of the White House. Albright completed a fellowship year at the Smithsonian Institution's Woodrow Wilson Center for Scholars and then joined the faculty of Georgetown University's School of Foreign Service as a research professor of international affairs and director of the school's Women in Foreign Service program.

According to her official State Department biography, Albright "taught undergraduate and graduate courses in international affairs, U.S. foreign policy, Russian foreign policy and Central and Eastern European politics, and was responsible for developing and implementing programs designed to enhance women's professional opportunities in international affairs." Georgetown students elected her best teacher on campus three times.

Albright's Georgetown position kept her involved in foreign policy issues and helped her augment the network of personal connections that later contributed to her appointments by Clinton. It also gave her a teacher-student relationship with the younger generation that has continued even while she is secretary of state. She has appeared frequently before student groups, eliciting questions from students and urging them to become involved in international affairs. Her record at Georgetown also drew later criticism because she never wrote groundbreaking books about history, strategy, or foreign policy, as Henry Kissinger had done at Harvard, but Albright always shrugged off such commentary. After all, most of her predecessors, including Christopher, Baker, Vance, and Rusk, had also become secretary of state without first producing great works of strategic analysis.

While at Georgetown, Albright also became president of the Center for National Policy, a nonprofit research organization founded in 1981 by out-of-power Democrats to study domestic and foreign policy issues. The chairman was Albright's former boss, Ed Muskie. Though modest in size and budget, the center was influential in Democratic circles, and its board included such prominent figures as Warren Beatty and Vernon Jordan. The center elevated her profile in Washington, enlarged her roster of influential friends, and gave her a platform beyond the classroom.

"I have had this fantastic life," Albright told an interviewer during that time. "For someone like me, who came to this country when I was eleven years old, to end up working in the White House and having all these amazing opportunities—I mean, I am kind of this American story. This is an amazing country."[12]

Clinton's victory over Bush in 1992 ended the twelve-year exile from power of Democratic party insiders such as Christopher and Albright; they returned from the law firms and universities where they had waited out the years of Republican rule. With Christopher in the top foreign policy job as secretary of state, Albright went to New York to represent the United States at the United Nations at a time when the organization—freed from the Cold War paralysis of the Soviet veto—was assuming broad new responsibilities around the world.

While serving in New York, Albright often appeared on television talk shows to represent the administration on foreign policy issues— a role that enhanced her value to President Clinton because Christopher and Anthony Lake, the national security adviser in Clinton's first term, were ineffective on television. In debates at the United Nations and on the Sunday talk shows, she showed a flair for crisp one-liners and punchy sound bites that contributed to her reputation as a tough negotiator and straight shooter.

Haiti's military rulers, she said, had a choice: "They can leave voluntarily and soon or involuntarily and soon." When the senior United Nations civil servant in Bosnia was quoted in the *New York Times* as saying that the Clinton administration was "somewhat afraid, timid, and tentative" about sending peacekeeping troops, Albright retorted, "International civil servants should remember where their salaries are paid—by member states. They should not even be thinking of criticizing the policies of member states. Frankly, I'm tired of it."[13]

She derided an address to the General Assembly by Iraq's senior diplomat, Tariq Aziz, as "the most ridiculous speech ever given by Iraq at the United Nations."[14]

When French defense minister François Leotard accused the United States of exaggerating the military threat when Iraqi troops moved toward the Kuwaiti border in 1994, Albright's staff encouraged reporters at the United Nations to ask her for comment. Sure enough, when Albright emerged from a Security Council meeting, she strode up to waiting television cameras to denounce an "ill-informed" Leotard for "giving comfort to a brutal dictator who is a repeat offender."[15]

And then there was the famous Cuban incident of February 24, 1996. Clinton was running for reelection, Florida was a key state in the campaign, and the Cuban-American vote there could be crucial. When two small planes operated by a Cuban exile group called Brothers to the Rescue flew close to Cuban airspace, Cuban fighter jets shot them down, killing the pilots. On tapes of the Cuban fighter pilots' conversations, recorded by U.S. intelligence, one was heard exulting about their feat, using the vulgar Spanish term for testicles.

Denouncing the Cubans at the United Nations, Albright turned their language against them. "Frankly, this is not *cojones,* this is cowardice," she exclaimed—a line that outraged straitlaced diplomats, especially those from Spanish-speaking countries, but delighted Cuban Americans, to the pleasure and amusement of Clinton.

Albright's statement was "probably the most effective one-liner in the whole administration's foreign policy," Clinton said. "The Cuban Americans loved it so much they had bumper stickers made up. I have a bumper sticker with Madeleine's quote on it."

When Clinton carried Florida in November 1996, the memory of 60,000 Cuban Americans on their feet at a rally in Miami's Orange Bowl cheering wildly for Albright—"Madeleine, Libertad!"—weighed in her favor as the president considered the composition of his second-term foreign policy team.

Some foreign diplomats who encountered Albright at the United Nations complained that she was a bully—they sometimes called her "the queen of mean." Her harsh reputation was enhanced when fellow delegates heard her shouting defiantly into a telephone in a common area they all shared, telling the White House that she was not prepared to carry out its instructions and could not achieve its objectives with regard to the Rwanda massacres of 1994. As she admitted years later, she completely lost her temper during that phone conversation because she was in an untenable position: The White House and many other people wanted the Security Council to pass a resolution that would do something, anything, toward stopping the killing. But Albright knew that no American troops would be available in the aftermath of the 1993 debacle in Somalia, in which eighteen American soldiers had died, and that no European countries wanted to contribute troops because of the murders of Belgian peacekeepers at the outset of the massacres. She did not want to be a party to a hollow resolution that would only expose the U.N.'s weakness, so she opposed any resolution. Philip Gourevitch, in his searing book on Rwanda, accused Albright of trying to scuttle the desperate efforts to stop the killing, describing this as "the low point in her career as a stateswoman." Perhaps it was, but not for the reasons he ascribed to her.[16] It was not that she opposed trying to save lives in Rwanda; it was that the Security Council's members were not prepared to back up their exhortations with muscle, and she knew that any such resolution would be hypocritical.

Her flair for trenchant one-liners and rhetorical challenges would not serve Albright well as secretary of state, a job in which people expected her to translate her words into action, but it took her half her tenure to learn that. At the outset, the blunt style she had displayed at the United Nations contributed to Albright's popularity with Congress; the Senate, in a collective fit of amnesia about her share of responsibility for the foreign policy missteps of Clinton's first term, would rush to confirm her nomination without dissent. And it contributed to the fact that at the time of her appointment she was probably better known around the world than she was at home. Her nomination provoked a flood of editorial comment and opinion in newspapers everywhere, much of it admiring, quite a bit not. Some of it was so adulatory as to be laughable.

El Tiempo, a Colombian newspaper, claimed: "The promotion of a woman to the second highest position of the world is a very significant act in advancing the feminine sex so that it may acquire positions of power and decisively influence the world's destinies from now on. A good performance in such a high political position could launch Mrs. Albright as a possible U.S. presidential candidate," a comment that overlooked the constitutional requirement that presidents be native-born citizens.

According to the *Manila Bulletin* in the Philippines, "Mrs. Albright will be not only the first woman Secretary of State but also the first naturalized American citizen to assume the job." Apparently Henry Kissinger, born in Germany, failed to make much of an impression in Manila.

Most of the substantive commentary, however, dealt with Albright's aggressive style and firmly held views, which drew praise from some commentators, apprehension from others.

"This iron lady, who is fifty-nine years old, is known as the most influential woman in the U.S. foreign policy establishment and as a supporter of using force instead of diplomacy to solve conflicts," said *Le Matin,* a French-language daily in Algiers. "So, Clinton made his choice. He preferred action to reflection and force to diplomacy."

"Albright is a heavyweight with outspoken ideas about the role the United States should play on the international stage," said *De*

Volkskrant, in the Netherlands. "She loves foreign policy, which is quite unusual for a woman."

"To get along with Madeleine Albright, one must be trustworthy, honest, and a person of his word," wrote a columnist in the Israeli newspaper *Yediot Ahronot* who had observed her at the United Nations. "Albright is a great believer in the direct approach. She can be blunt and tends to settle accounts on the spot. She is a person of multiple contradictions: She is at once a diplomat and a politician, tough, blunt, but also emotional and sentimental, a bitter enemy to her foes and a devoted ally to her friends."

"The most common knock against Albright is that she lacks a foreign policy 'vision,'" wrote Simon Barber in the *Sunday Times* of South Africa. "But that's the talk of academics who think that only academics are smart enough to become Secretary of State. . . . It's going to be interesting having a secretary who speaks her mind, has the admiration of the U.S. president and his wife and, unlike her predecessor, is not a doormat."

As Diana McCaffrey, the United States Information Agency editor who compiled such remarks from newspapers in fifty-three countries, noted in her summary: "A majority of analysts judged Ambassador Albright 'tough,' 'experienced,' 'loyal' and an 'iron lady.' Opinion was mixed, however, on whether or not such strengths would turn out to be her weakness in her role as the top U.S. diplomat and on what her appointment would mean for the conduct of U.S. foreign policy in the second Clinton administration."[17]

Not only journalists were divided about Albright's relative strengths and weaknesses. Sir John Weston, her British counterpart, cabled home a character sketch that described her as smart, friendly, modest, and skillful at cutting through complicated issues so that nonspecialists could understand them. "Inside the Security Council," Weston wrote, "she conveys a mixture of authority and insecurity. She is not good at devising a detailed game plan for pursuing broad objectives. This can make her look flat-footed, even gauche, in detailed handling. . . . And she is not always good at accepting the need to apply to the United States the same standards and expectations she requires of others."[18] That turned out to be a prescient observation: As secretary of state, Albright has always assumed that the United States' view of any issue is the correct one and that American motives and behavior are always honorable.

When Albright's appointment was announced, professional diplomats with whom she had worked at the United Nations, including many who had complained privately about her blunt style and uncompromising tactics, were suddenly unanimous in their praise; they understood that she was about to become the most powerful foreign policy official in the world, and it would be foolish to square off against her. Even away from New York, in reflective moments, diplomatic practitioners generally gave her high marks.

"I think she will be very successful because she's a smooth operator, a very smooth operator," said Egyptian foreign minister Amre Moussa.[19]

Eduard Balladur, a former French prime minister who had worked with Albright at the United Nations in trying to shape a response to the 1994 genocide in Rwanda, said that he found her "intelligent and a woman of strong character," an opinion he said was widely shared in Paris. He also said that she was "very competent" and that her ability to speak several European languages, including French, enhanced her standing in Europe right from the start.[20]

Similarly, an ambassador from one of the former Yugoslav republics said that "the central Europeans are absolutely happy with her. She has the background, she knows the region. We don't know yet about her management or her leadership of the department, but there is great acceptance and very positive reaction."[21]

Albright would address the issues of "management" and "leadership of the department" by retaining and installing strong, experienced deputies and assistants, including Strobe Talbott as deputy secretary of state; Thomas R. Pickering as undersecretary of state for political affairs, the number three job; and Stuart E. Eizenstat as undersecretary for economic and business affairs. Talbott, a friend of Clinton's from their days as Rhodes Scholars at Oxford, is an expert on Russia and on arms control, a thinker who hands out maps of the fifteenth-century Hanseatic League of German trading cities to illustrate his dream of a Russia integrated into northern Europe through Baltic commerce. Pickering was the most honored and experienced diplomat in the career foreign service before his 1996 retirement; he has been ambassador to Russia, Jordan, Nigeria, El Salvador, India, and Israel and was one of Albright's predecessors at the United Nations. Eizenstat, a colorless but creative veteran of the Washington policy wars, is a tireless worker who commanded respect in Europe. Albright demanded loyalty, but she showed no fear of strong subordinates.

In choosing Albright, Clinton nominated a person who was qualified, experienced, respected except by a few right-wing commentators who said her reputation for toughness was spurious, and above all confirmable in the Senate without controversy. That left only the question of her ability, as the first woman in the job, to deal effectively with foreign officials, in particular Arabs, who might be unaccustomed to accepting women as equals.

In reality, this was a phony issue. The list of women who have functioned effectively at the highest levels of international affairs in modern times includes Margaret Thatcher of Great Britain, Golda Meir of Israel, Indira Gandhi of India, and Tansu Çiller of Turkey. Many European countries have had female foreign ministers, as has Mexico.

But the media and some members of Congress behaved as if Albright's appointment represented a complete departure from the norm—as if she had been chosen to command the Marine Corps. Their comments focused on matters they would never have brought up with a male appointee—her clothing, her jewelry, her life as a divorced mother of three. She didn't object; in fact, she appeared to relish these lines of inquiry, because she wanted to be a pathmaker for women and was ready to confront the questions head-on. Still, there was an outburst of commentary that would not have been heard if she were a man; even when this commentary was admiring, it underlined the uniqueness of her position.

Representative Sonny Callahan, for example, a conservative Republican from Alabama who significantly influences foreign aid spending, called Albright "a flamingo in the barnyard of politics."[22] Senator John Kerry, a Massachusetts Democrat, said that he tried to shoo his three daughters out of his office so he could confer with Albright, and they refused to go: "They said, 'no, no, no, we want to meet Madeleine Albright.' And afterward they said, 'Boy, she's really cool.'"[23] A writer for *Vogue* noted: "Even when relaxing on her plane, [Albright] wears silk trousers and matching blouses, and she paid attention when someone said her makeup was too heavy."[24]

On the bulletin board in the State Department's press center, a journalist posted a photograph of a stern-visaged Albright in her trademark Stetson hat with the caption quoting Clint Eastwood in his *Dirty Harry* role: "Go ahead, make my day."

"Do you know the story of the Stetson?" Albright remarked about that photograph, taken during her first trip out of Washington as secretary of state—to Texas. "Only my daughter got it right. She called me up and she said, 'Mom, now tell me the truth. You put the Stetson on coming out of the plane on the first day because your hair didn't look right. Is that correct?' And that's exactly what it was." Besides, Albright said, she used to wear a Stetson as a young woman in Colorado, and she concluded: "I think I look pretty good in a Stetson."[25]

Washington custom dictates that a nominee for any office requiring confirmation by the Senate refrain from public comments or press interviews before the relevant Senate committee takes up the nomination at a public hearing. Albright adhered to the custom. In the six weeks between Clinton's announcement of her selection and the Senate Foreign Relations Committee's hearing, she stayed out of sight, studying the issues in preparation for questioning by the senators, visiting privately with committee members, and planning the staffing of the State Department.

"It quickly became apparent that Ambassador Albright was a voracious reader—good news for those of us who have toiled into the night on papers for the seventh floor, wondering if they're ever read," a member of the departmental transition team wrote afterward. "Secretary Albright reads them, and reads them closely." The term "seventh floor" is State Department jargon for the secretary and her most senior aides and deputies—those who have offices on the seventh floor of the department's depressing headquarters building in a part of Washington known as Foggy Bottom.[26]

At Albright's confirmation hearing, most committee members hailed the appointment of a woman to the post as long overdue; none suggested that her gender would be an obstacle to success in her job. On the contrary, most members expressed admiration for Albright's career, her successes, and her vigorous advocacy of U.S. interests at the United Nations. What was remarkable about that hearing was not that a woman had been appointed but that a prominent Democrat closely involved with some of the least successful foreign policy decisions of Clinton's first term was welcomed by all committee members of both parties as part of the solution rather than part of the problem.

"After twelve years of Ronald Reagan and George Bush," said chairman Jesse Helms, a conservative Republican often but erroneously derided as an isolationist, "the United States had once again become the undisputed leader of the world, certainly the free world. Our friends followed us, and the enemies of freedom, thanks to those presidents, feared and respected the strength of the United States. But many of those gains have been neutralized by a foreign policy [under Bill Clinton] too often vacillating, an insecure foreign policy that has responded to world events rather than shaping them."

Wasn't Albright a prominent member of the team that developed and carried out that "vacillating" and "insecure" foreign policy? Yes, but no member of the committee and few of the independent analysts and editorial writers commenting on her appointment blamed her personally. Her effusive, laudatory welcome from committee members of both parties was a testament to her ability to charm, persuade, cajole, and insulate herself from criticism.

As committee members raised issues of specific concern to them, Albright told them what they wanted to hear. She promised Senator Dianne Feinstein, a California Democrat, that Mexican drug trafficking would get "my special attention." She promised Senator Craig Thomas of Wyoming that she would pay close attention to the preservation of freedom in Hong Kong after the Chinese takeover that summer. When Senator Bill Frist of Tennessee complained that the Clinton administration had not sufficiently consulted Congress before sending American troops to Bosnia, Albright promised that the future would be different:

> Senator, my whole background, because I worked here and because my various previous administration jobs were involved with congressional relations, I believe that we should have close consultations and discussions about how to set priorities in foreign policy. I would hope that you would find, if I'm confirmed, that we will spend a lot of time together talking about foreign policy issues and consulting, and that you would not find us wanting in that.

Virtually without exception, the senators accepted these assurances and expressed eagerness to vote in favor of her nomination. Why was that?

In private meetings before the hearing, Albright had courted committee members and promised to work with them. They liked her reputation for bluntness and her fierce defense of the United States against all critics. They admired her unabashed affection for the United States and her belief that it held the moral high ground. Perhaps most important, however, she had given Helms and the other conservatives on the committee a human sacrifice in the person of Boutros Boutros-Ghali, the prickly Egyptian diplomat who was secretary-general of the United Nations until Albright and Christopher engineered his ouster.

Boutros-Ghali was the quintessential cosmopolitan, an Egyptian Christian with a Jewish wife; he spoke French and English as well as Arabic, and was not a career diplomat but an academic who specialized in African affairs. He was brought into the Egyptian Foreign Ministry by President Anwar Sadat at the time of Sadat's historic peace negotiations with Israel in the late 1970s. When I first met Boutros-Ghali, in 1976, he was still an obscure figure, toiling in a government-sponsored think tank in Cairo, but even then, although he was generally likable, it was clear that he gave great weight to his own opinions and had little patience for those whom he regarded as less well informed than he. Ordinarily amiable and polite, when challenged he became brusque and stern—rather like Albright herself.

When Albright took up her post at the United Nations early in 1993, Boutros-Ghali was serving a five-year term as secretary-general that was to expire at the end of 1996. Previously that job had been held by diplomats from Europe, Asia, and South America; Boutros-Ghali was selected in part because it was Africa's turn in this informal rotation, and Egypt qualified as an African country.

The Bush administration was unenthusiastic about his candidacy but accepted him because he promised to serve only one term. As it turned out, Albright, Christopher, and many Republicans in Congress, including Helms, came to view those initial American reservations as more than justified.

According to Christopher, Boutros-Ghali as secretary-general showed himself to be a "diplomat of the old school, a sophisticated operator who had all the moves." And he was wily: "He knew how to maneuver between the 'Perm Five' nations that had veto power in the Security Council and the developing nations that dominated the General Assembly."[27]

Many members of Congress blamed Boutros-Ghali for the 1993 military disaster in Somalia in which eighteen American soldiers assigned to United Nations peacekeeping duty were killed in a fruitless effort to capture Muhammad Farah Aidid, the leader of one of Somalia's warring factions. The eighteen who died were under the direct command of U.S. officers, but the overall mission in Somalia—which had evolved from a humanitarian deployment to feed starving civilians into an ambitious effort to rebuild the Somali state—was designed in New York.

"It had been on his watch," Christopher said of Boutros-Ghali, "that the U.N. mission to Somalia was disastrously broadened to include disarming the local warlords" and capturing Aidid.[28]

Albright was not blameless in the Somalia mess because she promoted the resolution demanding the warlord's capture, which was adopted at a time when she was supporting an expanded United Nations role worldwide. To a certain extent, the troops who engaged in the fatal firefight were sent there to do her bidding. Most of the blame, however, fell on the secretary-general, and Somalia was hardly the only blot on Boutros-Ghali's copybook.

American officials found him on the one hand overly ambitious, harboring plans for United Nations involvement in world affairs that exceeded his mandate from the members, and on the other hand insufficiently dedicated to enacting the internal administrative reforms that were obviously needed in the unwieldy United Nations bureaucracy. To his critics, Christopher later wrote, "Boutros-Ghali's name was synonymous with everything that was wrong with the organization. Rightly or wrongly, many perceived him as a symbol of a bloated and impotent United Nations."[29] That assessment reflected what Albright was reporting to Christopher from New York.

By the end of 1993, when Albright had been the chief U.S. representative at the United Nations for almost a year, it had become apparent to everyone except Boutros-Ghali himself that the secretary-general's penchant for solo diplomacy and his indifference to reform were alienating important constituencies, including Washington. When Clinton set a firm date for the withdrawal of American troops from Somalia, Boutros-Ghali criticized the decision in a five-page letter to Christopher in which the pronoun "I" appeared too many times for the Americans' taste.

Albright sent him a blunt early warning via a December 1993 *Washington Post* interview. "He is one of the world's most experienced diplomats," she said of Boutros-Ghali. "But his approach is often counterproductive." She revealed that in a recent conversation with Boutros-Ghali, in which he complained that the United States was not backing him up in his attempts to address numerous problems, she told him, "What you don't understand, Boutros, is that you are my problem."[30] Boutros-Ghali never took the hint.

To Albright, this was more than a personality issue. The United States was about $1 billion in arrears on payment for various U.N. peacekeeping operations, a fact that undermined her ability to persuade other members to see things her way. She often commented about the embarrassment she felt when a British colleague joked that the United States was enjoying "representation without taxation."

She felt that the United Nations could be more useful than ever in the confusing post–Cold War world, but only if the United States was able to wield the influence to which its size and financial contribution should entitle it. And she believed that Congress was unlikely to put up the $1 billion so long as Boutros-Ghali was in power, because influential members held him responsible for the Somalia mess and saw him as an obstacle to reform and budget cutting. In addition, Albright regarded Boutros-Ghali as an obstacle to effective international intervention in the war in Bosnia because he insisted on U.N. operational control of the multinational military intervention force there and refused to delegate to British or French officers the authority to order air strikes against the Bosnian Serbs.

As long as Boutros-Ghali was scheduled to leave office at the end of 1996, Albright could concentrate her energies on the search for a more effective—and more pliable—successor. But in 1995, she detected signs that he would back away from his one-term pledge and seek another five years in office. Boutros-Ghali was about to discover that behind the colorful suits, bright jewelry, and gregarious style Albright could be a relentless foe.[31]

In October 1995, Albright contacted Christopher and Lake to remind them that Boutros-Ghali's term was due to expire in little more than a year and ask about their strategy for selecting a replacement. In foreign policy, a scheduled event more than a year away is so far beyond the planning horizon as to be invisible to daily crisis managers, and Washington had yet to focus on the United Nations issue. Albright, who saw in Boutros-Ghali's travel schedule an incipient campaign to win support for a second term, forced the question onto Christopher's agenda.

At her request, the White House set up an interagency team consisting of James B. Steinberg, director of the State Department's policy planning staff and a confidant of Christopher's; James P. Rubin, universally known as Jamie, Albright's press spokesman, friend, and adviser; and Richard Clarke, who held the international organizations portfolio on Lake's National Security Council staff. They drafted a strategy paper that catalogued the reasons for opposing a second term for Boutros-Ghali and listed several possible successors—including Kofi Annan, a senior U.N. peacekeeping official from Ghana. That paper went to Christopher in late January.

The decisionmaking process moved swiftly, if secretly, for the next four months. First Christopher, then the president accepted the premise of Albright and the three-man interagency team that an effort to block the secretary-general from winning a second term was worth the risks. These risks included the possibility that the Security Council, on which the United States had only one vote, would reject Washington's position; the likelihood that African members of the United Nations would rally to the support of Boutros-Ghali; and the prospect that the campaign would be seen as an effort by the United States—the billion-dollar deadbeat—to impose its will.

Another problem was that the Americans had decided to promote Annan as Boutros-Ghali's successor. This choice could placate the Africans, who believed that the African in the top job was entitled to the same second term his predecessors from other regions had, but Annan's candidacy could be fatally undermined if he were perceived to be Washington's candidate. And Annan was precluded from campaigning for the job because he worked for Boutros-Ghali.

The plan adopted by Christopher and Albright involved behind-the-scenes, undeclared support for Annan coupled with an effort to negotiate a graceful exit for Boutros-Ghali. Christopher was willing to allow him to serve one additional year, until his seventy-fifth birthday, when he would announce his retirement. Albright, they decided, would stay out of the negotiations because she had to work with Boutros-Ghali on a daily basis.

Christopher met with Boutros-Ghali several times and thought they had a deal, but on June 18, the secretary-general rejected the compromise, and Christopher took the offer off the table. Three days later, in a background interview with the *New York Times*, Christopher revealed that the United States would use its veto power to block a second term for Boutros-Ghali.[32] This news drew the anticipated negative response at the United Nations and in foreign capitals, where officials accused the United States of acting arbitrarily, without consulting other U.N. members, and of going after Boutros-Ghali for political reasons without having a credible replacement candidate lined up.

The reason other countries suspected a political motivation was that Bob Dole, the likely Republican nominee to challenge Clinton for reelection that November, was campaigning against Boutros-Ghali, mocking his name and promising that he would never send American troops into battle under the secretary-general's command. Underestimating Albright's resolve, most diplomats at the United Nations—and Boutros-Ghali himself—believed that the issue would simply blow over if Clinton won reelection on November 5.

On the day the *New York Times* story appeared, Christopher came to the *Washington Post*'s offices for lunch with editors and reporters. He maintained the tactical fiction that Washington had no favorite candidate, saying that "my own preference would be to cast a very wide net." In fact, Albright was already at work in New York lining up support for the selection of Kofi Annan, courting colleagues at private dinners and buttering up Security Council president Paul Biya of Cameroon, a crucial figure because he represented a French-speaking African country. (France had announced that it would veto any proposed successor who did not speak French.) Although Albright's antipathy to Boutros-Ghali was common knowledge at the United Nations, she sought to depersonalize the issue, praising the secretary-general for his diplomatic skill but arguing that the giant organization needed new and more vigorous leadership.

Convinced at last that Washington was serious, some ambassadors at the United Nations began thinking about what to do once the United States carried out its veto threat. Others were reluctant to commit themselves until they saw the outcome of the U.S. presidential election. Christopher, during a tour of African countries in October, warned the Africans that they should unite behind a candidate or risk not having an African secretary-general at all, even if Africa was by tradition entitled to the second term. But still they held back until, on November 19—two weeks after Clinton was reelected—Albright vetoed a resolution to give Boutros-Ghali a second term. The vote in the Security Council was 14–1. Albright cast the only negative vote—a veto, meaning the resolution was dead no matter how many Security Council members voted for it.

The count seemed to show that the United States was isolated and that Albright had failed to rally her counterparts to the American position. But it turned out that Albright had been right all along in saying that Boutros-Ghali's support was "a mile wide and an inch deep." Faced with an unyielding United States, Cameroon's Biya released African delegates from their pledge to support Boutros-Ghali. And then on December 5, Clinton announced that he had selected Albright to be secretary of state.

"Suddenly she was someone who commanded new respect," a colleague said. "Everyone saw her as someone to fear, to be in awe of. . . . Everyone wanted to be able to present themselves as her special friend and not get on her bad side."

The denouement was that on December 13, the Security Council unanimously chose Kofi Annan to succeed Boutros-Ghali. Foreign diplomats who had been saying all summer that Albright was arrogantly leading the United States into a foreign policy disaster that would alienate everyone to no benefit suddenly were praising her as the mastermind of a campaign that achieved the twin goals of ousting Boutros-Ghali and installing a favored successor.

Administration officials, who had been smarting at the charge that they were going over a diplomatic cliff by campaigning against Boutros-Ghali without having a ready successor, revealed that the United States had privately supported Annan all along. One member of the White House National Security Council staff pulled from his files a 1994 photograph that showed Annan briefing Clinton, Albright, and Richard Clarke about U.N. peacekeeping activities. "We always had a lot of respect for him," the official said.

In Boutros-Ghali's account of this episode, published three years later, he gained a measure of revenge against Albright by accusing her of treachery, deceit, and racist tactics that alienated her colleagues. In his telling, he outwitted her at every turn; he had everyone's support, and these supporters stood fast in the face of her scheming and duplicity. Perhaps, but what was the outcome? Albright prevailed; the Security Council showed him the door.

The story of Boutros-Ghali's ouster merits retelling because it was crucial to Albright's standing in the White House and to her acceptance by the Senate, where Chairman Helms—who is strongly antipathetic to the United Nations—admired Albright's commitment to administrative reforms in the world organization. Albright's relationship with Helms would in turn be the cornerstone of her campaign the following year, as secretary of state, to win bipartisan support for a measure to pay off most of the United States' peacekeeping arrears in exchange for comprehensive organizational reforms. And the skill and tenacity with which she went after Boutros-Ghali rebutted the arguments of those who had criticized Albright as a short-term thinker with no strategic vision.

"That's why we killed Boutros: Boutros was the billion-dollar secretary-general," one of Albright's confidants said, referring to the amount of money owed to the world body by the United States. "You want to keep Boutros, you lose a billion dollars" because of congressional antipathy to him. "You get rid of Boutros, you have a shot at your billion. He was the billion-dollar man."

Albright was confirmed as secretary of state by a Senate vote of 99–0 on January 23, 1997, and was sworn in the same day. Considering the hostility with which the Republican-controlled Senate had treated some of Clinton's other cabinet nominees, the vote was an accurate measure of Albright's popularity. She was now free to undertake her self-assigned mission of storming the media in a campaign to convince the American people that international affairs mattered to them.

～

On her first full day in office, Albright held a news conference at which she promised to build good relations with the press.

"The press plays a vital role as educator, interpreter, and constructive, or usually constructive, critic of our foreign policy," she said. "I respect that role, and, as I do my job, I will strive to be open and available [and] thereby help you do yours." That same night, she appeared on *Larry King Live.*

This early outreach to the media was a sign of things to come: Albright was determined to get as much favorable coverage as possible for herself and her ideas because she saw personal popularity and public support as important tools that she would use in getting what she wanted from Congress. It would become apparent, however, that her idea of reaching out to the press meant delivering scripted messages in controlled settings as much as possible; it did not mean encouraging individual State Department officials to talk to reporters on their own.

One of the topics that inevitably came up in Albright's early media sessions was what it meant to be a woman in her job. She never dodged the question; on the contrary, she responded with relish. After a year or so, people in Washington stopped asking, but the question continued to surface when she was on the road.

Being a woman was actually an asset, she said, especially in the first big task she assigned herself, which was reconnecting the American people to American foreign policy through straight talk and an informal style:

> I think I just happen to have a personality that I hope makes people think they can talk to me, and that is true in the halls [of the State Department]. When I came here the first day I had my first meeting with everybody, I said, talk to me when I walk in the halls, you know, I'd like to have you talk to me. I'm not just kind of a figure that is the leader of the place, but I'd like to know more about the people that work here. I've gone to the cafeteria to have lunch.[33]

Like every cabinet officer, or president, or corporate executive, Albright found her early pledges of accessibility and informality hard to maintain as she came to understand the relentlessness of her job and the demands on her time. A chatty lunch in the cafeteria is a luxury that a secretary of state can seldom afford. She recognized this, saying that the one aspect of the job for which she was not fully prepared was "the inexorability of it. It just never stops. It's not like any other job in the world where you can say, all right, I'm taking the day off. . . . It doesn't stop at night, or in the middle of the night." But, she added, "It's the world's greatest job," and most of the time she was unmistakably having fun doing it, at least in the first year.

Albright addressed the gender issue with jokes and anecdotes in many of her public appearances, but also in less visible, unpublicized events, where she added a feminine touch, revealing a gregarious, informal style and a willingness to connect with people in personal ways that none of her male predecessors had displayed, as she did at the Black History Month celebration.

Albright had a serious message to deliver at that event, which was that the State Department had not done nearly enough to bring members of minority groups into its ranks. Indeed, the year before, the department had agreed to pay $3.8 million to settle a lawsuit by black foreign service officers who alleged that their careers had been cut short by racial discrimination. But it was Albright's style as much as the substance, the effervescent tone and personal touch, the self-deprecating jokes, that made clear that the office of secretary of state was occupied by a different type of person.

In formal diplomatic situations where jokes and personal comments are inappropriate, such as in public speeches at the United Nations, Albright plays her role as straight and deadpan as any gray-suited man. But in less formal settings, talking to students or among friends or at women's groups, she can be counted on to tell stories about what it means to be a woman in her job—such as the ability to turn her skirt around to hide an embarrassing stain.

The setting for this anecdote was Paris, where Albright was participating in ceremonies marking the signing of a landmark cooperation agreement between Russia and NATO, the former Cold War enemies. That was not an appropriate forum for girl talk, but Albright later addressed an audience of military wives and recounted an episode from the Paris event that they could all sympathize with.

"I had on a gorgeous new lavender suit," she recalled. "I thought I looked great." During lunch, however, as she chatted with German foreign minister Klaus Kinkel, "I looked down at my skirt and there's salad dressing all over it." Her first thought was, "Darn it, all these men have on dark suits, and even if they spilled everything all over them, no one would be able to tell, and this is a disaster."

Worse yet, the French foreign minister announced that right after lunch the participants were to gather outside for a group photograph, with Albright in the middle.

"So I sat there, and I looked, and I thought, could I put the menu over my skirt?" she recalled. "I don't carry a purse, because I forget it in places. So I really was debating what to do, and all of a sudden it came to me. I got up and turned my skirt around. Fortunately, it was not one of those very modern skirts with a slit all the way up."[34] These "between us girls" anecdotes were always good for laughter and applause. No one would say of Albright, as the British historian David Cannadine said of Margaret Thatcher, that she sought to be "an honorary man, tough, combative, determined and aggressive."[35]

Tough and combative, sure, but she never conceded that those were exclusively male traits.

Asked by students during one trip to the West Coast if she had ever experienced "gender discrimination," Albright said yes, of course, but she elaborated: "The most important thing is not to have a chip on your shoulder about it." She said, "If you go into it expecting a fight, that's what you'll get."

After a few months in office, Albright had developed her lines about the gender issue into a well-honed routine; reporters who followed her regularly could almost anticipate each utterance. She often began with a joke about her secret weapon: makeup. At a luncheon of the Women's Legal Defense Fund on June 13, 1997, she said:

> I'm often asked what it's like to be the first female secretary of state. Now that I've had the job for about five months, I have decided that being a woman has several important advantages. One is makeup. If a sixty-year-old male secretary of state has had a bad day, he has two choices—to look like a tired old man, or look like a tired old man with makeup. But with a little help, I can at least convince myself that I look as fresh as I feel right now.

As the transcript of this event noted, these remarks brought laughter and applause from her mostly female audience, but Albright wasn't finished.

Another advantage to being a woman in her job, Albright said, is: "We're just better at it. The scientists are saying that women are genetically inclined to be peacemakers, problem solvers, and basically well-adjusted. That may explain why I'm always so temperate in my language [laughter] and around the world there has recently been a bit of a boom in the appointment of new women foreign ministers."

Then she turned serious, offering her view that the status of women was an important international policy issue and that she intended to devote time and resources to it. That theme was to become the basis of some of her most creative and unorthodox diplomatic innovations.

> As we approach the new century, we know that we cannot build the kind of future we want without the contributions of women. And we know that,

around the world, women will only be able to contribute to our full potential if we have equal access, equal rights, equal protection, and a fair
chance at the levers of economic and political power. This isn't rocket science, or something that is even more difficult, like child-rearing; it is simple common sense. We know from experience, after all, that when women
have the knowledge and power to make our own choices, the cycle of
poverty, in which too many countries remain ensnared, can be broken.
Birth rates stabilize; environmental awareness increases; the spread of sexually transmitted diseases slows; and socially constructive values are more
likely to be passed on to the young.

With comments like these, Albright confidently set herself apart
from traditional diplomats who were trained to address such issues
as the strategic balance of power and the internal political dynamics
of foreign countries, rather than such lofty but vague ambitions as
instilling "socially constructive values" in young people. This emphasis on nontraditional, cross-border issues such as the status of
women was to become a fundamental building block of her foreign
policy agenda.

It came naturally to her. Once when I was riding with Albright
from one public appearance to the next, an aide handed her a cell-
phone and said that one of her daughters wanted to talk to her right
away. Albright was immediately anxious: Was something wrong? Was
it about the baby? No, it had to do with getting the fireplace at the
farm repaired before Thanksgiving. Albright's was the natural response of a mother and grandmother. That is who she is, that is her
personality.

This feminine—and sometimes feminist—approach to life, although refreshingly different and in many ways appealing, left open
the question of whether she would be helped or hindered in her
daily performance by the fact that she was a woman. The answer to
this came early, from an unlikely source: Saudi Arabia.

Over the past half century, Saudi Arabia, a conservative, theocratic society where the Koran, the holy book of Islam, is the constitution, has transformed itself physically from a primitive community
of mud-walled villages and animal transport into a modern country
of gleaming new buildings, space-age airports, and first-rate
telecommunications. But because of the Saudi monarchy's emphasis on social cohesion, the role of women has remained sharply re-

stricted: Saudi women are educated now, but they cannot drive cars, travel abroad without their husbands' permission, enter shops alone, or work alongside men. In accordance with Islamic law, Saudi men are permitted to have multiple wives.

It is hard to imagine a society that would be less appealing to Albright personally, other than the one created in Afghanistan by the cruel, misogynistic Taliban militia, whom she denounced as "despicable." But Saudi Arabia is also an important strategic and economic ally of the United States, a relationship that originated during the presidency of Franklin D. Roosevelt. Albright had no choice but to do business with the desert kingdom.

Accordingly, one of her first high-level official visitors was Prince Sultan bin Abdulaziz, the Saudi defense minister, brother of King Fahd and second in line of succession to the throne.

In preparation for Sultan's visit, his son, Prince Bandar bin Sultan, Saudi Arabia's immensely skillful ambassador to the United States, invited a group of reporters to the embassy to talk about what his father would be doing in Washington. He went through the schedule: this meeting, that dinner. Then I asked the inevitable question: "Does it matter to anyone in the delegation that the secretary of state is a woman?"

Bandar was ready. He broke into a huge grin, gave us a wink, took a big puff on his cigar, and proclaimed, "I am offended with this sexist question. If half the men in the State Department have the . . ." He paused; we laughed, knowing what was coming. ". . . the, what's that Spanish word, *cojones,* that Mrs. Albright has, America will be safe forever. We Saudis have dealt with Maggie Thatcher, a great leader, and I'm sure Mrs. Albright will be no less."

While Prince Sultan was in Washington, Albright gave a luncheon in his honor in the Thomas Jefferson room at the State Department. Seated at ten round tables, each adorned with a bowl of roses, were senior officials of both governments, including the Saudi foreign minister, Prince Saud al-Faisal, and the oil minister, Ali Naimi. Some of the Saudis, including Sultan, wore their traditional desert robes; others wore suits. Among the guests were Senator Arlen Specter, a Republican from Pennsylvania; executives from American companies with business interests in Saudi Arabia such as Steve Bechtel of the Bechtel Corporation; and Wyche Fowler, the American ambassador to Saudi Arabia.

Albright and Prince Sultan each spoke a few friendly, low-key words at a lectern and chatted animatedly, through an interpreter, over their chilled watercress bisque and potato-encrusted red snapper with pecan rice timbale. In her remarks, Albright referred to "my colorful outfits and your magnificent robes," getting that out of the way. It was unremarkable, as these events go, which was exactly the point. The Saudis declared themselves charmed and impressed by Albright's open and forthright style. As Bandar had predicted, the fact that she was a woman was not an issue.

That September, Albright visited the kingdom for the first time. Having been in Saudi Arabia when Rosalynn Carter went there with her husband, President Jimmy Carter, in 1978, I was struck by the difference in the way the two women were received. Mrs. Carter walked behind the president and the welcoming party, was excluded from official gatherings, and dined separately with Saudi women. But when Albright landed, prominent princes met her at the airport, with Saudi television filming the greetings. King Fahd and Crown Prince Abdullah received her in her official capacity, and local newspapers gave front-page display to pictures of her with her Saudi hosts.

The passage of time accounted for part of the difference. In the nearly twenty years that had elapsed between the arrivals of the two women, a new generation had come of age in Saudi Arabia, much more cosmopolitan than their elders. In some ways, the country has accommodated itself to the fact that in the modern world many governments and businesses will be represented in the kingdom by women. Nowadays there are even some public buildings with restrooms for women, a feature notably lacking in government buildings in the past because women were never expected to visit them.

But most of the difference between Albright's reception and Mrs. Carter's was that Albright was in the kingdom in her official capacity, as the chief foreign policy representative of the United States. The Saudis have long made it a practice to address the position rather than the person, just as they did when they received Henry Kissinger in the 1970s even though Jews were not normally welcome.

When Albright descended from her airplane, she wore a black suit with long sleeves and a skirt that reached nearly to her ankles, along with a broad-brimmed hat, in deference to Saudi sensitivities about female attire. Otherwise, the event was not much different from an arrival in any other country, thus demonstrating again that the fact of Albright's femaleness was not an obstacle to job performance.

King Fahd bin Abdulaziz accorded Albright the full reception bestowed on the kingdom's most distinguished visitors. They met in his white marble palace, the floors covered with rich oriental carpets, the air scented with incense, and the tables decked with pots of flowers.

"I want to welcome you to Saudi Arabia," the king said. "This meeting as usual is a meeting between friends."

A year later, she would tell interviewers from a high school newspaper that she had found Arab leaders such as Crown Prince Abdullah "much more accepting than others. I think it's because they know it's a question"—that is, the Saudis were going out of their way to show that they were able to deal with a woman.

Still, this question kept coming up, at least outside Washington, even after Albright had demonstrated to most people that it was irrelevant. More than two years after she took office, back in Saudi Arabia, Albright met with American troops stationed at Prince Sultan Air Base. When she asked for questions from the audience, a sergeant rose to inquire about her reception by leaders of countries where women are not regarded as equals.

"Well, they're learning," Albright cracked, to the delight of the troops.

Just as happened when Geraldine Ferraro became the first woman to run for vice president, in 1984, and when Sandra Day O'Connor became the first female justice of the U.S. Supreme Court, in 1981, Albright was able to demonstrate that there was no inherent anomaly in having a woman in the job of secretary of state. Far more than O'Connor, Albright chose to emphasize her gender in her public conduct—joking about makeup, holding babies, flashing her trademark jewelry—and in some of the policy issues she elected to stress, such as the plight of women refugees. This approach stems from the fact that she has never regarded her gender as a liability; on the contrary, it proved to be quite useful as she took on with zest the first major task she set for herself as secretary of state, which was to maximize her personal popularity so she could use it as a tool to forge support for the administration's foreign policy.

Albright knew that having her picture on the cover of *Newsweek* with the headline "Mad About Madeleine" was the kind of asset that would command attention as she embarked on the first big job of her tenure: selling the administration's program to a skeptical, Republican-dominated Congress.

Chapter 2

THEY CAN CALL ME MADELEINE

I N THE ORNATE, chandeliered sanctum of the Senate Foreign Relations Committee on the first floor of the U.S. Capitol, Senator Jesse Helms was running the meeting.

Helms, a conservative Republican from North Carolina, is widely regarded in Washington as a know-nothing and an isolationist, but neither appellation is accurate. He maintains strongly held views that are often irreconcilable with those of colleagues such as Richard Lugar of Indiana who are interested in foreign affairs above all else, and he is a longtime critic of the United Nations, the institution where Madeleine Albright made her name. But Helms in his own way is quite engaged in international issues that affect the well-being of Americans, such as the rise of drug traffickers in Colombia and the uncompensated seizure of American property by the Sandinista government in Nicaragua.

During Albright's entire tenure as secretary of state, Republicans have controlled both houses of Congress and chaired all committees. Helms presides over the Senate Foreign Relations Committee, which has jurisdiction over treaties; the appointments of undersecretaries, assistant secretaries, and ambassadors; and part of the State Department budget. If he wished, he could have made Albright's life miserable—but he did not wish to do so, as he signaled at her confirmation hearing. He regarded her as a refreshing antidote to chronic squeamishness in the White House.

While still at the United Nations, Albright telephoned Helms to congratulate him on his reelection to the Senate in November 1996. That seemed a bizarre move for a Democrat, but for Albright it was just one step in a campaign to forge a working relationship with a senator whose views clashed with hers on almost every subject.

On this day, July 30, 1997, Helms was chairing a conference of Senate and House members over a bill to reorganize the government's foreign policy bureaucracy. One issue was how many undersecretaries the Department of State would be authorized to have. Albright wanted six. Helms wanted to permit no more than five; after all, he had noted the day before, the Defense Department, with more than ten times the State's budget, has only four. But he began this session by stating that he had had two conversations with Albright overnight on the subject, and as a result, he announced: "I'm going to yield to her. I want her to continue the good job she's doing."

This positive outcome did not just happen. In her first year in office, Albright worked assiduously not just to cultivate Helms but to build bipartisan support for the administration's foreign policy agenda and for her department and its budget. This was not her idea alone; Clinton began his second term with an appeal for bipartisanship in foreign policy as well as in domestic affairs, believing that the partisan wrangling that had temporarily shut down the federal government the previous year had further alienated the American public from politics. Albright commented:

> I felt it was important that I had a new opportunity to re-engage a bipartisan spirit. It's a fairly pragmatic thing to say, given the fact that everybody I have to deal with on the Hill in chairmanship positions is a Republican, and therefore it is one thing that I believe is the right thing to do but it's also the smart thing to do and so I worked to get the bipartisanship.[1]

She said many times that upon becoming a diplomat, "I had all my partisan instincts surgically removed." Still, for a lifelong Democrat, Albright put on an amazing display of cozying up to Republicans.

Her first official trip out of Washington as secretary of state was not to a foreign country but to Texas, to see former president George Bush and his secretary of state, James A. Baker III. A few weeks later she journeyed to Grand Rapids, Michigan, to attend a dedication ceremony at the library of former president Gerald R. Ford, which gave her the opportunity to discuss foreign affairs with such pillars of the Republican foreign policy establishment as former secretary of state Alexander M. Haig, former defense secretary Dick Cheney, and former White House national security adviser Brent Scowcroft, Republicans all. She was thrilled, she said, when Ford introduced her as "the Tiger Woods of foreign policy," because it meant that she was as popular as the young golf champion.

One of Albright's first public meetings with members of Congress was an appearance to testify before the House appropriations subcommittee chaired by Representative Harold Rogers, a courtly Kentuckian. His subcommittee's jurisdiction includes the State Department's operating budget, so Albright needed to be on good terms with him. For the occasion, Albright carried with her a big box, gift wrapped in red, white, and blue ribbon. Inside was a book of photographs. Albright had learned that Rogers had lost all his papers and photographs in a fire at his home, a disaster that had erased many souvenirs of his career and compounded the grief caused by the recent death of his wife. Albright instructed embassies in countries he had visited to provide copies of photos taken on those occasions and compiled them in an album, which she presented right there in the committee hearing room.

She turned the charm on Representative Sonny Callahan, too. When the GOP seized control of Congress, Callahan, who represents the Mobile, Alabama, region, became chairman of the Appropriations subcommittee that allocates foreign aid money. When the Democrats controlled the subcommittee, he had voted against every foreign aid spending bill that came along, but those were free votes aimed at the folks back in Mobile; he knew that the bills would pass anyway, so his vote was a symbolic one intended for home consumption. But now he was chairman, and he knew that his subcommittee had to produce a bill—he was not going to "zero out" foreign aid all by himself. The question was, how much?

This was the key question for Albright as she courted Callahan, Rogers, and other Republicans who had input into the federal budget. She wanted more money. The House has no jurisdiction over treaties or State Department nominees, but the conservative GOP House leadership was crucial to Albright's determination to halt the long slide in what is known as the 150 Account, the budget term for all international affairs spending: State Department operations and diplomatic missions, embassy security, foreign aid, language training, the United States Information Agency—everything that goes into the machinery of American diplomacy.

For some years, as Cold War anxiety receded, Congress had been cutting the 150 Account, much to the dismay of foreign policy practitioners. Warren Christopher had pleaded eloquently and publicly for more money, and had watched unhappily as budget cuts forced the department to close consulates overseas. The breakup of the former Soviet Union and the former Yugoslavia created a score of new nations where the United States was committed to establishing embassies; without new funds, putting embassies in outposts such as Tashkent and Skopje meant cutting back somewhere else.

In the 1980s, Congress funded the 150 Account at well over $20 billion annually. By the 1997 fiscal year, the amount was down to $18.2 billion, and the long-term projections of congressional budget cutters envisioned an eventual drop to $15 billion or less. Moreover, the United States owed the United Nations at least $1 billion in back dues and assessments for peacekeeping activities—the arrearages that were undermining U.S. influence at the United Nations and had spurred Albright's campaign to get rid of Boutros-Ghali. Alarm bells were sounding all through the administration and particularly in Washington's foreign policy establishment.

A study published in the summer of 1996 by Georgetown University's School of Foreign Service found "plentiful" anecdotal evidence of the strains on American diplomacy caused by inadequate resources:

> Staffing gaps during transfers are now routinely several months. Large consular sections in Latin America are chronically understaffed in terms of their ability to carry out U.S. visa law. The key positions of political and economic counselors at embassies have become difficult to fill because congressionally mandated ceilings in senior personnel, coupled with reduced promotions, have limited opportunities and make these positions no longer "career enhancing." Seasoned experts in European, Asian and Middle East affairs have been reduced to a handful.[2]

The Brookings Institution and the Council on Foreign Relations issued similar findings in January 1997, just as Albright was taking office. An all-star team that included three former secretaries of state and two former national security advisers concluded:

> The State Department and its 260-plus overseas posts constitute the basic and indispensable infrastructure upon which all U.S. civilian—and many military—elements rely to protect and promote American interests around the world. The Task Force found unmistakable evidence that the readiness of this infrastructure has been seriously eroded. Some 30 posts have been closed in the past three years for lack of operating funds. Many of the remaining posts are shabby, unsafe and ill-equipped. All are handicapped by obsolete information technology.[3]

"I agree with you that the decline in spending on international affairs is troubling, and I am committed to working to secure the resources we need to sustain America's international engagement," Clinton wrote to Senator Lugar. In a handwritten postscript, the president added: "I will work hard with you on this."[4]

Thus the money issue was inescapable as Clinton began his second term and as Albright took over as secretary of state. On his way out, Christopher had done most of the heavy lifting on this issue within the administration, convincing the Office of Management and Budget (OMB) that the political goal of balancing the federal budget could not be met by further shaving federal spending on diplomacy and foreign aid; he induced the OMB to allocate more funds to diplomacy in the president's annual spending proposal. Now it fell to Albright to persuade Congress to give the administration what it asked for.

In his proposed budget for the 1998 fiscal year, sent to Congress in February 1997, Clinton kept his promise to Lugar and his commitment to Christopher by asking for $19.45 billion for the 150 Account, with an additional fund of $921 million to pay the overdue bills at the United Nations. And the White House signaled that further increases could be expected in subsequent years, just as Albright wanted.

In a fact sheet distributed with the proposed budget, the White House argued:

> Maintaining American leadership is critical to safeguarding the security and interests of the American people. The downward spiral in interna-

tional affairs funding—*a real dollar cut of 14 percent in just the past 2 years*—compromises our leadership. The President's budget request of $19.451 billion only partially restores this damaging cut and sets a level needed to maintain American strength.[5]

Callahan was a key figure. He likes to say that he is "just an appropriator," interested in responsible spending, not in foreign policy. But as chairman of the subcommittee that controls foreign aid spending, one of the biggest components of the 150 Account, he clearly had the authority to swing a few hundred million dollars this way or that.

Conservative southern politicians like Callahan generally have little in common with liberal Democrats such as Albright who supported the presidential candidacy of Michael Dukakis, but her popularity was such that it made political sense for the Republicans to be seen working with her in bipartisan style.

Callahan and Albright appeared together at a chamber of commerce dinner in Mobile that developed into a virtual love-in. This was the event at which Callahan used his "flamingo in the barnyard of politics" line. Callahan responded to her prepared remarks by saying:

> My area of jurisdiction as chairman of Foreign Operations includes half of your operation in the State Department but it also includes some operations in the Treasury Department. I want to tell you, I'm not going to invite [treasury secretary] Bob Rubin down here. You have so impressed all these people, and me as well, that we're going to cut that [spending] bill, but we're not going to cut you!

After Albright took a few questions from the audience, he picked up the theme again:

> You are a compliment to this administration, a compliment to this country. We are very happy to have you in Mobile. When you came to my office in February, shortly after you were confirmed by the Senate, I, as I do many times when I visit foreign countries, I gave you a book written by Harper Lee, *To Kill a Mockingbird*, which was written by a famous author from my district. Since I've already given you that copy, we have another famous author here in Mobile by the name of Winston Groom. Winston

Groom wrote a book called *Forrest Gump*, which was made into a movie. I want to present you with an autographed copy of that book from Winston Groom, personally autographed to you.

Albright, who was a political activist long before she was a diplomat and knew what the moment required, responded with some crowd-pleasing treacle of her own: "Well, taking a line out of this book, dealing with Sonny is a little bit like having a box of chocolates," she said. "In the book it says, 'You never know what you're going to get,' but with Sonny you always know you've got a very sweet center."

At least she didn't hold hands with Callahan, as she did with Helms when she journeyed to North Carolina to visit his alma mater, a former junior college that has since grown into Wingate University, and an affiliated institution, the Jesse Helms Center, which houses the senator's papers and memorabilia.

The two flattered each other, praised each other, and promised to cooperate when they could and disagree respectfully when necessary. Helms, sitting at a front-row desk, beamed like an infatuated schoolboy as Albright discussed world affairs with Wingate students. On two occasions during her visit, once while disembarking from her car and once while seated together onstage at the university, they were photographed hand in hand. The pictures were published in many newspapers the next day, with predictable comments about this political odd couple, and surfaced months later in a newspaper advertisement placed by a group supporting the expansion of NATO. Above the picture of Helms and Albright smiling as they sat hand in hand, the advertisement carried the headline, "An Unlikely Couple. A Common Cause."

Albright spent a productive day at Wingate, buttering up Helms, flattering him for his patriotism, telling audiences about their mutual respect, touring the Jesse Helms Center, and chatting with students.

When Laura Welsh, a Wingate student from West Virginia, asked Albright what her "toughest negotiation" had been when she was at the United Nations, the secretary paused a moment and then replied, "with Jesse Helms." The senator grinned broadly and flashed a thumbs-up.

In the "Jesse Helms Lecture" she delivered that evening in the university's auditorium, she noted that some people were puzzled by her friendly relationship with the senator. After all, she said, "the senator is from rural North Carolina. I was born in the capital city of Czechoslovakia. He can square dance. I've done the Macarena—and unlike Vice President Gore, I actually move. He's a Republican, and before I became a diplomat and had all my partisan instincts surgically removed I was a Democrat. So, what gives?" She said the answer could be found on the first page of a book Helms wrote, where he proclaimed that "being an American in the twentieth century is the greatest fortune that can befall a human being."[6]

At the end of the day, these unlikely allies appeared together at a news conference, and Albright got her payoff. Helms announced that he would bring up for a vote a treaty known as the Chemical Weapons Convention, which barred the production, possession, or use of poison gas weapons. Helms opposed the treaty and did not endorse it, but he promised, in effect, to get out of the way and let the Senate vote on it.

Helms said that he not only welcomed Albright's quest for bipartisan cooperation, he initiated it, and indeed he had written to Clinton expressing a desire to avoid the partisan bickering over foreign affairs that had marked the president's first term. The vehicle for forging a new relationship was one of the most complicated and significant pieces of foreign policy legislation in the 105th Congress. This measure, sponsored by Helms and Senator Joseph Biden of Delaware, the Foreign Relations Committee's senior Democrat, aimed to reorganize the government's foreign policy agencies, which had not been restructured since the Cold War, and to pay $819 million of the more than $1 billion owed by the United States to the United Nations, mostly for past peacekeeping assessments, conditioned upon substantial internal reform at the United Nations. Enactment of this legislation would benefit both Helms and Albright: He would achieve the elimination of two government agencies he thought had outlived their usefulness, the United States Information Agency (USIA) and the Arms Control and Disarmament Agency, and impose a cleanup on the United Nations, which he regarded as a cesspool of waste, incompetence, and fuzzy one-world thinking. She would gain a great enhancement of her authority as secretary by assuming the functions of the eliminated agencies, and she would also realize her goal of paying the debt to the United Nations—the goal that had prompted her campaign to oust Boutros-Ghali.

When the Foreign Relations Committee met in June 1997 to take final action on the bill and send it to the full Senate, Helms said:

> From the beginning, it has been my hope that this effort would be a bipartisan one, dedicated to the reorganization and revitalization of our foreign policy institutions. Unfortunately, in the 104th Congress the effort degenerated into a partisan battle. When Congress finally enacted legislation and sent it to the President, the President vetoed a bill that would have eliminated just one federal agency which had "temporary" status for half a century [the USIA]. . . . This year I was determined that this spectacle should not be repeated. Shortly after the November 1996 election, I spoke with the President, and I expressed the hope that we would work together this time around, thereby forging a proposal giving the American taxpayers a more efficient and effective foreign affairs apparatus. The President agreed. I also conveyed this hope, both publicly and privately, to Secretary of State Albright, who readily agreed that it was essential that this be a bipartisan effort. Thereby, we together sent the administration a clear message that there must be no repeat of the unsuccessful battles waged in 1995 and 1996.

In the end, the problem with getting this legislation passed lay not with Helms or with Albright but with the Republican leadership in the House, which allowed right-to-life crusaders to attach to it unrelated language on abortion that was unacceptable to the administration. Clinton vetoed it, even though it contained almost everything Albright wanted, in what Helms called "an astounding display of administration priorities. The White House chose to block this reform bill at the end of the first session of this Congress after the House added a single provision protecting unborn babies from deliberate mass destruction."[7]

The most subtle and nuanced issue on which Albright was able to maintain good relations with Helms even while disagreeing with him involved Cuba. By most definitions Cuba is not a national security issue at all—it is a poor country of negligible economic or strategic interest to the United States—but is instead a political issue, the passions driven by Cuban Americans dreaming of liberating their homeland from Fidel Castro's communist rule. For anticommunists such as Helms, the perpetuation of Castro's regime represents a never-ending challenge to liberty and to American values, a challenge that must be confronted.

The visit to Cuba of Pope John Paul II in January 1998 focused worldwide attention on the island, on Castro, and on Cuba's relationship, or lack of a relationship, with the United States. And it raised corresponding questions about the long-standing and unremitting U.S. policy of trying to bring down Castro by isolating him diplomatically and undermining him economically.

Given that Castro had kept a solid grip on Cuba for nearly forty years, it was reasonable to question the effectiveness of Washington's policy—and the pope did so. At the time of the visit, the United States was trying to ensure that food and medicine were flowing to Iraq, an international outlaw, while barring most such shipments to Cuba. Washington was pursuing economic engagement with China and Vietnam, both of which had killed many thousands of American troops in war, while refusing to try engagement with Cuba.

Albright has been questioned throughout her term about just these sorts of inconsistencies: Why get involved in Kosovo, a separatist province of Serbia, and not Chechnya, a separatist region of Russia? Why impose human rights sanctions on Burma and not China? Her answer has been that a powerful, globally involved country such as the United States "can't have a cookie-cutter foreign policy." The case of Cuba, however, involves domestic electoral politics as much as foreign policy. When I asked one of Albright's senior Cuba policy staff people about the Vietnam versus Cuba inconsistency, he responded that the difference was the domestic political context. "Congress has a strong voice on Cuba policy and that's appropriate, that's how it should be in a democracy," he said.

Christopher had given a similar explanation for Clinton's decision in his first term to sign an anti-Castro bill known as the Helms-Burton law after its principal sponsors, Helms in the Senate and Representative Dan Burton of Indiana in the House. The administration opposed this piece of legislation as unnecessary and unworkable until the Cubans shot down two unarmed light planes operated by a Miami-based anti-Castro exile group. (That was the incident that had inspired Albright's *"cojones"* line.) After the shootdown, Christopher believed that congressional anger at Castro ran so high that Helms-Burton would have been enacted over Clinton's veto anyway, so there was no point in suffering the political wounds that a veto would have caused.

Helms-Burton turned out to be a serious nuisance. All the reasons the administration had given for opposing it before the shootdown of the planes were valid. Provisions that imposed economic sanctions on foreign companies that invested in certain properties in Cuba—and on executives of those companies—infuriated the Europeans and Canadians, who regarded the law as American interference with their freedom to do business. The European Union threatened retaliatory action; it took considerable diplomatic skill for Stuart Eizenstat, the undersecretary for economic affairs, to negotiate a cease-fire agreement in which, essentially, the Europeans pretended to get serious about human rights in Cuba and the United States pretended to enforce the law. Even worse, Helms-Burton wrote into law the long-standing embargo on trade with Cuba. Once Clinton signed Helms-Burton, he no longer had the authority to end the embargo. Only Congress could do so, upon a presidential certification that Cuba had become a democracy. Clinton had ended the American embargo on trade with Vietnam, but he could no longer do so on Cuba even if he were so inclined.

As a second-term president, Clinton might have had little to lose politically from a reappraisal of Cuba policy, and in fact a few modest changes were in the works—Albright would reveal them in a background briefing for a few journalists a couple of weeks after the pope's visit—but any show of softness on Castro would have torpedoed Albright's carefully nurtured relationship with Helms, one of Castro's most relentless opponents in Congress. Clinton and Albright would have liked to end the embargo, but any effort to do so would have been political dynamite, and in any case Castro gave them little to work with, continuing to rule the island with an iron grip and to suppress all dissent.

Several months after the pope went to Cuba, in the fall of 1998, a bipartisan group of senators, led by John Warner, the Virginia Republican who chaired the Armed Services Committee, proposed the creation of a presidential commission to evaluate all aspects of U.S. policy on Cuba, including the question of whether the trade embargo had outlived its usefulness. This proposal offered Albright an opportunity to promote modifications in Cuba policy if she wished; the senators' recommendation carried with it the implication that the policy should be revised, and its bipartisan origins provided insulation against criticism from the right wing.

"I think everybody would like to have a different policy on Cuba," she said when I asked her about it. "The problem is Cuban actions," in reference to Castro's tendency to do something outrageous to discourage any overtures toward better relations. As for Warner's proposal to create a commission, she said, "We have obviously heard about it but have not yet formulated a response, nor can I make any judgment yet whether it's a good idea or not."[8]

This hardly fit the image of straight-talking bluntness that Albright had promoted for herself. Congress has a right and a duty to be heard on foreign policy issues, and the secretary must respect congressional sentiment, which in the case of Helms means relentless opposition to Castro, period. But the bipartisan commission proposal could have provided an opening, had she wished to embrace it.

Instead, she recommended—and Clinton approved—another modest set of revisions to the embargo. These included provisions allowing any American citizen—not just those with relatives in Cuba—to send money to people on the island, an expansion of air service between the United States and Cuba, and a resumption of direct postal service. The president even authorized the Baltimore Orioles to play two exhibition baseball games against the Cuban national team, one game in each country. The president rejected the Warner plan for a bipartisan commission.

Some lobbyists on both sides of the Cuba policy issue thought that the president's package would upset Helms, and in a way it did, but not for the reasons they expected. Helms was not opposed to the increased flow of people and dollars to Cuba; he favored such commerce, on the theory that the more Cubans knew about democracy and the more they could become economically independent of the Castro government, the sooner change would come to Cuba. What bothered Helms was that the changes did not go far enough. Helms was delighted that Albright nixed the commission proposal because appointing such a commission was tantamount to seeking an end to the trade embargo, an outcome that would have been anathema to Helms.

"The proposed commission was the latest project of the appease-Castro crowd," the senator said in a statement. He further stated that the commission proposal was a "Trojan horse for lifting the Cuba embargo" and that the administration, by turning it away, had "opened the way for us in the Senate to say 'yes' to a lot of creative ideas for bringing change to Cuba."

There have of course been occasions when Albright openly challenged conservative GOP sentiment on important issues—most notably in a passionate defense of arms control policy after India and Pakistan conducted tests of nuclear weapons in the spring of 1998. Those tests prompted calls from hawkish Republicans to scrap as outdated the 1972 Antiballistic Missile Treaty, a cornerstone of arms-control efforts for a whole generation, and to reject as useless the Comprehensive Test Ban Treaty, which banned all future nuclear weapons tests and which Clinton and Albright strongly endorsed. To the nuclear hawks, including Helms, the Pakistani detonations showed that a nation could develop nuclear weapons without testing—after all, the weapons Pakistan exploded had been designed and assembled without prior detonations—and therefore the Test Ban Treaty was useless.

"I say that is dangerous nonsense," Albright said. "Efforts to halt the spread of nuclear weapons do not come with a guarantee. But to abandon them because they have been dealt a setback would be a felony against the future."[9]

Albright has generally refrained from public criticism of individual Republicans, especially Helms and his House counterpart, Representative Benjamin Gilman, a New York moderate who obtained the chairmanship of the House International Relations Committee by carrying water for Speaker Newt Gingrich and other right-wingers in the House Republican leadership.

Albright largely ignored Gilman, a weak chairman of a weak committee, and he complained about it in public. At one hearing, he griped:

I regret that especially in recent months, we've been having difficulties obtaining administration witnesses to explain and defend their policies before the Congress. From the failure of the Secretary of State who had agreed to appear here and continuing on down through the department, this phenomenon is not consonant with this or any other administration's obligation to explain, to defend, and to sustain a democratic basis of foreign policy.[10]

That was nonsense. Albright was well aware of—indeed, reveled in—her obligation to explain and defend the administration's policies. She just chose not to do so before Gilman's committee, a collection of mediocrities and posers from both parties with little real power. She preferred to work with members of Congress who had power over things that mattered, such as Helms and Rogers, and to shape opinion on Capitol Hill by taking her case to the public, directly and through the media.

At her first news conference after her swearing in, Albright told the gang in the State Department briefing room: "The press plays a vital role as educator, interpreter, and constructive—or usually constructive—critic of our foreign policy. I respect that role and, as I do my job, I will strive to be open and available, and thereby help you to do yours." The reality turned out to be much more complicated. Albright's relationship with the press in many ways resembles that of her pal, Hillary Clinton. On the road, she is often genial and friendly, though she is also guarded and alert for any perceived slight. On most extended trips, she schedules an informal dinner with the traveling reporters; at those events, the conversations are off the record and the atmosphere is generally relaxed. She is wary of one-on-one encounters with journalists who know what they are talking about, and she has little tolerance for journalistic efforts to go beyond what she wants us to know.

The tradition of taking members of the press corps aboard the plane when a secretary of state travels abroad goes back at least to the tenure of Dean Rusk in the administration of Lyndon B. Johnson. The arrangement serves the needs of both the State Department and the press corps. For the secretary of state and her staff, such proximity to selected members of the press corps ensures extensive coverage by reporters whom they know—reporters who can be counted on to avoid the bombastic and ideologically loaded questions fired at secretaries of state by journalists from other countries—and allows them to provide unofficial background information to guide the press coverage in the direction most favorable to them. The arrangement also has the practical benefit for a cash-strapped State Department of filling up otherwise empty seats with journalistic passengers paying top dollar.

For the press corps, these trips are an essential component of diplomatic news gathering. They ensure that reporters will be present, with front-row seats, at all of the secretary's public events in the countries to be visited. Because State Department reporters travel on the secretary's plane—unlike White House reporters, who except for a small pool travel separately on a chartered aircraft and have no access to the official staff—we have access to background briefings and informal conversations aboard the aircraft that we would otherwise not hear. The unwritten rules of these trips allow us opportunities to meet, talk to, and sometimes even socialize with State Department and National Security Council officials to whom we might not have immediate access back home. At the State Department, as at the Defense Department, the job of the journalist is not just to record events but to penetrate a culture that does not lend itself to penetration; traveling with the secretary and her party is essential to doing that.

When an overseas trip by the secretary is announced, a sign-up sheet is posted in the press office, and journalists who want to make the trip put their names on it. In theory, any correspondent with State Department credentials can go, but most of the time the number of applicants exceeds the number of seats that will be available—usually ten to fifteen or so—and the State Department selects the organizations that will be taken aboard.

The three major international wire services, Associated Press, Reuters, and Agence France-Presse, make almost every trip. Cable News Network (CNN), the *Washington Post,* the *New York Times,* the *Los Angeles Times,* the *Wall Street Journal, USA Today, Time,* and *Newsweek* are pretty much guaranteed seats if they want them—although on her first trip abroad as secretary, Albright booted the French news agency to make room for Fox Television, a clear sign of the importance she attaches to communicating with domestic audiences. If all those organizations want to send correspondents, as they often do on major policymaking trips or in times of tension, that leaves little room for other news organizations, a source of endless frustration for correspondents from the *Boston Globe,* the *Chicago Tribune,* Voice of America, and other media outlets who can never be certain of getting on the plane. Occasionally Albright will reserve a seat for an organization that is doing a profile of her or giving in-depth coverage to a specific issue, as she did for *Vogue* and the *New Yorker.*

The ground rules for the press on these trips are unwritten but well known, and seem to have changed little since I first traveled with Henry Kissinger in 1976. At gathering places on the ground, such as an airport waiting room or a hotel checkout line, reporters are free to approach members of the official party and talk to them; it is up to the official to decide whether to talk at all, and if so whether to talk substance or limit the conversation to chitchat.

An official having breakfast in a hotel restaurant is fair game; a reporter can approach and ask permission to sit down and talk, and the official is free to say yes or no. Often, in the peculiar culture of policymaking Washington, a reporter will know a member of the official party from a previous incarnation, on Capitol Hill or in some think tank, or through a parents' association at a school, and the trips thus provide opportunities for tennis games or late-night dinners where the conversations are informal but useful.

Aboard the plane, reporters sit in the rear compartment along with members of the diplomatic security staff. We are not free to enter the forward cabins except by invitation; but lavatories and the galley are in the rear compartment, and officials who come back to use those facilities may be approached for questions. Occasionally these officials give formal briefings. Otherwise, whatever they say is protected: We can use whatever information they give us but we cannot attribute it to them.

For veteran correspondents who already know the officials in the traveling party, these informal encounters provide an opportunity to talk with sources who are comfortable because they have worked with us in the past and know we will play by the rules. For newcomers to the press corps, these trips provide the opportunity to meet officials whom they will need to know—the deputy assistant secretaries and National Security Council directors who do the heavy lifting in foreign policy. Often the fact that we are all far from home together inspires a willingness among senior officials to socialize, perhaps over dinner, even though we rarely have such extended access to them at home.

These trips are not junkets, despite the occasional opportunities for sightseeing or shopping. For every convivial dinner at Castelli's in Addis Ababa or some other exotic spot, there are two overnight flights and four crack-of-dawn departures. The trips are tightly scheduled and often involve stops for meetings with foreign officials in several countries in a single day. For a grandmother in her early sixties, some of the trips have become grueling tests of stamina—

which Albright has always passed, beating back pressure and fatigue that have worn down younger colleagues and the traveling press.

One extreme example was her trip to East Africa after the terrorist bombings of the U.S. embassies in Kenya and Tanzania in August 1998. We took off from Andrews Air Force Base outside Washington on a Monday morning and flew all day and then overnight to Dar es Salaam, Tanzania, arriving about 9 A.M. Tuesday Tanzania time. Albright visited the damaged embassy, spoke to the staff and the American community, and met with security officials and FBI agents investigating the bombing. After about three hours, we flew up to Nairobi, Kenya, for a similar but even more moving program—the damage there was greater, the death toll higher, and the shock and grief of the citizenry more palpable. At about 8:30 P.M., we headed back to Nairobi airport for the long flight home.

The reason Albright and her aides gave for not staying overnight in Nairobi was that her presence would put an additional burden on an embassy staff and host government already overwhelmed by the disaster. But there was another reason: Albright knew that President Clinton had already given the order for cruise missile strikes the next day against encampments in Afghanistan suspected of harboring terrorists and a pharmaceutical factory in Sudan believed to be producing chemical weapons. She wanted to be out of Africa and back in Washington when the trigger was pulled.

Her plane, however, had developed a mechanical problem and could not take off. So she commandeered a U.S. Air Force C-141, a giant cargo jet that happened to be in Kenya after hauling relief supplies and medical equipment down from an air base in Germany. Being a cargo plane, it was cold, noisy, and dimly lit. The portable seats, bolted in for passengers, had evidently been designed by torturers. There was no separate cabin, and no separate restroom, for a traveling VIP such as Albright. No matter—we clambered aboard and headed for home, another eighteen hours in the air, refueling in flight. We were back in Washington less than forty-eight hours after we had left. Most of us took the next day off, but Albright was in her office just a few hours after our landing.

Despite outward similarities, Christopher and Albright developed quite different approaches to these trips. Christopher, although personally reserved and uncomfortable at scheduled social events with the press, placed virtually no restrictions on other members of his traveling party, who were free to talk, eat, and socialize with reporters as much as they chose in the time available.

Albright, by contrast, routinely organizes dinners and other social events with the press corps and seems to enjoy them—the best that I participated in was a boat ride down the Zambezi River below Victoria Falls in Zimbabwe, on which we joined the secretary in drinking beer and watching hippos—but restricts the opportunities for us to talk to other officials in her party. On one particularly tense trip to the Middle East, reporters joked that nobody in the official party ever went to the bathroom, because no senior officials came to the back of the plane, so reporters could not question them. That was symptomatic of Albright's approach to the media: welcome at official events such as news conferences but unwelcome to develop sources of information outside the secretary's control.

At one of her press dinners, in Hong Kong, she scolded me and Steve Erlanger of the *New York Times* for what she saw as "tendentious" reporting in our newspapers and in the press overall. What she meant, it was clear from her comments, was that she did not appreciate analytical stories that probed at motives, personalities, internal debates, or possible outcomes that were not part of the official message. It seemed to surprise her when I countered that we are not stenographers: It is our job to look behind the official announcements and the controlled timing of staged events to discern what is really going on.

Albright and members of her inner circle—especially her spokesman, Jamie Rubin—have been willing to tolerate critical reporting about the administration's foreign policy, even though they don't like such coverage, but they are sensitive to the point of absurdity about any reporting that suggests that she herself might have failed to deliver, or done or said anything inappropriate.

When Albright visited a muddy, hilly camp for returned refugees in Rwanda, for example, Laura Myers of the Associated Press noted in her story that the secretary "tottered over rocky passes in red high heels."

That was a fact; Albright had gone to the camp directly from a meeting with government officials and nobody had remembered to throw more comfortable footwear into her car. But Rubin was furious; he apparently thought that Myers was suggesting that Albright somehow lacked respect for Rwanda's suffering. Long after midnight, he flagged me down in the corridor of our hotel to complain about what Myers had written and ask me what to do about her. This was preposterous; had Myers really wanted to suggest some inappropriateness on Albright's part, she could have pointed out that the secretary had worn black for cocktails with the press the night before and red to visit a mass grave and the refugee camp. Besides, Albright always dresses so colorfully and wears so much jewelry that her attire invites comment. And beyond that, Rubin should not have been talking to me about what Myers wrote; if he had a problem with her, I said, he should take it to her.

During that same stop in Rwanda, I inquired about the developing pattern of showing tolerance for, and a desire to work with, African leaders with less than stellar human rights records. The administration had decided on pragmatic grounds to follow such a course; Clinton and Albright wanted to promote economic, military, and environmental cooperation with the Africans, and in order to accomplish this they were willing to pull a few punches on human rights. One of the American officials I talked to summarized this policy in a wisecrack: "We don't do Mary Robinson." Robinson, a former president of Ireland, is the U.N. high commissioner for human rights; for her, human rights is the only item on the agenda. The wisecrack was just a shorthand way of saying that Albright's agenda was more complicated. When I quoted the comment in my story the next day, without identifying the speaker, Albright and Rubin were angry because they thought I was implying that the secretary tolerated disrespect for Robinson. They sent Susan Rice, the assistant secretary of state for African affairs, back to the press section to find out who had made the comment. There was no way I was going to tell them, because that person had been talking to me on a background basis, trying to help me understand the policy—not commenting for attribution. I had often spoken to Rice on the same basis; it is standard practice in Washington, for better or worse, and she always expected me to honor the unwritten agreement not to name her. Albright's sending her to inquire was a reflection of the secretary's desire to control communications and to silence anyone who said anything unauthorized.

The *Washington Post* of July 23, 1998, featured two long stories about developments in American foreign policy. One, written by me, said that the United States had suffered "a spectacular diplomatic defeat" when delegates to a conference in Rome resoundingly rejected American conditions for the establishment of a permanent international war crimes court. The other, by my colleague Barton Gellman, was a nuanced evaluation of Middle East peacemaking efforts, saying that Albright had concluded there was "no hope" of persuading Israel to accept the deal with the Palestinians that she was promoting, and that she had been forced to retreat from an ultimatum she had issued to Israel two months earlier.

Nobody at the State Department complained about the strong language in my article, but Rubin went over the top about what Gellman had written, accusing him of being a "hype artist" who refused to listen to what department officials told him. He called Gellman, and our editor, to complain. Then he went public at the daily State Department briefing.

"It is always an interesting phenomenon to read in the newspaper what appear to be fictional accounts to those who are participants," he said. "This was a classic hype job." He said that Nabil Shaath, a veteran Palestinian negotiator whom Gellman had quoted in his article, "does not represent the views of the Palestinians"—despite the fact that Albright had invited Shaath to Washington the week before so he could tell her the views of the Palestinians.

The difference in response to the two articles, of course, was that Gellman's piece suggested some personal failure by Albright, whereas mine did not.

To her credit, Albright is aware of her sensitivity and occasionally jokes about it. "Some say the secretary of state is thin-skinned and can't take criticism. I can't stand people who say that," she deadpanned at a charity event, evoking laughter from her knowledgeable audience.[11]

Nor is she the first secretary of state who has lacked understanding about how the press corps really works and what reporters are after. Richard Valeriani, a correspondent for NBC who logged more than 500,000 miles in the air with Henry Kissinger, recalled a conversation during Kissinger's Middle East peace shuttle after the 1973 war in which Kissinger fretted about news coverage:

> Kissinger suggested that perhaps he was briefing us too much. He was worried about how the stories out of Alexandria would look, what kind of signals would be sent to the Israelis. Perhaps it would be better if he didn't see us quite so often.

"That's up to you," I said. "We all know that you're in control of the flow of information. We try to find out as much as we can on the ground, but everybody recognizes that you set the tone for the reporting in your briefings. And," I reminded him, "if you don't brief frequently—if you leave an information void—it will be filled by others."

After pondering this for a moment, Kissinger told Valeriani that he could not really complain about the press coverage, which had been generally favorable—not surprising, since most of the information had been coming from him—and added, "I know all of you are back there rooting for me to succeed."

There Kissinger, smart as he was, was completely wrong about the press, and Valeriani called him on it:

"Mr. Secretary," I said immediately, "I don't want to sound harsh about this, but there's something I ought to explain. As American citizens, we may be sitting back there rooting for you to succeed. But as professional journalists, we don't care whether you succeed or fail!" It came out a little more blunt than I intended.

Kissinger looked as though I had just told him the plane was landing in Albania. "You can't be that objective," he argued.[12]

Yes, we can, or least we can try to. From the perspective of the back of the airplane, a secretary of state's failure is at least as good a story as a success. As Americans, we want to see our country peaceful and prosperous. But as journalists, we don't care—or at least we don't show that we care—what the outcome of any particular diplomatic mission is.

Albright took office proclaiming her intention to reconnect the American people with foreign policy. With the Vietnam War a generation past and the Cold War slipping into history, she felt and said repeatedly that Americans were losing their sense of involvement with the world. They needed to be reminded and persuaded that foreign policy matters to them, that they are connected to the world by trade, immigration, overpopulation, the global environment, international crime, the development of chemical and biological weapons that could easily cross borders and be used against civilians, and the expanding threat of terrorism. She wanted Americans to believe so strongly in the importance of American leadership in world affairs that they would urge Congress to put up enough money to support effective diplomacy. These were constant themes in her public appearances:

> I thought and still do that one of my prime jobs here is to reconnect the American people with foreign policy and to make it understandable and to make it interesting and to make it meaningful on a very particular basis. So in terms of what my goals have been, one of my prime goals initially was to create a platform for being able to do the basic foreign policy issues. And that platform included going out to the American public and presenting the case as clearly as possible and relating it to whatever area I was in at the time.

Many people, she said, think of foreign policy as an "arcane science" practiced by "stuffy diplomats." She wanted to break down that image. "I think I'm a fairly accessible person, and the woman part I think makes me more accessible, and people feel they can kind of have an understanding of the way I explain things and the fact that they can call me Madeleine and there's something about it that makes me more accessible and I think that helps."[13]

Valeriani recalled: "The stroking of the press and the Congress played a major role in Kissinger's rise to superstardom; he understood that they were the keys to a successful career in Washington."[14]

Albright, who lived in Washington for many years before taking on a prominent diplomatic job and who had been married to a journalist, knew at least as well as Kissinger that the news media were indispensable to the dissemination of her message. She held her first news conference the day after she was sworn in. She was a regular on the Sunday morning television talk shows, on *Larry King Live,* and on *NewsHour* with Jim Lehrer.

Unlike other cabinet officials, a secretary of state has few "deliverables" that can demonstrate results to ordinary people. The State Department cannot provide housing or health care or crop subsidies or roads or schools, the tangible products of government that win constituents. But when opportunities arose to show Americans directly that the State Department mattered to them and that diplomats worked hard on their behalf, she seized them.

Just a few weeks after she took office, for example, Albania, the poorest country in Europe, disintegrated into violence and chaos after thousands of citizens lost their savings in unregulated pyramid schemes. Albright allowed reporters and television camera crews into the State Department operations center to see the work of an Albania task force she had created, under the direction of deputy assistant secretary of state Rudolf Perina, a veteran of Eastern European diplomacy.

Working in shirtsleeves, with boxes of snack food and empty soda cans strewn about, the task force was scrambling frantically to get information about the situation in Albania, arrange the evacuation of American citizens, and provide information to the anxious relatives of Peace Corps volunteers and other Americans stationed in Albania, who were deluging the department with inquiries.

Classified documents were lying on the conference table, and staff members were talking on secure telephone lines. This was not the sort of gathering accustomed to being televised. But Albright understood the market value of this scene, showing people around the country that their State Department was working hard for them.

"I'm very grateful to all of you for what you are doing," she told Perina's team. "You are doing real people work."

That same day, Albright went to a public school in Washington to read to first graders. "The purpose of the secretary's visit," said spokesman Nicholas Burns, Jamie Rubin's predecessor, "is to create awareness even at an early age of the connection of the United States to the larger world around us."

It was not as if Albright had nothing else to do. The previous day, a Jordanian soldier had murdered seven Israeli schoolgirls, endangering Middle East peace negotiations; the following day, Russian foreign minister Yevgeny Primakov was due in Washington to complete arrangements for an upcoming summit meeting between Presidents Clinton and Boris Yeltsin. But to Albright, this outreach effort was as important as the other events on her crowded calendar because she believed that her personal popularity and the engagement of the public were the keys to success, especially on Capitol Hill.

"The bottom line is her popularity, which is real—you've written about it, others have written about it," one of her aides said. "She recognizes it and she intends to exploit it." Naming members of Congress with influence on the foreign affairs budget, the aide continued:

> What makes Pete Domenici and Mitch McConnell or Hal Rogers or Bob
> Livingston give us more money is not because they suddenly think foreign
> policy is great. It's because when they come into a room with Madeleine

Albright, there are ten TV cameras there. And when they bring her to their district, Sonny Callahan goes to his district, the whole county comes out and thinks it's great. Jesse Helms has never been as popular as the day he was leading Madeleine Albright around his home town. He had five thousand people in a stadium cheering, and those people didn't all vote for him. That's power. That's what makes these guys, when push comes to shove and they have to figure out where the money is going to come from, it's, "Oh, God, I don't want to hear from Madeleine on this, she just called me yesterday, she's going to call me tomorrow if I don't do this." Who wants to piss off Madeleine Albright? She's popular! That's how you get money. There are techniques that one uses, and she does them better, she's a natural at it, but at its core, what this is about is, she's popular. You've seen the polls—she's as popular as Colin Powell, or more. That matters.

What this official referred to as "techniques" included Albright's and Rubin's use of the news media and new tools such as the Internet in innovative ways that have gone far beyond the traditional daily briefing in the State Department press room.

That briefing, conducted by the spokesman, has long served as the principal channel of communication between the department and the world. Officials in each regional or functional bureau— African Affairs, for example, or Population, Migration, and Refugees—spend much of the morning preparing "guidance" on every conceivable development in world affairs for the spokesman to read if asked, and coordinating this guidance with the White House and with other departments to ensure consistency throughout the administration. To the annoyance of the State Department, reporters from the *New York Times,* the *Wall Street Journal,* and the *Washington Post* rarely attend the briefing. It takes place at lunchtime, and we often have lunch appointments with officials, scholars, or foreign diplomats who may provide exclusive information; we don't need to be present at the briefing because we can read a transcript on our computer screens as soon as we return to our offices. In addition, we are often working on what we hope are exclusive stories, and we don't wish to tip our hands by asking about them at an open briefing.

Albright knew that the major news organizations would track her activities one way or another. She was interested in reaching a larger audience, capitalizing on her popularity to engage ordinary people outside the Beltway in international affairs. She wanted to get to Americans who don't read the *New York Times* or the *Washington Post.* For much of her first year in office, it seemed that the woman was everywhere, spreading the foreign policy gospel and promoting her image.

With the politician's innate understanding of the value of images, Albright was photographed on her hands and knees, talking to children from Afghanistan in a refugee camp on the Pakistan border, to show her support for Afghan women and her contempt for the religious zealots in Kabul. In a camp in northern Uganda, she cradled a baby conceived in rape. She charmed the French, with whom Christopher had had a difficult relationship, by speaking to them in their own language. Claiming to be too old to learn any new vocabulary, she told students at the Bronx High School of Science in New York that "foreign policy is awesome, foreign policy is cool."[15] Often she appeared in public wearing her Stetson hat, which somehow contributed to her tough-guy image.

In the Krajina region of Croatia, she flew in by helicopter, accompanied by journalists, to stand before a burned-out house and publicly dress down Croatian reconstruction minister Jure Granic. In language rarely heard from diplomats, she said she was "disgusted" by Croatia's failure to halt violence against Serb refugees and added, "You should be ashamed of yourself. How can you allow such things to happen?"[16]

Later, she acknowledged that the burned-out house was prop, a site that had been selected before her arrival for its visual impact. "Obviously the house was set up," she admitted. "What I said was not. And they can testify to that. You find a background and everything, but I believe that the strength of the United States is to be a leader and speak out, that if we don't speak out, then nobody will speak. Then my own personality is such that I—I didn't make it up."

She said that she was outraged by what had happened to two couples who epitomized the peaceful, multiethnic population of prewar Yugoslavia:

> I mean, there was a Serb married to a Muslim and a Croat married to a Serb, and all they were trying to do was to come back to the house they lived in and they were beaten up not by their real neighbors but by im-

ported neighbors. . . . I sat in this hovel of a house with this eighty-year-old grandmother who'd been beaten up and four little children and I was appalled. . . . I was in a fit in the car, saying this is really awful.

She was still steaming when she encountered Granic. "I could have been in front of a totally put together house, I still would have said it. The image was set up, but I was not programmed. . . . I don't abjure the idea of using images to tell the story, because to me telling the story is part of how you get the American public to support the foreign policy."[17]

There was an important subtext to that incident that went well beyond the burnishing of her reputation for straight talk. Albright was trying to overcome the reluctance of the Defense Department to keep American troops in Bosnia beyond the arbitrary July 1998 deadline set by Clinton for their withdrawal. She believed that the United States had a responsibility to help enforce the 1995 Dayton agreement that had ended the war, and that if Washington pulled out, the agreement could collapse. Undiplomatic outbursts like the one in Krajina reinforced the sincerity and vigor of her arguments, and she prevailed—so convincingly, in fact, that there was little political outcry from any domestic faction when the president eventually decided to keep the troops in place indefinitely.

~

Meanwhile, Albright was working the home front, too.

She appeared on *60 Minutes,* in a flattering profile that reinforced her reputation for forthrightness and an ability to connect with ordinary Americans. Asked by interviewer Ed Bradley what she wanted people to know about her, she replied, "Actually, I want them to know everything about me," which of course was not true—nobody would want that—but which sounded sincere. Asked what she did when not working, she said, "I have a farm not far from here, and nobody would ever recognize me on the farm as I play around in my garden barefooted. And I go to the movies, and I knit." The profile included a film clip of Albright dancing the macarena. And she assured Bradley that she had never had a face-lift. No stuffy, tradition-bound diplomat here.

On opening day of the 1997 major league baseball season, Albright went to Camden Yards in Baltimore to throw out the ceremonial first ball. Wearing an Orioles cap and jacket, she took the mound, ball in hand—and jokingly shook off the sign flashed by catcher Chris Hoiles. She said later that the moment clearly separated her from her predecessors: "As far as I am aware, none of those distinguished gentlemen ever walked out in front of fifty thousand screaming baseball fans wearing a Baltimore Orioles jacket and jewelry."[18]

On March 16, 1997, less than two months after she took office, Albright appeared as the star and subject of "The Mini Page," a children's supplement to the Sunday comics that is distributed with newspapers all across the country. "First Woman Secretary of State Madeleine Albright Talks to Kids," the headline read. There were photographs of Albright with Hillary Clinton and Czech president Vaclav Havel; of Albright as a girl, in traditional Czech clothing, with her mother, sister, and brother; and of Albright as a young mother, with her twin baby daughters. The connect-the-dots puzzle was of the face of Madeleine Albright. Drawings of cute animals illustrated items about the State Department, including a word jumble that featured such terms as "treaties," "visa," "policy," and "cabinet." In a "Message from the Secretary of State," Albright delivered in simple language the same homilies about herself, her past, and her role that grown-ups were hearing in other forums:

> By the time I was 11, I had lived in five countries and knew four languages. In my parents' home we talked about international relations all the time, the way some families talk about sports or other things around the dinner table. As a child, living in so many foreign countries made it easier for me to adjust to different situations and to make friends—the essential skills of diplomacy. My mother always taught me to be open and friendly with new people. She said I could learn a lot from them, and she was right.

She told her young readers: "Today, it is more important than ever to know what is happening around you. . . . You will find that we live in a time of vast change, and that because of developments in technology, communication and international trade, the world is shrinking. Our jobs, safety and prosperity depend more than ever on events that happen thousands of miles away."

Albright delivered variations on this theme through multiple channels—speeches to university audiences and student groups, appearances on television and radio talk shows, and unorthodox presentations such as the "Global Connections" mailing.

This last was a project developed by InterAction, which bills itself as "the nation's largest coalition of international humanitarian aid groups." With a grant from the Pew Charitable Trusts, InterAction set out to engage Americans in thinking about the larger world outside their borders. An initial mailing to "opinion leaders" in September 1997 featured a "Dear Friend" letter from Madeleine Albright. "Since becoming Secretary of State," she wrote, "I have tried to reach out to the American people to explain the importance of foreign affairs to our country's continued greatness. Our nation stands preeminent in the world today: our values, powerful economy, dominant military, and faith in the future make us truly the world's indispensable nation."

Acknowledging that many Americans understood this in principle, she continued:

> Unfortunately, I have been struck by how little many Americans really know about our efforts overseas. Many are surprised (and perhaps you will be too) when I say that foreign affairs spending represents only one percent of the federal budget. Yet that one percent may well determine much of the history written of our era, and affects 100% of Americans. . . . I urge you to take advantage of the opportunities offered by *Global Connections: A National Conversation About a Changing World* to make your voice heard and help us all better understand the critical issues facing Americans around the globe and how we can respond to them.

Through the Internet, Albright put the State Department—and herself—on-line to millions of consumers around the world. The State Department's site on the World Wide Web (www.state.gov) replaced mailings and faxes as the principal channel for informing the public—for issuing travel warnings, for example, and providing passport information. The site also includes a home page for the secretary, with such features as "What the Secretary Has Been Saying" and "Travels with the Secretary."

People were invited to communicate with Albright by sending e-mail to [secretary@state.gov]. When they do, the department announced, their messages "will be reviewed by the Bureau of Public Affairs; foreign policy opinions and concerns will be carefully recorded and given to the Secretary each week along with a representative sampling of the mail."[19]

The public affairs staff also created a special section of the web site aimed at young people. That's where I learned that Albright's favorite color is blue and her favorite poet is Robert Frost; that she fills quiet moments with "needlepoint and sewing"; and that her favorite food is "Czech dumplings," which are made of "shrimp, artichokes and mushrooms in a cream sauce." (That seemed to me to be an odd choice, since she is allergic to shrimp. When I asked one of Albright's young aides to check on it, she reported that the wrong recipe had indeed been posted. The Czech dumplings Albright likes to eat are pastries with fruit inside. "She thought it was hysterical," said the aide who had relayed my query.)

In addition to publicizing her general message about the importance of world affairs to Americans, Albright has used the media in creative ways to advance specific items on her agenda, such as the expansion of NATO.

Enlarging the Atlantic alliance to take in Hungary, Poland, and the Czech Republic, former members of the Warsaw Pact liberated from Moscow's domination by the collapse of communism may turn out to be the most significant foreign policy undertaking of Clinton's presidency. Albright, her views shaped by her background, believes passionately that NATO, which binds democratic countries with shared ideals, is the key to stability in a historically volatile Europe. But the need to enlarge the alliance by taking in new members was debatable; the very events that made expansion possible— that is, the end of the Soviet Union and the evaporation of the communist threat—led some opponents to question its necessity. After all, they argued, NATO was created to defend free Europe against the Soviet threat. Now that there was no Soviet threat, these analysts said, it was more important to nurture the developing relationship with a reforming Russia than to risk alienating Russia by expanding an anti-Soviet alliance toward the East. Critics further argued that expansion would cost too much, dilute the alliance by taking in fragile countries of dubious reliability, and create new lines of division in Europe.

The arguments against enlarging NATO were not trivial, and the people advancing them were not lightweights. At one point, fifty prominent members of the foreign policy and national security establishment, including former secretaries of defense, retired generals and ambassadors, and respected political and academic figures, told Clinton in a letter that he was making "a policy error of historic proportions." (One of the signatories was Morton H. Halperin, who had failed to win Senate approval for a posting as an assistant secretary of defense in Clinton's first term. Despite this opposition to one of Albright's cherished objectives, she later appointed him to head her policy planning staff, a position that does not require Senate confirmation.)

To Clinton and Albright, the opposition's arguments posed a potential threat to an initiative on which they placed the highest priority. To accomplish their goal of enlarging the alliance, they needed to win approval from the Senate, which would have to ratify the modifications to the treaty, and from the parliaments of the fifteen other NATO members. Domestically, the issue was never in serious doubt because NATO expansion had strong bipartisan support. It was, in fact, the major foreign policy plank in the so-called Contract with America promulgated by conservative Republican House candidates in the 1994 election campaign. To reach the European audience, Albright used a media channel that she knew would guarantee a large and respectful audience throughout the continent: the *Economist,* a London-based newsweekly read in every foreign ministry and university in Europe. The *Economist* gave Albright three full pages for a cogent essay arguing the case for expanding the alliance. She wrote:

> NATO and its members have laid out the reasons for enlargement. It is high time that critics come forward with a rationale that might possibly support a policy of fossilised immobility in the face of Europe's sweeping changes. Now that democracy's frontier has moved to Europe's farthest reaches, what logic would dictate that we freeze NATO's eastern edges where they presently lie, along the line where the Red Army stopped in the spring of 1945?
>
> Those who ask, "where is the threat?" mistake NATO's real value. The alliance is not a wild-west posse that we trot out only when danger appears. It is a permanent presence, designed to promote common endeavours and to prevent a threat from ever arising. That is why current allies still need it and why others wish to join. NATO does not need an enemy. It has enduring purposes.[20]

Albright also used the "wild-west posse" line in an essay promoting NATO expansion that she wrote five months later for the *Washington Times*. To the regulars in the State Department press corps, that was nothing new. All of us could by then recite from memory a dozen lines that Albright used over and over as she hammered home her themes in speeches and articles: "We are doers, not world-class ditherers." "We can't do foreign policy on the cheap." "We want to ensure that the Hong Kong of tomorrow is like the Hong Kong of today." "There is a new Russia, but there is also a new NATO." "We are indispensable as the pathfinder nation." We got the message—and so did the Senate, about NATO at least, if not other issues. Expansion of the alliance was approved by a comfortable margin, 80 to 19.

Another of Albright's priorities upon taking office was persuading the Senate to ratify the Chemical Weapons Convention, which bars the possession or use of poison gas weapons. This multinational treaty created an international enforcement agency, based in the Netherlands, with the authority to inspect chemical factories in the member nations to ensure that their output is not being misused. Albright wanted prompt ratification so that the United States could participate in the operations of the enforcement agency. Arms-control advocates favored ratification, as did the trade association representing large American chemical manufacturing companies, which did not want to be omitted from a global arrangement and thus face losing some export markets. But many senators, including Helms, opposed the treaty, arguing that it would not stop rogue governments such as Iraq from acquiring or using chemical weapons and that it would subject American citizens—the operators of chemical plants—to intrusive inspections by foreigners.

The Clinton administration, fighting many other fires during the president's first two years, did little to promote ratification of the treaty while the Democrats still controlled the Senate. By the time Albright became secretary of state and moved ratification to the top of her agenda, Jesse Helms and the GOP were in charge, making her task considerably more difficult.

Albright authorized the senior Democrat on the Senate Foreign Relations Committee, Joseph Biden, to negotiate with Helms on behalf of the administration over a resolution of ratification that would satisfy some of the objections raised by Helms and the Senate majority leader, Trent Lott of Mississippi. Then, in an effort to put pressure on reluctant members, she took her case to the public by going straight into their living rooms through their television sets.

The State Department rented a commercial television studio in downtown Washington, featuring a set that looked like an office. There, without leaving her chair, Albright gave a rapid-fire series of live interviews to local news anchors all across the country, talking up the chemical treaty. The local anchors, of course, were thrilled to get live interviews with the secretary of state, who normally wouldn't give them the time of day.

Shortly after 10 A.M. on a Friday, she took questions about the treaty from John Lomax of WKRC-TV in Cincinnati and told him that the agreement was "good for the American people." Seven minutes later, she gave virtually the same interview to Steve Gullien of WBRC-TV in Birmingham. Next in line was WMC-TV in Memphis, followed by local stations in San Antonio, San Diego, Seattle, and Denver. For each interview, aides placed a placard in front of her showing the first name of the interviewer, so she could address "John" or "Steve" as if she knew them well and talked to them all the time.

Like a political campaigner delivering the same simple, catchy message at every stop, Albright ignored the subtleties of the chemical weapons issue in favor of easily digested, broad language that might inspire viewers to write to their senators:

"This is a treaty that has 'Made in USA' written all over it. We thought this treaty up!"

"This is not a political issue. This is an issue where the national interests of the United States are at stake."

"Can you imagine what it would be like for us to be on the same side as Libya and Iraq?" That was the camp in which the United States would find itself, she said, if the Senate refused to ratify.

This serial-interview technique was reused many times when Albright wanted to deliver an uncomplicated message to the widest possible audience. When King Hussein of Jordan died in early 1999, for example, Albright gave reassuring interviews to the three major network morning shows, Voice of America, and the Associated Press, telling them all that Hussein's successor, Abdullah, was smart, competent, and friendly to the United States. She could have addressed all those news organizations at once to save time, of course, but doing so would have reduced the chance that they would give extensive play to her message. By talking to them serially, she created for each news organization a pseudoexclusivity that made it more likely she would get airtime.

Her single-message, keep-it-simple comments in such sessions demonstrated the premium Albright places on talking to people in terms they can understand.

"I think you know that one of my objectives has been to try to bring foreign policy to the American people," she said as we rode back to the State Department in her official car after the chemical weapons interviews. "Having me out there talking in very plain language on an issue that is important has its own value, but also it projects the fact that American foreign policy can affect their lives. I think we'll have a payoff for this [in Senate ratification of the treaty], but we'll have a larger payoff in terms of people understanding what we do."[21]

Albright told me and others that her ability to speak effectively on television did not come naturally. She developed it through years of practice while she was at Georgetown, appearing in relatively obscure media outlets in friendly circumstances. She appeared regularly in the 1980s, for example, on a Public Broadcasting System show called *American Interests,* moderated by a Georgetown colleague.

Because Albright's name begins with "A," it was near the beginning of the directory of faculty experts that Georgetown distributed annually to the news media. (Many universities and research institutions produce such directories; they want their experts to appear on television and be quoted in respectable newspapers. It enhances their stature, and their ability to raise money.) Because of that happy alphabetical accident, she said, organizations such as Finnish TV would call seeking her comment on this issue or that—comments that no one in Washington or New York was ever likely to hear, which made it less risky to utter them. She said that she learned to keep her hands still while talking and not to alter her demeanor because on television, physical activity detracts from effective delivery of the message. Even today, when she appears on a Sunday morning talk show, she rarely allows her facial expression to change.[22]

Former undersecretary of state George Ball once wrote that the State Department had declined in public esteem since the days of

George C. Marshall and Dean Acheson because "it is inarticulate. Sensible advice based on solid experience gets so deeply buried in a blancmange of clichés and bureaucratic jargon that it suffers by comparison with the glib views of less experienced academics."[23] Albright did not have that problem. Initially at least, the blunt style and verbal quickness that had distinguished her years at the United Nations served her well as secretary of state, although by the middle of her second year her flair for laying down rhetorical markers would come back to haunt her.

Her ability to articulate difficult issues in terse, straightforward language not only helped her promote the administration's policies, it helped her cut off lines of questioning she did not want to pursue. In one notable example, on April 22, 1997, she appeared in the State Department briefing room to announce the imposition of new economic sanctions against the corrupt, repressive military government of Burma. She was asked the inevitable question: Why is it not hypocritical or inconsistent to lower the boom on Burma for human rights violations while simultaneously courting China, a notorious violator of human rights? Her answer:

> We have consistent principles and flexible tactics. We will continue to speak out about human rights violations whether they're in China, Burma, or Cuba. We, however, have a flexible approach to how we deal with it, depending upon what our national interests are. And we have to understand where we have a strategic relationship that requires us to take a different approach. I guess the easiest way to describe it is, Different Strokes for Different Folks.

This facile response had the desired effect: It flummoxed the press corps. How could we dispute her point? No general would fight a war the same way in the desert as he did in the swamp. The outcome was a spate of news stories that focused on the unhappy situation in Burma without dwelling on the perceived inconsistency of the administration's policy, which was essentially to strike at Burma because it was weak and economically irrelevant while cozying up to China, powerful and economically vibrant.

～

Although effective at the moment, over time such inconsistent responses to arguably similar situations would become a chronic problem, subjecting Albright to the criticism that foreign policy decisions were based on politics or commercial considerations or opportunism rather than on durable principles.

Early in Albright's tenure, she and Jamie Rubin sent a clear signal of the importance they attach to press coverage of the secretary as a person, as opposed to coverage of the issues. The daily package of news clippings about world affairs compiled by the press office was revised to feature a new section that was placed first: The Secretary in the News. The package thus gave the most prominence to articles that were about the secretary herself, ahead of articles about South America or central Asia. For all this focus on what reporters write, however, Albright's relations with the press have not always been cordial, partly because of her attempts to control information. It was understandable that she wanted favorable coverage. But she attempted to use the press to convey her message of the moment, while seeking to cut off press access to State Department officials who might give out information not supportive of that message, or information about some other issue that she did not want publicized at that time. Most of us found that we could gain access to the officials we needed to talk to in pursuit of our news stories, but only by first going through Rubin's staff. That way, Rubin and Albright knew who had talked to us, and if they didn't like the articles we wrote, they knew whom to blame. Another tactic Albright and Rubin adopted was to suggest—which meant insist—that we interview officials other than those we asked to talk to. The suggested officials were, of course, knowledgeable about whatever issue was at hand; but they could also be counted on to hew closely to the preferred version of events and the approved iterations of policy. Freelance contact with the press and commentary through unauthorized channels were strongly discouraged; it still occurred, of course, because many reporters had long-standing relationships with individual State Department officials, but such meetings became steadily harder to arrange as contacts were restricted. This effort to limit contact and control the message was understandable, given the "message chaos" of Clinton's first two years, but it also heightened the natural tension between the freewheeling culture of the press and the cautious, controlled targets of our inquiries.

A month after taking office, Albright gave an official luncheon at the State Department for Prince Sultan bin Abdulaziz, the defense minister of Saudi Arabia. This was a big event for her, an early test of her ability to work with an important but difficult ally from an alien culture. To demonstrate her prowess, she invited a few reporters. I was one; Elaine Sciolino of the *New York Times,* one of the most dogged and creative reporters in Washington, was another.

At each table was a mix of Americans and Saudis, business executives and officials, with the few reporters scattered around the room. One of the guests at Sciolino's table was Louis Freeh, the director of the FBI.

Freeh, a former federal judge, was in charge of the American side of the investigation into a terrorist bombing at an air force housing compound in Saudi Arabia known as Khobar Towers, in which fifty-six Americans died. At the luncheon, with Sciolino listening to every word, Freeh sounded off about the lack of Saudi cooperation with the American investigators. This was real news, because the official U.S. position was that the Saudis were being fully cooperative, so Sciolino put it in her newspaper.[24]

She did not quote Freeh's words directly; rather, she wrote coyly that although prominent Saudis were seated on either side of Freeh, his complaints were "part of a conversation with another guest seated at the table." Still, Albright was angry because she thought that Sciolino had broken the ground rules and betrayed the department by reporting an informal conversation at a social event. This reaction was unjustified, because Freeh has plenty of experience in Washington, and he knew that he was talking to a reporter for the *New York Times.* But Albright, uncomfortable with conversations she could not control, responded by cutting the press out of most such events after that.

She also greatly reduced press access to her at State Department events known as photo ops. These are a long-established part of the diplomatic ritual: The secretary of state is receiving the prime minister of Country X or the foreign minister of Country Y. Before the meeting, they pose for photographs and take a few questions from reporters. Most of Albright's photo ops, however, have been billed as "cameras and stills only"—that is, still photographers and television camera crews were welcome, but reporters who might ask questions were not.

Albright, unlike Kissinger, rarely engaged with the traveling reporters on an intellectual level; when she talked substance, she generally hewed to ideas and language on which she had settled in ad-

vance. When she engaged in small talk, the topics were mostly informal—children, gardening, her years as a teacher. She was hardly
ever willing to freelance on an important point of policy or strategy
on which she had not boned up beforehand. In many other ways,
however, her attitude toward the press was much the same as
Kissinger's. Richard Valeriani's account of Albright's predecessor
could apply equally well to Albright: Kissinger "had an obsessive
aversion to news leaks except for those he perpetrated himself."[25]
Further, "One aspect of reporting that drove him up the wall . . . was
the unauthorized 'leak,' the unofficial revelation of information,
sometimes classified, in the media. He wanted the State Department
to be a ship that 'leaked' only at the top. . . . Non-Kissinger leaks
brought retribution."[26]

One afternoon in early 1998, Albright—the same woman who had
threatened to fire a senior foreign service officer because he had
confirmed an important but inconvenient story that a journalist had
uncovered elsewhere—summoned a few of us to her office to hear
news about U.S. relations with Cuba.

President Clinton was planning to announce the next day a modification in long-standing restrictions on travel to Cuba and on sending money there. The idea was that Pope John Paul II's visit to the island might have created conditions in which Castro could be
circumvented through such institutions as the Catholic Church, and
Clinton wanted to open some channels for people in the United
States to communicate with and send help to individual Cubans and
nongovernmental Cuban organizations.

Albright invited reporters from the five daily U.S. newspapers that
the State Department takes most seriously to her office for a sneak
preview. The five are the *Washington Post,* the *New York Times,* the
Wall Street Journal, the *Los Angeles Times,* and *USA Today.* (*USA Today*
had only recently made the list, thanks to the relentless hounding of
the department by its correspondent, Lee Katz. He kept pointing
out that his paper had a bigger circulation than any of the others
and was a prime source of news for people all over the country, even
if nobody at Harvard or the Brookings Institution took it seriously.)

On condition that she not be named as the source, Albright told
us in considerable detail what the president was planning to announce, including the authorization for the Orioles' baseball
games. Putting the news out in this fashion had several advantages

from her point of view. By inviting us to her office, Albright could be sure she got our attention. Whatever else we were working on, we had to drop it when summoned by the secretary. It enabled her to present the initiative in the light most politically favorable to the administration—that is, as an attempt to find new ways to undermine Castro rather than as a softening that might be helpful to him. It ensured that she personally would not be upstaging the president because her name would not appear as the source. And it reduced the possibility of a confrontation with Helms on an issue that mattered deeply to him.

Should the five of us have acquiesced in this? Should we have allowed ourselves to be used in this fashion? That is an eternal Washington question to which there is no easy answer. Our job is to get as close as possible to the secretary and other senior officials so as to acquire information that might not otherwise be available. More often than not, this requires receiving the information on the conditions dictated by the source. (Kissinger carried this practice to the point of absurdity; when he was traveling, which was most of the time, reporters attributed information to "a senior official on Kissinger's plane" or "a senior official in the traveling party." Everyone in Washington, and Moscow, knew the identity of the source.) In the case of the Cuba story, we probably did not need to accept Albright's ground rules because the information had already begun to circulate around the Cuban exile community and among Cuban-American members of Congress, and, with a little more work, we could have obtained it from them. George Gedda of the Associated Press, who has been following Cuba for many years, was not invited to Albright's briefing, but by the end of the day he had the whole story anyway.

In the Bureau of Near Eastern Affairs, which is responsible for some of the most sensitive issues on the diplomatic agenda, such as the Israeli-Palestinian peace negotiations, the containment of Iraq, and the evolving relationship with Iran, Albright conducted a virtual reign of terror to silence officials she suspected of talking to reporters, telling them that their jobs were on the line. I and my press corps colleagues found that people we had known for years and considered friends now refused to talk to us; our calls to them were often returned by intermediaries from the public affairs staff asking what we wanted to talk about. One veteran foreign service officer whom I had known since he was a junior diplomat in the Middle East twenty years earlier continued to take my calls and even met me for lunch, but he did not list these appointments on his calendar and insisted that we return separately to the State Department so that he would not be seen with me.

There is nothing unusual, of course, in a cabinet officer's desire to control the flow of information. Presidents, military commanders, and corporate executives do the same thing. But after thirty years in Washington, Albright should have known that imposing restrictions and threatening to fire people only make staff members and reporters resentful. She should have known that information would come out through channels she could not control—from Congress, from the Pentagon, from foreign diplomats, even from political operatives in the White House whose objectives in a crisis were not necessarily the same as hers. And she should have understood that her efforts to curtail contacts with the press sowed confusion in the ranks, because foreign service officers are taught during their training that talking to responsible journalists is necessary and desirable. I know, because I had been asked many times to lecture on the subject at the Foreign Service Institute, the State Department's diplomatic training school, where instructors joined me in telling junior diplomats that thoughtful conversation with responsible reporters could be valuable—not that it would derail their careers.

Albright is, to put it bluntly, a control freak. Once while traveling abroad she called a senior official from her plane to berate him over an article I had written describing the administration's difficulty in deciding whether to impose economic sanctions on French and Russian oil companies that were preparing to invest billions of dollars to develop an offshore natural gas field in Iran. The article was accurate; she was not complaining about the content but about the fact that it had appeared at all. The subject was one she did not wish to see in the public domain because it illustrated differences of opinion among the president's senior advisers. The official she scolded was an obvious suspect, but in fact I had not talked to him for that very reason. So many agencies of the government—State, Treasury, Commerce, the White House—and so many foreign diplomats and well-placed lobbyists were working on the issue that there was no way to trace where my information had come from.

It was understandable that Albright and Sandy Berger and Mike McCurry, the White House press secretary, did not want a return to the chaos of Clinton's first two years as president, when confused policymaking and mixed signals created an impression of incompetence in foreign policy. It was better for them and perhaps better for the country that the administration speak with one voice and release information in a planned manner that advanced policy objectives. The issue was one of balance. There was no point in throwing tantrums and threatening to fire people when the press refused to play ball. Refusing to provide information only stimulates good reporters to redouble their efforts to get it elsewhere.

This is not to suggest that reporters expect State Department employees to volunteer secret information or deliver classified documents, although that sometimes happens. But on the other hand reporters will not accept what the State Department says at face value or pursue certain lines of inquiry only when it suits the secretary of state. Journalists want informed explanations of events and policies from people in a position to know what they are talking about; they are not stenographers transmitting the message du jour. Limiting access to information is counterproductive because it raises suspicions about motive, and it inclines reporters to give more audience to critics of the administration's performance.

In undertaking to engage the public in foreign policy, Albright was breaking away from traditional self-congratulatory attitudes in the State Department and the East Coast foreign policy establishment. In those environs, ordinary citizens are widely regarded as uninformed and uninterested in world affairs, and as people whose periodic attempts to influence foreign policy are a nuisance that interferes with the work of the professional practitioners. As Eric Alterman put it in his study of public input into foreign policy decisionmaking:

> Even James Madison worried about democratic participation in foreign policy because so much could be easily "concealed or disclosed, or disclosed in such parts and at such times as will best suit particular views." The modern-day foreign policy establishment is less concerned with its own ability to conceal or disclose selectively than with the public's ability to muck up its work with inconvenient interference and ignorant objection.[27]

Alterman reproduces devastatingly snobbish and elitist comments from such hallowed figures as Walter Lippmann, George F. Kennan, and Albright's former mentor, Zbigniew Brzezinski, to the effect that the public should be anesthetized rather than energized on foreign policy lest annoying dissent be voiced or independent judgments rendered. And he tars "the elite foreign policy media" with the same brush, citing the careers of "reporter/policymakers" such as Strobe Talbott and former *New York Times* reporter Leslie H. Gelb, now president of the Council on Foreign Relations. These foreign policy professionals, according to Alterman, "are unwilling to own up to increasing amounts of evidence that the values they believe should underlie the nation's foreign policy are at odds with those of the people in whose name they profess to speak."[28]

Other studies have found that the culture of elitism flourishes not only among the foreign policy mandarins in the universities and research institutes but in the professional foreign service corps within the State Department as well. Nearly two years into Albright's tenure, the Center for Strategic and International Studies examined the State Department's performance in the era of instant global information flows and found it crippled not just by obsolete equipment but also by obsolete attitudes similar to those observed by Alterman. The study concluded:

> Ending the culture of secrecy and exclusivity is a requirement for developing a collaborative relationship with the public. The first and highest priority is to end the culture of secrecy and exclusivity, to embrace the notions of openness and trust. The sense that diplomacy takes place in a closed universe of privileged intellectuals must change. Diplomacy must move from a *mandarinate* system to one which recognizes the permeability of borders in formation. Embassies must not become the monasteries of the 21st century.[29]

Albright hates the notion that she—divorced single mother, grandmother, avid gardener, popular teacher—is part of some exalted foreign policy cult insulated from the real life of Americans. She has certainly understood that public apathy about foreign affairs and the public's sense that cloistered elites control the decisionmaking process undercut the State Department's influence on Capitol Hill and make difficult foreign policy choices, such as dispatching troops to Bosnia, harder to sell politically. She has invested countless hours with groups of citizens all across the United States, trying to explain why foreign affairs matter to them and to win support for the administration's decisions. With the exception of one infamous "town meeting" on Iraq at Ohio State University in February 1998, she has been warmly received.

On the other hand, Albright has undercut her message of openness by her efforts to limit her diplomats' contacts with the press. Her relationship with the press could hardly be described as hostile, but after a difficult 1998 she and Rubin sensed that it needed improvement. Early in 1999, they initiated a new avenue of contact: periodic informal conversations between the secretary and a small group of reporters, perhaps five or six at a time. That winter, these conversations were literally "fireside chats"—we sat with the secretary on comfortable chairs and sofas before a big fire in the hearth in her office. The idea was that in such a setting we could get around the barriers imposed by formal events and have direct access to the secretary's thinking. But even at these fireside sessions, she was reluctant to let down her guard. At the first of them, which I attended, she pulled out a sheet of "talking points" when the subject turned to Iraq. So much for informality. In her office, as on the plane, she was reluctant to freelance on any substantive topic. Kissinger enjoyed bantering with the press, throwing up trial balloons, soliciting and challenging reporters' ideas and inviting them to challenge his, showing off his wit and occasionally throwing a tantrum. He telephoned State Department reporters and foreign affairs columnists early in the morning and late into the night, often returning their calls before those of foreign officials. That is not Albright's style. An engaging conversationalist on subjects other than foreign policy, she always has her game face on when the topic is world affairs.

As the 105th Congress headed for adjournment late in 1998, consumed by the Monica Lewinsky scandal, the results of Albright's relentless efforts to marshal public support to produce results on Capitol Hill could best be described as mixed.

The administration failed to win congressional approval for one of its highest foreign policy priorities, authorization for the president to negotiate "fast track" trade agreements with other countries. "Fast track" is Washington shorthand describing negotiated trade treaties that are submitted to Congress for approval on an all-or-nothing basis, not subject to amendment. Trade negotiators, supported by Clinton and Albright, argued that they could not complete the free trade agreements they wanted with Chile and other countries because, without fast track, the negotiators could never promise that a deal was final. The death of fast track was a rebuff to the administration, but in this case Democrats, swayed by the opposition of organized labor, were as much responsible as Republicans.

Meanwhile, the facade of comity between Helms and Albright was cracking. The dossier of letters from Helms and other senior Republicans to Clinton and Albright expressing unhappiness over foreign policy issues kept growing. Helms and Gilman, for example, objected to the agreement that Stuart Eizenstat had negotiated with the European Union in which the Europeans promised to turn up the human rights heat on Castro in exchange for a relaxation of the Helms-Burton law. Helms and his counterpart on the Senate Banking Committee, Alfonse d'Amato of New York, complained about the administration's decision not to impose sanctions on French, Russian, and Malaysian oil firms that had agreed to develop an offshore natural gas field in Iran; they predicted that the Iranians would use the revenue to promote terrorism. Helms objected vehemently to the administration's support of a U.N. Security Council decision to impose new sanctions on the Angolan opposition army led by Jonas Savimbi, who had held the American proxy when Angola was a Cold War battleground but who now is regarded in Washington as a dangerous nuisance.

On the other hand, congressional opposition to keeping troops in Bosnia dissipated. If there was one case where Albright's determination, commitment, and clear vision prevailed over the political obfuscators and the cautious analyzers, this was it. Shortly after taking office, she recognized that not enough was being done to bring about implementation of the Dayton agreement, which after all had been virtually imposed on reluctant parties, none of whom had been vanquished on the battlefield. She appointed Robert S. Gelbard, a no-nonsense career diplomat experienced in dealing with thugs and criminals, to accelerate compliance. And she prevailed in the administration's inner debate about keeping the troops on station—important in itself, because they kept the lid on a violence-prone country, but also important symbolically because

Russian troops were participating in what was officially a NATO-directed operation. The NATO mission reinforced Albright's argument that the Atlantic alliance still had important security duties in the post–Cold War era, and the Russian involvement supported her argument that expansion of NATO would not preclude cooperation with Russia on other fronts. Many senior members of the U.S. intelligence community believe that the entire effort to stabilize Bosnia as a multiethnic society is doomed and that Serbia and Croatia are only waiting for an opportunity to carve it up. Events may prove these analysts correct; the Bosnian elections of September 1998, in which hard-liners generally prevailed, were not a good sign, from Washington's perspective. But if Dayton ultimately fails, it will not be because Albright let it fail.

In its final hours, the 105th Congress passed the bill to reorganize the foreign policy bureaucracy and provide more than $900 million for the United Nations arrearage. Getting that money had been one of the foremost goals of Clinton's second term, and it had been Albright's objective when she set out to replace Boutros-Ghali. It was fundamental to restoring and preserving America's influence in a United Nations that was assuming more responsibility around the world as the Cold War paralysis faded. Albright had begged and pleaded with members of Congress to accept the compromise legislation negotiated by Helms and Biden. But Clinton vetoed the bill the same day it arrived at his desk because it still came with restrictive abortion language that would prohibit funding of groups overseas that lobbied their own governments to liberalize abortion laws. The restrictions, referred to as "Mexico City language" because of their origins at a conference there, were so watered down in the final version of the bill that Washington insiders jokingly called them "Tijuana language," but Clinton, who owed his reelection largely to female voters, was not going to accept any antiabortion provision.

Helms publicly urged Clinton to sign the legislation. In the *New York Times,* he argued:

> Twice, the House leadership has significantly watered down the abortion language the president opposes to try and reach a compromise. Yet the president doggedly continues to insist that he will not make even a symbolic concession on abortion. Clearly, Mr. Clinton is desperate to keep the support of groups like the National Organization for Women and

Planned Parenthood. But is the president really so desperate that he is willing to put his political needs ahead of paying the United Nations arrears?[30]

The answer was yes. In his veto message, Clinton said that he had nixed the bill "for several reasons, most importantly, because the Congress has included in this legislation unacceptable restrictions on international family planning programs and threatened our leadership in the world community by tying our payment of dues to the United Nations and other international organizations to these unrelated family planning issues." Despite the modifications, Clinton said, he could not accept two provisions: one prohibiting U.S. assistance to voluntary organizations abroad that use their own money to fund abortions, and one that would ban funding for organizations that lobby for liberalization of abortion laws. The result of these provisions, Clinton said, would be more unwanted pregnancies and more abortions, not fewer.[31]

Not long after Clinton vetoed the bill, Albright was chatting with pupils at George C. Marshall Elementary School in Vancouver, Washington, during a brief tour of the Pacific Northwest. When one of them asked what had been her hardest problem as secretary of state, her answer was, working with Congress to get "the money we need to do our work." The next day, she predicted: "It's going to get much more serious [at U.N. headquarters] in New York. I've been reading some of the cable traffic: there's no question everybody's getting fed up with this. It's going to play into questions about reforming the Security Council, how many jobs will be given to Americans, the way contacts are made up there."

She said that she had already felt tension and resentment over the U.S. arrears when she was at the United Nations, and that tensions had built up even more in the two years since her departure—an assessment reinforced by Kofi Annan, who made no secret of his own disillusionment over the issue. He thought that by getting a start on reforming the bloated, duplicative bureaucracy of the United Nations, he was doing Washington's bidding and would be rewarded by Washington's support.

"I must say we are all disappointed, very disappointed, and we feel deceived," he said, in unusually blunt language for an international civil servant. "Lots of promises were made to us—'reform and we will pay'—and I think we have delivered on our part of the bargain. We have conducted enough reform for anyone with good faith to see that we are serious about reform, and reform is an ongoing process and it will go on. We have not received the money."[32]

Albright did not dispute him. "There's got to be a way to separate these two issues," namely the U.N. and abortion, she said.

> Nobody understands how we can hold up our funding over an emotional issue such as family planning. We're going to have to try to figure out some new strategy for trying to get the arrears problem taken care of. It's going to be a very high priority item for the president and me. I mean, the president whenever we talk about this is quite appalled by it, and I know he wants to take that on very strongly.[33]

She refrained from speculating on how a president politically undermined by a sex scandal and impeachment proceedings would be able to accomplish in the 106th Congress what she and an untainted president had been unable to do in the 105th, and I refrained from asking because I knew about her aversion to discussing the Lewinsky affair.

It was academic anyway, because the man most responsible for appending the Mexico City language to the bill, Representative Christopher Smith, a New Jersey Republican, was unmoved by Clinton's veto message, just as he had been unmoved by personal appeals from Albright while the bill was under consideration. He issued a statement saying that Clinton's veto "showed that [the president] cares more about funding the international abortion industry than he cares about the U.N." According to Smith, the bill in question,

> like most major foreign policy legislation, represented a series of compromises among deeply and sincerely held views on important issues. None of us agreed with every provision in the bill. That is what compromise is about. Pro-life Republicans and Democrats in Congress voted for compromise and moderation. We even voted to allow the U.N. to receive $1.4 billion from the United States in fiscal year 1999 payments. But the President chose to let the foreign policy of the United States take second place to the demands of his most extreme pro-abortion supporters.[34]

In a way, Smith's statement was disingenuous. Many conservative Republicans voted in favor of the U.N. funding bill only because they knew that Clinton would never accept the abortion rider and that the money would therefore never actually be delivered; they could pretend to have done the right thing, knowing there would be no cost. No one, however, doubts Smith's personal commitment on the right-to-life issue. Moreover, Clinton and Albright made the task of getting the U.N. money more difficult the following spring by cutting the Security Council out of the diplomacy over Kosovo, undercutting their own arguments about the indispensability of the United Nations.

As for foreign aid and the State Department's own budget, Congress responded to the administration's appeal to stop cutting the 150 Account by funding it at $19.1 billion in fiscal year 1998. The president sought still more for 1999, basing his request for $20.15 billion partly in anticipation of a giant influx of cash to the federal treasury from a proposed settlement of tobacco liability legislation. But the settlement never occurred, and Congress balked at providing additional funds out of general revenue. Fiscal conservatives who wanted to hold fast to their budget-balancing agreement with the administration sought to slash the 150 Account, not increase it further.

Albright appeared before the Senate Appropriations Committee on June 16, 1998, to press the administration's funding request, but the chairman, Ted Stevens, an Alaska Republican, was not so easily charmed as Helms or Callahan.

"We deal with hard dollars," he said. "We cannot deal with prospective streams of revenue. As a consequence, it is my sad duty to tell you that there is just no more money."[35] Of course, the government was on its way to a budget surplus for that year of some $80 billion, but the White House and congressional leaders had not agreed on what to do with that money, and none of it was made available for foreign affairs spending.

In the last hours before adjournment, the 105th Congress enacted a massive, multiagency spending bill to fund government operations for the 1999 fiscal year. Determining whether or not Albright got what she wanted is difficult, because the numbers depend on what items one chooses to include in the total. Onetime special allocations, such as money for security upgrades at threatened embassies abroad, show up in the budget totals but do not give the secretary of state more money to spend on diplomatic activities. Here is the State Department's assessment:

> From FY [fiscal year] 1995 to FY 1997, America's International Affairs program resources were reduced in real terms by over 14 percent. With the introduction of the FY 1998 budget, the Administration proposed a new agenda for enhancing America's international leadership through federal government–sponsored and supported programs. The proposed FY 1998 budget for Function 150 programs was $19.451 billion, while Congress appropriated $18.721 billion for FY 1998. Again in FY 1999, the Administration requested adequate funding to maintain America's investment in international affairs programs and activities that support America's national interests. The FY 1999 base budget request for $19.648 billion was about $1 billion more than the FY 1998 enacted level. Congress appropriated $18.662 billion in base programs, and provided additional appropriations of $1.014 billion for arrears payments to international organizations and financial institutions [mostly international development banks, not the United Nations], as well as supplemental appropriations in the amount of $1.899 billion for emergency security requirements in the aftermath of the 1998 embassy bombings [in Kenya and Tanzania] and for anti-narcotics activities. Including supplemental appropriations, total enacted FY 1999 appropriations were $21.556 billion.[36]

The 1999 funding was enough to stop the slide but not enough to ease cost-cutting pressure that limited, for example, the number of delegates the department could send to international negotiating conferences.

The problem for Albright lay not just in a parsimonious, Republican-dominated Congress but in the administration's political commitment to a balanced federal budget. In Christopher's tenure, congressional leaders such as Senator Mitch McConnell of Kentucky, who controls foreign aid allocations on the Senate side, had offered to provide more foreign affairs funding if the administration would agree to cut equal amounts somewhere else. Christopher always rejected this offer, saying that it was not up to him to reconfigure the president's spending priorities. Albright was less reticent, and McConnell congratulated her for her success at persuading the White House to boost her budget. "Your fresh perspective has made a decisive difference, and we thank you for that," he told her.[37]

Having won that internal fight for Fiscal 1999, Albright had to fight it all over again when the administration was planning its budget for Fiscal 2000—a budget that would be sent to Capitol Hill by a scandal-tarnished president and received by a Congress dominated by conservative Republicans furious at Clinton and antipathetic to international spending.

Albright was relatively successful in the administration's internal deliberations over how much money to ask for in Fiscal 2000; the growing federal budget surplus made it easier for Clinton to dole out budgetary goodies. In the proposed budget, sent to Congress in January 1999, the White House asked for $21.31 billion for the 150 Account, including "$19.906 billion for base programs, $1.244 billion more than enacted in FY 1999." Even in Washington, a billion dollars is real money, and the inclusion of the extra money in the 150 Account gave Albright a little running room to seek funding for some pet projects, such as regional environmental training programs for foreign government officials.

Helms and other congressional leaders still believed, however, that Albright could find plenty of additional maneuvering room within the spending limits they had set, if she was a skillful manager and bureaucratic infighter. The restructuring of the government's foreign affairs bureaucracy, which was implemented in 1999, greatly increased the secretary's power to set priorities and allocate resources.

Two independent agencies—the Arms Control and Disarmament Agency and the United States Information Agency—were abolished, their functions and resources transferred to the State Department. The annual budget for these two agencies is well over a billion dollars, about 5.7 percent of the 150 Account, and there is a considerable amount of overlap, duplication, and bloat that can be trimmed to provide more money for essential programs. The full effects of this reorganization will not be felt until after Albright has left office, and the decisions she and her management team still must make before she steps down will affect the State Department's operational capability for years to come.

There seems to have been virtually no response among the general public to Albright's appeals for increased spending on diplomatic activities. One of the most comprehensive surveys of public attitudes about international relations, the quadrennial study sponsored by the Chicago Council on Foreign Relations, found a surprisingly high level of interest in the subject in the fall of 1998, but no desire to spend big money on it. Education, health care, and efforts to fight crime far outdistanced international relations and defense among the public's priorities.[38]

On other issues, too, Albright achieved mixed results in Congress. She probably did as well as anyone could have, given that Congress was controlled by the opposition party and gripped by the White House sex scandal.

NATO expansion sailed through the Senate with little difficulty, because Helms and other conservative Republicans supported it just as much as Clinton and Albright did. The Senate also ratified the Chemical Weapons Convention, and Congress in its last hours enacted legislation to implement it. Some critics said that the implementing legislation violated key provisions of the treaty, but neither Clinton nor Albright raised public objections, and the president signed the bill.

Other treaties endorsed by the administration went unratified, most notably the Comprehensive Test Ban Treaty, which bans the testing of nuclear weapons, and the Law of the Sea Treaty, an international compact regulating maritime commerce, traffic, and exploration that President Ronald Reagan had rejected but that Clinton accepted after extensive modifications satisfied U.S. objections.

Helms made clear that he saw no strategic reason to approve the Test Ban Treaty, no matter how much he was willing to defer to Albright on other matters, and in any case, he informed her, he would not consider doing so until the administration submitted for ratification two agreements to which he was opposed: the Kyoto climate change agreement and modifications to the 1972 Antiballistic Missile Treaty with the Soviet Union. Helms accused administration officials of holding these treaties back from the Senate because they knew that the treaties would not be ratified, while complying with the treaties administratively as if the Senate had in fact approved them. In October 1999, Helms abandoned all pretense of cooperation with the administration by joining forces with other conservative Republicans to reject the Test Ban Treaty outright—the first major multinational treaty to be voted down since the Treaty of

Versailles after World War I. There were indications that this vote was not about the treaty itself, or about Albright, but about Republican rage at Clinton and his survival of the impeachment process earlier in the year; but whatever the motivation, the outcome was a stunning repudiation of one of the administration's cherished foreign policy goals, and it came despite energetic last-minute appeals from Albright.

Congress did give the administration the authority it sought to pump $18.2 billion into the International Monetary Fund to help stabilize the battered global economy, and the authority to waive what had been mandatory economic sanctions on India and Pakistan after their nuclear weapons tests. The administration wanted the waiver authority as a negotiating tool in trying to persuade the two South Asian countries to accept the Comprehensive Test Ban Treaty and limitations on deployment of nuclear warheads.

After Clinton vetoed the bill authorizing payment of the United Nations arrears because of Chris Smith's abortion rider, the United States faced the prospect of losing its vote in the General Assembly because of the debt. Albright proclaimed her determination to rally public and political support to get the money. "The time has come to stop treating the United Nations like a political football," she told a business group that supports the United Nations.

> The United States is not a failed state. We have no excuse. Plain and simple, we should pay our U.N. bills. As the business community well knows, we have important interests throughout the U.N. system. That is why I am calling this evening for a fresh start. Whether or not the immediate impasse is settled during the final days of this congressional session, we have to do more next year than just run around the same flagpole chasing our tail.[39]

A fine appeal—good, blunt words from Madeleine Albright. But it remained to be seen whether the Republican leadership in the incoming House under Representative Dennis Hastert of Illinois would do what Gingrich never did: persuade Chris Smith to back off. Through the summer of 1999, as the months of Albright's tenure slipped away and Congress wrestled with health care and other unrelated issues, the question went unanswered. To the distress of some nongovernmental groups that sought to rally political support for paying the debt, Albright said little in public on the subject; the war in Kosovo and then a new effort to reach a Middle East peace agreement consumed much of her time. Publicly she stayed on good terms with Helms, at least until the Test Ban Treaty fiasco, but he wasn't the problem—he had already signed off on repayment and negotiated the deal with Biden. The problem was in the House, where sulfurous resentment of Clinton limited the leadership's willingness to accommodate the administration on this or any other issue.

The issue festered until the very last days of the 1999 congressional session. Richard Holbrooke, finally confirmed as ambassador to the United Nations, Albright's old job, roamed the halls of Congress for weeks, "begging," as he said, for the money. Albright quietly prodded the president, looking for some graceful way for him to step back from the absolute position he had taken in his veto message the year before. The outcome, as usual in Washington, was a compromise that allowed both sides to claim the high ground.

A modified version of the restrictive language on abortion remained in the bill, but a provision was added allowing the president to waive it, at the price of a reduction in funding each time he did so. Pro-choice absolutists such as Representative Nancy Pelosi, a California Democrat, cried capitulation, but Albright brushed them off.

At a news conference in Ankara, Turkey, she welcomed the compromise as a successful outcome to a quest that had preoccupied her and the president for seven years. "I expect that as details of the agreement emerge," she said, "it will meet our goal in minimizing the practical impact on U.S. support for women's health programs around the globe."

That, of course, was exactly the argument Helms had made the previous year—but the previous year had been an election year.

Chapter 3

A MARINE CORPS
KIND OF GIRL

MORE THAN ANY other secretary of state in modern times, Madeleine Albright has worn her heart on her sleeve, diplomatically speaking. Unlike, say, Henry Kissinger, a student and practitioner of unemotional geostrategy, or Warren Christopher, a lawyer and conciliator, Albright has unabashedly set policy and made recommendations to the president based on her personal experiences as a woman, a refugee, and a teacher.

"My mindset is Munich, not Vietnam," she has often said, a shorthand statement of her belief that the consequences of inaction, as exemplified by the appeasement of Hitler before World War II, are a more valid lesson for international policymaking today than the consequences of misplaced action, as in the Vietnam War.

This conviction, coupled with a belief that she must work hard at all times because she has four years at most to achieve her aims, has produced a commitment to energetic involvement all over the globe. In sharp contrast to the caution of Christopher or the hard-eyed detachment of Jim Baker, she wants to grasp every nettle.

"She is always conscious of her limited tenure," one of her senior aides said. "That's the basic difference between us political appointees and the career people. We'll be gone in a few years, and we don't want to look back and say, 'If only we had worked harder, if only we had made that extra phone call.' We'll have more vacation time than we want pretty soon." Another senior staff member told me:

I've had the opportunity to spend a month with her in really close quarters. I have been remarkably impressed by the fact that what you see is what you really get. I had been familiar with her tough talk, like everyone else, but it's a genuine reflection of what she believes in. She truly believes that the United States has to take a leadership position. She sets the bar high for the United States; it probably comes from her immigrant past.

When the Vietnam War was at its height and American university campuses were in turmoil over it, Albright was already a mother and a part-time graduate student. Her children were girls; military conscription and the war were no threat to them. The war that had shaped Albright's attitudes about global affairs and America's role in them was World War II.

The "Munich, not Vietnam" slogan became a familiar shorthand for her view that action is better than inaction, that great powers have an obligation to intervene against evil, and that the unique history of the United States gives this country the moral standing to weigh in on the side of good in almost any global trouble spot. The unstated assumption, of course, is that the good side of any conflict is the one supported by the United States, which overlooks the history of such places as Guatemala and Iran.

Today's world is "a viper's nest of terrors," Albright said in a typical speech. "We know that small wars and unresolved issues can erupt into violence that endangers allies, wreaks economic havoc, generates refugees, and embroils our own forces in combat. American diplomacy, backed by military power, is the single most effective force for peace in the world today."[1]

But "Munich, not Vietnam" turned out to have another, more subtle, effect on Albright's outlook and policies.

In the spring of 1968, when the United States was reeling from the impact of the Vietcong's Tet offensive and campuses—including Columbia, where Albright was pursuing her Ph.D. in political science—were aflame with protest, she wasn't paying much attention to Vietnam. She was a young mother with a busy social life whose personal and academic interests lay in other parts of the world. As a result, she missed one of Vietnam's crucial lessons for modern policymakers: the ability of relatively weak countries or groups to defy the powerful, to reject the collective advice or instruction of the big powers, and to use unconventional methods to gain their objectives. Saddam Hussein in Iraq, Slobodan Milosevic in Serbia and the rebels in Kosovo, the Taliban militia in Afghanistan, Jonas Savimbi's UNITA rebels in Angola, the clan chiefs in Somalia, Burma's military rulers—all had formulated their own objectives and made their own risk-reward assessments, which they would not amend despite exhortations from Albright or well-intentioned resolutions of the U.N. Security Council.

As Tony Judt of New York University observed:

> The incomprehension of democratic nations is especially apparent when they are faced with small, weak dictators. Whereas Stalin and Mussolini recognized real-world constraints and preferred bluff to action whenever possible, the same does not hold for their modern micro-successors. Shortly after the start of the NATO bombing of Yugoslavia, an official at the National Security Council spoke of making Slobodan Milosevic pay an unacceptable price for his behavior. But the only unacceptable price for Mr. Milosevic is the loss of power.[2]

Milosevic was willing to let his country be bombed to rubble for the same reason Kim Jong Il was willing to let untold thousands of his North Korean compatriots starve: Retention of power was the overriding consideration.

Albright regularly recounts her childhood as a double refugee and relates those experiences to her current view of the world. She generally omits, however, reference to a crucial part of her family history that came to light only after she was sworn in as secretary of state. This was the fact that her grandparents were Jewish, and three of them perished in Nazi concentration camps.

Raised as a Roman Catholic, Albright was profoundly flustered and upset when my *Washington Post* colleague Michael Dobbs unearthed the truth about her family and confronted her with it shortly after she took office. She said that it was news to her, that she had never inquired about what had happened to her grandparents, and that her parents had never volunteered the truth. She was furious at Dobbs, whose only offense was brilliant, dogged reporting, and hurt by critics such as Frank Rich of the *New York Times* who said that she must have known the truth all along. "I'm deeply hurt that people think I'm lying," she told Rich. "I have never been secretive about anything in my life. If a shrink wanted to deal with me, it would be primarily about the fact I talk too much."[3]

No one can discern any particular Jewish orientation in anything Albright has done on the job, whereas her European refugee background comes up all the time. There has never been a foreign policy issue in which her Jewish past appears to have been a factor in her decisionmaking—not even in dealing with the Middle East. Her overall support for Israel has been consistent with a half century of American policy, and yet she has worked hard to develop a comfortable rapport with Yasser Arafat. On issues such as the expansion of NATO to take in countries that had once been under the yoke of Nazi and Soviet dictatorship, she proudly proclaimed her refugee experience, not her Jewish ancestry, as a factor in her outlook. This was never more evident than on the dreary March day in 1999 when she traveled to the Truman Library in Independence, Missouri, to preside over the ceremony in which Hungary, Poland, and the Czech Republic, the land of her birth, officially joined the Western alliance. Her joy and exhilaration were palpable in her "Hallelujah!" as she signed the documents with a flourish and hugged her counterparts from the three countries, all former dissidents who, like her, had spent much of their adult lives seeking the liberation of central Europe from Soviet domination. The issues for her that day, as throughout the campaign to take new members into NATO, were liberation, independence, fortification of the Western alliance, and European stability. Her Jewish roots appeared largely irrelevant; they have come up mostly during her visits to such sites as Yad Vashem, the memorial to victims of the Nazi Holocaust in Jerusalem.

Visiting the Jewish Museum in Prague not long after Dobbs had uncovered her family history, Albright delivered a personal statement of the sort rarely heard from professional diplomats. "Now that I am aware of my own Jewish background, and the fact that my grandparents died in concentration camps, the evil of the Holocaust has an even more personal meaning for me, and I feel an even greater determination to ensure that it will never be forgotten." As she looked at the names of Jewish victims of the Nazis carved into the walls of Prague's old Pinkas Synagogue—including the names of her grandparents—she said that she "not only grieved for those members of my family whose names were inscribed there, but I also thought about my parents. I thought about the choice they made. They clearly confronted the most excruciating decision a human being can face when they left members of their family behind, even as they saved me from certain death."[4] Most often, however, she described her parents as refugees from oppression who fled Europe because they aspired to freedom; she did not describe herself—and apparently did not think of herself—as a child of Jews who fled for their lives.

The closest she came to a public reckoning with her history and with the impact of learning the truth was at a Washington event that did not require any policy input from her, only empathy with the cause under discussion. This was a conference sponsored jointly by the State Department and the Holocaust Memorial Museum in Washington on the subject of art treasures and insurance policies looted from their rightful owners—mostly Jews—by the Nazis in the 1930s and 1940s.

In addition to government officials and art experts from forty-four countries, the participants included Holocaust survivors and their heirs, and representatives of Jewish groups from the United States and Europe. Everyone in the State Department's Loy Henderson conference room that day knew Albright's story; in that setting, she could not fail to address it.

In a speech that electrified the audience and earned her a standing ovation, she exposed her private anguish over what she had learned about herself and what her family had lost:

I cannot leave this subject without addressing briefly a subject for which I have not yet found, and may never find, exactly the right words, and that concerns my grandparents, who I learned recently were Jewish and died along with aunts, uncles and cousins in the Holocaust.

When I was young, I didn't often think about grandparents. I just knew I didn't have any. I was an infant when I separated from them. Now I too have become a grandparent, and I look at my children's children and the love and pride literally overflows.

I am sure now that I was once the object of such affection, not only from my parents, but from those who gave them life. And as I think of my life, now in my sixty-second year, I think also of my grandparents' lives in those final years, months and days. I think of the faces at the Holocaust Museum and Yad Vashem and the long list of names on the wall of the

Pinkas Synagogue in Prague, among them, those of my grandparents, Olga and Arnost Korbel and Ruzena Spiegelova.

I think of the blood that is in my family veins. Does it matter what kind of blood it is? It shouldn't. It is just blood that does its job. But it mattered to Hitler, and that matters to us all, because that is why 6 million Jews died.

And that is why this obscenity of suffering was visited on so many inno-cent irreplaceable people, people who loved and enriched life with their warmth, their smiles and the embrace of their arms, people whose lives ended horribly and far too soon; people whose lives and suffering we must never forget or allow to diminish, even if we must from time to time inten-tionally shock our collective memory.

The peoples of the world differ in language, culture, history and choices of worship. Such differences make life interesting and rich. But as the Holocaust cries out to us, we must never allow these distinctions to ob-scure the common humanity that finds us all as people. We must never al-low pride in us to curdle into hatred of them. Remembering that lesson is what this effort at research and restitution of Holocaust-era assets is really all about, for it is about much more than gold and art and insurance; it's about remembering that no one's blood is more or less precious than our own.[5]

No one in the room moved or coughed or shuffled papers while Albright was delivering these remarks. Participants saw a secretary of state speaking as none had previously spoken: as a mother and grandmother, as a refugee, as an individual whose sense of who she was and where she came from had been profoundly shaken, as a person who reflects in public on the richness of life and the para-doxes of human nature. I can recall only one occasion on which Warren Christopher spoke reflectively about his boyhood in Depression-era North Dakota, and that was at an off-the-record farewell dinner with reporters at the end of his tenure. Most of the world's diplomats never speak in personal terms at all, at least not in public; but to Albright, who she is, where she came from, what she stands for, and what the United States is all about are all woven to-gether.

As long ago as the Carter administration, when Albright was on Zbigniew Brzezinski's National Security Council staff, she was a voice arguing for more, rather than less, projection of American power in the world—a hard sell in a country and a Democratic party then still traumatized by Vietnam. "I think that's one of the legacies of Vietnam—we are afraid to use power," she said then. "The tragedy of Vietnam is that there are a series of people that were in the government who felt that the use of power was something alien to America, because it had been misused. I think that what we needed to do was to get at the selective use of power instead of saying, 'We can't do that.'"[6]

In his 1976 study of U.S. foreign policy—published during the cynical aftermath of Vietnam and the Watergate scandal—former undersecretary of state George W. Ball wrote:

> To exercise effective leadership, we must once more come to believe in ourselves, in our uniqueness as a nation, and in our special mission; we must, in other words, recapture that faith in our own exceptionalism that assures us that we had something special to offer the world, that we were, as a nation, destined by history and geography and bountiful resources to show the way to others.[7]

For Albright, believing in the exceptionalism of America and its special place in the world is not difficult. The country that took in her family, fought the fascists, and defeated the communists in the Cold War holds, by definition, a unique place in global affairs that carries with it responsibilities as well as privileges. "If evil is not dealt with early, and if steps are not taken to stop the advance of evil people, then the problem gets to be much worse," she said during an appearance before the Commonwealth Club of San Francisco in June 1997. "And while it is easy for this great nation to be able to take a high road because we are, in fact, behind two great oceans, when problems are not dealt with by America early on, they come home to America, and we have to deal with them when they are more serious."

This attitude has drawn criticism from self-proclaimed pragmatists and moral relativists who see Albright—and Clinton—as global busybodies, inserting the United States into problems it need not have taken on and pushing their vision on others. But Albright was proud of her outlook and her commitment. She sometimes sounded like Ronald Reagan in her unabashed belief that the United States was a special country with a special mission and a special responsibility. In a commencement address at Harvard University in June 1997, she told the graduates:

> You will compete in a world marketplace; travel further and more often than any previous generation; share ideas, tastes and experiences with counterparts from every culture; and recognize that to have a full and rewarding future, you will have to look outward.
>
> As you do, and as our country does, we must aspire to the high standard set by [George C.] Marshall, using means adapted to our time based on values that endure for all time, and never forgetting that America belongs on the side of freedom.
>
> I say this to you as Secretary of State. I say it also as one of the many people whose lives have been shaped by the turbulence of Europe during the middle of this century and by the leadership of America throughout this century.
>
> I can still remember, in England during the war, sitting in the bomb shelter, singing away the fear, thanking God for American help.
>
> I can still remember, after the war and after the Communist takeover in Prague, arriving here in the United States, where I wanted only to be accepted and make my parents and my new country proud.
>
> Because my parents fled in time, I escaped Hitler. To our shared and constant sorrow, millions did not. Because of America's generosity, I escaped Stalin. Millions did not. Because of the vision of the Truman-Marshall generation, I have been privileged to live my life in freedom. Millions have never had that opportunity.
>
> It may be hard for you, who have no memory of that time fifty years ago, to understand. But it is necessary that you try to understand.

In that same speech, and on many other occasions, Albright warned that the greatest danger facing the United States was that Americans would forget the lesson taught by President Harry Truman and his secretary of state, George Marshall, half a century earlier: the need for the United States to take the lead in making the world a better, safer place. Marshall is one of two former secretaries of state whose portraits hang in Albright's office. The other is her mentor, Edmund S. Muskie, who as a senator from Maine gave Albright her first political job.

"We are doers," Albright likes to say, urging her audiences to support American involvement in the world and not to become "world-class ditherers" or "neoprotectionists" who fail to act when action is needed to "forge alliances, deter aggression and keep the peace."

The day after NATO began bombing Yugoslavia, Albright was asked at a State Department news conference to evaluate what was happening in the Balkans in light of her experience. She didn't hesitate for a second.

> Here we are in 1999, at the end of what historians agree has been the bloodiest century in the history of the world. We know how the blood was created and why it happened. It happened because there were evil dictators or aggressive leaders in countries who felt that their own space was not big enough and that they had to expand it. It took a long time for those with good intentions to understand that without their direct involvement, those dictators would be able to not only spread fear among their neighbors, but also systematically murder the people within that they did not like for ethnic reasons. . . . I think that we have an opportunity to learn from the mistakes that our predecessors made, the slowness of responding, of not dealing with wars or problems when they were small and coming in—I am somebody that was liberated by Americans, but I think that if things had been done earlier, not so many lives would have been lost.[8]

As one of the country's most experienced diplomats put it, "More than anyone else in the administration, Madeleine is driven by her own biography. Time and again she raises the sights to the moral and historic issues."

In practice, this view of the world has inclined Albright to inject the United States into problem areas around the globe even when there has been no demonstrable U.S. security interest, commitments she has sought to validate by expanding the definition of national security. This outlook inevitably drew her into conflict with the Defense Department, whose primary mission is always to protect the security of Americans and their commerce, and whose resources and personnel have been stretched thin by deployments from Korea to the Persian Gulf to Bosnia. This conflict was the source of her famous testy exchange with Colin Powell when he was chairman of the Joint Chiefs of Staff. In perhaps the most quoted passage of his memoirs, Powell wrote:

> My constant, unwelcome message at all the meetings on Bosnia was simply
> that we should not commit military forces until we had a clear political ob-
> jective. [Les] Aspin shared this view. The debate exploded at one session
> when Madeleine Albright, our ambassador to the U.N., asked me in frus-
> tration, "What's the point of having this superb military that you're always
> talking about if we can't use it?" I thought I would have an aneurysm.
> American GIs were not toy soldiers to be moved around on some sort of
> global game board.[9]

By the time she was appointed secretary of state, Albright understood that such exchanges had given her a reputation in the
Pentagon as being a bit trigger happy. This was odd because she had
opposed the Persian Gulf War of 1991; but during her tenure at the
United Nations, she had repositioned herself, at least rhetorically, as
a tough global activist, and that was her reputation when Clinton
named her secretary of state.

At Albright's confirmation hearing, Senator Chuck Hagel, a
Republican from Nebraska and a thoughtful combat veteran, asked
for her views about the deployment of American troops abroad. She
replied, "I would never advise using American forces where other
means are available; where there is not the support of Congress and
the people; where there is not the possibility of—where there is no
exit strategy and where there is not the likelihood or the reality of
winning."

Her "exit strategy" comment was fashionable nonsense, inspired
by the fear in Congress that commitments such as those in Somalia
and Bosnia might be open ended. It overlooked the fact that the
United States already maintained open-ended troop commitments
abroad, such as in South Korea. These continuing deployments are
fundamental to U.S. global strategy. Still, her answer helped assure
the senators that she would not casually advocate the deployment of
American troops.

By Albright's second summer on the job, some of the concern
about her alleged cavalier attitude toward military deployment appeared to have dissipated. During the debates over whether it might
be necessary to send NATO troops to Kosovo to stop Serbian abuses
of the ethnic Albanian populace there, we saw few indications of the
differences between her and the Defense Department that had surfaced during the deliberations over extending the troop commit-

ment in Bosnia. Her acceptance by the defense establishment was validated by a tribute in the inaugural edition of *Defense Business,* a magazine dedicated to the propositions that military contracting is the most important activity in the world and that defense spending benefits everyone. The magazine gushed:

> Madeleine Albright clearly symbolizes the unprecedented era dawning in defense, aerospace and national security. It is no longer solely a man's world, even at the highest levels of government. She has proved herself to be a highly influential, clear thinking, fast moving, aggressive leader. She forged an easy rapport with world leaders as well as with troops in the field, and has no trouble confronting rogues such as Iraqi thug Saddam Hussein. In addition, Albright, more than most of her predecessors, has taken a keen interest in the state of the military, and she privately pushed the Pentagon to take better care of its forces in Bosnia.[10]

If the Pentagon did seem more comfortable with Albright—and with the Clinton administration in general—one reason was the promulgation in the summer of 1997 of Presidential Decision Directive 56, a comprehensive policy directive issued by Clinton after extensive review and debate by Albright, Secretary of Defense William Cohen, National Security Adviser Sandy Berger, and senior military officers. The purpose of PDD 56 was to set down terms, conditions, and procedures for noncombat U.S. military deployments abroad, easing the military's fear of overeager political responses, open-ended commitments, and murky missions. Its publication culminated a process that began in the early months of Clinton's first term, when the well-intentioned humanitarian mission in Somalia turned into a military and political nightmare.

The administration sought to codify, politically and operationally, the conditions under which the United States would get involved in peacekeeping and other complex political-military operations abroad, and how it would proceed once it was committed. PDD 56 and two earlier documents, PRD 50 and PDD 25, assume that combined military-civilian operations such as those in Haiti and Bosnia will continue to be required and in fact will represent the most frequent type of military mission in the future.

If followed, the procedures laid down in these papers would prevent open-ended, unfunded commitments that failed to define "mission accomplished," such as what the administration had inherited in Somalia.

According to State Department and National Security Council officials, most of the doctrine laid down in PDD 56 and its predecessors aims at easing the sort of Pentagon concerns expressed by Powell after his conversation with Albright. The Defense Department is uncomfortable using military personnel for nonmilitary tasks, such as police work, and wants civilian agencies to pay for their own share of combined operations.

As one official put it, any deployment plan has to include "notwithstanding" money—that is, money that everyone knows will be available for this purpose and this mission no matter what else is going on.

PDD 56 "establishes how we do these things, on the assumption that we do them all the time," said one senior official who participated in the drafting process. Although the text is classified, the document's contents are known in broad outline. It specifies, for example, that each operation be coordinated by a senior official who knows all aspects of the operation, that each participating agency report through that senior official, and that each participating agency develop a timetable and funding plan so that everyone knows how the operation is to proceed. Detailed interagency planning is necessary, administration officials said, because the armed forces and civilian agencies have totally different cultures and methods of operating that do not lend themselves to easy coordination. Except in Vietnam, where military and civilian officials worked closely together in designing and carrying out the so-called pacification program, civilian agencies in the past have generally entered an area of operations overseas after the military's task has been accomplished, not simultaneously. That pattern is now changing.

Several officials who worked on the development of PDD 56 said that the administration had two models to work with: Somalia, a bad model because of the open-ended commitment, the vague and shifting objectives that led to "mission creep," and the lack of an exit strategy; and Haiti, a good model because the objective was clear and the duration of the mission was specified.

"For Bosnia, we were looking at Haiti as a model," said Robert L. Gallucci, the administration's original point man on seeking compliance with the Dayton peace agreements. "Whether it was good for all contingencies was a question, but it was a template and we were working off that."

In the months that preceded the dispatch of U.S. troops to Haiti, "the U.S. government created, perhaps for the first time in its history, a formal political-military operations plan," according to a paper by James F. Dobbins, at that time the administration's Haiti policy coordinator and later the senior coordinator for the Balkans. "The objective of this planning exercise was to impel civilian agencies toward the sort of precision, discipline and forethought that military establishments routinely demand of themselves."

For example, according to Dobbins, plans for operations such as those in Haiti and Bosnia call for participation by the U.S. Agency for International Development (USAID), which is responsible for humanitarian relief, reconstruction assistance, elections training, and other civilian activities. Yet the aid agency is required by law to "follow procedures for the design and delivery of assistance that maximize accountability and cost effectiveness at the expense of speed, precision and flexibility," Dobbins wrote in his study of the lessons of Haiti. To the military, "these can be false economies." In Haiti, Dobbins said, "we were able to break out of this mold, to a limited degree," partly because of the long lead time—several months—when it was apparent that a military intervention was in the works. The planning and recruiting of the international police force that would be needed to supplement the troops were well advanced by the time the troops landed.[11]

"If you have enough foreknowledge, you can apply resources to the problem of planning, write down on paper what you would do, where you would get the money, how many people you would send, all that sort of stuff," a senior official said. That was the reason NATO troops were poised at the border, ready to move into Kosovo, when the air war there ended in 1999: The bombing lasted eleven weeks, and by the time it was over the troops were in place, relief planning was under way, and Congress had already appropriated money.

Conversely, when events unfold swiftly and unexpectedly, as in the outbreak of genocidal war in Rwanda in 1994, the military remains the only organization capable of moving quickly enough to affect the situation on the ground. In such cases, the military can find itself doing—and paying for—unexpected tasks such as running field hospitals for refugees or operating civilian airports until USAID and other government agencies, along with nongovernmental organizations, can catch up. Naturally, the Pentagon wishes to limit the number of such emergency deployments and the extent to which Defense Department funds are used to pay for nonmilitary activities.

The principles laid down in PDD 56 helped the administration prepare for and implement the daunting challenge of stabilizing and rebuilding Kosovo after the air war against Yugoslavia ended in the spring of 1999. By the time Serbia capitulated and pulled its security forces out of Kosovo, Congress had already appropriated enough money to finance U.S. participation in the international relief effort and the deployment of American troops as peacekeepers. No Pentagon funds were diverted for police training, food assistance, or reconstruction. The military units to be deployed had already been designated, and many were already in the Balkans. Within a few days after the U.N. Security Council voted to approve the cease-fire agreement and assume responsibility for the civilian administration of Kosovo, the U.S. government submitted a fifty-page implementation plan—scripted by Dobbins and incorporating all he had learned in Haiti—which the United Nations generally followed. In a lawless environment with no government and few functioning civilian institutions, violence and revenge killings continued for weeks after the cease-fire; but in comparison with Bosnia during Clinton's first term, the deployment of peacekeeping troops and international civilian administrators in Kosovo was quick, well organized, and politically trouble-free.

In the late summer of 1998, when Albright and the administration were facing difficult times in Africa, the Balkans, Russia, Iraq, and East Asia all at once, the secretary of state reassured the military that she understood and respected the armed forces' role in American history. In a speech to the national convention of the American Legion, she said:

> Long ago, when Hitler invaded my native Czechoslovakia, my family sought and found refuge in London. Europe was our world then, and the war was a battle for survival. When my family was not in a bomb shelter, we were glued to the radio. Through the darkness, we were sustained by the inspiring words of Eisenhower, Roosevelt and Churchill, and by the courage of Allied soldiers. I was just a little girl; even then, I developed

deep admiration for those brave enough to fight for freedom. And I fell in love with Americans in uniform. The story of my family has been repeated in millions of variations over more than two centuries in the lives of those around the world who have been liberated or sheltered by American soldiers, empowered by American assistance or inspired by American ideals.[12]

Albright seized every opportunity to reaffirm her esteem for the military and her reluctance to see troops sent casually into harm's way. Her line, "I fell in love with Americans in uniform," popped up again and again. On her trips to Saudi Arabia, she has made a point of visiting the American troops at Prince Sultan Air Base, in the middle of nowhere south of Riyadh, and reassuring them that they are admired and respected, not taken for granted.

On one occasion, she appeared in the State Department auditorium with General Charles C. Krulak, commandant of the Marine Corps—in his dress blues, with a chest full of medals—for a ceremony marking the fiftieth anniversary of the Marine Security Guard Program. About 1,100 marines serve as security officers in 122 American embassies and consulates around the world, some in extremely dangerous environments.

Albright again told her story about living in wartime London as a child and falling in love with Americans in uniform, and she recalled meeting a marine hero at the bombed-out embassy in Kenya. The marines, she said, are "the thin blue line standing between America's diplomats and an often perilous, sometimes hostile, always uncertain world. In doing this dangerous job with grace and valor, the marine guards themselves are superb ambassadors, showing the world much of what is right and good about our country."

She recalled being honored at a Marine Corps parade, and firing the starter's gun at the beginning of the annual Marine Corps marathon. "I have a K-bar knife on my desk," she said. "I have a sword with my name on it on the wall. I guess you could call me a Marine Corps kind of girl."[13]

This sort of flattery of the military establishment is harmless, and it probably helped Albright burnish her reputation with the troops. She was well received during the two visits to the base in Saudi Arabia that I observed, for example (though not as well received as

Tipper Gore, who wowed the troops with tales of hanging out the family laundry on a communal line as a young army wife living on an enlisted man's pay). But it didn't do much to placate critics in Congress and in the Pentagon who continued to believe that President Clinton had been too quick to dispatch troops on uncertain missions of dubious importance to American security.

The military is "becoming a police organization rather than a military organization," Representative Pat Danner, a Missouri Republican, complained at a House committee hearing shortly before the start of NATO's air war against Yugoslavia.

"Well, let me just say," Albright replied, "that I have the highest respect for the U.S. military, and I would never for a moment waste them in something that was not important to U.S. national interests."[14]

One of Albright's closest confidants at the State Department rejected as "just plain bullshit" any suggestion that she somehow overrides a reluctant Pentagon to dispatch troops here and there despite objections from the military leadership. "Madeleine doesn't do that," he said. "That's not the way she does business. She states her position and then works with people. She's a consensus builder."

Less than a week after Albright's metaphoric enlistment in the marines, Clinton announced his readiness to send up to 4,000 Americans to enforce a political settlement in Kosovo, setting off a new round of complaints on Capitol Hill—complaints that quickly became irrelevant as NATO warplanes began the air war against Yugoslavia and the issue evolved into whether the air assault could succeed on its own or whether ground forces would have to be sent not as peacekeepers but as combatants.

Of course, most U.S. input into the world's problems does not involve military intervention. Albright likes to travel the world trying to rally support for good causes, such as protecting the environment and stamping out corporate bribery, and taking on diplomatic challenges even when there is little prospect of success, such as finding a solution to the division of Cyprus.

Albright is "passionate about democracy" and "believes that a great nation can do great things," a trait that has inclined her to activist policies, according to Maureen Steinbrunner, her longtime colleague at the Center for National Policy.[15]

An effusively laudatory editorial in the *Economist* said that Albright "has an immigrant's special passions, which drive her to exert American power whenever there is a chance that it may right a wrong. . . . After the radical blandness of her predecessor, Mr. Christopher, Mrs. Albright is a gale-force blast of fresh air."[16]

In late June 1997, Albright was asked during a long flight across the Pacific how she could reconcile her hands-on, get-involved approach with the perception in many quarters that the United States—rich, powerful, and secure—was more scolding bully than friend. This question was about to become a serious issue in Asia, as an international financial crisis erupted and the United States stirred considerable resentment by insisting that the affected countries swallow the harsh medicine prescribed by the International Monetary Fund regardless of the short-term pain it inflicted on their citizens or their political systems. She answered:

> I think what is very important—and it's not true just with our dealings with Asia, but throughout the world—as I have said many times, is that the United States has a special role in the world. One, by our own choosing because we are a country that has very fixed ideas about political rights and human rights and the fact that we believe that democracies do not go to war with each other but provide a very good climate for their own people as well as the American public. Another reason that we have this leading role is that others have asked us to have it. They find our presence in places useful in terms of providing a secure environment. The 100,000 troops we have in Asia, as well as in Europe, are there primarily because the countries in the region welcome it.
>
> I am very proud of the role the United States plays, whether in Asia or in Europe. We need to be true to our principles in describing how we believe various societies should operate for the benefit of their people. But there are different ways of making those points, in terms of tone and how one addresses people. I believe that the best role for the United States is as a partner and as somebody who respects the operating procedures of various countries.

Throughout her tenure, the "different ways of making those points" have created an appearance of inconsistency as she tailored her relations with different countries to fit their political or strategic importance, as with China, or their domestic political standing, as with Cuba. But her assessment of other governments, if not her response to them, has always developed through a clear differentiation between right and wrong.

It was Albright's "moralistic" view of the world, one of her senior aides said, that led her to insist on developing a special relationship with Latvia, Lithuania, and Estonia, the three tiny Baltic republics that regained independence after the breakup of the Soviet Union. Accepting them into NATO would clearly have been a provocation to Moscow; at the 1997 Helsinki summit meeting in which he grudgingly acquiesced in the eastward expansion of NATO, Russian president Boris Yeltsin unsuccessfully sought a commitment from Clinton to keep the Baltic states out of NATO forever.

The three little countries, which have energetic political constituencies in the United States, are members of NATO's Partnership for Peace security group, but they are unlikely to earn full membership in NATO for the foreseeable future. Albright could have left it at that, as many State Department officials and regional specialists urged her to do. But "Madeleine Albright instinctively understood small states that have been overrun," one of her senior aides said. She and Strobe Talbott devised the Baltic Charter, signed in Washington in January 1998, that gave the three countries, if not the promise of NATO membership, the guarantee that they would not be excluded and the prospect that they could join at some unspecified time—with no veto power by Russia.

"A lot of people said it was too hard" to find a formula that would respond to the concerns of the Baltic states without provoking Russia, said a State Department official who helped draft the charter. "They said, 'You can and should ignore this.' But she said, 'Let's try to tackle it.'"

In truth, Albright was hardly alone in the Clinton administration in her willingness to sally here and there trying to influence events. The president had set an example in his first term, leaping into the intractable conflict in Northern Ireland with his decision to allow Gerry Adams, leader of the political wing of the Irish Republican Army (IRA), to visit the United States. Washington has no strategic interests and few economic interests in Northern Ireland, and America's closest ally, Great Britain, was peeved that Clinton would wade into what London regarded as a domestic problem. But

Clinton felt vindicated when his decision gave Adams the credibility he needed with his constituents to persuade the IRA to declare a cease-fire and enter negotiations over the province's future, which produced an unlikely peace agreement in 1998.

In one way or another, the Clinton administration inserted the United States into the affairs of Sudan, Paraguay, Cambodia, Nigeria, Burma, Macedonia, and other countries of which most Americans are barely aware and which have only peripheral or theoretical impact on U.S. interests.

The results of these efforts have been mixed at best but, despite predictable setbacks, the administration kept trying because it is in the nature of Albright, and Clinton, and Strobe Talbott, to do so.

In the summer of 1997, for example, the administration took on a new assignment: trying to resolve the dispute between Armenia and Azerbaijan over the Nagorno-Karabakh enclave, largely populated by Christian Armenians but located in Muslim Azerbaijan. Its citizens wanted either independence or union with Armenia. Azerbaijan wanted to preserve its territorial integrity. After a brief war, an uneasy cease-fire was established, with Armenia in the stronger position. The United States joined France and Russia as cochairs of the so-called Minsk Group of countries seeking a resolution.

This scenario might sound like some collegiate humorist's parody of diplomacy, especially because the Minsk Group never met in Minsk, the capital of Belarus. But in fact, Talbott and others made a credible case that the conflict was sufficiently important to the United States—mostly because of Azerbaijan's centrality to the development of Caspian Sea oil and gas resources—to justify the diplomatic effort. The administration's policy called for shoring up the political and economic independence of the former Soviet republics to limit Russian influence, while at the same time incorporating Russia into the political mainstream of the West. Taking part in the work of the Minsk Group alongside Russia furthered these aims.

On June 20, 1997, the leaders of the Group of Seven, or G-7, the seven biggest industrialized nations, gathered in Denver for their annual meeting. They were joined by Russia's Boris Yeltsin, whose economically feeble but potentially powerful country became an informal eighth member as a reward from President Clinton for its progress, however halting, toward economic reform. Clinton,

Yeltsin, and President Jacques Chirac of France issued a statement calling for a quick end to the conflict in Nagorno-Karabakh, saying that it had "seriously undermined economic and social development and prosperity throughout the Caucasus region" of the former Soviet Union. I had been told that such a statement would be issued only if the three leaders were convinced that a solution was achievable, so I wrote an article for the *Washington Post* about the Nagorno-Karabakh issue and the diplomacy behind the statement.

Some weeks later, I heard that Talbott had made a bet with James B. Steinberg, the deputy White House national security adviser, on whether anyone in the American press would report on the issuance of that statement. Talbott won when I did so, but he had the advantage of knowing that I had been briefed on the subject and was prepared to write an article about it. As it turned out, nothing came of the Minsk Group's efforts—almost two years later, on the margins of NATO's fiftieth anniversary summit in Washington, Albright was still trying, as she met with the presidents of Armenia and Azerbaijan to no visible effect—but the American participation showed once again the administration's penchant for getting involved in conflicts and disputes that for most Americans were somewhere behind the back burner.

The administration is "active . . . on every continent," Albright said proudly in a September 30, 1997, appearance before the Council on Foreign Relations,

> striving to heal the crisis of confidence that has arisen in the Middle East peace process; preventing a new war in Bosnia; offering our help in mending long-standing disputes in the Caucasus, the Aegean and South Asia; preparing with our partners for the second Summit of the Americas; recognizing and supporting the new promise of Africa; and combating the horror of terror, the plague of illegal drugs, the peril of international crime and the national security threat posed by environmental degradation, including global climate change.

Nowhere was this thirst for involvement more clearly evident than in sub-Saharan Africa, where Albright traveled in December 1997 to unveil what she described as an aggressive new policy of engagement with the continent, based on a realistic assessment of its problems and prospects.

Since the end of the Cold War, Defense Department doctrine has held that the United States has no strategic interests in sub-Saharan Africa. The era when Washington supported corrupt dictators like Zaire's Mobutu Sese Seko and rebel opportunists like Angola's Jonas Savimbi just because they presented themselves as anticommunist had ended before Clinton took office, and in his first term the administration generally behaved as if it embraced the Pentagon's view that the region was essentially irrelevant. Washington joined the world in celebrating the end of white minority rule in South Africa, but aside from a few events that compelled the United States to pay attention—most notably the genocide in Rwanda in 1994—the administration was generally content to stay out of the continent's seemingly endless upheavals.

Christopher, who declared shortly after taking office that he would give Africa "the attention it deserves," waited more than three years before going there.

Sentiment for staying out of Africa was especially strong after the Somalia debacle of 1993, when a U.S. army ranger unit on peace-keeping duty lost eighteen men in a botched effort to capture the leader of one of the warring factions. President Bush had sent the troops to Somalia on a humanitarian mission; Clinton pulled them out in an ignominious end to a fruitless effort to rebuild the Somali state. After that, no one in Washington had much stomach for further adventures in Africa.

As the chief U.S. representative at the United Nations at the time the mission to Somalia collapsed, Albright bore some responsibility for Somalia, which was perhaps the biggest foreign policy pratfall of Clinton's first term: the breakup in disarray of a U.N.-sponsored effort to save a broken country that had embodied Albright's vision of "assertive multilateralism" as the key to stability in the post–Cold War world.

It was on Albright's watch at the United Nations that the original humanitarian military mission evolved into a U.N.-controlled effort to rebuild the Somali state, an effort in which the duties of the American troops became increasingly complex and muddled. According to Elizabeth Drew's detailed account, it was Albright who promoted the U.N. Security Council resolution calling for the arrest of "those responsible" for an attack in which twenty-four Pakistani peacekeeping troops died. It was in an effort to carry out that resolution that the Americans were killed a few months later. As Drew noted, Albright's diplomatic handiwork thus "led straight to the disaster" of the bungled raid, a poorly planned and ultimately fatal effort to capture a local warlord, Muhammad Farah Aidid.[17]

A few weeks before the raid, Albright had taken an uncompromising stance in support of the American military effort in Somalia. She wrote:

> By seeking to disarm Mr. Aidid, the U.N. is fulfilling its mandate in Somalia. The earlier, American-led intervention ordered by President George Bush was limited to humanitarian relief. But the currently applicable Security Council resolutions call explicitly for the disarming of Somali factions because humanitarian and political goals cannot be assured unless a secure environment is created. . . . The decision we must make is whether to pull up stakes and allow Somalia to fall back into the abyss or to stay the course and help lift the country and its people from the category of a failed state into that of an emerging democracy. For Somalia's sake, and ours, we must persevere.[18]

That commitment blew away with the smoke from the fatal firefight. The Somalia experience traumatized the administration and forced Clinton and his foreign policy team to abandon "assertive multilateralism." According to Richard Holbrooke, who was assistant secretary of state for European affairs in Clinton's first term and later Albright's rival for the top job, Somalia was a "catastrophe" for the administration. He recalled:

> The events of October 13, 1993, when 18 Americans were ambushed and killed in 10 minutes on the streets of Mogadishu, one of them dragged through the streets and shown on CNN, is [*sic*] so profound you can hardly imagine it if you weren't there. It shattered the administration, almost brought it down internally, led to the resignation of the Secretary of Defense and was a cloud over everything that I was trying to do in Bosnia.[19]

And not only Bosnia was affected. Just over a week after the deaths in Mogadishu, Clinton ordered a U.S. Navy ship carrying military police personnel to Haiti to turn back because a handful of pistol-waving thugs had gathered at the pier there to protest. In effect, a small group of lightly armed Haitian civilians had scared off the U.S.

Navy because the navy's commander wanted more than anything else to avoid casualties. That was the lowest point in the dismal foreign policy performance of Clinton's first two years.

"The deaths in Somalia so affected [Anthony] Lake that he offered to resign, but Clinton would not allow it. A lesson had been learned: Seven months later Lake recommended against sending any peacekeepers to Rwanda," according to historian Douglas Brinkley—a recommendation that Clinton followed, allowing the death toll to mount in the Rwandan genocide. Albright later acknowledged that the administration had mishandled this situation as well.[20]

The Somalia debacle reinforced the Vietnam-based squeamishness of Clinton and most of his team. It touched off a long struggle within the administration to define and limit the circumstances in which U.S. troops would be committed to peacekeeping and humanitarian operations worldwide, of which the most visible effect was Clinton's refusal until after the Dayton peace agreement to put any military personnel on the ground in Bosnia.

Clinton closed the political books on Somalia by pulling out the troops and writing the country off. Albright also put it behind her; in an impressive display of political dexterity that baffled some of her administration colleagues, she walked away politically unscathed. She paid no political price for it, mostly because the troops had originally been sent to Somalia by President Bush, not by Clinton.

At her confirmation hearing before the Republican-controlled Senate Foreign Relations Committee in January 1997, only one member even mentioned Somalia. Chuck Hagel, who had been in the Senate just twenty-four hours, asked her to "reflect a little bit on your concept of committing American troops."

"I along with everybody else, am deeply regretful of the lives lost in Somalia," Albright responded, noting that the Somalia incident had prompted the review of the circumstances under which U.S. troops would be committed in the future. But she said nothing to acknowledge that any responsibility for those deaths fell upon her personally.

"Thank you," Hagel responded, and that was the end of it.

Thus Albright became secretary of state free to pursue greater involvement with Africa, as if she had an entirely clean slate. Her perspective, not surprisingly, was very different from that of the cautious George Moose, an amiable but conventional career diplomat who was the assistant secretary of state for African affairs in the first term. Moose was never inclined to go looking for trouble.

At one point in the late spring of 1993, crises of different cause and intensity erupted simultaneously in five African countries: Somalia, Liberia, Togo, Angola, and Zaire. Pressed by Congress to back up the administration's stated commitment to a more dynamic involvement with Africa, Moose responded with carefully crafted explanations why, in each case, it was not in the interests of the United States to intervene, or why the problem should be dealt with by others. In anarchic Liberia, for example, Moose told the Senate Foreign Relations Committee that a regional peacemaking effort by neighboring countries, "supported by the Organization for African Unity and the United Nations, offers by far the best prospect for achieving a settlement that will restore peace."[21]

That passive response reflected the policy of "assertive multilateralism," in which the United States would generally let others take the lead in designing, and pick up most of the cost of executing, collective intervention in the world's crisis spots, while retaining the right to act unilaterally in its own interests where necessary. The failures in Somalia and Bosnia obliterated assertive multilateralism, and the term vanished from the American diplomatic lexicon; in its place emerged a doctrine of activism based on Albright's conviction that U.S. leadership is essential to calming the upheavals of an unruly world. Anyone whose acquaintance with Madeleine Albright began when she became secretary of state would never know that she once championed assertive multilateralism; the expression was expunged, like an entry in the Great Soviet Encyclopedia about a notable person who had since been purged.

While still at the United Nations, Albright traveled in January 1996 to four of Africa's most depressing trouble spots—Rwanda, Burundi, Liberia, and Angola—and came away convinced that it was not only wrong but dangerous to stay on the sidelines while Africa consumed itself with violence. The legacy of Somalia precluded direct American intervention, but it did not preclude political and economic efforts to stabilize the continent.

"I think it was the worst trip I've ever been on," she told high school students in Addis Ababa, Ethiopia, on the first day of another

Africa tour almost two years later, because she saw endless suffering in four countries that ought to have been capable of allowing their citizens to lead normal lives. In each of the countries, State Department officials said later, Albright also saw the malign influence of Zaire, then still ruled by the corrupt Mobutu Sese Seko, which was selling weapons and fomenting trouble throughout central Africa. And she concluded that the United States, already a major investor in the oil fields of Angola and Nigeria, could capitalize on economic opportunities if Africa could be stabilized. Moreover, Albright was becoming increasingly convinced that some of Africa's chronic problems—infectious diseases, corruption, degradation of the environment, displaced populations—could in time pose direct threats to the well-being of Americans, and therefore warranted attention. All these elements combined to persuade her that the United States should engage more aggressively with Africa.

During Albright's first months as secretary of state, a profound and unexpected change in the African political landscape in a generation gave her the opening she wanted. Without warning, an armed insurgency arose in the remote eastern provinces of Zaire, where hundreds of thousands of Rwandan refugees had upset the regional balance of power. The rebels quickly picked up support from neighboring countries that were fed up with Mobutu and swept across one of the continent's biggest states. Mobutu's unpaid army and hollow government collapsed, and by May 1997, after thirty-two years in power, he was gone. He died of prostate cancer in exile in Morocco a few months later.

In his place was an alliance of little-known leaders and groups who had neither the resources nor the technical competence to govern effectively a vast nation whose physical and social structures had been destroyed by Mobutu's corrupt rule. They restored the country's original name, Democratic Republic of the Congo, but seemed to have little idea of what to do next.

During the months when the rebel forces, led by a former Maoist named Laurent Désiré Kabila, were sweeping across Zaire, the response from Washington was basically to watch in amazement. Administration officials expressed concern that chaos in Zaire, which borders nine countries, might engulf all of central Africa, but Washington had no control and little influence over what was happening on the ground. In fact, Kabila was aided by troops and weapons from several of those nearby countries, especially Rwanda and Angola, where leaders who understood that Mobutu had outlived his Cold War usefulness to the West seized the opportunity to bring down a regime that had caused them trouble for many years.

In that outcome, Albright and her assistant secretary for African affairs, a brilliant young academic named Susan Rice, who had worked on African issues for Tony Lake at the National Security Council during the first term, found both opportunity and challenge.

The opportunity lay in the fact that African leaders such as Yoweri Museveni of Uganda and Paul Kagame of Rwanda had been able to cooperate in their own collective interest by aiding Kabila's rebellion. They had clearly put aside the postcolonial African doctrine of noninterference in the affairs of other African countries, however odious their governments, and showed that they could work together for the betterment of the continent. The challenge lay in trying to stabilize Congo so that it could develop an effective government, rebuild its economy, and use its vast resources to create an engine of development for all of central Africa.

Albright concluded that the United States could play a useful role in nurturing that transformation only by developing a new way of dealing with African leaders and governments. They could no longer be appraised in terms of their value as Cold War proxies, good if inclined toward Washington, bad if inclined toward Moscow. Nor, she concluded, could the way they ran their countries be measured by Western standards of performance. Many of the brightest new African leaders were struggling to keep themselves and their countries afloat in the face of economic collapse, military insurgency, and tribal rivalries. They were not interested in hearing lectures from Washington about human rights or, if they could avoid it, from the International Monetary Fund about their interest rates and monetary policies.

Albright decided to accommodate the presidents and prime ministers she met and make an effort to treat them as equals, tolerating if not approving of certain counterinsurgency and crowd control tactics that would have outraged human rights purists, and avoiding putting public pressure on leaders such as Museveni and Ethiopia's Meles Zenawi to hold elections and ensure political openness. Albright concluded that security and stability in the continent's Great Lakes region, including Congo and Rwanda, were the keys to progress in Africa; regression there could doom much of the continent to violence and poverty for decades to come. In an address to the Organization of African Unity in Addis Ababa that served as a keynote for her tour of the continent in December 1997, she said:

> Africa's new leaders come from varied backgrounds. They are as diverse as the continent itself. But they share a common vision of empowerment, for all their citizens, for their nations and for their continent. They share an energy, a self-reliance and a determination to shape their own destinies. They are moving boldly to change the way their countries work and the way we work with them. They are challenging the United States and the international community to get over the paternalism of the past; to stop thinking of its Africa policy as a none-too-successful rescue service; and to begin seizing opportunities to work with Africans to transform their continent.

Perhaps these new African leaders sometimes resorted to tactics of which Americans might disapprove, Albright said, but their circumstances left them little choice. "Those who would build democratic institutions and market-based economies in the Great Lakes face tremendous obstacles: societies weakened by protracted and brutal conflicts; devastated government institutions; and the legacies of authoritarian rule," Albright continued, adding that if these leaders sometimes failed to meet the political standards expected of stable Western countries, it was understandable.

Furthermore, Albright said, the United States and other Western countries bore some share of responsibility for Africa's problems. Promising to help Africans overcome the "culture of impunity" that allowed violence to rage unchecked, she said, "Let me begin that process here today by acknowledging that we—the international community—should have been more active in the early stages of the atrocities in Rwanda in 1994, and called them what they were— genocide." With that, she became the first high-ranking American official to acknowledge that Washington had behaved cravenly as innocents were slaughtered for weeks on end. President Clinton made a similar statement during his own six-nation Africa tour the following year.

Albright and Rice were convinced that future U.S. credibility in Africa required an acknowledgment of what had happened in

Rwanda and a public pledge not to sit by if the ethnic violence there erupted anew. An essential component of their new policy was to overcome the ingrained attitudes that had allowed the continent's malefactors to go unpunished.

According to aides, Albright accepted Rice's argument that they should view the African glass as half full rather than half empty. Albright knew perfectly well that some of these "new" leaders she was courting had been in power a decade or more; and she knew that with the possible exception of Angolan president José Eduardo dos Santos, none of these energetic leaders about whom she spoke so enthusiastically could claim to hold power as the result of a free election, nor was any of them much inclined to risk giving up power at the ballot box. Given their collective record, a case could be made that Albright had turned to a Kissinger-style realpolitik, the hard-nosed, reality-based policy that Clinton's critics on the right were always chastising him for failing to pursue.

But Albright and her senior advisers on the trip insisted that it was not as complicated as all that. Convinced that Africa matters, she simply decided to play the cards the continent had dealt her, including the biggest card of all, Kabila.

The Congolese leader, an enormous, moon-faced man who favors leisure suits over jacket and tie, had a long and checkered history as an unsuccessful Maoist of the African bush, but he was an unknown quantity as a national leader. He came to power in one of Africa's most important countries more or less by accident, as the nominal leader of the ad hoc alliance that had seized control of the country from the terminally ill Mobutu in the spring of 1997.

Some human rights groups argued that the United States should keep its distance from Kabila until he proved his good intentions; their suspicions had been aroused by reports that his forces had massacred civilians in their drive toward Kinshasa. But Albright and Rice felt there was too much at stake to permit a wait-and-see approach. According to a senior official assigned to relay Albright's views to reporters riding in the back of her plane:

> The Congo can essentially go one of two ways. It can yet again be unstable, export instability across its borders, fail to revive its economy and therefore put a drag on the economies of all of central and southern Africa . . . or it can pull out of the bog that it's been in, implement something ap-

proaching responsible government, be a force for peace and stability in
the region, respect the rights of its people and be a part of a national and
regional economic revitalization that could have better consequences for
all of east, central and southern Africa.

Under Mobutu, the country had been a rotting mess for years,
contributing to the continent's general misery, to no visible detriment to the interests of the United States. There really was very little
evidence that a continuation of Congo's pitiable condition under
Kabila would have presented any greater threat to Americans.

But that was not the way Albright looked at it. She saw an Africa
gripped by violence and poverty as a source of disease, overpopulation, environmental degradation, and lost economic opportunity,
as well as human misery, and she believed that the United States
had a duty to help turn the continent around. The senior official
continued:

> We feel very strongly that the United States can't afford to be indifferent
> to the outcome, that it serves our long-term interests, as well as obviously
> the interests of the region, that this window of opportunity end in success
> if at all possible. Therefore we have made a policy decision that rather
> than sit on the sideline and keep score as events unfold, we would try to
> use our influence to bear on the fragile new inexperienced government.
> The reality is that after thirty years of Mobutu there is no infrastructure,
> there is no responsible government and not even a real clear-cut concept
> of what responsible governance is.

So rather than criticize or "sit on the sideline," Albright offered
help. Washington would try to come up with $35 million to $40 million to assist Congo in public health, sanitation, and financial management. The United States would contribute to a World Bank trust
fund for Congo and consider relieving the country of some of the
massive external debt rung up by Mobutu. Washington would pay to
rebuild an important bridge. Peace Corps volunteers would return.

Albright announced this aid package after meeting with Kabila in
Kinshasa, Congo's shabby, chaotic capital. At a joint news confer-
ence in an open-air pavilion on the banks of the mighty Congo
River, the two presented a fascinating contrast: the diminutive
Albright in her bright suit and flashing jewelry alongside the im-

mense Kabila in a monochromatic leisure suit. Albright said that she was there "because there can be no doubt that what happens in this vast country will do much to shape the future of Central, Eastern and Southern Africa, and because we have an unprecedented opportunity to build a new relationship between our two nations." With Kabila beaming at her side, Albright proclaimed: "The United States is committed to supporting the people of the Congo as they seek to build the peace, freedom and growth they have been so long denied."

But then one of the traveling American reporters, Roy Gutman of *Newsday,* cast a shadow over the happy scene by asking about political prisoners. Had Albright brought up the subject with Kabila, and if so how did he respond?

"Yes," she said. They had "talked quite a bit about the importance of elections and the importance of dealing with numerous political views." And she told Gutman that she, Clinton, and the Congress would be "very interested in how Congo and President Kabila do in fact carry out obligations on issues of human rights and democracy."

That should have been the end of it. If Kabila were at all smooth, he would simply have nodded in agreement or added a few anodyne words. Instead, he took the microphone and challenged Gutman to give him the names of any supposed political prisoners.

"The name I've heard is Zaide Ingoma; [it was] in one of the leading publications," Gutman replied. "Is he now free, or where is he?"

To our amazement, Kabila responded that Ingoma was not a legitimate political figure but a rabble-rousing pamphleteer who had incited the citizenry to violence in conspiracy with "foreign embassies."

"Do you let people like that free on the street?" Kabila said. "Those who incite people to violence will go to jail. Long live democracy," he said with a sneer.

Members of Albright's team acknowledged afterward that they would have preferred that Kabila express himself differently, but they ascribed his crude performance to lack of experience in the spotlight and lack of political acumen. Those excuses were not available when Albright went through a similar session a few days later with President Robert Mugabe of Zimbabwe.

Mugabe, who has run the former Rhodesia since independence in 1980, is as polished as Kabila is crude, but he demonstrated the same instincts at his joint news conference with Albright.

A week before their meeting, Mugabe's riot police had provoked the country's deepest political crisis in years by crushing an antitax demonstration, blocking a planned peaceful march through the capital city, Harare, and clubbing and tear-gassing participants despite an order from the country's highest court to allow the demonstration to proceed so long as it remained peaceful.

Asked about this by the indefatigable Gutman, Albright said that she had learned on her tour of Africa that "we need to make sure that human rights continue to be the bedrock of our whole relationship, but we have to recognize that the countries are not identical to each other and that there is a local context and that we have to do everything possible to make democracy sustainable." This gentle response amounted to a passing grade for Mugabe despite the events of the previous week, and Mugabe ought to have let it go at that. But, like Kabila, he had more to say.

The police were just doing their duty, he said, defending the city against people who were common looters, "people who from the very onset of the demonstration would want to commit acts of violence, people who would want to rob others of their property. . . . Government has the right to prevent all these things happening." Whereupon Albright restated her "benefit of the doubt" theme:

> There is a local context. Rule of law is essential. Reform of the judicial system is essential. The development of democratic institutions is essential in order to make democracy sustainable. But I do think we have to recognize the difference in these countries and various evolutions they are going through, and it is only appropriate that the United States, while pressing our agenda, respect the agendas in these countries as they are moving forward into the twenty-first century.

Thus the Clinton administration and the woman who promised at her confirmation hearing to "Tell It Like It Is" on human rights went through a policy shift with regard to Africa similar to the one they had gone through with regard to China in Clinton's first term. Faced with the need to deal with China as a strategic and economic power, the president decided that he could not allow those ties to be held hostage by China's dismal human rights record. In Africa, the administration recognized that much of the continent simply could not be fairly judged by Western standards of personal and political freedom—people have to survive first. But China is an inescapable global force, demanding Washington's attention and making it possible to justify retreats from principle in the interest of a stable relationship. The imperative of Africa is less clear, as was reflected in reviews back home of Albright's tour.

Some commentators gave her credit for taking the continent as she found it and for trying to deal with it as best she could. Others faulted her for being insufficiently vigorous in pressing the leaders she met on the rights issue. That split was probably inevitable, given that there was not—and probably could not be—any consensus on the nature of U.S. interests in Africa. In the Albright view, the United States is obliged to be involved with Africa because millions of people live there, suffering and violence are widespread in what should be bountiful lands, chaos in Africa could affect the rest of the world, and a stable Africa offers economic opportunity to the United States. There, as elsewhere, a clear demonstration of manifest U.S. strategic interests was not necessary to attract Albright's attention.

The least that could be said was that the United States had little to lose from pursuing a policy of engagement in sub-Saharan Africa. It required no military investment—burned by Somalia, the administration was not going to send troops into African conflicts, and in fact was training African militaries to conduct such interventions on their own—and it involved a minimal investment of taxpayers' money.

The themes of Albright's tour reappeared in Clinton's visit to the continent the following March. He offered some new economic development aid, but mostly he stressed investment and a commitment by the United States to remain engaged. Like Albright, Clinton stressed the importance of a transition to democracy but refrained from an overly fastidious scrutiny of the democratic credentials of his African interlocutors. He included Kabila in a summit meeting with African heads of state in Uganda and had a long telephone conversation with Charles Taylor, who had fomented a brutal civil war in Liberia and taken power amid the ruins.

"The people of Africa should understand—and many of them need convincing—that when the United States says it wants to work with them on the basis of shared interests and mutual respect, we're not just blowing smoke," Albright said of the president's visit.[22]

She described an approach that represents a complete reversal from the Cold War era, when Washington viewed Africa mostly as a proxy battlefield for containing the ambitions of the Soviet Union. Henceforth, she said, Washington's policy in Africa would emphasize economic, political, and social development through expanded trade, support for credit cooperatives, public health initiatives, and new opportunities for women. She explained:

An increasing focus of our programs is the empowerment of African women. We have found that when women gain the knowledge and power to make their own choices, they are often able to break out of the cycle of poverty. Birth rates stabilize; environmental awareness increases. The spread of sexually transmitted diseases slows, and socially constructive values are more likely to be passed on to the next generation. This is how social progress is made and how peace and prosperity are built.

Today, throughout Africa, we find grass-roots organization made up of women and health-care practitioners, educators and small farmers, who are reaching out to create the foundations of a civil society, to build a future from the ground up, often despite great hardship and poverty and prejudice. American policy is to support these efforts and to strengthen them.

This is about as far as a secretary of state can get from traditional balance-of-power diplomacy, but it represents the core of Albright's approach to the world. The problem, in Africa as elsewhere, is that such an approach often seems divorced from reality. All the time Albright and Clinton were talking about a new relationship with an evolving continent, Africa seemed to be sliding backward: war in Congo, war in Angola, war and mutilation of innocents in Sierra Leone, war between Ethiopia and Eritrea, war without end in Sudan. These unhappy circumstances prompted a memorable wisecrack from Georgetown professor Peter Krogh, Albright's longtime colleague, who said that the African renaissance Albright talked about was more like a Renaissance Weekend.

Some months later, the scene in Africa appeared somewhat less grim, as settlements were announced in the Congo and Sierra Leone conflicts. Nevertheless, Africa stands as Exhibit A in support of the charge that Albright sees the world not as it is but as she would like it to be.

Late in Albright's first year in office, her effort to engage with yet another remote corner of the world, South Asia, led indirectly to the first serious criticism of her performance—not about South Asia, but about Iraq, which intruded on and finally overtook her ambitious plans for building a new relationship with India, Pakistan, and Bangladesh.

Because the main lines of the Clinton administration's foreign policy had been forged the time she took office, Albright was not seriously tested—and encountered little criticism of her performance—during her first ten months on the job. When the test came, it was from an unlikely source: Saddam Hussein, the dictator of Iraq.

The decision by President Bush and Colin Powell at the end of the 1991 Persian Gulf War to halt the advance of alliance troops well short of taking Baghdad left Saddam Hussein in power. His ability to make trouble for his neighbors was drastically curtailed by the most stringent sanctions ever imposed on a country by the United Nations Security Council, but he still controlled Iraq's armed forces and retained the country's levers of power, which he wielded ruthlessly.

Every six to twelve months, Saddam Hussein would make some move to test the will of the United Nations, and of the United States. One time he moved large numbers of troops toward the Kuwaiti border, pulling them back when the United States responded with its own deployment, and made clear that no threat to Kuwait would be tolerated. Another time he sent troops north, into the city of Irbil in the Kurdish zone of northern Iraq, a strike that violated cease-fire rules and rolled up a major CIA operation. The Clinton administration's response was to fire a few cruise missiles at relatively insignificant targets in southern Iraq, a limp-wristed response that deserved the ridicule heaped upon it by critics.

In the fall of 1997, Saddam Hussein offered a more serious challenge. He ordered that American citizens be excluded from the teams of U.N. inspectors then searching his country for nuclear, chemical, and biological weapons. Iraq's acceptance of the inspection regime and declared willingness to abandon its weapons development programs were conditions of the cease-fire that had halted the 1991 war; when Saddam Hussein challenged the teams dispatched by the U.N. Special Commission, or UNSCOM, the United States and other members of the Security Council took the position that he could not dictate the membership of the inspection teams. It was tantamount to letting the criminal select the policemen.

With Americans barred by Saddam Hussein's order, Ambassador Richard Butler, the Australian diplomat then running UNSCOM, pulled all the teams out of Iraq. For the first time since before Clinton's election, Iraq was free from the scrutiny of the arms-control experts, setting off fears in Washington and other capitals that the country would quickly reconstitute some of the lethal weapons programs it was believed to be concealing, including development of weapons potentially capable of wiping out whole cities in Israel, Saudi Arabia, and southern Europe by spreading anthrax or other deadly biological agents.

Washington's position was that Iraq had to be compelled to allow the inspectors, including those who happened to be American, to return, with unfettered access. As for the sanctions, which had essentially excluded Iraq from political and economic contact with the rest of the world for more than six years, the Iraqi challenge had only demonstrated and reinforced the need to maintain them, in the American view.

Britain was the only permanent member of the Security Council to endorse Washington's position unequivocally. Russia and France had long sought some relaxation of the sanctions—several Russian and French oil companies had signed lucrative deals with Iraq that could be implemented only after the sanctions were lifted—and the Chinese appeared ambivalent.

Clinton, Berger, Albright, Cohen, and Bill Richardson, Albright's successor at the United Nations, devised a two-tier strategy for dealing with what the news media insisted on calling a "crisis." The United States moved an aircraft carrier and other military reinforcements to the Persian Gulf to show Saddam Hussein that Washington meant business if it came to that; but at the same time, the administration expressed a desire to resolve the situation diplomatically by shoring up the collective will of the Security Council and making it clear to Saddam Hussein that he had no choice but to comply.

The administration stated publicly that it was willing to allow Russia to be the Security Council's interlocutor with Saddam Hussein because the Russian foreign minister, Yevgeny Primakov, had extensive experience in the Arab world and a record of sympathy for Iraq that presumably made him more acceptable and credible to the Iraqis.

Meanwhile, Albright had been convinced by Talbott that the United States had paid insufficient attention to India and Pakistan during Clinton's first term. Talbott had visited the volatile, nuclear-capable neighbors carrying a regional security proposal aimed at lowering tensions between them but had gotten nowhere. The two countries are deeply suspicious of each other and regard any effort by the United States to mediate as a zero-sum game: Any gesture by Washington toward one is taken as a slight by the other. Albright wanted a new beginning in which the United States would engage this teeming part of the world on a much broader front, politically and economically as well as strategically. India and Pakistan had new leaders who were saying conciliatory things, and Albright wanted to seize that small opportunity. On November 13, 1997, she set out from Andrews Air Force Base on what quickly became a nightmare journey.

Albright was trying to do too many things at once; she had multiple missions on that trip and she was not in control of the agendas or the outcomes. On her way to South Asia, she was also going to meet Israeli prime minister Benjamin Netanyahu and Palestinian leader Arafat in Europe at a crucial moment in the Middle East peace negotiations, and she was trying to shore up support for U.S. policy toward Iraq among the Persian Gulf Arab states at a time when they were all unhappy over Washington's perceived refusal to lean on Netanyahu to be more forthcoming with the Palestinians. She was aiming to build new relations with India and Pakistan just as the governments in both countries were facing domestic political tests that could bring them down (and indeed the government of Indian prime minister I. K. Gujral fell just two weeks after Albright left New Delhi). She was trying to give Primakov something to say to Saddam Hussein without letting it appear that Washington had agreed to negotiations with the Iraqi leader or that Primakov had Washington's proxy. And by the time she arrived in Europe on her way to South Asia, she was operating several time zones removed from Washington, a fact that kept her and her aides up much of the night making telephone calls during working hours in Washington—a situation that grew more acute as she made her way eastward.

The planned itinerary for that trip included a stop in Qatar, on the Persian Gulf, for a Middle East regional investment conference aimed at developing economic relations between Israel and the Arab countries. The United States had begun sponsoring these annual affairs three years earlier, when a comprehensive regional peace had seemed a possibility. Now that Israel under Netanyahu appeared to be pulling back from its deal with the Palestinians, Arab enthusiasm for commerce was fading. Attendance at the Qatar session would be the smallest of the series, several important Arab countries having declined to participate; rather than promoting regional integration, the conference in Qatar had turned into an embarrassment because it would inevitably dramatize the deterioration of the Arab-Israeli peace process. Once the government of Qatar overcame its qualms and committed itself to hosting the event, Albright was obliged to attend, but the Iraq issue was muscling aside all other concerns. She reduced her schedule in Qatar to a token appearance (obliging all of us in the traveling party to shell out $600 for reserved hotel rooms we never saw) and then on the same day hustled around the Gulf to Kuwait and Bahrain to consult their leaders about Iraq and visit the exiled American inspectors. Then she headed for Riyadh, Saudi Arabia—the fourth country of the day. We stayed overnight there only because air force rules required that the flight crew on her plane get sixteen hours of ground time, then resumed this bizarre flying carpet ride through exotic lands.

At one point in that hectic day, a member of Albright's staff came back to give us some information about what was going on. He said that although the United States insisted that Iraq comply unconditionally with U.N. rules and allow the inspectors to return, Washington was also willing to consider expanding the U.N. program that allowed Iraq to sell limited quantities of crude oil and use the money to buy food and medicine, and that Primakov was conveying this information to the Iraqis.

That indicated to us that the Americans were in fact negotiating the terms of the inspectors' return, even though they denied it. (When some of my press colleagues filed accounts of this briefing at our next stop, talking of "carrots" for Saddam Hussein along with sticks, there was a furor back in Washington, where White House officials ordered Albright and her exhausted staff to somehow correct what the White House said was a false impression. That only made this ill-fated trip more difficult, for the secretary and her aides, and for us.)

Moreover, Primakov received a senior Iraqi official in Moscow and talked openly about a Russian plan to resolve the situation, compounding the impression that Albright had allowed the pro-Iraq Russian to seize control of the diplomacy.

From Riyadh, we flew on to Islamabad, Pakistan, but much of Albright's ambitious South Asia schedule was sacrificed to the Iraq crisis. She scrapped a stop in Bangladesh, curtailed her public appearances in Pakistan and India, and undermined the impact of her stop in Pakistan with an anemic, distracted performance in her only news conference there.

At that news conference, with Pakistani foreign minister Gohar Ayub, whom she dislikes, Albright missed an opportunity to speak forcefully and in new ways to the Pakistanis. She wanted to talk about a new era in relations between the United States and the countries of South Asia. The Pakistani journalists, however, were as always obsessed with India, formulating zero-sum questions suggesting that any American gesture toward India must be at Pakistan's expense and demanding to know why Washington tolerated this or that alleged atrocity by the Indians.

What Albright could have said was, "Look, those attitudes are part of the problem here. We want to be friendly to Pakistan but not at India's expense, and vice versa. It is time for new thinking." Instead, she gave bland and formulaic responses that would not have any perceptible impact on Pakistani public opinion. Her tone was flat, her style uncharacteristically wooden.

At the time, I attributed this to fatigue and to the strain of trying to focus on Pakistan when the real problem was the unfolding drama with Iraq. Since she couldn't give Pakistan her full attention, she did not want to risk a misstep by deviating from her scripted answers. But when I asked her about it later, she offered a different reason. The press conference was indeed "boring," she acknowledged, but the reason she had held her verbal fire was that it was her first visit to Pakistan as secretary of state and she did not want to start by hurting anyone's feelings.

Albright wanted to meet with Primakov to find common ground on Iraq, but she was in South Asia and he was in Moscow. He was willing to meet her but insisted that he had to go ahead with a long-scheduled trip to Brazil, on which he was about to embark. To accommodate him, Albright canceled a speech before the Indian Parliament and a sightseeing trip to the Taj Mahal and headed for Geneva. It was the third time in a week she had flown through the night. Two of her senior aides, hustling out of their hotel in New Delhi on the way to the airport, complained that they had never left the hotel the entire time they were in the country—all their waking hours were spent on the phone dealing with Iraq and arranging the Geneva meeting.

We arrived in Geneva after midnight, Swiss time, and Albright went to a meeting of the foreign ministers of the five permanent members of the Security Council—the United States, Russia, France, Britain, and China—that began at 2 A.M. So hastily was that session arranged and so uncertain the agenda that no one had been designated chairman; Britain's Robin Cook took it upon himself to chair the meeting because someone had to do it. Diplomats abhor improvisation, and this was as improvised as diplomacy can get.

The outcome—announced by Albright at a 5 A.M. news conference—was the best she could hope for under the circumstances: Primakov told her and the other foreign ministers that Iraq would back down and allow the inspectors to return to work unhindered. He said that Baghdad would make a formal announcement later that morning. And then he took off for Brazil, his schedule intact.

Baghdad did make the promised announcement; but there was no escaping the fact that Iraq and Russia had scored gains at the expense of the United States. Saddam Hussein not only went unpunished for his defiance, he gained a promise of increased oil sales. He had forced the secretary of state to truncate a major foreign policy initiative. And the episode underlined his ability to seize the agenda and, more or less at will, to force the United States to deploy troops. As for Primakov, he was able to claim that the outcome was a victory for Russian diplomacy, achieved without the threat of force, and that he had prevailed over Albright in the arm wrestling over the schedule. Around Washington, it was said that if Primakov had tried such a ploy with Jim Baker, Baker would have responded, "Fine, Yevgeny, you go to Brazil. And the next time you need economic help, you call the Brazilians."

Here is an excerpt from notes I drafted during that trip.

Well, this is first time Ms. Tell It Like It Is, the Media Queen, has been under real pressure on one of these trips, and she goes to ground. Trip billed as start of new era in U.S. relations with the nations of the subcontinent, but most time spent figuring out what to do about Saddam Hussein. Negotiations on Iraq being conducted on the fly thru Russia, Saddam defying the United Nations, Albright trying to salvage truncated program in India and Pak while getting pushed around by Iraqis. This is the trip of the famous flying carpet ride thru the Gulf, four countries in one day, trying to find some coordinated policy of opposition to Saddam to make him back down on the weapons inspections. Traveling press gets nowhere near her.

She cancels press dinner in New Delhi; OK, that can happen, dinner time in Delhi is full work time in Washington and she and all her aides are working the phones. But the next night she is flying to meet Cook, [French foreign minister Hubert] Vedrine, and Primakov in a meeting set for 2 A.M. in Geneva. And knowing that we all have to file, all our papers and stations are waiting to hear from us, on the entire seven-hour leg from Delhi to a refueling stop in Cairo, she doesn't even make an appearance in the back of the plane—not even to tell us why she can't tell us anything.

This is a symptom. She wants to be in control of the events and the message, and in this case she's not in control. It would have been easy to offer some anodyne commentary—"These are difficult negotiations and I'm sure you'll understand if I can't go into details but I can say we're not altogether satisfied with what we are hearing,"—something like that, anything that holds on to the press corps rather than alienating them and arousing their suspicions. This is not a good sign.

Albright said later that she had been irked earlier in the trip by some inaccurate reporting in the world media about what was happening with Iraq. She said that she could not understand how CNN could go on the air and report that a meeting was taking place between her and Primakov to discuss the Iraq situation when it had not yet been firmly scheduled. She did not make clear, and perhaps could not articulate, exactly how that CNN report had affected events or complicated her mission.

In an informal conversation, we reporters had to explain to her that in contrast to, say, her earlier trips to Croatia or Vietnam, where her presence and her message were the whole story, the Iraq drama was unfolding in many places at once. In the absence of informed input from us, given her inaccessibility, our colleagues at the White House and the Pentagon, and in Paris and Moscow and at the United Nations, were all doing their jobs, finding out what they could, and some of them were going to get information she did not like.

That incident confirmed my impression that although Albright is interested in using the media to convey messages and is friendly with many journalists, she doesn't really understand how we work. The fact is that when a secretary of state cuts short a major diplomatic initiative in an important part of the world to participate in a crisis-management negotiation with the Russians, British, French, and Chinese at 2 A.M., that is big news, and the media are going to publish articles about it and put news stories on the air. The *Washington Post* has a publication schedule, and I had a deadline to meet; CNN is on the air and its correspondents have to say something. By refusing to talk to us or send one of her senior aides to do so, she essentially forced our organizations to scramble for information from other sources—information that she could not control.

As bad as that trip was, it was only a preview of greater difficulties soon to come. The three subjects that occupied her time as she scrambled here and there—the Middle East, Iraq, and South Asia—would all plague Albright throughout her second year in office and deal her the most serious setbacks of her tenure.

Chapter 4

I WAS QUEEN OF THE MAY

A FEW DAYS BEFORE the first anniversary of Albright's swearing in, I ran into a senior member of the Bureau of Near Eastern Affairs at the lunch line in the State Department cafeteria. He was gloomy, and did not seem happy to see me. I asked what was wrong, and he responded that he and his colleagues were upset because "We're getting hammered in the press."

Hammered in the press? What could he have been talking about? Certainly Albright, Berger, and the president himself were being criticized by many columnists and editorial writers at the time for the fact that Saddam Hussein was again defying the international weapons inspectors with whom the U.N. Security Council had ordered him to cooperate, and the Clinton administration did not seem to know what to do about it. But by historical standards, and in comparison with Albright's predecessor, Warren Christopher, Albright and her team were not only not "getting hammered," they were getting a virtual free ride from the Washington media. It has been said that Washington is a city that runs on protocol, alcohol, Geritol, and vitriol, but Albright had been mostly spared the vitriol except from a few snipers on the far right.

One reason was that Albright and her senior advisers—Strobe Talbott, Tom Pickering, and Stuart Eizenstat in particular—had earned generally good grades in their first year. Talbott, a friend of Clinton's from their Oxford days, is a former *Time* correspondent who entered the administration in the first term as Clinton's princi-

pal adviser on Russia. After the departure of the hapless Clifton
Wharton, Talbott became deputy secretary of state. Albright wisely
kept him on in that capacity. An indefatigable worker, he kept
adding tough assignments to his portfolio, including Haiti, Kosovo,
the Caucasus, and South Asia, to the point where he seemed to be
shrinking physically from exhaustion even as he grew professionally.
His influence on Russia policy would wax and wane with events—diminished by the repudiation of the economic reformers Talbott
championed, reinforced by his crucial diplomacy in the Kosovo
campaign—but his "friend of Bill" access to the president was always
valuable.

Pickering, an affable career diplomat called out of a brief retirement, had been an ambassador to six countries as well as to the
United Nations. As undersecretary for political affairs, the number
three job at State, he offered experience in almost every part of the
world, and sported an air of confidence. More than any other diplomat I have ever met, Pickering has a talent for talking to the press
and public in what seems to be a frank and forthcoming manner,
without revealing any new information. An interview with him is the
diplomatic equivalent of Chinese food: An hour later, you're hungry
again. Early in his tenure with Albright, he made one uncharacteris-
tic blunder—he instructed a public affairs officer to tell me that
American diplomats would soon return to Khartoum, Sudan,
whence they had withdrawn the year before, in an effort to put this
decision into effect before it had been cleared by the White House.
Alerted by my brief news article, the White House promptly nixed
the move and ordered Pickering to accept responsibility for the
snafu, which he graciously did. Aside from that misstep, which was a
symptom of deep fissures within the administration over Sudan,
Pickering contributed to the aura of competence that surrounded
Albright's first year.

So did Eizenstat, who as undersecretary for economic affairs sup-
plemented Pickering's diplomatic background with extensive political and economic experience. He had been domestic policy adviser
in Jimmy Carter's White House in the 1970s and an undersecretary
of commerce before taking his State Department assignment. A colorless personality but a creative negotiator, he took on difficult assignments in which economics was a major component, such as
managing the global warming and climate change negotiations in

Japan and finding a compromise with the European Union over American efforts to keep foreign corporations from investing in Iran and Cuba.

Another key figure was James P. Rubin, Albright's spokesman and confidant. Rubin was an arms-control specialist who had worked for Senator Joseph Biden of Delaware before becoming Albright's spokesman at the United Nations. Many of us in the State Department press corps were dubious about Albright's decision to select Rubin as assistant secretary of state for public affairs and chief spokesman; we thought he was too thin-skinned and too much of a New York smart aleck to handle the job. Rubin exhibited a flair for stunts, such as bungee jumping off the Zambezi River Bridge below Victoria Falls or standing on his head in the aisle of the secretary's plane; he would never do, many thought, as the public voice of foreign policy for the administration. But despite a few gaffes—at one point Rubin was forced to write an apology to Israeli president Ezer Weizman when Rubin's background account of Weizman's meeting with Albright was intercepted by the Israeli press—Rubin turned out to be a deft and forceful spokesman for the administration and a skillful defender of Albright.

As in any large organization, the State Department's official ranking of titles did not necessarily reflect the true lineup of power. The real hierarchy was exhibited in a set of matrushka dolls that Talbott had made in Russia. These are the uniquely Russian dolls that come in sets of five or six, packed one inside the next. Older matrushka dolls in traditional Russian styles are true works of art, but after the Cold War, as visitors poured into Moscow carrying hard currency, enterprising Russians began creating new ones with Western political or social themes. (The Russians even made matrushka doll sets about the White House sex scandal; the big doll on the outside was President Clinton, but the next one was Monica Lewinsky.) Talbott brought back a set of dolls representing the State Department power lineup: Albright, of course, was the biggest doll, on the outside. Next came her chief of staff, Elaine Shocas, a wisecracking former federal prosecutor. Then came dolls representing Talbott, Pickering, and Eizenstat, presumably in descending order of clout. Next was Timothy E. Wirth, a holdover from the first term as undersecretary for global affairs, who was soon to resign, followed by Dennis B. Ross, the indefatigable Middle East negotiator. The last and smallest doll depicted Rubin.

Through most of Albright's first year, with the country's principal international relationships on an even keel, this team generally had demonstrated vigor and creativity in the management of foreign policy; except for some briefly visible differences between Albright and Secretary of Defense William Cohen over Bosnia, there was little sign of the animosity among the top people that had plagued Clinton's first term. Talbott and the others had few blots on their copybooks.

But the larger reason Albright was able to skate through the first year without taking any serious criticism from Congress or the press was that most of the really hard foreign policy decisions the administration had to make had already been made in Clinton's first term, when Albright—who was a key member of the foreign policy team but based at the United Nations and not in Washington—did not take much political heat for them. And most of the bitter lessons the Clinton administration had to learn about the American role in the world had already been learned. Albright of course was an important part of the policymaking team in that first term and had much to answer for in the Somalia debacle of 1993. But as ambassador to the United Nations, she was less vulnerable than Christopher, Anthony Lake, Les Aspin, CIA director James Woolsey, or Clinton himself when things went wrong. They, much more than she, were perceived as responsible for the administration's decisions in international affairs.

Christopher in particular had suffered criticism and even ridicule for his cautious, lawyerly style. But his problem was not a lack of diplomatic skill; it was that he was a lawyer with an indecisive, erratic client. By the time Albright took over, Clinton was considerably more surefooted, and the government's entire apparatus of international affairs, including the CIA, the National Security Council, and the Defense Department as well as State, was operating much more smoothly. With the team functioning competently and the world mostly at peace, there was little reason for criticism of Albright. But then, she had not been seriously tested.

Just as the United States and Great Britain were preparing for military strikes against Iraq early in 1998 because of Iraq's defiance of United Nations weapons inspectors, Clinton suffered a potentially crippling political blow with the emergence of allegations that he had had a sexual affair with Lewinsky, a young White House intern, and urged her to lie about it to a grand jury. Many Washington analyst believed that this development could undermine Clinton's credibility if he did indeed order a military attack against Iraq; such an attack would be a tough sell at home because it might appear to be an attempt to divert attention from the scandal, some analysts and members of Congress said.

Jim Hoagland, the veteran foreign affairs columnist for the *Washington Post,* saw it differently. He saw the scandal as an opportunity for Albright:

> This in fact can be Madeleine's hour. A combination of circumstance and her own outgoing, highly visible personality now make Secretary of State Madeleine Albright the key figure in Bill Clinton's cabinet. She has a golden opportunity to reach for and attain a goal that has eluded her in her first year in office: putting her personal stamp on U.S. foreign policy.[1]

The reason that goal had eluded her was that until the confrontation with Iraq in February 1998, after she had been in office more than a year, there had been few if any truly neuralgic foreign policy decisions that she had had to put her name on, and she had offered no groundbreaking initiatives of her own. There was no equivalent to the Somalia disaster, or Christopher's unhappy trip to Europe concerning Bosnia, or the dithering and squabbling with allies while untold thousands died in Rwanda. Albright built a powerful team, but once assembled, the members had the luxury of thinking things through and setting their policies in place without much crisis or public pressure.

This is not to say that there was no criticism of the administration's policies. Enlargement of the Atlantic alliance, for example, stirred opposition from an impressive array of political and academic leaders who thought it unnecessary or counterproductive. The administration's initial response to the financial crisis that swept across Asia in the second half of 1997 provoked some unhappiness on Capitol Hill, where it was perceived as a "bailout" of reckless bankers at taxpayers' expense. But even if that criticism had some merit, as President Clinton acknowledged it did, the person taking the heat for it was not Albright but treasury secretary Robert Rubin, because the president believed that Rubin had the confidence of Wall Street and decided that Treasury, not State, should do the administration's talking.

There was little sustained criticism of Albright herself; on the contrary, she emerged from her first year a popular and widely respected figure. Nobody blamed Albright, at least in public, for the biggest foreign policy setback of her first year, the administration's inability to win "fast track" trade negotiating authority from Congress. That was a political setback for the president, but no U.S. troops died because of it and no fundamental relationship with any foreign country or group of countries was threatened by it.

One side effect of this generally benign environment in which Albright operated was that it contributed to dinner-party chitchat to the effect that she was not a strategic thinker, not a profound conceptualizer—not, in other words, Henry Kissinger.

John F. Kennedy Jr. asked her about this in an interview for his magazine, *George*.

"You've often been criticized for lacking a global vision," he said. "Is that fair, and is a grand vision suitable for today's world?"

"Obviously, I don't like it when people say that because I don't think it's true," she replied. "I do think that a global vision is very different than it would have been during the Cold War. It was much easier then to make stark statements about the world, the good versus the bad, arcs of crisis and various things."[2]

Albright inherited both the overall outlines of the Clinton administration's approach to world affairs—enlarging the circle of democratic societies, rehabilitating failed states, and promoting free markets and unfettered flows of capital—and policies toward specific countries, including China, Russia, and Iran. In both arenas, the administration had survived trials by fire in the first term.

The president had sent American troops to force the departure of Haiti's military rulers and restore the elected president, Jean-Bertrand Aristide, to power. In Bosnia, after Clinton and Christopher were pilloried in Congress and the press for dithering, the president had backed up the Dayton peace agreement by sending U.S. troops to police it—a deployment that began as a one-year effort but evolved into an open-ended commitment. Clinton had allowed a visit to the United States by Gerry Adams, the political voice of the Irish Republican Army—a decision that angered Britain but energized a political process that led to a peace agreement in Northern Ireland in 1998.

Responding to the entreaties of the aerospace industry, Clinton had modified a long-standing ban on the export of sophisticated armaments to South America, allowing American aircraft makers to compete for military sales in Chile and other countries. Over the objections of European allies, Clinton signed measures aimed at blocking foreign companies from investing in Iran and Cuba.

In addition, the president had committed himself to the expansion of NATO, pressing the alliance eastward toward an unhappy Russia even as he sought to establish a "partnership" with Russian president Boris Yeltsin that would withstand the vicissitudes of politics and economics in postcommunist Moscow.

Clinton's administration has often been charged with lacking a coherent strategic vision. This is certainly not true in regard to Russia. Richard Holbrooke's assessment was accurate, even if his syntax was garbled, in this summary:

> From the second month he was president, Bill Clinton focused on Boris Yeltsin, and sustained a support for democracy and reform in Russia through the last four and a half, five years, despite Chechnya, despite the massive corruption in Russia, despite the attempted coup against Yeltsin, despite Yeltsin's own collapse in his health occasionally, and all sorts of other problems, because this administration believed that engaging Russia and bringing it into Europe was essential.[3]

It was not easy for Clinton to maintain this commitment while Russian troops were pulverizing the breakaway Chechnya region of the Caucasus or interfering in the conflict in Georgia—and eventually, in fact, it would fall to Albright to engineer a substantial shift in relations with Moscow after the Russian economic collapse in the summer of 1998. When she took office, however, the "Yeltsin first" commitment devised by Clinton and Talbott was firmly in place.

Perhaps the most controversial foreign policy decision of Clinton's first term was the abandonment of the linkage between trade and human rights in China. As a candidate for the presidency, Clinton had sharply criticized George Bush for his pursuit of good relations with Chinese rulers who had blood on their hands after the Tiananmen Square massacre of 1989; as president, he sought to soften China's repressive domestic policies by linking human rights issues to trade concessions. But that approach failed for many rea-

sons, including the opposition of the American business community, which did not want restrictions on trade with China, and
Clinton abandoned it, to much criticism, in May 1994. In its place,
he installed a commitment to expanded economic, military, and
diplomatic engagement with China in the hope, if not the conviction, that China would naturally evolve into a more modern and responsible member of the world community.

Each of those decisions was the subject of intense debate and criticism; none was made easily, and none was without potential negative consequences. But for better or worse, the decisions had all
been made and the policies put in place by the time Albright became secretary of state. In Clinton's first term, of course, she was
deeply involved in most of these issues. As the voice of America at
the United Nations, as a member of the cabinet, and as a member of
the "principals committee," the highest-ranking members of the
president's foreign policy and national security team, she was there
when the decision papers were drafted for the president. But after
the Somalia debacle, she mostly kept her fingerprints off the outcomes while Christopher and Lake took the heat. As a result, she
was able to begin her tenure as secretary of state with a virtual clean
slate. The relatively benign state of world affairs enabled her to
spend much of her first half year in office focused on relations with
Congress.

Albright did have one sensitive decision to make that was closely
watched: whether to participate in the return of Hong Kong to
Chinese control after a century of British rule. She chose to go, and
to speak out while there in support of Hong Kong's promised special status within China; but she boycotted a reception for the territory's new legislature, which was installed by Beijing over local opposition. This compromise prompted some grumbling on both sides
of the China debate in Washington, but essentially it was a tactical
decision, not a strategic one. The strategic decision to "decouple"
the human rights issue from the trade issue and to press ahead with
relations with China despite Beijing's odious domestic policies had
been made during Christopher's tenure.

This relative lack of controversy, together with her personal popularity, combined to enable Albright—like the president she served—
to plow through 1997 in very good shape. Of course there were arguments, for example over the administration's decision to certify

Mexico as fully cooperative with American efforts to combat narcotics trafficking; it seemed that everyone in Washington knew that this certification was a political gesture to President Ernesto Zedillo, not a factual assessment. And there was some criticism of her reluctance to go to the Middle East—from many of the same pundits who had criticized Christopher for going there too often—but there was nothing remotely resembling a crisis, and no American blood was being shed in overseas adventures. The gloomy predictions from critics of the U.S. troop deployment to Bosnia proved utterly unfounded. Not only did troops from the United States, other NATO countries, and Russia survive their peacekeeping mission in Bosnia virtually unscathed but they actually made progress in carrying out the Dayton peace agreement. By the time Clinton dropped any deadline for a U.S. withdrawal and accepted an open-ended commitment, the move aroused little controversy because it was clearly the right thing to do.

In the late spring of 1998, this period of relative tranquillity came to an abrupt end. Albright and her senior colleagues were stretched very thin as they scrambled to confront crises, major and minor, that sprang up suddenly in every region of the globe. So much was happening at once that the diplomatic press corps barely noticed what in quieter times would have been an important story, the outbreak of war between Ethiopia and Eritrea. This bewildering and seemingly inexplicable conflict matched two countries that the administration had courted and that were indispensable to Washington's efforts to stabilize the Horn of Africa and neutralize Sudan. Albright sent Susan Rice, her assistant secretary for African affairs, out to the region to mediate, and when Rice came back empty handed the president recalled Anthony Lake, now a Georgetown professor, to take on this assignment. The fighting went on for months, on a scale that Eritrea's president, Isaias Afwerki, said rivaled that of the World War I trenches. This was a serious setback for the administration's aspirations for a better Africa, but it coincided with other fastbreaking events that the media found even more compelling.

There was no pattern to the developments of that late spring. Some involved issues in which Albright had already taken a direct hand; others came out of the blue. What they demonstrated in the aggregate was that the world is and probably will remain unruly and surprising, no matter what any American president or secretary of state does. Albright and her senior colleagues worked themselves to exhaustion, but new fires kept breaking out. Far from achieving stability in the post–Cold War era, the world was "a viper's nest of terrors," as Albright put it.

The outcomes of these upheavals mattered to the United States on an individual basis, but collectively they posed another kind of test for Albright and her colleagues. On Capitol Hill, Republican critics often said that the administration lacked the depth and commitment to deal with more than one crisis at a time. If the administration was going to prove them wrong, this was the time. The problem Albright and her colleagues faced as they grappled with the events of that spring was more than just one of resources and organization. As had been true throughout Clinton's presidency, the administration gave the impression of lacking any theoretical basis or coherent policy framework that would enable its diplomatic practitioners to calibrate their responses or pick their areas of concern. The State Department felt that it had to fight every fire and take on every villain. In truth, the problem was more complicated than that; there was indeed a comprehensive policy framework in place, but it provided insufficient guidance on how to respond to specific events or establish a hierarchy of interests when two or more fires broke out at the same time.

Consider what was happening more or less simultaneously, the issues listed here in no particular order.

The administration's effort to resolve the quarter-century-long impasse over the division of Cyprus and thus stabilize the volatile southeastern quarter of Europe ran aground on the rocks of Turkish intransigence. The Turks were furious at the refusal of the European Union to list their country as a candidate for future membership—a decision over which Washington had no control and little influence—and responded by hardening their position on Cyprus. With the Greek Cypriot government planning to take delivery of a battery of Russian-made ground-to-air missiles by late summer and the Turks threatening to prevent that deployment by force if necessary, Albright and the U.S. special envoy for Cyprus, Richard Holbrooke, faced a deteriorating situation that could lead to armed conflict between two NATO members, Greece and Turkey, and explode the rationale for further expansion of the Atlantic alliance. Senior aides to Albright acknowledged that her reliance in this matter on Holbrooke, who had been her chief rival for the job of secretary and who was a skillful self-promoter, was a measure of how much she was overcommitted elsewhere.

The story of Cyprus is too long and painful to retell here, but the fact was that the Clinton administration's strategy of using Cyprus's application for admission to the European Union as a lever on the Turks, who kept more than 30,000 troops in the northern part of the island, backfired—as Holbrooke admitted—and made the impasse more volatile and dangerous than it had been before the Clinton administration waded into it. As the summer of 1998 approached, Turkey was threatening military reprisal if Cyprus took delivery of a Russian S-300 ground-to-air missile defense system, and the administration appeared to have no credible plan for heading off the conflict between two NATO allies that would ensue.

At the same time, another conflict that could destabilize much of Europe loomed in Kosovo, a province of Yugoslavia where the population, mostly ethnic Albanians, had grown increasingly restive under the rule of the Serbian regime in Belgrade. The Serbian leader, Slobodan Milosevic, was proving just as truculent in Kosovo as he had been during the war in Bosnia, and he was just as resistant to threats and blandishments from the United States or the United Nations. When shooting broke out between Serb police and Kosovar separatist guerrillas, Albright again called in Holbrooke, who joined another tough talker, Robert S. Gelbard, the career diplomat assigned by Albright to implement the Bosnia peace agreement, in an effort to prevent the fourth Balkan war of the 1990s.

It was eerie to be reading *To End a War,* Holbrooke's account of his Bosnia diplomacy, at the same time he was trying to head off a recurrence of violence in another part of the former Yugoslavia. Milosevic, the same Serbian leader who had fomented wars in Slovenia, Croatia, and Bosnia, was behind the trouble in Kosovo, and in the crucible of Bosnia, the Clinton administration had learned that Milosevic responds only to force. Bosnia, however, was an independent country and a member of the United Nations when the war there broke out; Kosovo was a province of Yugoslavia, and thus the conflict there was legally an internal Yugoslav affair, even if it did threaten to draw in several neighboring countries. France and other allies were reluctant to use military force in Kosovo without

United Nations authorization, but a request for such authorization would probably provoke a Russian veto, calling into question the value of all that Clinton had done to establish a partnership with Boris Yeltsin—and of everything that Albright had done to bolster support for the United Nations. For Albright, the risk in this situation was that she laid down a very tough rhetorical marker on Kosovo, saying that a repetition of Bosnia would not be accepted, but she appeared to lack the means to back it up.

The spectacle of the "ethnic cleansing" in Bosnia replaying itself in another part of the former Yugoslavia refocused international attention on the issue of war crimes. But at this very moment, the administration's effort to construct a permanent international system for investigating and prosecuting war crimes blew up in a diplomatic fiasco that left even close U.S. allies angry and frustrated. After months of intense negotiations over a treaty that would establish a permanent, independent war crimes court to deal with the perpetrators of the Bosnias, Rwandas, and Cambodias to come, the United States declined to sign the final document because other countries refused to give an absolute guarantee that no Americans would ever be subject to the court's jurisdiction. This outcome left Albright and her team open to criticism from supporters of the court, who said that the U.S. position was arrogant and counterproductive, and from opponents of the court, who said that the United States should not have supported it in the first place.

Meanwhile, Albright made what appeared to be a serious tactical error in the long-running Middle East peace negotiations. Faced with Benjamin Netanyahu's refusal to give up control of as much of the occupied West Bank as Albright thought would be the minimum necessary to satisfy the Palestinians, she issued what everyone in Washington took to be an ultimatum, although she insisted that it was not.

After yet another round of fruitless conversations with Netanyahu and Yasser Arafat, she announced that she had invited both to Washington on Monday, May 11, to meet with President Clinton and begin the so-called final status negotiations, which were to determine the most sensitive and inflammatory issues of all: the final eastern borders of Israel, the scope of Palestinian self-government, the fate of Palestinian refugees, and the future of Jerusalem, a city sacred to Muslims as well as to Jews and Christians. Since Netanyahu had proposed accelerating these "final status" talks, which were scheduled to conclude by May 4, 1999, Albright portrayed herself and Clinton as trying to give the Israeli leader what he wanted. But she made the invitation conditional upon the acceptance by both sides of the West Bank territorial terms offered by the Americans. Since Arafat had accepted these terms and Netanyahu had rejected them, her ploy was understood to be an ultimatum.

With the 1998 congressional elections looming and Vice President Al Gore already seeking Jewish support as he prepared to run for president in 2000, this was a politically risky move, and it didn't work, or at least it didn't work as quickly Albright had calculated.

Netanyahu, who is nothing if not a shrewd political bargainer, rejected the summons to Washington. Congress, where support for Israel is entrenched, backed him up. Leaders of Jewish groups blasted Albright in a conference telephone call, saying that it was inappropriate for the United States to issue ultimatums to an ally or to make security decisions that only Israel could make for itself. Worst of all, the failure of this maneuver appeared to leave Albright with nothing left to offer in her attempts to break the Israeli-Palestinian impasse. She and her senior aides had said repeatedly that if the impasse continued, the administration would have to "reevaluate" or "reassess" its role, suggesting that it would walk away, but that threat was unrealistic because it would expose the United States throughout the Arab world as a faithless friend and diplomatic paper tiger.

Thrown on the defensive by the criticism, Albright called a news conference to defend herself and the administration's policy. This was a curious event because of the site, the ballroom of the National Press Club in downtown Washington. Normally when a person of Albright's prominence speaks in that room, it is at a breakfast or luncheon event attended by journalists and a wide variety of people from other professions. For Albright's news conference, there was nobody in the room but the Washington diplomatic press corps, except for a group of young journalists from countries such as Angola and Ukraine who were in Washington on a tour sponsored by the United States Information Agency and who had come to see the spectacle.

Albright's opening remarks at that event came across as one of the most forthright challenges to Israel offered by any senior-level

American official since James Baker, secretary of state in the Bush administration, confronted the Jewish state over the issue of settlements in the West Bank. Albright said that the proposals laid down by the Americans were "balanced, flexible, practical, and reasonable," that the Palestinians had accepted them and had met Israel more than halfway, and that Israel was on the brink of throwing away the Arab goodwill and the prospect of regional cooperation that had been in the air just two years before—that is, before Netanyahu was elected and soured the atmosphere by turning away from the Oslo peace process.

The focus of press coverage and congressional response to her remarks, however, was not on substantive issues but on Albright's negotiating tactics, which she felt obliged to defend at some length.

"We are not giving any ultimatums," she said. "We are not threatening any country's security. We are not trying to make any party suffer at the expense of another. All we are trying to do is find the path to peace, as the parties have repeatedly asked us to do." She argued that the U.S. proposal was "not a take-it-or-leave-it deal." But then she added, "We're not going to water down our ideas."[4]

The outcome, at least in the public perception, was to leave Albright and the administration in a worse position than before. Netanyahu rejected the U.S. position, Congress and many prominent American Jews backed him up, and Albright—having reiterated that she would not "water down" the U.S. proposal—appeared to have left herself with no fallback position. This assessment underestimated Albright, who by changing her tactics and lowering her sights was able to prevent an irreparable breach between the two sides, but at the time this episode contributed to her diminished luster.

In that same hectic month, May 1998, President Suharto's government in Indonesia was in its death throes. Here was a country of some 200 million people spread out across a vast archipelago in Southeast Asia, rapidly modernizing and a major exporter of oil and natural gas, which with President Clinton's encouragement had become a focus of U.S. business investment. But it was also thoroughly corrupt; its wealth was controlled by Suharto, his family, and their business cronies, to the detriment of the mass of the population. When Indonesia's currency collapsed in the Asian financial crisis of 1997 and the International Monetary Fund (IMF) dictated the adoption of austerity measures that had their greatest impact on the country's ordinary citizens, the regime's fate was sealed after more than thirty years of virtual one-man rule by Suharto.

The unraveling of a vast and friendly country put Albright in an uncomfortable position. As America's chief foreign policy official, and as a person accustomed to speaking her mind, she would be expected to deliver the views of the Clinton administration on events in Indonesia. But because the roots of the crisis there were perceived in Washington as primarily economic—and linked to related economic problems in Thailand and Malaysia—the administration decided to let treasury secretary Robert Rubin take the lead on the U.S. side. Senior officials said that this decision reflected Rubin's credibility in global financial markets, his clout with the IMF, and his sensitivity to the impact any comments from Washington could have on an already spooked investment community.

As a result, the State Department, in the persons of Albright and Jamie Rubin, had little to say about the unraveling of Indonesia other than urging that country's armed forces to exercise restraint in confronting demonstrators and looters until after Suharto had agreed in principle to relinquish power. Once the aging ruler accepted the inevitable, offering a transition process that could have extended for months, Albright was free to encourage a rapid transition without fear that doing so would upset the financial markets. But even then she stopped short of calling for his immediate resignation.

She said that Suharto "has the opportunity for a historic act of statesmanship, one that will preserve his legacy as a man who not only led his country but who provided for its democratic transition. In this delicate and difficult time, we strongly urge the Indonesian authorities to use maximum restraint in response to the peaceful demonstrations."[5] She did not say what she thought his legacy was, but it hardly mattered because Suharto resigned less than twelve hours later—not because of what she had said, but because his position was no longer tenable.

The departure of Suharto was undoubtedly a major international event, but it had little direct impact on American security interests. If China had threatened to intervene on behalf of the ethnic Chinese in Indonesia, whose shops were being torched by Indonesian looters, or if the demonstrators had appeared to be Islamic religious activists supported by Iran, the stakes for

Washington would have been much higher. They were, in fact, much higher in another immense Asian country where events shocked the Clinton administration that month—India, which conducted five underground nuclear tests. A known nuclear power for more than twenty years, India had tested only one previous device, in 1974, and had refrained ever since from demonstrating its nuclear muscle.

Because India was not a party to the Nuclear Nonproliferation Treaty (NPT) and had not signed the Comprehensive Test Ban Treaty, its tests did not violate any international law. Nevertheless, this unexpected development was extremely bad news for the administration and for Albright in several ways.

By definition, it torpedoed the Albright-Talbott strategy of forging a new, broadly based post–Cold War relationship with India. Under a United States law that left President Clinton no room to maneuver, the Indian tests triggered the imposition of wide-ranging economic sanctions, including a requirement that the United States oppose all lending to India by institutions such as the World Bank, which undercut a parallel Commerce Department effort to expand trade and investment ties with India. The tests ruined the administration's ambitions for a rearrangement of the Asian security chessboard to defuse tensions between India and China. And they exposed the administration to accusations of a massive intelligence failure, because they caught Washington utterly by surprise—even though the Hindu nationalist government that rose to power in early 1998 had campaigned on a platform of declaring India's nuclear capability, and even though there had been extensive open-source coverage of these plans. It seemed to astonish everyone in Washington that a political party would actually carry out its campaign promises. Foreknowledge of the tests probably would not have affected the outcome because India was committed to them and Washington had little leverage, but it would have spared the administration considerable embarrassment. As discouraging as these developments were, however, worse was to follow.

As soon as the Indian tests were announced, the administration undertook an intensive and highly visible effort to dissuade Pakistan from matching them. The president telephoned Pakistani prime minister Nawaz Sharif on several occasions to urge him to resist pressure from Pakistan's aroused citizenry to match India's action.

Talbott, accompanied by Karl F. Inderfurth, the assistant secretary of state for South Asian affairs and a favorite of Albright's, and Bruce Riedel, the senior official on the National Security Council responsible for South Asian affairs, flew to Tampa, Florida, where they met up with General Anthony Zinni, the four-star marine commander of the U.S. Southern Command. The delegation boarded a military jet and flew more than seventeen hours, refueling in the air, to Islamabad, the Pakistani capital.

While they were meeting with Prime Minister Sharif and other senior Pakistanis, Clinton and Albright were appealing in public for Pakistan to show "restraint" by refraining from testing. In the private talks in Pakistan and in their public appeals, the Americans forwarded several arguments: By testing, Pakistan would fall into a trap set by India, forfeiting the moral high ground and deflecting international outrage away from New Delhi; Pakistan would draw the same economic sanctions as India, and was much less able to withstand them; and Pakistan would accelerate a dangerous arms race that it could not afford and could not win. A show of restraint, however, would restore Pakistan to the good graces of the U.S. Congress, which had cut off U.S. economic and military aid to Islamabad years earlier because of its nuclear weapons program. And Pakistan did not need to test anyway, because everyone, including the Indians, already knew that the country had nuclear capability.

All these arguments were legitimate, but none proved persuasive. One reason was that the United States had little leverage over Pakistan; most Pakistanis believed that the United States had used their country as a proxy army to contest the Soviet occupation of Afghanistan in the 1980s and then turned its back when this marriage of convenience ended. But the main reason to move forward with nuclear testing, as Pakistanis at every level explained over and over, was that their country was now a democracy, and the will of the people had to be respected. And the will of the people dictated that Pakistan do whatever was necessary to stand up to India. On May 28, 1998, despite a last-minute appeal from Clinton to Sharif, Pakistan announced it had detonated five weapons. Another test followed two days later.

Everyone outside Pakistan deplored this outcome, of course. It was hard to recall an international event that provoked so much predictable and ineffectual deploring. Albright, who was at a NATO meeting in Luxembourg at the time, joined the chorus, issuing a statement saying: "The United States deplores Pakistan's decision to test. Although Pakistan did not start this arms race, its decision to join it is a serious error."

The world now faced a situation of unparalleled danger: two nuclear-armed countries, locked in hostility for fifty years, facing each other down along a common border and racing to develop the missiles by which they could attack each other. There was no evidence that India and Pakistan had worked out the kind of tense modus vivendi, the network of communications and command-and-control structures, that had kept the United States and the Soviet Union from launching nuclear strikes, whether planned or inadvertent, during the Cold War. "The United States and the Soviet Union spent a lot of time getting this problem right, and we had a lot of hairy moments along the way," Talbott said.[6] Looking drawn and exhausted, he made no effort to play down the seriousness of the setback that the two sets of tests represented. "The back-to-back tests by India and Pakistan unquestionably represent a setback for the search for peace and security and stability in the South Asian subcontinent and indeed a setback for the global cause of nonproliferation and moving toward a world where fewer and fewer states are relying on nuclear weapons for their greatness or for their defense," he said.[7]

In those comments, Talbott hinted at the body blows inflicted on the Clinton administration's overall approach to world affairs by the two sets of nuclear tests. Because both countries were ruled by democratically elected governments, their tests undermined the administration's conviction that democracy is the cure for war—a conviction that had earlier formed the rationale for the expansion of NATO and that was now also being challenged in the eastern Mediterranean, where Turkey and Greece, democracies and members of NATO, were working themselves up into a new confrontation over Cyprus and other issues.

In addition, the South Asian tests provided powerful new ammunition to congressional Republicans and conservative defense analysts clamoring for development of a national missile defense system—including Jesse Helms, whom Albright had worked so hard to court and who declared in a statement issued after the second round of Indian tests that they "revealed the stark reality that the

Clinton administration's six-year cozying up to India has been a foolhardy and perilous substitute for common sense." Helms said that the Indian tests provided "compelling additional evidence pointing to the need for a national missile defense to protect the United States and the American people."[8]

The United States has never constructed a defense system against a missile attack—whether space-based, like the defenses proposed by Ronald Reagan and ridiculed at the time as "Star Wars," or land-based—because a 1972 treaty with the Soviet Union prohibited it. Clinton and Albright were defenders of that Antiballistic Missile Treaty, but critics now were in a position to argue that the imminent ability of developing countries in South Asia to fire nuclear warheads on long-range missiles, coupled with the fact that there was no longer a Soviet Union, made the ABM Treaty a dead letter.

The administration would in fact soon modify its position on missile defenses and propose modifications to the ABM Treaty; but in the immediate aftermath of the South Asian tests, Albright issued her "dangerous nonsense" challenge and argued that the tests showed the urgency of Senate ratification of the Comprehensive Test Ban Treaty.[9] She was fighting an uphill battle on that issue, because Helms and other critics of the Test Ban Treaty said that the Pakistani detonations had pointedly shown that it was possible to develop nuclear weapons without testing. Therefore, they said, there was no point in depriving the United States of testing, a tool that remained useful in guaranteeing the safety and readiness of the American nuclear arsenal. These arguments aided the treaty's foes in the Senate as they laid the political groundwork for its rejection in the fall of 1999.

And beyond these specific blows to its cherished policies, the administration collectively seemed to be thrown onto the defensive by the events in the Middle East and South Asia. Having had their bluff called by Netanyahu and their entreaties spurned by Sharif, Clinton and his foreign policy team appeared at a loss as to what to do next. These were not problems that could be minimized by spunky commencement speeches from the secretary of state. On the contrary, much of the administration's self-confidence in global affairs that followed the Dayton peace agreement in Bosnia evaporated, as brave talk about the mandate for American leadership gave way to expressions of frustration about Washington's inability to control events in an unruly world.

"We hope that as the American people and those who comment on American foreign policy examine this issue, they bear in mind the fact that the United States is not in a position to control every event that occurs in the world," Jamie Rubin said after the Pakistani tests. "There will be bad things that happen in this world that we have not been able to stop, regardless of what we do."[10]

Albright was successful in orchestrating an international response of criticism and rejection of the South Asian tests. In Geneva on June 4, the five permanent members of the U.N. Security Council "condemned" the tests—strong language in diplomacy—and pledged that India and Pakistan would never be admitted to the global network of nuclear nonproliferation agreements as nuclear weapons states. Under the terms of the Nuclear Nonproliferation Treaty, only five countries are permitted to have nuclear weapons: the United States, Russia, France, Great Britain, and China. All other signatories agreed to forswear nuclear weapons in exchange for controlled access to civilian nuclear technology and a commitment from the five nuclear states to work toward eventual nuclear disarmament.

The Chinese cooperated with Albright in crafting the communiqué that the five nuclear powers issued after their Geneva meeting. That made it a diplomatic success for her, because the administration wanted to highlight indicators of Chinese goodwill as President Clinton's state visit to China approached. But the declaration was seriously flawed as an effort to influence India, for two reasons.

First, India developed its nuclear program in large part because it felt threatened by China, a nuclear-armed communist state that had thrashed India in a border war in 1962 and that provided crucial assistance to the nuclear weapons program in Pakistan. India was not about to alter its security strategy in response to admonitions issued by any group that included the Chinese. Second, the Indians believed that the entire diplomatic exercise was hypocritical because the five nuclear powers, in India's view, had done little if anything to meet their commitment under the NPT to work toward global nuclear disarmament.

The Indians resented the fact that the United States made common cause with China, a politically oppressive state with a long history of nuclear proliferation, while orchestrating the global pummeling of India, a democracy with no history of proliferation that had refrained from testing for twenty-five years after a first detonation in 1974. Never having signed the NPT, India had not violated it and specifically rejected the notion that it was up to the five declared nuclear powers to decide whether or not to accept India as a legitimate member of their exclusive club.

"India is now a nuclear weapon state," Prime Minister Atal Bihari Vajpayee declared. "This is a reality that cannot be denied. It is not a conferment that we seek; nor is it a status for others to grant. It is an endowment to the nation by our scientists and engineers. It is India's due, the right of one-sixth of humankind."[11]

Furthermore, the Indians—always proud and prickly, even in the best of times—resented Albright's rhetorical thrusts at them. In fairness to Albright, the administration's quick move to impose economic sanctions on India because of the tests was not her doing; under the law, the sanctions were mandatory, and the decision to move quickly to levy them was Clinton's. But Albright laced her public commentary with sarcasm and caustic commentary about the Indians that was bound to reinforce their aversion to tutelage from Washington.

Specialists in Indian affairs, and the Indians themselves, said that a principal reason for the Indian tests was a collective feeling that India did not receive the respect from the rest of the world to which it was entitled as the second most populous country, a nuclear power, and a potential economic giant. Albright's remarks in response to the tests only compounded Indian resentment. At a news conference after the Geneva meeting, she said:

I think what has happened is that India has lost the respect of the international community. A nation that has the tradition of Gandhi, of nonviolence, and of Jawaharlal Nehru, who had great moral authority throughout major portions of the Cold War—that good name of India has been lost.

As far as making their people more secure, they have earned nothing, zero, zilch, by what they have done. They have only earned themselves the opprobrium of the international community across the board and have made their people less secure—not to speak of poorer—and not to speak also of having lost the respect of the international community.[12]

"My goodness," she said, pressing that theme in a CNN interview, "they had more moral authority than many countries in the world. They blasted away that respect. So nobody should think they gained by that."

According to Naresh Chandra, India's ambassador to the United States, the reference to the legacy of Nehru, which Albright repeated several times over the next few weeks, rubbed India exactly the wrong way. Nehru, the first prime minister of independent India, provoked the United States throughout the 1950s by calling for global nuclear disarmament even as the United States was building its nuclear arsenal to meet the Soviet challenge.

"I didn't know she admired Nehru so much," Chandra said sarcastically. "He was never listened to by the United States back when he was calling for a nuclear standstill. I'm so glad he's been discovered." He said that Gandhi and Nehru "would never forgive us if we did not provide for the security of our people."[13]

Albright also raised Indian suspicions because of her views on Kashmir, the mostly Muslim region of northern India that has been disputed by India and Pakistan ever since the two countries gained independence from Britain in 1947. Resolution of the Kashmir dispute would have been an especially sweet triumph for Albright because her father worked on the same issue as a representative of the United Nations a generation earlier, but the Indians have told the Clinton administration repeatedly that they regard the separatist insurgency in Kashmir as an internal affair because Kashmir is and will remain part of India, and New Delhi has therefore rejected all outside mediation offers. Albright remarked:

> Let me say on that issue, I think there is no question that Kashmir has really been a very serious, long-running problem. In fact, in stepping into this room [at the Palais des Nations in the United Nations compound in Geneva] this time, I remembered that the first time I was introduced to this building was actually when I was ten years old and came here with my father, who was the Czechoslovak representative to the original India-Pakistan commission to deal with Kashmir. He's dead and I'm old, and it's

still going on. I think that the flash-point aspect of the Kashmir issue is very serious.[14]

She was correct about the importance of the issue, of course; a border war provoked by Pakistan a year later brought alarming threats of wider retaliation from India in which the nuclear threat was clear, if unspoken. A few months after that skirmish, in October 1999, Sharif was overthrown in a military coup, an event that further heightened fears of a nuclear confrontation in the region and terminated the administration's hope of building a democratic, peaceful South Asia. Once again the harsh realities of a dangerous world overcame the Clinton administration's lofty visions.

Moreover, Albright's personal commitment to resolving the Kashmir issue only bolstered India's determination to resist such efforts by outsiders. When the Indians were forced to take military action to repulse the Pakistani troops and Pakistani-sponsored Islamic militants who had occupied heights along the line of demarcation in the spring of 1999, they resolved anew to deal with the Kashmir issue on their own terms.

The net result was that one of the most important policy initiatives of Clinton's second term, an effort to forge a new, cooperative relationship with an emerging India that offered immense opportunities for American investment, ran aground. This development was especially disappointing for Inderfurth, the assistant secretary for South Asian affairs, who had worked for Albright at the U.N. and had spent a year developing the approach to India that began with Albright's aborted trip to the region and was to climax in a visit by President Clinton. That visit finally took place, in the spring of 2000, because Inderfurth and some of his senior colleagues were unwilling to let that effort be wasted. By the time Clinton and Albright had put in place economic and diplomatic sanctions on India for testing, the secretary's colleagues were already looking for ways to salvage the relationship. Recognizing that India was not going to cave in and was too important to cut off entirely, senior members of the administration's foreign policy team quickly adopted a more conciliatory tone than Albright's. Sandy Berger said:

We have to keep in mind our long-term interest in the way India evolves. Listen to the president as he talked about the tests: He talked about the greatness of India and the potential of India and the tremendous benefits that could come from a closer relationship with India. . . . I don't want to lose sight and the president doesn't want to lose sight of the opportunity after the Cold War to develop a fitting relationship with the world's largest democracy.[15]

Strobe Talbott added:

We want to see India prosper and thrive and attain its aspirations for itself in the next century. One of the reasons for the intensity of President Clinton's feelings, of Secretary Albright's feelings, is because it was particularly disappointing, and I would say even dismaying, coming from a country which otherwise seemed to be moving in the right direction in so many ways. So in no sense is our policy intended to be directed against India, or anti-Indian.[16]

Throughout that summer, Talbott pursued an effort to persuade India and Pakistan to cut a deal in which both would commit themselves to refrain from further tests, sign the Comprehensive Test Ban Treaty, and undertake to settle their long-standing differences over Kashmir. These negotiations were so difficult and so volatile that Talbott decided not to say anything about them in public, but his Indian counterpart, a smooth, soft-spoken diplomat named Jaswant Singh, who later became foreign minister, had no such compunction. In late August, he published an article in *Foreign Affairs* restating India's commitment to the nuclear option.

"Nuclear weapons remain a key indicator of state power," Singh wrote. "Since this currency is operational in large parts of the globe, India was left with no choice but to update and validate the capability that had been demonstrated 24 years ago in the nuclear test of 1974." Not only did Singh defend India's nuclear policy, he attacked one of the Clinton administration's most cherished diplomatic achievements—the unconditional and indefinite extension, in 1995, of the Nuclear Nonproliferation Treaty. According to Singh, the effect of that agreement left India with

no option but to go in for overt nuclear weaponization. The Sino-Pakistani nuclear weapons collaboration—a flagrant violation of the NPT—made it obvious that the NPT regime had collapsed in India's neighborhood. Since it is now argued that the NPT is unamendable, the legitimization of nuclear weapons implicit in the unconditional and indefinite extension of the NPT is also irreversible. . . . This fatal setback to nuclear disarmament and to progress toward delegitimization of nuclear weapons was thoughtlessly hailed by most peace movements abroad as a great victory.[17]

The United States wanted India to sign the Comprehensive Test Ban Treaty, promise not to be the first to use nuclear weapons in South Asia, refrain from selling nuclear technology or fuel to other countries, and hold off on deploying actual warheads. If the Indians did all that, I asked Talbott, would it not strengthen their case to be admitted to the nuclear club as a responsible nuclear power? "No," he said, "but you're doing a good job of making their case for them." He said that the United States would never agree to amend the Nuclear Nonproliferation Treaty to accept India as a declared nuclear state because doing so would break faith with Japan, Germany, Brazil, South Africa, and other nations that had foregone the nuclear option, with the understanding that no more countries would develop such weapons. He said that he would respond to Jaswant Singh's arguments in his own *Foreign Affairs* article, which he did a few months later.

Talbott's rebuttal essay rejected Singh's arguments and insisted that India could not be allowed to blast its way into the fraternity of legal nuclear weapons countries.[18] Neither commentator was able to change the other's mind.

The flow of global bad news continued for months. War broke out anew in central Africa and Angola; this conflict, together with persisting hostilities between Eritrea and Ethiopia, undercut the validity of the administration's guiding premise that Africa was on the way up. North Korea made new noises about pulling out of its agreement with the administration and resuming its effort to develop nuclear weapons.

Inevitably, these events chipped away at Albright's image as a straight-talking woman of action, because some of the talk wasn't straight—for instance, her denials that she had issued an ultimatum to Netanyahu—and because promises of action went unfulfilled.

Direct criticism of Albright, previously voiced only by a limited cadre of Cold War defense hawks and political right-wingers, began to emerge among mainstream commentators. My colleague Fred Hiatt, of the *Washington Post's* editorial page, noted Albright's assertion that "we are not going to stand by and watch the Serbian authorities do in Kosovo what they can no longer get away with doing in Bosnia." When the Serbs began doing exactly that, driving thousands of ethnic Albanians out of Kosovo and torching their villages, Hiatt noted that the administration organized "Contact Group" meetings and devised some new sanctions on Belgrade but offered numerous reasons why it couldn't take more decisive action.[19]

Of course, there were plenty of valid arguments why the United States should not have intervened in Kosovo, especially unilaterally. French prime minister Leonel Jospin, visiting Washington in June 1998, deftly framed the dilemma facing the United States, France, and other members of NATO as they watched the Kosovo tragedy unfold: Because Kosovo was legally an internal Yugoslav matter, Jospin argued, "we don't want NATO to act without a United Nations mandate. But we cannot let the threat of a Russian veto [in the Security Council] be an excuse to do nothing."[20] No, as Hiatt and others indicated, the problem was not with the lack of intervention; the problem was that in Kosovo, as in the Middle East and elsewhere, the administration had laid down a rhetorical marker from which it then appeared to retreat. In reality, we all underestimated Albright. She did not retreat at all from her public commitment to thwart Milosevic's repression in Kosovo. Mostly behind the scenes, she labored for months to build an ironclad consensus within the NATO alliance to take military action if Milosevic persisted—a consensus that she held together, despite immense strain, to wage the air war against Yugoslavia the following spring. But the appearance of inaction on Kosovo and Iraq, along with the events in South Asia and the widespread perception that she had backed down from an ultimatum to Netanyahu, diminished the value of Albright's blunt talk. In her speeches she kept talking about the United States as being the world's "indispensable nation," but in that troubled summer her words rang increasingly hollow.

By late August, according to the State Department's own figures, nearly 300,000 Kosovars had been displaced from their homes in the ethnic violence Milosevic had ignited, and still no U.S. or NATO plan of action had been developed. In fairness to Albright and her team, there were no easy solutions in Kosovo. Unlike Bosnia, Kosovo was not an independent country; Milosevic had a legitimate argument that events there were an internal Yugoslav affair, not subject to intervention by NATO or anyone else. Nor could Kosovo be considered in isolation. Some NATO countries wanted a resolution of the U.N. Security Council as a prerequisite to military intervention, but the Clinton administration was not prepared to concede that any NATO decisions were subject to a U.N. veto—that would have been politically fatal in Congress. On the other hand, the administration did not wish to intervene in Kosovo without at least the tacit assent of Moscow. Russia was economically crippled and politically fragile, but Clinton was heading there for a meeting with Yeltsin in September, and the administration had no desire to inflame nationalist passions in Russia by going into Kosovo over Russian objections.

If there was one event, one moment, that stripped Albright of the virtual invulnerability to criticism she had thus far enjoyed, it occurred on the campus of Ohio State University on February 18, 1998. She, Berger, and Cohen were there to take part in a "town meeting" on the subject of Iraq.

Saddam Hussein was once again defying the inspectors sent by the United Nations to root out his nuclear, chemical, and biological weapons. This was the same issue that had disrupted Albright's important trip to India and Pakistan a few months earlier—the trip on which she had been snookered by Primakov into taking part in the infamous 2 A.M. meeting in Geneva.

By mid-February, the United States had assembled a powerful military force in the Persian Gulf region, ready to pound Iraq with bombs and cruise missiles and compel Saddam Hussein to cooperate with the inspectors. But there was a fatal flaw in the American position: There was no credible intellectual or strategic link between the objective Washington said it wanted to achieve, namely Iraqi compliance, and the tools available to obtain it, namely bombs and missiles. Had the United States unleashed its military power, Saddam Hussein in all likelihood would have survived to emerge triumphant from the rubble, trumpeting the inevitable civilian casualties and terminating the inspections altogether. This problem was well understood at the Pentagon, but at the time Albright gave no public sign that she grasped it.

The purpose of the Ohio State event, which was organized and televised by CNN, was to show that the administration's foreign policy team was united behind a coherent policy on Iraq and to win public support for that policy. The outcome was exactly the reverse.

A small but skillful group of hecklers opposed to the use of force against Iraq dominated the event, their outbursts magnified by television. The rest of the audience reserved its greatest applause for statements to the effect that Washington preferred a peaceful solution. The moderator, CNN's Judy Woodruff, lost control of the event. And Albright, who prides herself on her ability to communicate with students, lost her composure. This excerpt from the transcript of that event conveys the tone:

QUESTION: Yes, I have a question for Secretary Albright. Why bomb Iraq, when other countries have committed similar violations? Turkey, for example. [Applause.] Can I finish? For example, Turkey has bombed Kurdish citizens. Saudi Arabia has tortured political and religious dissidents. Why does the U.S. apply different standards of justice to these countries? [Cheers, applause.]

SECRETARY ALBRIGHT: Let me say that when there are problems such as you have described, we point them out and make very clear our opposition to them. But there is no one that has done to his people or to his neighbors what Saddam Hussein has done [hecklers shouting] or what he is thinking about doing.

QUESTION: What about Indonesia? Well, you've turned my microphone off.

SECRETARY ALBRIGHT: I think that the record will show that Saddam Hussein has produced weapons of mass destruction, which he's clearly not collecting for his own personal pleasure, but in order to use. [Hecklers shouting.] And therefore, he is qualitatively and quantitatively different from every brutal dictator that has appeared recently, and we are very concerned about him specifically and what his plans might be. Do you have a follow-up?

QUESTION: Thank you. My microphone is off. There we are. What do you have to say about dictators of countries like Indonesia, who we sell weapons to, yet they are slaughtering people in East Timor? [Cheering, applause from hecklers.] What do you have to say about Israel, who is slaughtering Palestinians, who impose martial law? What do you have to say about that? Those are our allies. Why do we sell weapons to these countries? Why do we support them? Why do we bomb Iraq when it commits similar problems? [Cheers, applause.]

SECRETARY ALBRIGHT: There are various examples of things that are not right in this world, and the United States is trying . . . [Hecklers shouting, booing.] I really am surprised that people feel that it is necessary to defend the rights of Saddam Hussein when what we ought to be thinking about is how to make sure that he does not use weapons of mass destruction. [Hecklers continuing to shout.]

MS. WOODRUFF: The people who are shouting—just a moment. [Shouting continues.]

QUESTION: [Inaudible] . . . Saddam Hussein. I am not defending him in the least. What I am saying is that there needs to be consistent application of U.S. foreign policy. [Applause, cheers.] We cannot support people who are committing the same violations because they are political allies. That is not acceptable. We cannot violate U.N. resolutions when it is convenient to us.

SECRETARY ALBRIGHT: We—

QUESTION: You're not answering my question, Madam Albright. [Applause, cheers.]

SECRETARY ALBRIGHT: I suggest, sir, that you study carefully what American foreign policy is, what we have said exactly about the cases that you have mentioned. Every one of them have been pointed out. Every one of them we have clearly stated our policy on. [Shouting begins again.] And if you would like, as a former professor, I would be delighted to spend fifty minutes with you describing exactly what we are doing on those subjects. [Applause.][21]

Ten months later, when President Clinton did order a heavy aerial bombardment of Iraq, all the questions thrown up by the hecklers remained unanswered—it was still unclear even to many experts on the subject how the Clinton administration proposed to change the situation in Iraq by hitting some factories, barracks, and communications towers with cruise missiles—but Albright and her colleagues made no further efforts to engage the public directly on this subject. When Ambassador Richard Butler, the Australian who headed the inspection team, reported that Iraq was again interfering with the work of his inspectors, Clinton—on the eve of an impeachment vote in the House—immediately ordered the air strikes, with no public debate. Only after they were concluded did Albright, Cohen, and Berger appear on television to explain them, in what were essentially one-way communications to the American public.

The missile strikes satisfied neither critics on the right, who clamored for more direct and vigorous action to get rid of Saddam Hussein, nor those on the left, who argued that the military action and relentless economic isolation of Iraq served only to impose suffering on innocent Iraqi people while leaving Saddam Hussein unscathed.

Both groups of critics were correct. The problem was that neither group offered a credible alternative. The standoff with Iraq can be seen as a classic illustration of the impotence of power. On the one hand, Saddam Hussein is a ruthless dictator who has started wars with two neighboring countries; he rules by terror and has used poison gas weapons against Iraqi citizens in his determination to crush the Kurdish minority. He is not amenable to the blandishments of diplomacy. But on the other hand, although the United States is militarily capable of driving Saddam Hussein from power, doing so would require an invasion and ground campaign by hundreds of thousands of American troops, and nobody wants to undertake such a mission—a fact that Berger pointed out after the December missile strikes. Joseph Biden, the senior Democrat on the Senate Foreign Relations Committee, said that he regularly challenged the Iraq hawks in the Senate by asking, "Who'll stand with me and commit American troops to go get Saddam?" No one stepped forward, Biden said.

What happened between February and December was that Clinton, backed by Albright, Cohen, and Berger, decided that the best course was to deprive Saddam Hussein of control of the agenda. They wanted to end the thrust-and-parry game in which he could force the Pentagon to deploy troops and ships and planes anytime he felt like it. If the only result of the U.N. inspectors' work was to give Saddam Hussein another opportunity to provoke a crisis by obstructing them, then the inspection regime was more trouble than it was worth. And if aggressive, confrontational inspectors accomplished nothing more than stoking sympathy for Saddam Hussein at the United Nations, those inspectors were part of the problem, not part of the solution. Albright understood that Saddam Hussein was his own worst enemy: Every time a country such as

Russia or France or Egypt tried to help him, he did something provocative or stupid that virtually forced the Security Council to unite against him, so why not let him continue to behave recklessly and keep the focus on him as the villain?

Bruce Riedel, the National Security Council's senior Middle East official, laid out the revised policy in unambiguous terms:

> After two years of repeated crises and broken Iraqi promises, it is clear that the inspectors cannot do their job the way it needs to be done. Inspectors without access, without required documents, without a cooperating partner, can only do so much. A Potemkin inspection process is worse than no inspection process. Inspectors confined to hotels in Baghdad may as well be in Baltimore. We will not be a party to a phony arms control regime.

This made sense. Riedel's argument was compelling. Iraq was not going to accept a serious inspection plan. When the U.N. Security Council finally reached agreement on a new inspection system, in January 2000, Iraq promptly rejected it, demanding that the sanctions be lifted first. That response validated the Clinton administration's assessment, but it did not overcome the administration's political mishandling of the original policy shift. Riedel delivered his lucid explanation of Washington's revised thinking in June 1999, a year after the administration had made the crucial change in Iraq policy without in any way preparing Congress and the public for it. By failing to level with the public at the time, Albright and her colleagues lit the fuse on the public relations disaster that would blow up in their faces later that summer.

~

Early in the morning of August 17, 1998, the State Department press corps gathered at Andrews Air Force Base outside Washington for the long flight to Dar es Salaam, Tanzania. Albright was traveling to Tanzania and Kenya to visit the U.S. embassies there, which had been shattered by terrorist bomb blasts ten days earlier, to show support for the embassy staffs, visit the wounded, and promise support to the host countries. The explosions killed 224 people, including 12 Americans.

This sad journey was Albright's third flight across the Atlantic in less than two weeks. She had traveled to Italy to attend the wedding of Jamie Rubin and Christiane Amanpour, the CNN reporter, but just hours before that event news of the bombings forced her to scramble back to Washington. A few days later, she flew to Germany to meet a plane carrying the American victims of the embassy attacks and accompany them back to Washington.

Albright appeared tense and grim as she delivered a brief departure statement at Andrews; the travel fatigue, the devastating loss of life in the bombings, and the disruption they caused in the State Department were only part of the reason. The global swamp seemed at the moment to be unusually full of alligators.

War was again raging in Congo and threatening to engulf much of central Africa; the Russian economy, viewed by the Clinton administration as the cornerstone of a democratic, post-Soviet Russia, was in a free fall. That morning's *New York Times* carried a report that North Korea appeared to be constructing a clandestine nuclear weapons plant, in contravention of an agreement with Washington that the administration had portrayed as one of its greatest diplomatic successes; and Albright had spent much of the weekend crafting a response to a devastating *Washington Post* story saying that she had duped the U.N. Security Council, and the public, by secretly putting pressure on Richard Butler not to stage challenge inspections that would force a showdown with Saddam Hussein. The clear implication of that story was that the political trauma of the Ohio State fiasco had led Clinton to waffle once again on an issue of principle, forcing Albright to back down from what had been an absolutist position. The reality was that the administration had changed its policy toward Iraq; having reached the conclusion that Saddam Hussein would never allow the weapons inspectors full access, Clinton and Albright fell back on a policy of isolation, hoping to keep Saddam Hussein bottled up until he was finally toppled from power. They never explained this shift publicly, however, and as far as anyone knew, the United States was still supporting a vigorous inspection program. The *Post*'s story appeared to expose the policy as a sham.

The newspaper followed that article with an editorial the next day accusing Albright of "deceitful diplomacy" and calling for a congressional investigation. On the morning the editorial was published,

Saturday, August 15, Albright sought through her public affairs office to place a rebuttal article in the *Post* on Sunday or at the latest Monday, the day she was flying to Africa. When the *Post* declined to accommodate her, she gave her rebuttal to the *New York Times,* which did print it that Monday morning.

In it, she did not dispute any of the facts reported in the *Washington Post* article, but she portrayed the administration's actions as tactical maneuvers in support of a consistent objective. (As one of her aides said privately, the *Washington Post* article was factually correct, but in this case "the facts and the truth are not the same thing.")

"Let's be clear," Albright wrote. "What Saddam Hussein really wants is to have sanctions lifted while retaining his residual weapons-of-mass-destruction capabilities. We will not allow him to achieve those objectives."[22]

If that exchange had occurred in isolation, her argument might have been persuasive. But after a six-month run of what were widely perceived to be hollow threats and proclamations of firmness that were not backed up by action, her saying so didn't necessarily make it so. A week later, Albright's rhetoric on Iraq was devalued further by the dramatic resignation of a U.N. Special Commission (UNSCOM) weapons inspector, W. Scott Ritter.

Ritter, a former U.S. Marine, had been one of the most persistent and creative leaders of the weapons inspections teams. One measure of his effectiveness was that Saddam Hussein went after him personally, accusing him of being a spy and demanding that he be removed from UNSCOM. On those occasions when, as the world now knew, Albright had secretly intervened to restrain UNSCOM because she did not want to ignite a confrontation with Saddam Hussein without sufficient support in the Security Council, it was Ritter whose team was pulled back.

In his letter of resignation, Ritter denounced the Security Council for what he called "the illusion of arms control." He said that the council's tolerance of Iraqi defiance "constitutes a surrender to the Iraqi leadership" and "makes a mockery of the mission the staff of the Special Commission has been charged with implementing."[23] He repeated these accusations in newspaper and television interviews.

Albright and her aides insisted that Ritter's account, although perhaps correct in narrative detail, omitted any of the complexities and subtleties of the diplomacy surrounding UNSCOM and the entire Iraq issue. "Ritter was a guy who saw only one leg of a very large elephant," one of them said. Albright herself told me that "Scott Ritter is a great American and he has been a great inspector, but he doesn't have the story."[24]

In this public relations battle, however, Ritter held the high ground. He appeared to everyone to be a courageous patriot who had taken risks to confront a bloodthirsty dictator. He came across as a straight-arrow former marine whose character and motives could not be impugned. The administration, on the other hand, was handicapped by its inexplicable refusal to explain what it was up to. Inside the State Department, Ritter was portrayed as either a simpleton with tunnel vision or an opportunist more interested in pointless confrontations with Saddam Hussein than in achieving credible objectives, but it would have been political poison to say so publicly. In fact, when Senator Biden addressed Ritter at a Foreign Relations Committee hearing as "sonny boy" and suggested that Ritter was trying to make policy when his assignment was to follow orders, callers to radio and television talk shows overwhelmingly sided with Ritter.

Administration officials offered a plausible argument that if Ritter and UNSCOM had been given a free hand, the result would have been counterproductive: Saddam Hussein would have blocked their planned challenge inspections and portrayed the inspectors as stooges of Washington, while Security Council support for the American position would continue to erode. Nevertheless, there was no disputing the fact that Saddam Hussein was defying UNSCOM and blocking inspections, and neither Albright nor anyone else in the administration was offering a credible response.

Regardless of the details or nuances of any specific situation, members of Congress, opinion columnists, editorial writers, and analysts in the think tanks were all by now keeping pretty much the same list of issues on which the administration's actions did not match Albright's rhetoric: threats to bomb Iraq, followed by a backdown, followed by the revelation of secret diplomacy that appeared to be at odds with stated policy; an ultimatum to Netanyahu with no follow-through; harsh words about Milosevic but no action on Kosovo; a commitment to extract a high price from India for its nuclear tests with little to show for it. Where was the beef?

Albright helped to devalue the credibility of her public statements when she told an incredulous Larry King on CNN that the nomination of Richard Holbrooke to be U.S. permanent representative at the United Nations, her old job, was her idea. Holbrooke, an outspoken and aggressive diplomat who had brokered the peace agreement in Bosnia, had been one of Albright's most serious rivals for the secretary of state job in Clinton's second term. Some commentators viewed Clinton's choice of Holbrooke for the U.N. assignment as a sign of diminished presidential confidence in Albright. The widespread view around Washington was that Albright and Holbrooke would inevitably clash, because the foreign policy arena was not big enough for two such outsize personalities. King asked her about this.

> KING: There have been reports in the press over the years about a rift between you and Richard Holbrooke. He will now be ambassador to the United Nations. What can you tell us about your relationship?
>
> ALBRIGHT: Well, I hate to say that anything that is in the press is wrong.
>
> KING: Impossible.
>
> ALBRIGHT: But Richard Holbrooke and I have been very good friends now since the Carter administration. And we work together very well. I'm very pleased that he's going to be part of our team. I am very proud of the team that I have at the State Department. I have been able to surround myself with very strong people. And I am glad to get another strong one on board.
>
> KING: Did the president ask you to sign off on his appointment?
>
> ALBRIGHT: It was my idea.
>
> KING: It was your idea?
>
> ALBRIGHT: Yes.[25]

Holbrooke is a showy, high-profile character who uses the press even more effectively than Albright. One member of Albright's inner circle said that the secretary overcame her initial reservations about him because she recognized his talents as an effective diplomat and needed all the help she could get in coping with multiple crises. Another said: "Of course Holbrooke was one idea she had for that job. How could he not be?" But these arguments were not persuasive, whether they were valid or not, because the wind in Washington had shifted.

After a first year in which she could practically do no wrong, Albright by late summer of 1998 was encountering the phenomenon of a media turnaround: Not only was it acceptable but it was almost becoming conventional wisdom to say that Albright talked a better game than she played. In her first year, even when there was criticism of the administration on a foreign policy issue, it generally was not directed at Albright personally. Now it was open season. Fueled by Congress, where members accused Albright of duplicity on Iraq and North Korea, conservative commentators, traditional big-power strategy analysts, and editorial writers began to snarl at the woman who had been the recipient of such widespread admiration just a few months earlier.

Here is a sampling:

"Madeleine Albright is the first Secretary of State in American history whose diplomatic specialty, if one can call it that, is lecturing other governments, using threatening language and tastelessly bragging of the power and virtue of her country."—former State Department adviser Charles Maechling Jr.[26]

"What you see is a Secretary of State with a highly visible role—and she has reveled in it. But as you look around the world, you have to ask, 'Where is she putting her mark?'"—former State Department counselor Robert Zoellick.[27]

"Clinton reached out to Holbrooke because he wanted a more decisive presence making foreign policy."—columnist Robert Novak.[28]

"Of course, concealing important truths is one of Albright's lifetime habits."—Martin Peretz, editor in chief of the *New Republic*.[29] This was a cheap shot that infuriated Albright and her aides. Peretz was writing about Iraq, but he was alluding here to the revelation of Albright's Jewish ancestry.

The very morning we assembled at Andrews for the flight to Africa, the *Economist,* a respected British weekly that had been a strong supporter of Albright, devoted a full page to the secretary's reversal of fortune, complete with an unflattering caricature:

When she became Secretary of State 18 months ago, things seemed splendid. She was the first woman in the job; she had an appealing personal story, as a childhood refugee from Hitler and Stalin; she exuded the charm and fluency so important in the age of television. She had more star power than any Secretary of State since Henry Kissinger, a fact especially noticeable because she succeeded plodding Warren Christopher. Yet these days almost nobody speaks well of her.[30]

Running down the list of reasons for this shift—the Israel ultimatum, the Ohio State debacle, the Holbrooke appointment—the *Economist* asked, "What to make of this humiliation? Some say it shows that charm and sound bites are no substitute for geopolitical grasp. This is unfair. Mrs. Albright, a former academic, grasps geopolitics as well as the next wonk; and she has deputies to worry about detail." No, according to the *Economist,* the problem lies in the nature of the job. If secretaries of state are vague and cautious, like Christopher, they forfeit the respect of Americans, who are generally indifferent to foreign policy. If they speak boldly, like Albright, they fall into a different sort of trap: "They may command admiring attention for a while. But they may fail to deliver on their bold words, in which case humiliation will follow."[31]

To say that Albright had been humiliated is going a bit too far. She remained personally popular and widely admired. But there was no doubt that a combination of events beyond her control in an unruly world, and her own rhetorical missteps, had diminished her stature. And it is a truism in Washington that sooner or later the press will turn on almost any successful, admired figure; this "prove our manhood" phenomenon almost requires us to go after those to whom we have given favorable coverage just to reestablish our own independence, even if the target has done nothing to deserve it. In different ways, this shift in reportage had targeted such figures as Henry Kissinger, Jimmy Carter, Oliver North, Hillary Rodham Clinton, Anthony Lake, and even General Norman Schwarzkopf, the field commander of Operation Desert Storm in 1991.

"We knew this would happen," said a member of Albright's inner circle who had been around Washington long enough to see this disenchantment overtake many others. "The only thing that surprised us was that it took so long. We have every confidence that it will be short lived."

That confidence was misplaced. In the five-day period from August 28 to September 1, 1998, the *Wall Street Journal,* the

Washington Post, and the *New York Times* all published front-page stories saying that Albright, after a strong first year, was struggling to
shore up her credibility, her clout within the administration, and
her team's track record. This theme became the journalistic flavor
of the month.

These articles pained members of Albright's inner circle, who
thought we were piling on in a display of pack journalism. They had
been able to shrug off a similar story in the *Baltimore Sun* a few weeks
earlier because the *Sun* does not have the same prominent reader-
ship in Washington and New York as the other newspapers. The
rapid-fire sequence in the *Journal, Post,* and *Times,* on the other
hand, commanded their attention.

"She doesn't deserve to be sniped at and picked off by a press
corps interested in protecting the world by screwing its leaders,"
one of them complained.

Members of Albright's team said that it was unfair and naive to
treat her sound bites and one-liners as if they were ironclad policy
statements that were meant to be precisely carried out. There was a
difference, they said, between Albright's efforts to talk to the
American people in what one called "kitchen table English" and the
implementation of complicated policies in difficult negotiating environments. And as for the criticism emanating from Congress, senior insiders said, it was to be expected as congressional elections
approached. In branding the criticism as political, they were taking
their cues from the boss.

After three decades in Washington, Albright told me, she recognized that the approbation of journalists ebbs and flows and that
criticism comes with responsibility. What will matter in the end, she
said, is not what the newspapers are reporting today but what the
outcomes of her efforts will be and how history views the Clinton administration.

"There have been times when I was Queen of the May and times
when I was the Ugly Duckling," she said, "but my whole sense of how
I do my job and my resolve to defend U.S. national interests is not
based on whether I'm Queen of the May or the Ugly Duckling. I get
up every morning and look at what needs to be done and feel very
proud to represent the United States."

She attributed the decline in her stature among members of
Congress to the facts that "we're in heavy-duty political season" as

the 1998 congressional elections approached and that the clout of her boss, President Clinton, had dwindled in the wake of the White House sex scandal:

> I'm old enough to know that the time between August and November of even-numbered years is not an easy time in Washington for anybody who has any public visibility whatsoever. But let me just say this: No matter what, Queen of the May, Ugly Duckling, August, April, May, June, there will never be any change in my resolve, or U.S. resolve, to carry out what we have to do to put America at the head of the international system and to protect U.S. national interests.[32]

The following week, while she was in Moscow participating in a meeting between Clinton and Boris Yeltsin, she gave an interview to Wolf Blitzer of CNN, who asked her about the spate of critical stories. "Why do you sense that you are getting this kind of criticism at this time?" Blitzer asked. She responded:

> Well, I've lived in Washington about thirty years, and I'm smart enough to know that when you fly high, there are times that people criticize you. If I weren't being criticized, I don't think I would be doing my job. I figure that I'm doing what I have to do, and that's life. I love what I do; I'm going to continue to love what I do. I expect the critics along with the praise.[33]

Outside the department, it was easy to see that a gap had opened between what Albright said she intended to accomplish and what she was actually able to accomplish; this was perhaps inevitable, given that the world was unruly and unpredictable and that her instincts for action were hemmed in by the political caution of the White House. "She made the classic mistake of a politician: She overpromised," a former assistant secretary said.

> Look at the title of Holbrooke's book, *To End a War.* That's all he promised to do, end the war, and he did it. He didn't promise to bring permanent peace or make America the indispensable nation. She promised to do that, to kick butt, to be involved in every dispute, but she's not the one who has to run for office. Her problem is, we're judging her by the standards she set.

Inside the department, naturally, the view was different. Albright's senior aides, such as Tom Pickering and Counselor Wendy Sherman, as well as Rubin, said that she and they understood perfectly well that the markers laid down in sound bites could not always be achieved in clear-cut terms over a short time. The purpose of uttering them was, in Sherman's words, to "plant the flag"—that is, to tell the American people and the world where the United States stood and where it wanted to go, not to make a commitment to reach a particular objective by a particular date. It was true that Netanyahu refused to come to Washington when summoned, they said, but in the months since that episode Israel had shifted its policy considerably, and an agreement with the Palestinians was more likely than before. It was true that Albright had reined in the UNSCOM inspectors, but only because letting them confront a defiant Saddam Hussein would have played into his hands—he would have portrayed them as cowboys, as provocateurs taking orders from Washington—whereas holding them back would have kept the onus of noncompliance on Iraq, where it belonged. Over time, they said, the United States would be seen as principled, unswerving, and effective in keeping Saddam Hussein bottled up. And it was true that NATO had been unable to decide whether or how to stop the bloodshed in Kosovo, but the issue involved larger, more important questions that had to be settled first, such as whether NATO had to defer to the U.N. Security Council in deciding whether to intervene.

"We have never felt it was a national obligation to explain ourselves in a way that provides a road map to our adversaries," Pickering said. "In diplomacy we don't set finite time lines. What we are being pilloried for is the failure to bring to conclusion a number of works in progress. But diplomacy isn't instant coffee."[34]

In fairness to Albright and her team, it had to be recognized that the year 1998 had overwhelmed them, and the international diplomatic system, with unforeseen and perhaps unforeseeable events, such as the South Asian nuclear tests, the increasing truculence of North Korea, the outbreak of multiple wars in Africa, and the collapse of the Russian economy. Nobody could have managed a response to all these developments without encountering criticism; the damage to Albright's credibility inflicted by Scott Ritter did not make the task easier.

Of course, as this sea of troubles deepened, the efforts by Jamie Rubin and the rest of Albright's team to shore up her image continued. One afternoon in early January 1999, for example, I got a call from Rubin alerting me to an event that would take place that evening. Albright was going to the Chinese embassy to offer a toast at a dinner celebrating the twentieth anniversary of the restoration of diplomatic relations between Washington and Beijing. Rubin provided an advance copy of her remarks, in which she recalled having been on President Carter's staff when ties with the communist government were first established. At that time, she said, "On fundamental issues, such as economics and controlling the spread of nuclear weapons, our philosophies were completely different. And on human rights, we were so far apart, there was nothing to discuss."

By the end of the century, she continued, the relationship had matured to the point where the two countries could speak frankly to each other and acknowledge their disagreements openly, which she then did, in strong terms.

> I am here as a representative of the American people. I could not fairly represent them if I did not emphasize America's belief that organized and peaceful political expression is not a crime or a threat. It is a right that is universally recognized and fundamental to the freedom and dignity of every human being. Accordingly, we are profoundly distressed by the unjustified prison sentences recently imposed upon a number of Chinese who tried to exercise that right.

For a secretary of state to say such things at a Chinese embassy celebration was newsworthy, and I wrote a brief article for the next day's paper.[35] But I also felt uncomfortable, because I was clearly being used. If I had decided on my own that the event was likely to be important and decided independently to cover it, the story would have been, shall we say, more legitimate. But in any case, it was clear why Rubin had alerted me: He wanted to get out the message that Albright was not backing down from her promise to challenge China on the human rights issue, and the fact that the administration was determined to forge a closer relationship with China would not deter the secretary on this point.

I think that such efforts were ill advised; they provided ammunition to the growing number of critics arguing that Albright talked a good game but failed to deliver. When the winds of disapproval are blowing in Washington, they can't be turned back by public relations work. It takes time, success, and the selection of a new target by the pundits.

Meanwhile, however much heat Albright was taking over Iraq, Kosovo, China, and other trouble spots, the hard work of nuts-and-bolts diplomacy went on every day. As if she didn't have enough on her plate, the indefatigable secretary of state was preparing an important new policy initiative.

Chapter 5

WE STAND READY
FOR A DIALOGUE

I N JULY 1998, halfway through Albright's difficult second year in office, a group of Iranian athletes arrived in New York to take part in the Goodwill Games, a made-for-TV event sponsored by Ted Turner that was similar to the Olympics. Their arrival attracted little notice because by that time the American public was becoming used to the idea of cultural and athletic exchanges with Iran. But only a week earlier, the Iranians had announced cancellation of their participation in the Goodwill Games. They were unwilling to undergo the same undignified treatment that had confronted Iranian wrestlers in Chicago a few months earlier—fingerprinting and other security checks by U.S. immigration officials, required because Iran is on the State Department's list of nations that sponsor international terrorism. A seventy-five-year-old scholar of Persian poetry, arriving in the United States shortly before the games, got the same treatment.

Albright didn't want the Iranian athletes to cancel. She was trying to manage one of the most creative and challenging diplomatic initiatives of her tenure, a rapprochement with Iran. The United States has not had diplomatic relations with Iran since 1979; except at the United Nations, officials of the two countries had virtually no direct contact. Under such circumstances, conventional diplomatic techniques such as meetings with ambassadors and exchanges of visits were not available. To reach out to the Iranians, Albright was required to send indirect signals through unconventional channels such as cultural and sports exchanges; cancellation of the athletes' visit would have been a setback. To assure them a smooth entry into the United States, Albright went directly to Attorney General Janet Reno, the country's highest-ranking law enforcement official, and persuaded her to waive regulations that would require the athletes to be fingerprinted upon arrival. State Department officials had already labored for weeks to obtain a waiver of the regulations; when their inability to do so led to the cancellation announcement, Albright took up the issue personally and went over everyone's head.

On the day the athletes landed in New York, the big news about Iran had nothing to do with sports. Iran had successfully test-fired an intermediate-range ballistic missile known as the Shahab-3, which according to intelligence reports was a variant of a North Korean model that the Iranians were developing with Russian help. With a range of 800 miles, the missile put Iran in a position to threaten Israel, Saudi Arabia, and Turkey, three countries with close military and political ties to the United States.

And on that same day word came from Tehran of the execution by hanging of a member of the Bahai religious minority, accused of inducing a Muslim woman to convert to Bahai, a capital offense in Iran.

These events showed that Iran to a great extent remained what it had been since the Islamic revolution of 1979: an intolerant, theocratic state bent on acquiring the military power to influence, if not dominate, the entire Middle East. Anti-Americanism—both political and social—and hostility to Israel were the cornerstones of Iranian foreign policy. Throughout the 1980s and well into the 1990s, Iranian agents left a bloody trail of death across Europe as they murdered opponents of the regime.

But Albright understood that Iran was not some backwater like Burma that could be neutralized through isolation and then largely ignored. Iran is a strategically located nation of almost 70 million people, half of them born since the revolution, rich in oil and natural gas resources and proud of the exalted tradition of Persian culture, symbolized by masterpieces of poetry, painting, and architecture that span centuries.

Unlike Warren Christopher, Albright is not personally hostile to Iran. Where others saw antagonism and terrorism, she has looked for opportunities to restore a semblance of normality in relations between the United States and this major regional power, and moved to seize the moment after the Iranian people changed their political direction in May 1997.

In Iran's presidential election that month, Sayyid Muhammad Khatami, a perceived moderate on social issues, triumphed with a shocking 69 percent of the vote over a reactionary hard-liner favored by most of the conservative religious establishment. Khatami is no radical dissenter; he is a mild-mannered theologian who wears the same turban and beard as the most implacable ayatollahs, and his candidacy had been approved by the religious leadership because he was not viewed as a threat to them. His triumph, widely attributed to the support of women and young people who wanted to break out of Iran's suffocating social and cultural repression, held the promise of a new era in Iran's relations with the world, even though he did not campaign on foreign policy issues.

Clinton pronounced the outcome "interesting," and shortly after Khatami was inaugurated in August, Washington and Tehran began a cautious process of feeling each other out.

An effort to break down the hostility between Iran and the United States was not to be undertaken lightly. This initiative was politically risky and diplomatically daunting. Animosity toward Iran runs very deep in Congress because of that country's seizure of the American embassy in Tehran in 1979 and the revolutionary government's complicity in the holding of American diplomatic personnel there as hostages for 444 days. Furthermore, Iran topped the State Department's annual list of nations that sponsor international terrorism.

On the Iranian side, hostility to the United States is not a random or arbitrary phenomenon. The Iranian people are deeply ambivalent about the United States. They are still bitter over Washington's role in restoring the hated shah to the Peacock Throne and undoing the populist triumph of Mohammed Mossadegh in 1953, American support for the shah throughout his oppressive rule, and Washington's preference for Iraq in the savage eight-year war that Iraq started in 1980. The Iranians are still aggrieved by the shooting down of an Iranian airliner over the Persian Gulf by a U.S. Navy warship in 1988, resulting in the deaths of 290 civilians. Iran's outrage over that incident was compounded when the ship's officers later received military decorations. Furthermore, many Iranians share the opinion of their religious leaders that American culture is excessively permissive and corrupt.

"This history is well-known in Iran and widely resented," according to a useful summary by Charles Kurzman. "Isolationists in the government cultivate this resentment through schoolbooks and public commemorations, and use it to mobilize popular sentiment for political goals."[1]

On the other hand, many Iranians have studied in the United States, have relatives in this country, and trained with the U.S. armed forces before the revolution; they generally like Americans if not American policy. Warren Christopher developed a deep antipathy to Iran's revolutionary government and its supporters when, as deputy secretary of state in the Carter administration, he negotiated the release of the American hostages. Even he, however, told me that he "consistently advised the president that we should have no permanent enemies" and that it would be appropriate to "assess what the possibilities are" if cracks appeared in Tehran's wall of hostility to the United States.[2]

A complicating factor is Iran's seemingly implacable hostility to Israel—another by-product of the 1979 revolution. Before that, during the shah's rule, Iran and Israel had been on good terms. In the 1990s, as Iran pressed ahead with its efforts to develop and deploy missiles capable of reaching Israel—an effort dramatized by the test flight of the Shahab-3—alarm in Washington about the threat to Israel grew. (A senior Japanese diplomat told me in the summer of 1998 that his government had urged Iran to extend diplomatic recognition to Israel, arguing that Tehran's objections to Israeli policies would be more credible if Iran at least accepted Israel's existence, but this Japanese line drew no response from the Iranians.)

Curiously, the same change in government in Israel that produced the stalemate in peace negotiations with the Palestinians produced a surprising bit of flexibility on the subject of Iran. American officials said that Benjamin Netanyahu, although concerned about the potential threat, was not obsessed about it, as the respected Yitzhak Rabin had been. One reason was that Uri Lubrani, Netanyahu's chief adviser on Iran, concluded in late 1997 and early 1998 that the political transformation in Iran represented by

Khatami's election was, in his word, "irreversible," and should be encouraged.

"Israel is not the enemy of Iran," Israel's ambassador in Washington, Zalman Shoval, told reporters over breakfast on August 6, 1998. "Israel must be very careful, and we are very concerned by Iran's support for Hezbollah [the Shiite Muslim militia in southern Lebanon], but Israel does not see Iran as an enemy per se." This modest relaxation of Israel's concern gave Albright a little running room to seek some accommodation with the mullahs' regime.

Those who say that no major foreign policy initiative has Albright's name on it may not appreciate the importance of her effort to rebuilt relations with Iran. If it succeeds, it will benefit the United States and the rest of the world in innumerable ways. Of course Albright could not have undertaken this effort without President Clinton's approval and encouragement, but it was up to her to devise the tactics. That meant finding a way to offer Iran goodwill and the prospect of improved relations without slackening efforts to limit Iran's access to nuclear materials and technology or its development of ballistic missiles.

Albright, Strobe Talbott, and Al Gore had been engaged for some time in an effort to persuade Russia not to assist Iran's nuclear and missile development programs, with only modest success. Aside from weapons and nuclear know-how, the cash-strapped Russians had few industrial products that other nations wanted to buy; they defended their contract to build a nuclear power plant in Iran as an economic necessity that was legal under the rules set down by the Nuclear Nonproliferation Treaty, a point the United States did not dispute. In January 1998, however, the Russians adopted export control regulations that satisfied Washington that they were serious about regulating the export of missile equipment and technology, and that summer Moscow announced that nine Russian companies were the subject of a criminal investigation into suspected unauthorized exports. Those moves convinced the Americans that Russia was getting serious about nonproliferation and gave Clinton the cover he needed to veto legislation that would have required economic sanctions on Russian private companies involved in the weapons commerce. Mike McCurry and Jamie Rubin said that the president vetoed the bill because it was flawed legislation; but it was clear in Washington that he was also motivated by the desire to maintain good relations with Russia and to signal Iran that the administration was aware of the signs of positive change there.

Albright tried a different approach with China, which was also supplying missile technology to Iran. She had had a long, discursive conversation with Chinese foreign minister Qian Qichen before President Jiang Zemin's state visit to Washington in the fall of 1997. She had known Qian for several years because they had been at the United Nations at the same time, and she described him as "a very interesting person . . . I had a feeling that if one could have an excellent discussion with him, that it would be very useful."

She told Qian that China, about to become an importer of energy and facing a growing dependence on oil imports as its economy expanded, should do what it could to minimize instability in the Persian Gulf region, and she found him responsive. "In terms of being dependent for their energy supply on the region, that potentially is dangerous, and I think they understand it," she said.[3] During the state visit, Clinton and Gore pursued the same theme with the Chinese.

These diplomatic discussions may have curbed the flow of some technology to Iran, but they did not halt the Iranian effort to develop ballistic missiles. After the Shahab-3 test, Martin Indyk, the assistant secretary of state for Near Eastern affairs, said that Iran would probably press ahead with its weapons programs even if Khatami changed the country's policies on supporting terrorism and opposing Middle East peace because Iran's neighbors—Iraq and Pakistan—are committed to modernizing their weapons systems and because Iran's regional ambitions in the Gulf require it.

But if it is inevitable that Iran will acquire longer-range missiles and perhaps nuclear or biological warheads to mount on them, it is all the more desirable to moderate Iran's strategic outlook and encourage better relations with the West. The problem for Albright was that doing so was as difficult tactically as it was politically because of Khatami's strange position in the Iranian system of government.

Under Iran's constitution, the president does not control the country's military or its security apparatus; that power lies with the supreme religious leader, Ali Khamenei, who sits at the pinnacle of a religious establishment propelled to leadership by Ayatollah Khomeini and mostly united in hostility to the United States. It was therefore not clear whether Khatami could deliver rapprochement even if he were so inclined. And for a related reason, some officials felt that an embrace by Washington would undermine Khatami's position at home as he sought to consolidate his position in the face of attempts by Khamenei and his allies to rein him in.

It seemed indisputable that Iran under Khatami wished to be a more responsible citizen of the world than it had been for the previous eighteen years. Khatami's government ratified the Chemical Weapons Convention. Tehran played host to a conference of all Muslim nations and used the occasion to begin a rapprochement with Saudi Arabia and to signal Yasser Arafat that it would not try to undermine him if he struck a deal with Israel that the Palestinian people accepted. The conference adopted a resolution, which Iran endorsed, condemning terrorism. Assassinations and terrorist attacks that could be traced to Iranian government sponsorship declined, especially in Europe. Iran agreed to work with Washington in the so-called Six Plus Two group of nations seeking an end to the conflict in Afghanistan, the eight being Afghanistan's neighbors plus Russia and the United States. And Khatami gave a long interview to CNN in which he expressed regret for the taking of the hostages at the U.S. embassy and said that Iran would welcome an increase in cultural and academic exchanges.

Albright and her colleagues were fascinated by these hints of change. They saw little that was encouraging in Iran's sustained efforts to acquire missiles and nuclear weapons, but the secretary seemed to agree with analysts who argued that the issue was not weapons so much as the policies of the country possessing them. Iran, still bitter about its inability to defeat the much smaller Iraq in their long war a decade earlier, is bent on acquiring missiles and otherwise modernizing its armed forces, whether Washington approves or not. Given that reality, the more promising approach is to reach some accommodation with the Iranian leadership. Albright recognized that this could not happen so long as Iran perceived the United States as irreversibly hostile.[4]

Looking for a constructive approach that would encourage Khatami without compromising on issues important to Washington, Albright invited several experts on Iran from universities and foundations to a dinner to solicit their views, a device she often uses to solicit input, recalling her pre-Clinton years as hostess of a

Democratic foreign policy salon. Among the guests were Gary Sick of Columbia University, who had been the White House point man on Iran during the revolution and had written a thoughtful book about it, and Geoffrey Kemp, a regional specialist at the Nixon Center in Washington, both advocates of a shift in policy toward Iran. Talk of rapprochement was no longer taboo in Washington.

For several months, the Clinton administration's willingness to reconstruct relations with Iran surfaced mostly in the form of small gestures and low-key but unmistakable changes in rhetoric and official language. The State Department sent a midlevel diplomat to a conference at Columbia University, organized by Sick, to participate with Iranian counterparts in a discussion about increasing cultural, athletic, and academic exchanges. For the first time in years, the State Department authorized a diplomat from Iran's United Nations mission to travel outside the New York area, to California, to make a speech.

American officials stopped saying in public that they suspected Iran of responsibility for the terrorist bombing of a U.S. Air Force residential compound in Saudi Arabia. Albright also ordered up a revised and much milder version of the State Department's warning on travel to Iran by American citizens. (The department routinely publishes advisories specifying the hazards of travel to hostile or dangerous countries.) The warning published in the summer of 1997—after Khatami had been elected but before he took office— began with this ominous message:

> Warning: The Department of State warns all U.S. citizens against travel to Iran, which remains dangerous because of the generally anti-American atmosphere and Iranian government hostility to the U.S. government. U.S. citizens traveling to Iran have been detained without charge, arrested and harassed by Iranian authorities.

It also warned of "fines, public floggings and long prison terms" for travelers who fell afoul of the Iranian authorities.

The revised version, issued less than a year later, omitted the references to harsh punishments and took a much less confrontational tone overall. In the new text, the department warned U.S. citizens merely "to defer travel to Iran." It noted that Khatami "has called for a 'dialogue of civilizations' and an increase of private exchanges between Iranians and Americans; some limited exchanges have taken place. There is, however, evidence that hostility to the United States remains in some segments of the Iranian population and some elements of the Iranian government."

In the language of diplomacy, the difference between the two versions is night and day.

In August 1998, when the Taliban militia in Afghanistan overran the city of Mazar-e-Sharif and seized Iranian diplomats at the consulate there, the State Department issued a statement deploring the action. "We would condemn any Taliban detention of official Iranians and call for their immediate release," the statement said. "The holding of diplomats for any reason and at any time is especially troubling, given their special protected status under international law."

This was a masterpiece of diplomatic understatement. It omitted any mention of the fact that the Iranians are the champion diplomatic hostage takers of the twentieth century, if not of all time, or any hint that the so-called diplomats seized by the Taliban were probably intelligence agents. The statement went on to urge "all of Afghanistan's neighbors to respect its borders," without singling out Iran, which at the time was massing troops at the frontier.[5]

What Iran wanted more than these gestures of outreach, however, was foreign investment to expand its oil and natural gas production, the country's main source of income. Clinton had banned all American firms from doing business with Iran, and he signed a law passed by Congress imposing stiff economic sanctions on foreign corporations that invested substantial amounts in Iran's petroleum infrastructure. A year after Khatami's election, Clinton exercised his authority under that law to waive the sanctions against three major foreign oil companies—one French, one Russian, and one Malaysian—that had signed a contract to develop a major offshore natural gas field in Iran.

Administration officials insisted that Clinton had waived these sanctions not to court Iran but to forestall a trade war with the European Union, which vehemently opposed what the Europeans regarded as an effort to impose American foreign policy on their companies. Nevertheless, the implications for Iran were clear: Clinton's gesture, along with a decision to refrain from sanctioning a Turkish company building a natural gas pipeline in Iran, removed a major obstacle to Iran's efforts to attract foreign capital.

Albright had wanted for some time to deliver a major speech systematically outlining her new policy on Iran. It would have been futile to do so while the sanctions decision was still pending, because the Iranians would have said, in effect, "Show us the money." With the sanctions issue out of the way, she used a previously scheduled appearance before the Asia Society in New York as the platform for her announcement. She began:

> One of the oldest civilizations in the world, Iran is at the center of a region which includes countries that contain three quarters of the world's population, three quarters of the world's proven energy resources and 60 percent of global GNP. These facts of life, and the critical role that Iran plays in that region, make the question of U.S.-Iran relations a topic of great interest and importance to this Secretary of State.

She gave no ground on opposition to Iranian sponsorship of terrorism or its efforts to acquire nuclear weapons and long-range missiles. Washington's efforts to block Iranian economic development would continue so long as any increased revenue in the Iranian treasury would be used for purposes of which Washington disapproved. "But let me be clear," Albright continued.

> These policies are not, as some Iranians allege, anti-Islamic. Islam is the fastest-growing religious faith in the United States. We respect deeply its moral teachings and its role as a source of inspiration and instruction for hundreds of millions of people around the world. U.S. policy is directed at actions, not people or faiths. The standards we would like Iran to observe are not merely Western but universal. We fully respect Iran's sovereignty. We understand and respect its fierce desire to maintain its independence. We do not seek to overthrow its government. But we do ask that Iran live up to its commitments to the international community.[6]

She offered the Iranians what she called a "road map" to improved official relations, by which each side would respond to positive actions of the other. A similar road map strategy, developed in the Bush administration, had led to the establishment of diplomatic relations between the United States and Vietnam earlier in Clinton's presidency.

Iran's official response—delivered by Foreign Minister Kamal Kharrazi in the same Asia Society venue three months later—was predictably negative. He took note of the "new tone" represented by Albright's speech, but argued that it was not matched by any change in American policy: "It is evident that the prolongation of outdated behavior, and sole reliance on variation in verbiage, can simply not provide the necessary basis for an invitation to political dialogue."[7]

This was hardly surprising. A brutal power struggle is unfolding in Iran, comparable to what happened in the Jacobin period after the French revolution. Kharrazi's New York speech reflected the fact that, at that moment, any public statement endorsing an official dialogue with Washington would be political suicide in Iran; but such may not always be the case. All revolutions exhaust themselves sooner or later.

And so Albright chose not to be discouraged by Kharrazi's negative initial response; the outreach continued. In December, Clinton notified Congress that he had removed Iran from the government's list of major drug-producing countries. Again, administration officials said that this was a technical move, prompted by intelligence data showing that Iran had ceased cultivating opium poppies, rather than a political gesture to Tehran. Nevertheless, it cleared away one more obstacle to the rebuilding of bilateral relations.

The new thinking about Iran that Albright encouraged among her Middle East advisers amounted to modification and then abandonment of the administration's long-standing policy of "dual containment," which meant keeping Iran and Iraq bottled up through economic and political pressure, including sanctions. American officials began differentiating between Iraq, where nothing positive was happening from Washington's perspective, and Iran, where they saw some encouraging signs. In testimony about Iran before a Senate Foreign Relations subcommittee on May 12, 1998, Martin Indyk never used the word "containment." Without saying so, Albright had deftly engineered a retreat from "dual containment," a policy that had strong support in Congress and that just a few months earlier had seemed politically inviolable even though it had outlived its relevance.

Indyk, the architect of dual containment when he was the senior Middle East policymaker on the National Security Council in Clinton's first term, formally consigned the policy to history in an address to the Council on Foreign Relations on April 22, 1999, several months after Albright had officially announced the effort to reach out to Iran. Different in language and history and hostile to each other, Iran and Iraq were nonetheless linked in isolation and opprobrium through most of Bill Clinton's presidency. The corollary of the outreach to Iran was its decoupling from Iraq.

Indyk said that the policy of isolating and hemming in the two countries always presumed that either or both could be restored to the world's good graces if they mended their ways. "Iraq, under Saddam Hussein, remains dangerous, unreconstructed, defiant, and isolated," Indyk said, and "will never be able to be rehabilitated or reintegrated into the community of nations" without a change of leadership. Not so the Islamic Republic of Iran, where the United States recognized the legitimacy of the regime.

"The evolution in Iran, and hence our response, has been markedly different," Indyk said. He stipulated that Washington remained concerned about Iran's weapons programs and its support for terrorist organizations. "We would be remiss, however, were we to fail to adjust our approach to the changing reality in Iran" by offering the possibility of a more forthcoming relationship, Indyk said.

Tehran and Washington continued this game of thrust and parry into 2000, Albright's last full year in office. It may be years before the outcome of her initiative is clear. She reluctantly acknowledged that it was not bearing fruit as quickly as she wished, but she was furious when lower-level State Department officials were quoted in press accounts as saying that it had petered out to no effect.

In her annual worldwide foreign policy assessment, submitted to the Senate Foreign Relations Committee in February 1999, Albright said that "the official Iranian response has thus far been disappointing, but we stand ready for a dialogue in which both sides would be free to discuss all issues of concern." And the gestures, including Martin Indyk's remarks putting an end to dual containment, continued—driven, State Department officials said, by Clinton's fascination with Iran's political evolution.

Because of the air war against Yugoslavia, nobody in Washington was paying much attention to Iran in April 1999, but it was not far from Clinton's thoughts. At a White House event on April 12, he delivered off-the-cuff remarks about the history of Iran's relations with the West that created a stir in Tehran, where arguments erupted in Parliament and on editorial pages about whether the president's words amounted to the apology for the past that Tehran has long demanded. Clinton said:

> It may be that the Iranian people have been taught to hate or distrust the United States or the West on the grounds that we are infidels and outside the faith. And, therefore, it is easy for us to be angry and to respond in kind. I think it is important to recognize, however, that Iran, because of its enormous geopolitical importance over time, has been the subject of quite a lot of abuse from various Western nations. And I think sometimes it's quite important to tell people, look, you have a right to be angry at something my country or my culture or others that are generally allied with us today did to you 50 or 60 or 100 or 150 years ago. But that is different from saying I am outside the faith and you are God's chosen.

Later that month, Clinton modified U.S. economic sanctions policy to permit American companies to sell food and medicine to Iran and other countries listed by the State Department as sponsors of international terrorism, a decision that made it possible for a Washington trading company to carry out a $500 million order for agricultural commodities that it had received from Iranian officials who had said that the order was a goodwill gesture.

In announcing the decision, Undersecretary of State Stuart Eizenstat said that it was part of an overall effort to reform sanctions to make them more effective, not "a signal to any country." But other officials told me that the administration had deliberately waited until the sanctions decision was ready before announcing another decision, reached earlier, to deny a request by the Mobil Corporation to engage in oil transactions with Iran. Clinton and Albright wanted to balance this bad news for Iran with the good news about the commodities order, they said.

They also told me to pay close attention to the section about Iran in the State Department's annual report on terrorism, which was due to be published a few days later. Sure enough, the report contained much softer language about Iran than had been used in previous years. Iran remained on the list of terrorist nations, but instead of calling Iran "the most active state sponsor of terrorism," as 1998's report did, the 1999 version said only that Iran "continued to be involved in the planning and execution of terrorist acts." It also noted that Iran "apparently conducted fewer anti-dissident assassinations abroad in 1998 than in 1997."[8]

It is true, as officials always say in public, that this language represents only an assessment of the facts. But it is also true that Tehran pays close attention to the language of Washington and that the wording was calculated to signal the Iranians that the United States was willing to move if they did.

In this case, Khatami's response was the diplomatic equivalent of a frozen mitten to the mouth: a meeting at which he joined hard-line rejectionist Palestinians from terrorist organizations in denouncing the Wye agreement between Israel and the Palestinians. Indyk made no effort to hide his dismay.

The Palestinians whom Khatami embraced "represent nobody on the Palestinian side," he said. "They're yesterday's men, who speak only the language of violence and terrorism and rejection. Why President Khatami would want to associate himself with these people is, I have to say, beyond me. And therefore, I'm at a loss to explain why."[9]

Albright never said that this initiative would be easy, and she never predicted positive results. Iran has embarked on a struggle to define its identity and its place in the world—a struggle that may be protracted and violent, as indicated by the student demonstrations that erupted in the summer of 1999.

It is still possible that the forces of reaction and obscurantism will prevail in Iran, but the triumph of reform candidates in parliamentary elections held in early 2000 was an encouraging sign. A few weeks afterward, on March 17, 2000, Albright responded with a major speech to a conference on American-Iranian relations in Washington in which she acknowledged Iran's grievances against the United States. She announced an end to the long-standing ban on imports of Iranian carpets, caviar, and pistachios and offered to move as quickly as Iran wished toward harmonious relations.

"On behalf of the government of the United States," she said, "I call upon Iran to join in writing a new chapter in our shared history."

Whatever the outcome of this quest to rebuild relations with Iran, the potential prize is worth the effort. If Albright's initiative fails, the United States will be no worse off than before; if it ultimately succeeds, she and Clinton can claim a historic accomplishment.

Chapter 6

I SOMEHOW LOST
MY INSTINCTS

BY LATE SUMMER of her first year as secretary of state, Madeleine Albright could no longer put off a direct encounter with the longest-running and most intractable issue on the U.S. foreign policy agenda, the standoff between Israel and its Arab neighbors. Her first trip to the Middle East as secretary that September merits examination at some length because it provided one of the first tests of her ability to function in a situation the United States did not control and the outcome of which was unpredictable. The way the trip was organized and the way her message was delivered offered a prototype of her technique.

In Clinton's first term, it seemed possible that the regional peace agreement Washington had been seeking since the 1973 war might finally be achievable. Jordan signed a peace treaty with Israel, joining Egypt as the only Arab countries to come to terms with the Jewish state. Israel and the Palestinians reached an agreement in principle in secret talks in Oslo, and even Syria said it was willing to make peace, entering negotiations on the basis of the land-for-peace formula that had underlain Middle East policy for three decades.

Israel and the Palestinians had crossed the previously unbreachable psychological border of mutual recognition, but crucial details of their future as neighbors remained to be settled. As projected in the Oslo agreements and envisioned by Washington, the road to full peace entailed a series of political, military, and economic steps designed to increase contact, promote understanding, and develop mutual economic interests that would overcome long-standing hostility.

Everyone in Washington, Jerusalem, and the Palestinian territories understood what the eventual outcome would be: an independent or quasi-independent Palestine, free of Israeli occupation after thirty years, which in partnership with Jordan and Egypt would establish friendly or at least correct relations with Israel, effectively ending the Arab-Israeli conflict. The details, however, were left to be worked out over a three-to-five-year period because the unresolved issues were so emotional, so freighted with history, symbolism, and fear, that they defied quick solutions.

These issues, such as the return of Palestinian refugees to their homeland and the political future of Jerusalem, were left to "permanent status" negotiations, which were to take place in tandem with interim steps designed to foster mutual confidence and respect. As Israel gradually pulled out of the West Bank and Gaza and turned control over to Yasser Arafat's Palestinian Authority, following a timetable agreed to in Oslo, the United States, the World Bank, and other donors would endeavor to stimulate cross-border economic development and investment, giving the parties incentives to cooperate and giving ordinary Israeli and Palestinian citizens reason to believe that peace was worthwhile.

By the summer of 1997, however, the core agreement between Israel and the Palestinians was falling apart, Syria and Israel had ceased talking to each other, and Arab states that had been cooperating in the economic program, including Egypt and Saudi Arabia, were threatening to pull out of the annual U.S.-sponsored regional investment conference, scheduled to be held that year in Doha, Qatar.

The principal reason for this unhappy turn of events was the 1995 assassination of Yitzhak Rabin, the Israeli prime minister, who was gunned down by a Jewish extremist opposed to peace with the Palestinians and to the surrender of Israeli-held land in the West Bank. Rabin's stature as military hero and political leader was such that most Israelis were willing to follow him down the risky road to peace, even if it meant giving up Zionism's biblical claim to the West Bank and perhaps even surrendering the Golan Heights, the strategic promontory on the Israel-Syria border captured by Israeli troops in the 1967 war.

Rabin was succeeded by his foreign minister, Shimon Peres, who for all his fame and distinction lacked Rabin's military credentials and iron will. Israelis simply did not feel as comfortable about the deal with the Palestinians under Peres as they had under Rabin. When Peres stood for election the following spring, he was narrowly defeated by the hard-line leader of the rightist Likud Coalition, Benjamin Netanyahu. Netanyahu campaigned against the Oslo agreements as a threat to Israel's security and opposed returning the Golan Heights to Syrian control.

During the campaign, Clinton and his foreign policy team more or less overtly supported Peres. When Netanyahu won, the entire picture changed. Washington now was dealing with an Israeli leader who was contemptuous of the Arabs, had no commitment to Oslo (although he kept promising that Israel would fulfill its legal obligations), and resented Clinton's backing of Peres. At the same time, Netanyahu had very strong support in Congress; the prolonged standing ovation he received when he addressed a joint session shortly after his election sent a message that was heard at the other end of Pennsylvania Avenue and around the Arab world.

This set of relationships was to present Albright with a conundrum she could not solve. Netanyahu was the democratically elected leader of a closely allied country that had strong support from every point on the American political spectrum. He could not be bullied or repudiated. But Albright believed that Netanyahu's policies were fundamentally wrongheaded and dangerous. If he snatched away the vision of freedom and independence that had inspired the Palestinian people after Oslo and that had made it politically permissible for other Arabs to accept the Palestinians' deal with Israel, he risked losing the peace and condemning Israel to further decades as a garrison state.

After several months of hesitation—and prodding from Washington—Netanyahu grudgingly fulfilled one of the Oslo requirements Likud found most painful, pulling Israeli troops out of most of the West Bank town of Hebron, where militant Jewish settlers had staked a religious claim and lived as a perpetual provocation to the Palestinian citizenry. With that move, Likud for the first time demonstrated that it could relinquish Zionism's historic claim to the West Bank, known to Israelis by the biblical names Judea and Samaria, in exchange for peace. This was "land for peace" as envisioned in every United Nations resolution and diplomatic initiative since the 1967 war, but to the Israeli right wing it represented the abandonment of a sacred commitment. It took some political courage for Netanyahu to take this step, and Washington was gratified.

In other ways, however, Netanyahu's government provoked the Palestinians, chiefly by undertaking—without consulting Arafat—housing and infrastructure development designed to cement the Jewish state's control of all of Jerusalem. Rabin had agreed to put Jerusalem on the table in the "permanent status" negotiations, and the Palestinians argued that the real purpose of Netanyahu's development projects was to preempt those negotiations by creating foregone conclusions. There was little reason to believe that even the most dovish members of Rabin's Labor party would have been willing to relinquish any of the holy city, but Oslo had at least opened the door for the Palestinians to assert their rival claim.

Clinton and Albright agreed that Netanyahu's moves impeded further progress toward peace. They said that the Israeli government's decision to construct up to 7,000 apartments for Jewish families in an area of Jerusalem known as Har Homa was "not helpful" and expressed disapproval of "unilateral actions" that violated the spirit of the peace negotiations. At the time, that was about as far as they could go politically.

These comments did not deter the Israelis and were of marginal comfort to the Palestinians. Before Netanyahu, the Palestinians thought they were within reach of their most cherished goal, an independent state. In Jericho, Ramallah, and other West Bank towns, the excitement was palpable as the Palestinians began building the functions of a state: They issued license plates, printed stamps and passports, recruited and armed their own police force, and built an airport in the Gaza Strip. There was talk of a Palestinian currency. After a year of Netanyahu, their aspirations seemed to have turned to dust. The standard of living in the Palestinian territories went down rather than up. Despair returned, and with it, violence.

Palestinian terrorists had struck in Jerusalem and other Jewish cities while Peres was prime minister, apparently in an effort to derail what was known as the "peace process." Netanyahu had promised Israel peace with security, but suicide bombings that sowed death and terror in Israel's streets and markets resumed in the summer of 1997. Netanyahu took the position that Israel could not move further toward peace while under the hammer of terrorism. The Palestinians and other Arabs retorted that his policies inspired the terrorism, and they accused him of using the bombings as a pretext for backing out of the Oslo commitments.

In her first six months as secretary of state, Albright received a steady stream of prominent Middle Eastern visitors—Netanyahu, Arafat, Crown Prince Abdullah and Prince Sultan of Saudi Arabia, King Hussein of Jordan, President Hosni Mubarak of Egypt—but the atmosphere in the region continued to deteriorate.

Albright resisted pressure from Congress, think-tank analysts, and editorial writers to go to the Middle East in an effort to reverse this ominous trend. There were several reasons for her reluctance. She was extremely busy with other items on her agenda that could not be postponed, such as the expansion of NATO and the evolution of relations with Russia; there was a high prospect of failure; and she believed that Christopher had squandered time and political capital by visiting the region two dozen times in his four years, often to no apparent effect. Her aides said repeatedly that she did not want to travel just for the sake of traveling.

According to one of the senior Middle East specialists on Albright's team, there was also a tactical reason to hold off. He said that it quickly became apparent to Albright that the "gaps" between Israel and the Palestinians had widened to the point that "we couldn't easily bridge them from the top down. So we began to think, is there a way to bridge them from the bottom up" by encouraging lower-level contacts to deal with technical issues such as the operating rules for the airport the Palestinians had constructed in the Gaza Strip but were barred by the Israelis from opening.

"The more profile we gave, the more we found resistance," the official said. "So to deal with the reluctance to have high-level contacts, we said, okay, let's try it in a lower-profile way."

Albright, ever image-conscious, was sensitive to the perception that she was ducking a fight she thought she could not win. On July 30, 1997, she was in Honolulu when she got the news that a Palestinian suicide bomber had killed thirteen Israelis in Jerusalem. When a reporter asked if the incident would "increase the need for you to get directly involved," she snapped back, "I am directly involved. Let me make this clear. I am directly involved in this. I have been from the day I became Secretary of State. I spend many hours every day dealing with this. . . . You do not have to be in the region in order to be directly involved."

But that posture was no longer tenable. The United States, and Clinton personally, were heavily invested in the Oslo process; losing Oslo would lead to years and perhaps decades of renewed tension in the region, undermine the domestic positions of Mubarak and King Hussein, and provide new ammunition for Iran and other centers of anti-Israel activism.

In a speech at the National Press Club a week later, Albright said that the situation had deteriorated to the point where energetic new input from Washington was required. Reviewing the depressing events of the preceding months, she announced that she was prepared to go to the region to exhort the two sides to redouble their efforts to cut a deal. "The Israeli-Palestinian crisis of confidence has cost the peace process six months," she said in her speech, which she knew would draw intense interest throughout the Middle East. She continued:

> Suspicions and mistrust are running high. The logic of Oslo, based on mutual recognition, is sound, but the incremental approach of the interim agreement needs to be married to an accelerated approach to permanent status. To restore momentum, we have to increase confidence on both sides about where the negotiating process is leading and what the outcome of permanent status talks might be.
>
> If the parties have a clear, mutual and favorable sense of the ultimate direction of negotiation, it will be easier for them to overcome setbacks and avoid distractions along the way. This will require accelerating permanent status negotiations. Today, this step is urgent and important. Accordingly, provided there is some progress on security issues, I am prepared to travel to the Middle East at the end of this month. I will consult closely with the leaders of the region—and especially with Israeli and Palestinian leaders—to improve the climate for negotiations, and to discuss the procedural and substantive aspects of the permanent status issues.

It then became necessary to define the objectives of her trip and to minimize public expectations to avoid the appearance of failure. This latter assignment fell largely to Jamie Rubin, whose line was,

"She's a realist, not a magician." About her own hopes for the up-coming trip, Rubin joked that "we've set the bar so low on this one, it's subterranean!"

According to Rubin and other senior aides, Albright had specific but narrow objectives for her first venture as secretary of state into these turbulent waters. She wanted to end the dangerous erosion in Israeli-Palestinian relations and find a way to resume implementa-tion of the Oslo accords. She wanted to shore up support for peace in Egypt, Jordan, and Saudi Arabia, where popular anger over Netanyahu's treatment of the Palestinians and over Israel's military activities inside Lebanon was putting pressure on the leaders to dis-tance themselves from the Jewish state. And she wanted to avoid en-tanglement in the shuttle diplomacy and incremental negotiations that had consumed so much of her predecessors' time and energy since the days of Henry Kissinger.

Albright recognized that Netanyahu's government was at least as responsible as the Palestinians for the breakdown of the Oslo process. Netanyahu was contemptuous of Arabs in general and Palestinians in particular. He did not want to give the Palestinians one square inch more than necessary, and the Palestinians inter-preted his attitude as a repudiation of Oslo. Albright was deter-mined not to accept an outright repudiation of that landmark agreement. But Israel's special relationship with the United States and its domestic support there precluded Albright from simply fly-ing in and taking Netanyahu to task, especially because Israel had just been traumatized by a new round of terrorist attacks and needed reassurance as much as it needed remonstrations.

Facing these conflicting imperatives, Albright and her aides, led by veteran Middle East coordinator Dennis Ross, scripted a trip that enabled her to employ all her favorite techniques. The theme would be "mutual responsibility," stressing that both sides were responsible for the situation and that it was up to both sides to take action to turn it around.[1]

Traveling with the secretary around the region in the second week of September 1997, we watched a performance that could be de-scribed as classic Albright. It combined conventional diplomatic dis-cussions, symbolic public events, communication to and with local people, news conferences, chats with students, frank talk, and eva-sive indirection in a package designed to communicate with many audiences.

About two hours out of Andrews Air Force Base, Albright came to the back of the plane to talk about her goals for the trip. She knew that the wire service reporters on board would file stories while the plane was refueled at Shannon, Ireland, which would be read in the Middle East while we were still flying over Europe, so she used the briefing to let people in the region know what her theme would be.

She began by talking about her reason for making the trip, which, after all, was by its nature and timing loaded with the kind of uncertainty and potential for failure that secretaries of state generally like to avoid. "Basically, as you know, a secretary of state has gone to the Middle East for two reasons," she said: "either because things are really good and it is possible for any secretary to close a deal and make a difference in that way or because things have deteriorated and it is important . . . to go in and see what can be done about putting things back on track."

(She used this introduction at so many of her public appearances on the trip that we who heard it on each occasion began to groan and roll our eyes as she launched into it one more time. At the end of the trip, when she joined us for a group picture at the airport in Larnaca, Cyprus, I jokingly asked her, "Madam Secretary, what are the two reasons a secretary of state goes to the Middle East?"

"If I didn't say the same thing every time," she responded, "you all would write that I was changing my message."

A few hours after that, in flight on the way home, when she came back to share with us her thoughts on what she had accomplished, she began, "I thought I would just start by telling you there are two reasons why a secretary of state goes to the Middle East . . ." Good politicians have always been skillful at disarming the press corps with self-deprecatory inside jokes.)

In her briefing on the outbound flight, stating the trip's theme, the key sentence was this: "Oslo has been and is a very important process that carries within it a lot of mutual responsibilities, and I am going to be speaking about carrying out mutual responsibilities in order to rebuild the confidence that is necessary for the process to go forward."

In other words, she was not going to give Netanyahu carte blanche to blame the Palestinians for everything that had gone wrong and to avoid carrying out the interim steps that his predecessors had agreed to. "Mutual responsibilities" became the code words for the entire trip.

Albright wanted the Israelis to be more forthcoming on the political and economic aspirations of the Palestinians, she wanted the Palestinians to cease acts of terrorism and stifle the anti-Israeli rhetoric flowing from the mosques and marketplaces, and she wanted other pro-peace Arab states, including Saudi Arabia and the Persian Gulf sheikhdoms, to continue down the road to normal relations with Israel upon which they had already cautiously embarked. Peace was everyone's job.

Because of the terrorist bombings, Congress was in a state of high outrage about the Palestinians. Several prominent members urged Albright publicly to limit the agenda for her trip to the single message that terrorism was unacceptable. Albright recognized that the situation was not so simple.

Her first event in Israel was a meeting with the venerated president, Ezer Weizman, not yet tainted by the political scandal that would besmirch his reputation early in 2000, followed by a brief joint news conference with him at which she announced that on behalf of President Clinton she had invited Weizman to visit Washington soon. The message was that Weizman, who had been much more responsive to the Palestinians than had Netanyahu, was in high favor in Washington.

Speaking into television cameras, Albright also delivered a message of support and reassurance to the Israeli people, pledging: "We are with you in the battle against terror and the struggle for security." She promised that "the terrorists will not succeed" in denying Israelis a peace she said they had earned through a half century of struggle and sacrifice. With that, she sought to establish herself with the Israelis as a sort of caring mother figure, from whom the stern words soon to come would be more acceptable because her audience already understood that she was devoted to them.

The stern words began that afternoon when she met privately with Netanyahu. For the occasion, Albright wore a dove-of-peace pin that had been given to her by Rabin's widow, Leah, a symbolic jab at Netanyahu that nobody in Israel could miss. She delivered her message about "mutual responsibilities," telling Netanyahu that the Palestinians were losing faith in peace because their economic situation was deteriorating and agreements already made that would enhance their self-rule were not being implemented. Netanyahu stuck to his theme that nothing could be done until the terrorism issue was resolved. Aides who worked closely with him said that Netanyahu, deep down inside, never believed that the Palestinians were committed to peaceful coexistence with Israel; he thought that once Oslo was fully implemented and they had their state, their hostility—and their demands on Israel—would resume. The terrorism gave him the tool he needed to avoid ever getting to that point.

At a news conference after their meeting, Albright and Netanyahu made little effort to disguise their differences.

"Real security depends ultimately on real peace," Albright said. "Achieving this peace turns fundamentally on a political process which meets, through a genuine process of give and take, the needs of both sides. Clearly, Israel also has a responsibility to shape an environment that will give that process a chance to succeed."

Asked if he was prepared to respond favorably and make some gestures toward the Palestinians, Netanyahu said, "We can talk, and you can ask me more questions of this nature, and they'll be largely irrelevant if we don't stop terrorism."

This basic standoff continued as long as Albright was in Israel. The next day she met with Arafat, and although he greeted her with a tirade about alleged Israeli violations of the Oslo agreement, he also offered some new counterterrorism initiatives that she found encouraging. Armed with that, she delivered a televised speech at a Jerusalem high school in which she called for a "time-out" in Israeli settlement building and other activities that the Palestinians found provocative.

Here was an unusual spectacle: an American secretary of state—with a long personal history of support for Israel—telling the Israelis in fairly blunt language that it was they, by their unilateral acts and contemptuous attitudes, who were driving the Palestinians into the anger and despair that undermined peace and stimulated terrorism.

She put herself in the camp of President Bush's secretary of state, James Baker, and a few other prominent Americans whose view of the Israelis could be summarized as, Yes, we love you and promise to protect you, but that does not mean you are always right. Baker, perhaps alone among American policymakers, had actually put his assessment into practice, persuading Bush to hold up U.S. guarantees that would have lowered the interest rates on bonds Israel wanted to issue to finance housing construction, to punish the Israelis for expanding settlements in the occupied territories.

Albright did not take any such direct steps to rein in Israel—after all, her boss was proud of his reputation of being strongly pro-Israel—but in the context of the Middle East her words immediately changed the atmosphere. During the rest of her trip and in the immediate aftermath, prominent Arabs including Egyptian foreign minister Amre Moussa, Saudi Arabian foreign minister Saud al-Faisal, and Hanan Ashrawi, a member of Arafat's cabinet and a former peace negotiator, said publicly that her words had restored some confidence on the Arab side in American impartiality and good faith.

That was not the same as progress in negotiations, of course, nor was it enough to dispel entirely the anger and despair that had overtaken hopes for peace among the Palestinian population, as Albright found out the following day. She traveled to an elite high school on the outskirts of the West Bank town of Ramallah to talk to a group of Palestinian students.

This was the kind of event Albright loves to conduct: a meeting with bright young people in which she can play the role of teacher, capturing their attention with stories of her own dramatic past and engaging them in the issues of the day. In Ramallah, however, the classroom event did not go well because Albright, hemmed in by domestic U.S. politics and congressional support for Israel, was unable to speak forthrightly. Long-standing American policies precluded her from telling the students what they wanted to hear; as a result, her answers rang hollow and the students sensed it.

Albright delivered her speech about the two reasons why a secretary of state would go to the Middle East, then took questions. The questions were tough but the answers were flabby. The first student, a girl, began:

> Madam Secretary, I am fifteen years old. I have lived under occupation all my life. Even though I was born in Jerusalem, I can't go there, not just a month ago [after the West Bank was closed off because of the terrorist bombings] but three years ago. I am looking toward a better future. Everyone is interested in bringing this peace process back on track and reaching a successful conclusion. Can you please tell me what a successful conclusion politically means?

The response she wanted, of course, was that the conclusion would be the establishment of an independent Palestinian state, free of Israeli occupation. But it has never been American policy to support an independent Palestinian state unless Israel agrees to it first, so Albright delivered a rambling summary of the status of the negotiating process, which she concluded by saying, "I have no specific answer for you as to what the political future is because we believe that it is up to the leaders here to determine that and not for the Americans to impose a plan because a plan that is workable here is only one that is created by leaders of the region." She offered nothing that even acknowledged the students' aspirations.

Then it got worse, when a boy rose to inquire about the terrorism issue. "We often hear about terrorism as related to bombings such as those in Jerusalem," he said, "but we never hear about the terror resulting from the midnight arrests of innocent people, pointed weapons, and humiliating remarks at roadblocks, attacks on our religion, destruction of homes and dreams. How does the U.S. view terror of all forms and their use?"

There was the Palestinian problem in a nutshell, the rage and humiliation of a proud people long abused by history, fate, Israel, and the incompetence and corruption of their own leaders. Albright's response showed barely a shred of sympathy. Instead, she delivered a lecture about the evils of Palestinian terrorism. "I think that it is very important that people understand that there is no moral equivalence between somebody who straps bombs around themselves and stands in the market and blows himself up and other innocent people along with him," she said, in uncharacteristically mangled syntax. "That is inexcusable, unacceptable and an evil form of terror that has no equivalence anywhere else."

She told her questioner that Israeli actions of the sort he asked about "may not be helpful" in reestablishing a constructive negotiating climate, but concluded that "they in no way resemble or have the same effect or [are] as despicable or unacceptable or dastardly as a bomb that hurts innocent people."

And when another student questioned the value of Albright's criticisms of the Israelis "when you are not putting any pressure on the Israeli government and they are not listening to you anyway," Albright repeated that "terror must stop."

After the secretary departed, reporters who stayed to talk to the students heard mostly irritation and bewilderment. Of course terrorist bombings are bad, they said; we knew that. What did she come here for if that was all she had to offer?

About a month later, I asked Albright to reflect on that meeting. She acknowledged that it had gone badly. "I somehow lost my instincts, which were that it was a lousy event, it wasn't set up right," she said. "It was set up in a very sterile way. What I should have done is what I would have done if I were being Madeleine Albright instead of being in this enormous entourage and said, 'Let's move the chairs around, let's do this differently.'"[2] In other words, the media layout was more significant than the substance of the conversation.

Observations such as these tended to reinforce the views of critics who said that Albright was more interested in sound bites than in substance, more attuned to the delivery of the message than to its content. But in the case of the Palestinians, the problem was deeper than that. Albright has never understood—or never showed that she understood—the depth of Palestinian despair, the rage born of years of weakness and unfulfilled aspirations. The same woman who would kneel in the dust to show her empathy with Afghan refugee women, the same woman who tenderly cradled a Ugandan baby conceived in rape, never exhibited the same human concern for the Palestinians. It is possible to be vigorous in support of Israel and sympathetic to the plight of the Palestinians at the same time; indeed, that is the stance adopted by many Israelis and their supporters in America, who believe Israel will never be secure if its neighbors are angry and resentful. Albright said that she accepted this premise, but I never saw her display to the Palestinians the kind of grandmotherly understanding that has been one of her most appealing traits.

When she was interviewed by high school students in Vancouver, Washington, a year later, she told them, "I have learned a genuine understanding of the difficult life of the Palestinian people. What makes me very sad is that I've gone into the West Bank and Gaza and seen how the Palestinians live, and I tell the Israelis it can't be good to have that disparity."[3] Even if she believes that her sanitized, security-escorted encounters with selected Palestinians have given her a genuine understanding of their plight, she has not conveyed that to the ordinary citizens of the West Bank and Gaza.

In October 1998, more than a year after that encounter with the students in Ramallah, the Arab American Institute in Washington arranged a conference call between Albright and prominent Arab Americans. According to James Zogby, president of the institute, the participants tried to get Albright to understand her own failure to connect with the Palestinians. Working out a compromise technical agreement with Israel over a few square kilometers was not the issue, they said; the issue was the desire and hope of the Palestinians to lead the lives of normal citizens of a country, free from the threat that Israel would bulldoze their houses or arrest their parents or rough them up at checkpoints. These were the ambitions the Palestinians thought would be fulfilled through implementation of the Oslo agreements; their despair was compounded by the fact that their hopes had been raised, then dashed—and the fact that their economic situation was deteriorating, while Israel was prospering. For the same reasons, disillusionment and cynicism about the United States were growing throughout the Arab world—a fact that Zogby said Albright simply did not grasp.

"I believe she has grown, and she's serious when she says she has learned a lot," Zogby said. "But we're only at the beginning of the learning curve, just at a time when we're coming to a crunch on policy. I told the secretary that she has to hold out to the Palestinians the possibility of a better future, the possibility that their aspirations may be realized." The institute issued a statement after the conference call that said:

> The Israeli Prime Minister has sucked the life and hope out of the peace process, offering the Palestinians only a compromise of a compromise of a compromise of a compromise. With the United States failing to provide any significant leadership, Palestinians have been left powerless and at risk without any leverage in an increasingly unfair and distorted process.[4]

Hillary Rodham Clinton seemed to understand exactly what the Arab Americans were talking about. She caused a sensation in the Arab world by saying publicly that the Palestinians would eventually have to have their own independent state:

> I think that it will be in the long-term interests of the Middle East for Palestine to be a state, and for it to be a state that is responsible for its citi-

zens' well-being, a state that has responsibility for providing education and health care and economic opportunity to its citizens, a state that has to accept the responsibility of governing. I think that is very important for the Palestinian people, but I also think it is very important for the broader goal of peace in the Middle East.[5]

The following summer, Mrs. Clinton, running for the Senate in New York, found her endorsement of Palestinian aspirations inconvenient and backed off from it. Albright, who had no political aspirations, was not similarly constrained. As secretary of state, she could not come out directly for Palestinian statehood. But she could have done more than lecture young Palestinians about the evils of terrorism; she could have said something to show she understood the accumulated grievances of thirty years of occupation. At a minimum, she could have traveled the few miles from Jerusalem to Ramallah by the main road, instead of allowing herself to be diverted onto the security bypass highway that Israel built to insulate Jewish settlers in the West Bank from their Palestinian neighbors. Not knowing the terrain, Albright needed a geography lesson.

On the main road from Jerusalem to Ramallah, the Jewish and Arab communities blend almost seamlessly a few miles north of the Old City. Arab shops and restaurants suddenly appear alongside Jewish establishments; then the landscape becomes entirely Arab, the streets thronged with Palestinians. Simply looking out the window of a car, one can see the daily life of poor but proud people struggling to make their way in a world where others control their destiny.

Albright did not travel to Ramallah by that road. She traveled by a roundabout security road, which skirts the Arab towns and passes through Jewish settlements that now stretch to the horizon as Israel has expanded into the West Bank. Vice President Gore took the same route during his 1998 visit—a route essentially dictated by Israeli security forces. Following the bypass road had the effect of insulating the American officials from contact—even eye contact—with any Palestinians other than those in their official scheduled meetings. As for the poverty and squalor of the Gaza Strip, the other Palestinian population center at the other end of Israel, senior American officials have rarely encountered it; conducting their business mostly at a border checkpoint, Albright and others have rarely gone into the mean streets where people actually live. The result is what Zogby calls an "asymmetry of compassion" in American policy toward Israelis and Arabs.

After delivering her message to Israel and the Palestinians, Albright flew to Damascus, Syria, to meet the famously cautious President Hafez al-Assad, the same man who had commanded endless hours of Warren Christopher's time without ever committing himself to the hard decisions that could bring peace with Israel.

As expected, Assad restated Syria's negotiating position. He was willing to resume peace talks with Israel, but only from the point to which they had advanced under Yitzhak Rabin and his successor, Shimon Peres, which basically meant only with the understanding that Israel would return all of the Golan Heights to Syria. Netanyahu had rejected that arrangement, seeking instead to negotiate more or less from scratch and find some accommodation that would retain Israeli security control of the Golan.

In Damascus, Albright ran head-on into entrenched positions, deep-seated fears, and ancient resentments that could not be neutralized by her style of diplomacy, or perhaps by any other style. She learned a lesson that American secretaries of state have been learning for a generation: The United States can change the balance in the region or move the ball down the field of peace only after some dramatic event beyond Washington's control alters the landscape. Washington can seize upon events to manipulate the players, but it can rarely initiate developments.

It was, for example, the unexpected death at age fifty-two of Egypt's Gamal Abdel Nasser and the ensuing war of 1973 that made it possible for Henry Kissinger to achieve the first direct Arab-Israeli negotiations and the postwar disengagement agreements. Anwar Sadat's 1977 visit to Jerusalem, which caught Washington flatfooted, made it possible for Jimmy Carter to bring the Egyptian and Israeli leaders to Camp David and negotiate their peace treaty. The secret negotiations between Israel and the Palestine Liberation Organization in Oslo, which had their genesis in a peace initiative by George Bush but went on for months without Washington's knowledge, made it possible for Clinton to induce Rabin and Arafat to shake hands on the White House lawn.

At the time of Albright's trip in September 1997, the rule-changing event that controlled the negotiating landscape was

Netanyahu's election the year before. Nothing that had occurred during her tenure as secretary of state broke through the lines established by that event, so she encountered confrontation, not compromise. Israel wanted to bottle up the Palestinians in as little of the West Bank as they could be coaxed or bludgeoned into accepting and to cement perpetual Jewish control over Jerusalem and its suburbs. The Palestinians, weak but not vanquished, were desperately trying to prevent such outcomes and get back on the path to an independent state that would free them from rule by the despised Jews. Similarly, on the Syrian front, nothing was happening. Assad was firmly in control, Israel was no longer amenable to giving up the Golan, and the stalemate in Lebanon was unbroken.

Under those circumstances, Albright had little leverage, other than the force of her personality and her status as a representative of the United States, to induce the parties to make decisions they were not ready to make. She let her exasperation show at a meeting with us before she left Israel for Syria. "We are at a point where hard decisions have to be made by the leaders," she said. "I will come back here whenever the leaders have made hard decisions, but I am not going to come back here to tread water."

Message to Israel and the Palestinians: Get serious, and I will be ready to help you over the bumps in the road. Message to Americans: I am not Warren Christopher, and you won't see me out here twenty times trying to squeeze out incremental gains.

She did obtain an agreement for Israel and the Palestinians to resume midlevel negotiations about implementation of Oslo, which at the time was no small accomplishment. "Madeleine Albright has started to make a difference," Egyptian foreign minister Amre Moussa said during a visit to Washington two weeks later. "She created new hope that the United States would be serious about many things."[6]

Hanan Ashrawi, one of the most articulate politicians in the Arab world, was less generous when she was in Washington not long after Moussa. Nice words, she said of Albright, but what had really changed? Unless the United States shored up the Arab commitment to peace by declaring its support for an independent Palestinian state, the rest was welcome but inconsequential. "The photo ops were okay," Ashrawi said, "but there are serious substantive issues" that in her view would not be addressed until Washington summoned the political will to put more pressure on Israel.[7]

At the time of Ashrawi's visit, Netanyahu and Arafat suddenly resumed direct meetings for the first time in months, but not because of anything Albright had done. Israeli intelligence agents carrying Canadian passports botched an attempt to assassinate a prominent leader of the Hamas terrorist organization in Amman, Jordan, infuriating King Hussein to the extent that peace between Israel and its best friend in the Arab world was jeopardized. To placate Hussein and the Palestinians, Israel released from prison Sheikh Ahmad Yassin, the leader of Hamas, who was turned over to King Hussein (not to Arafat) and allowed to return to Gaza a hero.

Faced with the prospect that Hamas, energized by this event and by collective Palestinian disillusionment with the peace process, might supplant Arafat and his team as the political leadership of the Palestinians, Israel had no choice but to reopen talks with Arafat, much the lesser of two evils.

Once again an event not of Washington's making altered the Middle East negotiating landscape. Whether the new talks would overcome the bitterness that had overtaken the region remained an open question. For Albright, there seemed to be no point in dwelling upon it. She had done what she could, and as she said during the trip home, she had other urgent matters to worry about. "If I can make a difference, I will be there," she said. "If there is not enough happening for me to make a difference, I'm going to concentrate on Cambodia or our [upcoming] summit with the Chinese, or on Bosnia, certainly NATO expansion and meeting with the Russians in New York. . . . The United States's responsibilities are so large, I can't be occupied with this full time."

For the next year and a half, Netanyahu and Arafat were never in the same room together. Far from sitting down to serious negotiations over the crucial "final status" issues, the two sides retreated into snarling stalemate. The annual economic conferences that had been envisioned as pathways to regional harmony ceased; the one in Qatar that Albright attended on her way to South Asia had been the last. Anti-Semitic commentary increased in the Arab press; nasty columns lumped together Albright, defense secretary William Cohen, Middle East coordinator Dennis Ross, and Martin Indyk, the assistant secretary of state for Near Eastern affairs, into some imagined Zionist cabal. For Albright and Ross, this was a period of damage control. Their mission was to keep the lid on, to keep either side from doing something irretrievable that would provoke new violence, to create an illusion of progress, however incremental, that would somehow hold things together until the political landscape changed again. Nobody wanted an outright repudiation of Oslo.

Arafat had accepted an American proposal for breaking the impasse, never made public but well publicized because of press leaks in Israel, that called for Israel to return another 13 percent of the West Bank to Palestinian control in exchange for demonstrable and effective Palestinian efforts to stop terrorism. Albright's objective was to cajole or browbeat Netanyahu into going along. Even if this deal was done, it would be only an interim step; it fell well short of resolving the "final status" issues. Albright recognized, however, that there was no prospect of opening serious "final status" talks without first achieving the interim step proposed by Washington because mistrust between the two sides had completely overtaken the optimism that prevailed at the time of Oslo.

Albright thought she saw a window of opportunity at the annual meeting of the United Nations General Assembly in New York in September 1998. That event brings into proximity leaders of many countries who would not otherwise talk to each other or be welcome in the United States; Netanyahu and Arafat would both be there.

"We had been pushing, pushing, something had to happen to add some new dynamic to it," Albright told me. "In the back of my mind, at the end of August, I knew both of these guys were going to be there at the same time. I thought it would be an opportunity to see if we could mix up the process and if there were any chance of having a trilateral."

She met Arafat and Netanyahu separately and secretly, asking each if he was willing to meet the other. "I didn't want any publicity before it happened because I wasn't sure it was going to happen. I was trying to figure out how it could happen without everybody knowing about it," she said.[8]

It was close to midnight when the two men arrived separately at her suite in the Waldorf-Astoria Hotel. Albright greeted them, then left them together, with no one else in the room except the State Department's Arabic interpreter. When she returned after forty-five minutes, she had to make a snap judgment: Were they sufficiently interested in getting negotiations back on track to justify inviting them to Washington to meet with Clinton? She gambled that they were.

That invitation began a month of white-knuckle diplomacy, one side or the other repeatedly threatening to walk out, in which the amount of time and effort expended by Clinton and Albright seemed disproportionate to the tiny stakes on the ground in the Middle East. Technically, the negotiations were about a sliver of land on the West Bank, the airport and an industrial park that the Palestinians wanted to open in Gaza, and the arrest of a modest number of Palestinian extremists. In reality, Albright understood that unless the deal got done, the outcome could be the unraveling of the entire Oslo process, a resurgence of violence and Arab hostility to Israel, and the possible evaporation of Israel's hope for a peaceful future. Only seven months remained until May 4, 1999, the deadline set by Oslo for completion of the "final status" negotiations; everyone recognized that the deadline would now be impossible to meet, but to walk away from it without at least the appearance of a good-faith effort was to invite a new cycle of despair, extremism, and violence. This was the argument Albright pressed upon Netanyahu again and again; since Arafat had already agreed to the 13 percent deal, the task was to put pressure on the arrogant, pugnacious Netanyahu without breaching the tradition of American support for Israel.

Clinton was prepared to summon Arafat and Netanyahu to the United States one more time for an extended trilateral summit meeting to get the deal done, but only if Albright calculated that there was a reasonable possibility of success. To gauge the prospects, she went back to the region in mid-October. On the plane, I reminded her of the two reasons a secretary of state supposedly goes to the Middle East and asked her which applied here. "I guess you can say there is a third reason," she responded with a grin. "What I'm going to work on is so that we can close the deal, so it's 'The preclose 2-A.'"

There was big news on that trip: Arafat spontaneously invited Netanyahu to lunch, and Netanyahu accepted. The occasion for this was Albright's meeting with the two men at a border crossing point where Israel adjoins the Gaza Strip. We, the traveling reporters, were killing time, standing around in the sunshine and chatting with friends in the local press corps, when we became aware of a wave of excitement among local Palestinian officials and Palestinian reporters: Netanyahu was going inside the Gaza Strip for lunch!

This wasn't exactly like Nixon going to China, but in the context of that time it was a breakthrough. For Arafat, the invitation was a reaffirmation of his stated commitment to peace. For Netanyahu, who had criticized Rabin for shaking Arafat's hand, acceptance was an important symbolic gesture. By traveling the short distance to the guest house where lunch was served, he for the first time entered territory under Palestinian control, and Arafat showed his appreciation by giving him a box of cigars.

Albright, who with that meeting brought the two men together for the third time in two weeks after more than a year in which they had had no contact, was delighted. "I don't want to overstate my optimism," she said. "But I would like to say one more time that I had a sense after the meetings here that there really is a new spirit of cooperation and a sense of urgency and a desire to move forward. On the other hand, I wasn't born yesterday."[9] A few weeks later, Albright told me:

Something serendipitous happened at Gaza. They were meeting, and sometimes meetings take a long time. Netanyahu said, "Should I bring in sandwiches for lunch?" And Arafat said, "Well, no. I've invited the secretary to have lunch with us, do you want to join us?" And Netanyahu said yes. And I know very well that if we'd planned that weeks in advance, there would have been all kinds of security questions and, you know, all kinds of second guessing about whether the Israeli prime minister should be in Gaza.

Did she mean it just fell into place on the spot, she had no idea going in what the outcome would be?

"That's exactly right," she said.[10]

Through persistence, calibrated public statements, and behind-the-scenes pressure, and with well-timed intervention by President Clinton, Albright had staved off the complete collapse of the Oslo process, which had seemed not only possible but likely a year earlier. The two sides were talking again, and reaching specific—though quite limited—agreements. The most they were aiming for was a partial implementation of Oslo. No one, and certainly not Albright, was talking anymore about a comprehensive regional peace that would include Syria and end the Arab-Israeli conflict once and for all. Her objective was to achieve modest progress, the illusion of progress on more complicated matters, and the hope of further progress down the road, with the aim of keeping the lid on until some future, unspecified event or combination of events might make the larger agreement possible once again.

Moreover, Albright had salvaged something of the peace process by putting considerable pressure on Netanyahu without abandoning the fundamental American relationship with Israel. The ultimatum she issued to Netanyahu at one point, when she threatened that the United States would abandon its mediating role if Israel did not assent to the 13 percent plan, angered some prominent Jewish leaders in the United States and contributed to the tension and criticism of Albright's difficult spring in 1998. But that turned out to be a momentary setback in a year-long process in which Netanyahu ultimately accepted what he had pledged never to accept: the return of much of the West Bank to Arab control. He may have had little choice, given the strong sentiment in favor of Oslo among the Israeli public and American Jews, but his decision was denounced by Israeli hard-liners as an abandonment of their dream of "Greater Israel" and contributed to his political downfall in 1999. With Clinton's encouragement, Albright put Netanyahu between a rock and a hard place, and squeezed him there.

Albright's report of a "new spirit" at the Gaza meeting led Clinton to invite Arafat and Netanyahu to an extended meeting at the secluded Wye River Conference Center on the eastern shore of the Chesapeake Bay. The objective was to finalize the 13 percent deal. Israel would agree to evacuate that much more of the West Bank in exchange for demonstrable and effective Palestinian cooperation in combating terrorism—that is, the two sides would accept and agree to implement the American-drafted plan that Arafat had accepted and Netanyahu had rejected months earlier.

It took nine days of brinkmanship and high drama, the most sustained and extended diplomatic effort of Clinton's tenure. Both sides threatened to walk out, and at one point the Israelis actually packed their bags and called for transportation to the airport. A new terrorist attack in Israel almost terminated the conference. Tempers flared as the exhausted participants haggled late into each night. It was 2:30 A.M., a week into the session, when Albright called Netanyahu to say that the Palestinians had moved as far as possible and it was up to him to say yes. "We want to get your comments by morning, and if you don't think this does it, we don't know what else we can do," she said.[11] Even then, Clinton had to call in reinforcements in the person of King Hussein, near death from cancer, gaunt and bald from his chemotherapy treatments, but holder of the moral high ground and respected by all sides. The king's passionate appeal to the Israelis and Palestinians not to squander this opportunity spurred them to close the deal.

At the White House signing ceremony on October 23, 1998, Sandy Berger went out of his way to give credit to Albright:

> I think it is important to remember that the person who launched this initiative, this American initiative, for breaking the logjam was Secretary of State Madeleine Albright eighteen months ago. She has been the engine that has kept this process going forward not just in the ups and downs of the last nine days, but the ups and downs of the last eighteen months. And she has brought to this a steel backbone, a steel-trap mind and an absolute determination that this will go forward. This is a very tough person to say no to.[12]

As part of the Wye agreement, Clinton promised to visit the Middle East in December 1998, in particular Gaza, where he would preside over a meeting at which the Palestinians would repudiate the sections of their national charter that called for the elimination of Israel. Although overshadowed by Clinton's difficulties at home, where impeachment proceedings loomed in the House of Representatives, that presidential visit represented a watershed in the history of relations between the United States and Israel and in the role of the United States in the region.

More than any other president, Clinton stepped back from the American image of Israel as a plucky little country surrounded by powerful enemies. Without in any way retreating from the long-standing policy of support for Israel's security, the president recognized that the roster of victimized people in the Middle East today must include the Palestinians, and he understood, as his wife did, that only by alleviating Palestinian grievances can Israel and the region achieve permanent peace.

"For the first time in the history of the Palestinian movement, the Palestinian people and their elected representatives now have a chance to determine their own destiny on their own land," the president said. "I am proud to be the first American president to stand with the Palestinian people here as you shape your future." To cheers and applause, the president recalled the generations of Palestinians who had known only "dislocation and despair"; he spoke of olive trees and the Palestinians' attachment to their land. "America wants you to succeed," he said.

Those words of empathy from an American president exhilarated the Palestinians and contributed to a political crisis in Israel; a month after the president spoke, Netanyahu—facing an irreconcilable split at a crucial moment in Israeli history between those who wanted to keep the West Bank and those who understood that if the Palestinians remained a subjugated people, Israel would never know peace—was forced to call early elections.

Clinton did what Albright has never done: He told the Palestinians, to their face and in their land, that the United States understood their grievances and their aspirations. Had Albright given the students in Ramallah half the empathy Clinton delivered fifteen months later, she would have stronger credentials as a leader of compassion.

As Berger noted during the signing of the Wye agreement, Albright had worked doggedly to break the impasse between Israel and the Palestinians that she had encountered on that first visit. In particular, she made it her business to work with Arafat, calming him down during his outbursts of frustration and persuading him to accommodate Israel's concerns about security. Still, Albright seems never to have responded as emotionally to the Palestinians as she did to other victims of history, such as the kidnapped children of northern Uganda.

That is not to say that she caved in to Netanyahu—far from it. It was relentless pressure from Albright and Clinton that forced Netanyahu to abandon his party's commitment to retaining the entire territory of Judea and Samaria. In retrospect, it can be seen that the tactics Albright and Clinton followed throughout 1998—mollifying Arafat while squeezing Netanyahu into taking incremental steps toward the implementation of Oslo—staved off a complete collapse of the negotiating process just long enough for another balance-changing event to occur.

Netanyahu scheduled the election for May 17, 1999. Arafat, frustrated by Israel's refusal to carry out most of its Wye commitments, had been threatening to issue a unilateral declaration of statehood on May 4, the date originally set at Oslo for completion of the permanent status negotiations. Those negotiations had never really begun, let alone addressed the issues in a serious way; but if Arafat declared Palestinian statehood over the land he controlled and sought international recognition, Netanyahu made it clear that Israel would respond forcefully, perhaps by annexing the West Bank and putting an end to Palestinian aspirations forever. When Israel's internal political turmoil forced Netanyahu to call early elections, the possibility that he would lose gave Clinton and Albright leverage to persuade Arafat not to do anything irreversible.

With Arafat wisely staying his hand, Netanyahu was resoundingly repudiated by the Israeli electorate; his successor, Ehud Barak, immediately promised to resume the negotiations Netanyahu had repudiated. The atmosphere in the region was transformed almost overnight.

Once again, an unexpected event over which Washington had no control had shifted the sands of the Middle East. With Netanyahu's departure, not just from the prime ministership but from Parliament, the unhappy details of the negotiations of the two previous years receded in importance. It no longer mattered whether Albright had actually delivered an ultimatum to Netanyahu, or whether she had failed to back it up. What mattered was that she had breathed enough life into the peace process to give Barak something to build on. When she returned to the region on a temperature-taking trip in September 1999, after Barak's election and the resumption of negotiations between Israel and the Palestinians, she could not guess the outcome but she could travel with the satisfaction of knowing that her efforts had helped make further progress possible.

Chapter 7

WE DID NOT
BLOW IT

MADELEINE ALBRIGHT BECAME secretary of state at a time
when the job, the world, and diplomacy itself were changing.
In President Clinton's first term, it became apparent that the
post–Cold War world was more confusing and in some ways more violent than it had been during the half century when the struggle
against communism had guided all thinking. In the words of
Monteagle Stearns, a career diplomat and former U.S. ambassador
to Greece, "the loss of an enemy can be as disorienting as the loss of
a friend. The collapse of communism has revealed a world that existed virtually unseen while the attention of Americans was riveted
on the superpower confrontation."[1]

In Clinton's first term, the war in Bosnia, the genocide in Rwanda,
and the Russian bombardment of Chechnya exposed the paralyzing
difficulty of setting a coherent policy for responding to unantici-
pated events and building the domestic and international support
required to carry it out. Washington's inability to formulate any focused response to the 1997 uprising that swept away the regime of
Mobutu Sese Seko in Zaire resulted largely from the lack of a Cold
War prism through which the events could be viewed.

As the threat of nuclear extinction diminished, the relative significance of other threats—terrorism, international crime, degradation
of the environment—increased, without clear guidelines or tested
procedures for responding to them. In the absence of the threat
from the Soviet Union, issues that would once have been sec-

ondary—the environment, air traffic rights, sweatshop labor, peace-keeping, the building of ad hoc coalitions for specific situations—took on correspondingly greater importance. The supersonic bombers, mechanized divisions, and nuclear submarines that had defined power and protected the United States and its allies from the Soviet threat were essentially irrelevant to the problems of Haitian poverty, African instability, or Balkan hatreds. As analyzed by John Ruggie of Columbia University:

> The core problem American leaders faced in 1919 and 1945 once again has become pressing: devising a coherent rationale to ensure continuous and active international engagement by the United States in support of a stable international order. *A la carte* interest calculations are unlikely to suffice, as Kissinger now agrees. But what are the grander alternatives? Fear of a Russia gone mad? Threats posed by rogue states? The clash of civilizations? The doctrine of enlargement? Jobs, jobs, jobs? No overarching framework equivalent to the Cold War is likely to reappear in the foreseeable future . . . and attempts to define one in the abstract are destined to prove futile.[2]

Albright has straight-ahead instincts, but many of the issues she has had to deal with in this newly complicated world do not lend themselves to straight-ahead responses, a dichotomy with which she has struggled throughout her tenure.

The primal struggle in the world today, in Albright's view, "is a confrontation not so much of armies as of values and emotions; of reason versus hate; of faith versus fear. It is not as much a clash between cultures and civilizations, it is a clash between civilization itself and anarchy, between the rule of law and no rules at all."[3] Albright is unabashed in believing that the task of American diplomacy is to advance civilization and American-style rule of law, coaxing along those who have yet to adopt democratic values and isolating the forces of anarchy and repression. "The challenges we face, compared to those confronted by previous generations, are harder to categorize, more diverse, and quicker to change," she observed in a *Foreign Affairs* article summarizing her view of the world after nearly two years on the job.[4]

In a speech she delivered at about the same time she was writing the *Foreign Affairs* piece, Albright said, "We're learning, as former

Secretary of State Dean Acheson once said, that 'The problems of American foreign policy are not like headaches, when you take a powder and they're gone. We've got to understand that all our lives the danger, the uncertainty, the need for alertness, for effort and for discipline will be upon us.'"[5]

Sandy Berger, whose job it was to sort out the varying views of all executive branch departments involved in foreign policy decision-making—not just State but Defense, Energy, Treasury, Commerce, Justice, and others—summarized the difficulty he faced in any given crisis:

> While we have been freed from the compulsions of containment, we have inherited a more demanding task, particularly in a world where conflict instantly is thrust upon a global stage. We must balance interest and risk, achievability and cost, clarity of mission and support from others in what ultimately is an exercise in prudent judgment. We can't be everywhere and shouldn't do everything. But we must be prepared to engage when important interests and values are at stake and we can make a difference.[6]

In practice, these are subjective standards, open to evaluation, interpretation, and differing outcomes—and applied in a political landscape in which, as one study put it, "Many leftists' conviction that the U.S. is not morally fit to lead in the world combines with some neoconservatives' tendency to believe that the world is not worthy of American efforts."[7]

In deciding what to do about Iraq, for example, the Clinton administration had to take into account not only the interests of Kuwait and Saudi Arabia, which wanted protection from Saddam Hussein, but also the interests of Russia and Turkey. Russia, destitute, wanted Iraq restored to commercial viability so it could repay billions of dollars owed to Moscow for armaments. Turkey, battling Kurdish separatists encamped at bases in northern Iraq, wanted a strong central government in Baghdad that could reassert its control over the north—even if that government were run by Saddam Hussein. At the same time, the administration wanted Turkey's cooperation in the expansion of NATO and in efforts to end the division of Cyprus. These objectives require cooperation with the Turkish armed forces, but the Turkish military is a perennial target of civil rights groups that object to the army's treatment of Turkey's Kurdish minority.

Similarly, as the administration tried to line up NATO allies in support of a bombing campaign to halt Serb repression in the separatist province of Kosovo, Washington encountered resistance from Italy and other members of the alliance that did not favor military action and so insisted on obtaining specific authorization from the U.N. Security Council. The United States did not want to take the issue to the Security Council because Russia would have vetoed a resolution authorizing the use of force. In addition, the United States did not want to validate the principle that the Security Council held an effective veto over NATO decisions, a position that Congress would never accept. These considerations prevailed over equally valid competing arguments: for example, that the United Nations should not be bypassed because it remains the most useful forum for resolving international disputes; and that circumventing the Security Council would undermine relations with Russia, which values the leverage that goes with its veto power.

For months, Albright and her colleagues took criticism from members of Congress, human rights groups, and newspaper editorialists as Serb troops wiped out villages in Kosovo; but responding to the violence required first resolving these overlapping and difficult considerations. In the end, Albright was gratified that it took her only four months to assemble a credible threat of NATO military action—not four years, as in Bosnia.

At the same time, in shaping relations with Pakistan after that South Asian country defied U.S. warnings and tested nuclear weapons, the administration had to factor in the value of Pakistan's cooperation with American efforts to isolate and capture terrorists and end the conflict in Afghanistan—cooperation Washington did not want to cut off. When Angolan rebel leader Jonas Savimbi scuppered a carefully crafted peace agreement and went back to the bush to resume the civil war in his country, his decision had the potential to destabilize much of Africa and threatened once again to truncate economic development throughout the region. What should the United States do, if anything? Savimbi had been a useful ally during the Cold War, when he fought against an Angolan government backed by the Soviet Union and Cuba. But in Washington now it is no longer useful or even possible to evaluate foreign policy decisions through the disciplinary optic of the Cold War. In these and dozens of other examples, Albright together with the administration's defense and national security policymakers faced a world of growing complexity and murkiness, where the arguments for or against any particular decision seemed always to multiply.

In the case of Angola, for example, the administration decided in the summer of 1999 that the civil war, raging again after a decade of diplomatic efforts to stop it, was simply not ripe for a new effort, and decided to do nothing. This was perfectly reasonable; but given the administration's repeated pronouncements about peace, democracy, and the value of innocent lives, a decision to redouble peacemaking efforts would have been equally rational.

The competing concerns that complicate decisionmaking are compounded by conditions at American embassies in the field, which have become steadily more difficult for a secretary of state to control because so many other government agencies are represented there. In some embassies, a majority of the U.S. government employees are not foreign service officers; they represent the FBI, the CIA, the Drug Enforcement Administration, the Treasury and Agriculture Departments, and other agencies that have interests abroad. These people do not work for the secretary of state. Even though all embassy personnel are theoretically under the supervision of the ambassador, the State Department and the ambassador have only limited say in the agendas—and no control over the paths to promotion—of these employees from other agencies. Melding embassy personnel into a cooperative team requires trade-offs just as does policymaking back in Washington, where other departments often have more effective advocates than State.

According to no less a personage than George Kennan, the venerable sage of foreign policy widely credited with forging the U.S. strategy of containing Soviet communism after World War II:

> It has gradually been borne in upon everyone familiar with the foreign affairs process that of all the government departments and agencies in Washington, the State Department has the least developed domestic political constituency—a situation that leaves it largely helpless in relations with the rest of the official community. . . . Not only has the State Department been largely deprived of its traditional role as the spokesman for and coordinator of foreign policy, but hundreds of other areas of in-

ternational relations have been abandoned to the desires and whims of the numerous forces on the Washington scene.[8]

Kennan commands respect, but this is overstated, to say the least. No one should think that a State Department under the leadership of Henry Kissinger, James Baker, or Madeleine Albright is "largely helpless" in asserting itself in policymaking. Still, Kennan's point— the proliferation of participants in foreign policy decisionmaking and the relatively low esteem of diplomats in the public perception—was reflected in Albright's effort to build a domestic constituency and increase her clout on Capitol Hill.

Furthermore, as Albright was to discover, the most daunting international crisis of Clinton's second term was one over which the secretary of state had no control and little influence. The economic meltdown that began in Thailand in 1997, spread across Asia and Russia, and threatened the stability of South America was a crisis of capital flows, unwise credit decisions, currency speculation, and investor confidence, all matters that landed in the in-box of the secretary of the treasury, not the secretary of state.

In Indonesia, for example, the State Department was virtually silent as economic collapse swept away the government of President Suharto, because the White House gave the lead to Robert Rubin's Treasury Department. Only when it was obvious to the world that President Suharto had to go before order could be restored did Albright call on him publicly to step down—and even then she used oblique language that ignored his record of dictatorship and corruption.

By late 1998, as hundreds of thousands of wretched Asians were snatched out of middle-class comfort and middle-class aspirations and thrust back into a subsistence economy, and as economic hardship threatened stability in Russia, serious analysts were questioning a fundamental tenet of the Clinton administration's global policy: the primacy of free markets and the unfettered flow of capital. For the first time since the Great Depression of the 1930s, the overriding issue in global affairs was economic rather than strategic.

Of course, in Clinton's view, economic and strategic were in many ways the same thing. Throughout his presidency, Clinton energetically advocated free trade, open markets, and unfettered flows of money and ideas as the keys to a more stable and prosperous world.

The informal slogan of his 1992 campaign—"It's the economy, stupid"—might have been applied to his worldview as well. That is why, as Richard Melanson noted in his study of American foreign policy:

> As president he [Clinton] threw himself into the effort to win passage [of the North American Free Trade Agreement] with an intensity not evident in his handling of Bosnia, Somalia, or Haiti. Clinton's near obsession with "national competitiveness" accounts for his "lifelong learning" investments, his creation of a national economic council, his tireless promotion of American exporters, and his elevation of the Commerce Department to a foreign policy stature not seen since the 1920s. This administration equated economic policy with security policy to an almost unprecedented degree.[9]

That is also why American policy toward countries such as Poland, India, and South Africa is now determined at least in part by their designation as "big emerging markets"—a designation applied by the Commerce Department, not the State Department. Clinton's belief that open markets lead to open societies shaped his decision to establish diplomatic and commercial relations with Vietnam and prompted the controversial "decoupling" of human rights from trade relations with China. There is abundant testimony from senior officials who served during both of Clinton's terms that the president would have forged a similar economic opening to Cuba if it had been politically acceptable in Congress.

Thus it would be up to Albright not only to conduct American diplomacy but to redefine it. What is the purpose of diplomacy and how should it be practiced in an era of instantaneous round-the-clock communication? Inevitably, the globalization of the world's economy and President Clinton's emphasis on economic development have elevated the diplomatic profile of the Treasury Department at the expense of State, not just in the Asian crisis but in bailing out the Mexican peso, stabilizing the Brazilian and Russian economies, managing the U.S. response to the single European currency, and rewriting the rules for the International Monetary Fund (IMF). Some analysts went so far as to say that diplomacy as traditionally conducted by the State Department and envoys overseas no longer has much value at all—an argument that Albright indirectly validated by expanding the definition of diplomacy to take on issues far outside the traditional agenda, such as women's rights. In the contemporary world, the mission of diplomacy, of the secretary of state, is not to build an empire or subjugate colonies; it is not to forge balance-of-power alliances when there is no rival power to be balanced; it is not to protect commodity supply lines when all markets are global. No, in the new era, as seen from Washington in the administration of Bill Clinton, the purpose of diplomacy is at once broader and vaguer: the advancement and protection of American national interests, through the opening of markets; the establishment and protection of democracy and the rule of law; the defense of the homeland through overlapping security and arms-control agreements; and stewardship of the air, water, and earth to preserve the planet for future generations.

Unhappily for Clinton and Albright, by the middle of 1998, the economic meltdowns in Asia and Russia were threatening to undermine the most fundamental tenet of the administration's global policy—namely, that open markets inevitably lead to better living conditions and freer societies. This inescapable circumstance forced Albright to do two difficult things: Get engaged in the economic issue, and reevaluate the administration's relationship with Russia.

In the summer of 1998, what began as a purely economic crisis involving currency exchange rates, defaults on debt, and bank restructurings metastasized into a political crisis that threatened to undermine the administration's objectives on other fronts as well.

Albright recognized the daunting sweep of negative consequences that could flow from the economic meltdown. Hard-pressed factories in Asia might resort to child labor. Cash-strapped militaries might be tempted to export dangerous weapons. Fragile new democracies facing economic hardship could present opportunities to demagogues and advocates of state control. Consensus on environmental issues might vaporize under the pressure of economic desperation. Young people would be forced to drop out of school, forfeiting future earning power and possibly aligning with undesirable political movements. And in many societies, the first victims of the collapse of the middle class would be women, driven out of jobs and classrooms by the need to feed their children.

Clinton rejected State Department proposals for a major new program of direct economic assistance to Asia. His decision to have Treasury assume leadership of the American response to the financial crisis limited the State Department's public role to minor tasks such as arranging for Thai students to stay in the United States instead of returning home to a bleak future and enabling the Thai government to back out of a contract to buy American combat jets it could no longer afford.

Nevertheless, according to Stuart Eizenstat, Albright's low-key but influential undersecretary for economic affairs:

> We realized, fairly early on, that this crisis was not just a financial crisis, that it was a political crisis with several dimensions. Dimension number one, which has particularly attracted the secretary, is the social fallout from the financial crisis, the devastation which has been done in terms of unemployment, the drop in growth, bankruptcies, and the absence, the utter absence in most of these countries, of any modern social safety net. Unemployment insurance, job retraining, welfare benefits, food stamps, indeed to some extent these are all almost contrary to the sort of Asian ethic.[10]

The United States of course has no control, and limited influence, over the domestic social welfare policies of other countries. So what Eizenstat set out to do, with Albright's encouragement, was to join forces with the Treasury Department in attaching social welfare considerations to the economic aid packages being assembled by the IMF, the World Bank, and other international financial institutions (known in the trade as IFIs), and at the same time to provide individual countries with technical assistance to establish safety-net programs if they wished to or were compelled to by the IFIs.

"We must ensure," Albright wrote in her midterm policy review essay, "that international financial institutions operate and are seen to operate in ways that benefit broad segments of the world's population."[11]

Grafting social considerations onto the technocratic analyses of the IMF has been recommended by some analysts for more than twenty years. I first encountered the issue as a correspondent in Cairo in 1977, when overnight price increases on basic foodstuffs—dictated by the IMF—ignited destructive riots that threatened the government, which rescinded the increases a few days later. Now, according to Eizenstat and other officials, the Clinton administration was determined to reshape the balance of considerations before the president's second term expired. "We're working with the World Bank in developing sort of a social code," Eizenstat said. "Part of the emerging new [international economic] architecture will be a better integration of World Bank social programs with IMF austerity programs so they work more hand in glove, and encouraging where possible that austerity programs ought not to be at the expense of social investments."[12]

"A viable strategy must not only facilitate the adjustments of corporations and banks, but also should help families," said Alan Larson, assistant secretary of state for economic and business affairs. He continued:

> One of the tragedies we want to avoid in the current financial crises is to lose a whole generation of young people to economic hardship. I'm talking about students forced to drop out of school to assist their families; young entrepreneurs forced to abandon new businesses, many of which might import American inputs, because they cannot get credit. We cannot ignore the risk that large segments of a country's population may lose faith in economic reform and open markets if they lack the tools to secure the basic necessities of life. I can assure you that there is little support anywhere in the world for economic reform that only seems to bail out bankers and the well-connected.[13]

Some senior officials on Albright's staff also recognized that in many countries where democracy is new—including Russia—democratic government actually contributed to instability because their fragile institutions lacked the deep roots necessary to survive economic hard times. The most obvious example was Albania, where the fledgling institutions of a nascent democratic state collapsed after thousands of citizens lost their savings in pyramid schemes from which the government failed to protect them. Conversely, the shift from autocratic rule to democracy meant that the IMF could no longer simply dictate the economic path it wished a country to follow. The citizens of that country were entitled to be heard. According to Jeffrey E. Garten, a former Commerce Department official:

> It is now better understood that a successful stabilization and restructuring package cannot be forced down a country's throat. One of the endur-

ing images of a mistaken approach is likely to be the photo carried in major newspapers of the IMF's managing director, Michel Camdesus, arms defiantly crossed over his chest, standing over former Indonesian president Suharto as the latter reluctantly signed an IMF agreement that was soon to collapse.[14]

Of course, Indonesia under Suharto was no democracy; but the IMF was also dictating tough terms to South Korea and Russia, two vital countries whose citizens have only recently gained the right, and the expectation, to be heard.

Fearing that economic turmoil would undermine democracy in countries where democracy was new and untested, the administration selected eighteen such countries, including Russia and Brazil, and designated senior officials from State, Treasury, and the president's National Economic Council to consult regularly about developments in these countries in an effort to ensure that political and economic policies were coordinated. The administration did not want countries seeking debt relief, for example, to be able to play off State against Treasury; it did not want rigid economic reform prescriptions to inflict such hardship on the citizenry that they would be susceptible to antidemocratic or protectionist appeals.

Interagency meetings by definition are closed-door affairs; the press and public often are unaware that they are taking place until the outcomes are announced, often months or even years after an issue is first raised. That was the case with the economic crisis meetings, a fact that contributed to the widespread perception that Albright had no role in responding to the economic crisis.

In October 1998, I got a call from Jamie Rubin, who offered a rare invitation. Albright was going to the West Coast, to Silicon Valley in California and to Seattle, to talk to business executives and other groups about the Asian economic crisis. Normally the secretary does not take reporters on her plane for domestic trips, but this time one seat would be available if I wanted it. The purpose of the trip was to talk to, and hear from, Americans on the Pacific Rim—Americans whose livelihoods in the computer industry, shipping, agriculture, and finance depended on doing business with Asia—about the impact of the economic meltdown there. Albright wanted to show them that she understood the potential consequences of the economic turmoil in Asia and that she was involved in formulating constructive American responses. And she wanted me to witness her performance on the West Coast and write about it in the *Washington Post,* so that people back home would understand that she was not a mute figure or a bystander as the administration grappled with the Asian mess.

The only unusual thing about that trip was that Albright invited me. The secretary routinely conferred with business groups around the country and frequently invited bankers, economists, and business executives to dinner to discuss their concerns. Right from the beginning of her tenure, she made it a point to visit corporate offices and business groups on her travels, pledging to fight hard to open new markets abroad for their products and services and promising that embassies would vigorously represent American business interests overseas.

On the West Coast trip, she did not have to offer bold new solutions; what she had to do was demonstrate competence in understanding the situation and speaking credibly about it on behalf of the administration. A few weeks earlier, President Clinton had laid out a six-point prescription for global recovery that featured debt restructuring, the development of a social safety net for Asia's poor, and increased U.S. government support for private investment. Once Clinton had done that, Albright could speak openly within the margins he had established, without fear that she would inadvertently exacerbate the problem by saying the wrong thing.

Albright delivered public speeches in San Jose, Seattle, and Vancouver, Washington. She also met privately with business executives, bankers, and trade lawyers, with whom she was able to speak freely because her comments would remain within the conference rooms. I was permitted to sit in on one of the sessions, with the understanding that I would quote her directly only with her approval. Albright told the group that she shared their frustration at the Japanese government's inept response to that country's recession, and she admitted her anxiety about the discouraging signs emanating from the new government in Russia. On some detailed points involving currency markets and trade rules, she deferred to Al Larson, who specialized in such matters. But she certainly held her own in the conversation; if the participants found her ill grounded in the issues that mattered to them, they gave no sign of it.

Here is the beginning of the article I wrote in the *Washington Post* describing that trip:

> Helping Asian countries recover economically is not charity, it's enlightened self-interest because they will again be among the best customers for U.S. products when they get back on their feet.
>
> The "best international vehicle" for aiding that recovery is the International Monetary Fund, despite all the recent criticism.
>
> And even in hard economic times, "Protectionism is not the answer, for them or for us."
>
> Says who? Says Secretary of State Madeleine K. Albright, sounding almost like a secretary of commerce last week as she toured the Pacific Northwest and California's Silicon Valley with a "stay the course" message, promoting the Clinton administration's policy of free trade and unfettered flows of capital in a region hit hard by Asia's economic meltdown.

As I noted in that article, "The fundamental premise of the Clinton administration's global policy—that free markets and open societies lead to prosperity and stability—is under challenge, and she was out to defend it."[15]

During that trip, I asked Albright about her supposed lack of expertise on economic issues and on Asia, as she knew I would. She replied:

> Look. I have never pretended—you know, I was a Soviet expert, an expert on communist systems, and a professor of international relations, not an economist. But anybody who has watched and listened can see that I have integrated aspects into what I think are U.S. foreign policy goals and, as importantly, I think I've figured out a way to explain the connection to businesspeople and nonbusiness Americans. On the Asia thing, I have to say I've always thought that was a rather peculiar argument. I've now spent more time going to Asia, I think, than previous secretaries of state, an unbelievable amount. I have good relations with the Koreans and the Chinese and the Japanese. I understand the economic argument [about her lack of expertise] because my Ph.D. is in a different subject, but I've never understood the Asian one. Nobody ever mentions that I speak more languages than any other secretary of state ever.[16]

I was baffled by this last comment. Nobody was challenging her linguistic skills, and in any case it was irrelevant. She could speak twenty languages and still be an incompetent secretary of state, or ignorant of economics. Overall, however, she made the case, not just to me but to the public, that although she was not a specialist in economic matters, she was quite capable of understanding the issues and responding to them. She would never speak with the authority of Jim Baker, who had been secretary of the treasury before he was secretary of state, but she was not completely out of her depth, either. For her West Coast trip, her mission was accomplished. The unstated bargain of the trip had been carried out: She got an article in the *Washington Post* saying that she was on top of the economic case, and I got an extensive interview and other exclusive opportunities to see her in action.

Formulating a new policy in response to the turmoil in Russia was a different matter. Guided by Strobe Talbott, the administration had from the outset sought to promote a transition to democracy and capitalism in a country that had little experience in either. In practice, this policy came to mean a commitment to supporting Boris Yeltsin, no matter how much his compatriots turned against him and no matter how autocratic his conduct became. And it came to mean support for the radical economic reformers in Russia such as former first deputy prime minister Anatoly Chubais, even as their policies beggared the country and led to unspeakable hardships for millions of Russians.

From Washington's perspective, the choice at the beginning of the Clinton administration was clear: Yeltsin, reform, and the free market, nudging Russia into a place at the table of the industrialized democracies; or Yeltsin's rivals, including the communists, holding Russia back as a truculent, unpredictable rival to the United States, a rival still equipped with a powerful nuclear arsenal.

Those who argue that the Clinton administration has been characterized by murky objectives in foreign policy have no case when it comes to Russia. Warren Christopher stated the policy as forcefully as possible in one of the earliest speeches of his tenure, less than two months into Clinton's first term:

> These three pillars of American foreign policy—building America's prosperity, modernizing America's armed forces and promoting democratic

values—form the core of the Clinton administration's new diplomacy.
. . . These three pillars converge and form the basis for one of our highest
foreign policy priorities, and that is helping the Russian people to build a
free society and a market economy. This, in my judgment, is the greatest
strategic challenge of our time. Bringing Russia, one of history's most
powerful nations, into the family of peaceful nations will serve our highest
security, economic and moral interests.[17]

This speech reflected not just Christopher's own views but
President Clinton's deepest convictions. "Upon his election," Christopher wrote later in describing the context of his speech,

President Clinton decided that we should make an early, all-out effort to
engage Russia's reformers and support their efforts. Russian hard-liners,
most of them former members of the Soviet elite, were resisting market
reforms and posing a direct political threat to President Boris Yeltsin. Our
assessment was that America's national interest lay squarely in supporting
the process of reform—that this was a key payoff of the end of the Cold
War. Moreover, we were determined to avoid repeating the Bush
Administration's slow start; in 1989, its policy toward the then–Soviet
Union had become bogged down for months in a "strategic review," resulting in delays that produced early tensions with the Soviets. The
Russian economy was now in dire straits, and the president believed that it
needed and deserved our support without delay. He gave this support his
highest priority in the foreign policy field. . . . The president and I wanted
to stress that as long as reform moved in the direction of democracy, civil
liberties, and free markets, we would be there to help.[18]

It may be that the administration's aspirations for a post-Soviet,
postcommunist Russia were never realistic. As early as 1951, George
Kennan had said as much. "Perhaps the first thing to get straight
here," Kennan wrote, "is the sort of Russia there is no use looking
for. And such a Russia—the kind we may NOT look for—is easy to
describe and envisage, for it would be a capitalistic and liberal-
democratic one, with institutions closely resembling those of our
own republic."[19]
But that was a generation ago, when the dissolution of the Soviet
Union seemed inconceivable. Once that dissolution occurred, the
Clinton administration seemed to have little to lose and much to

gain by trying to shepherd Russia down the exact path Kennan had said it would never follow. As Richard Melanson noted, "For an administration routinely accused of foreign policy incoherence as it lurched from crisis to crisis in Bosnia, Somalia and Haiti, its approach to Russia appeared quite consistent and even sophisticated."[20]

What did Christopher's words and Clinton's commitment mean in practice?

First, it meant allegiance to Yeltsin personally. Clinton embraced him as the one Russian who could lead his country through the transition from communism and along the path of economic reform.

Through the brutality in Chechnya, through the bouts of drunkenness and illness, through Yeltsin's ham-handed abuse of his rivals, through his open opposition to U.S. policy in Iraq and his sale of nuclear equipment to Iran, Clinton, Talbott, and others stuck with the Russian president long after his own people had given up on him. "No truly democratic government would ever have dared impose on its citizens measures as harsh as those implemented by Yeltsin," Soviet-born Dimitri K. Simes wrote in a penetrating analysis of Washington's commitment to the erratic Russian leader. "Despite this, and after the predictable backlash, the administration endorsed Yeltsin's unconstitutional dissolution of the Congress of People's Deputies in 1993, his shelling of the Russian White House (where the parliament was located), and his virtual imposition of a new constitution granting the Russian president almost dictatorial powers." This policy, Simes said, amounted to supporting "economic reform over democracy, and . . . Yeltsin's personal fortunes over respect for Russia's constitution."[21]

Eventually Albright came to share Simes's opinion that the sufferings and aspirations of ordinary Russians had to be taken into account in the formulation of American policy. But even as she was revising her assessment of the situation in Russia and as conditions there continued to deteriorate, Yeltsin rewarded Clinton for his support by acceding to Washington's wishes on important issues. Yeltsin had basically decided after visiting a Houston supermarket in 1989 that communism was futile, and he no longer wanted it for Russia.[22] Clinton's embrace encouraged him in his commitment to dismantle the remnants of communist economics and communist thought in

Russia. Moreover, Yeltsin was capable of compartmentalizing his differences with Washington over issues such as NATO expansion and cooperating where it suited his interests—in policing the peace agreement in Bosnia, for example, and in nuclear arms control. At one point Albright went so far as to say that on strategic issues, "we are on the same side."[23]

In late January 1998, the Energy Department published a document with the uninspiring title "MPC&A Program Strategic Plan." The initials stood for "Material Protection, Control, and Accounting," the material in question being nuclear material and bomb components in the former Soviet Union. On the centerfold of the document was printed a remarkable full-color map showing every nuclear production, plutonium separation, and bomb testing site in the former Soviet Union, from the nuclear naval base at Vladivostok on the Pacific coast to the Khlopin Radium Institute in St. Petersburg.

During the Cold War, spies were shot for trying to obtain even small pieces of the information displayed on that map. But by early 1998, American scientists and security specialists were working at virtually every one of those sites to improve their security, account for radioactive material, and train technicians how to handle and secure material and equipment.

"We're in every site we know about and we think we know about every site," said Rose E. Gottemoeller, director of the Energy Department's Office of Nonproliferation and National Security, briefing reporters on the program. "We really have a shot at getting 650 metric tons [of Soviet plutonium] fully under control by 2002." Gottemoeller wrote the following in her introduction to the MPC&A document:

> This partnership for nuclear material security is built upon new confidence and trust that has evolved between the United States and the states of the former Soviet Union. Nuclear experts from these countries are now cooperating to adopt effective MPC&A methods and technologies, as well as to develop comprehensive and self-sustaining MPC&A programs consistent with international standards. Significant progress has been made since this historic cooperation began in 1993, first to build trust and confidence and later to install fully operational MPC&A systems to improve security. However, much work remains to be done.[24]

What this meant was that the United States and Russia, working together, were beginning to get a handle on the so-called loose nukes problem, the frightening prospect that the indiscipline produced by the breakup of the Soviet Union would enable rogue countries, individual terrorists, or common criminals to get their hands on nuclear explosives. Conceived at the end of the Bush administration and financed by Congress, the intimate nuclear security cooperation between Washington and Moscow represented one of the big payoffs of Clinton's decision to support Russia and stick with Yeltsin through good times and bad.

In every assessment of its global priorities, the Clinton administration put at or near the top its desire to limit the proliferation of what were collectively known as "weapons of mass destruction": nuclear, biological, and chemical weapons and the missiles or other means to deliver them. This was the imperative that led Albright to spend so much time and effort during her first spring in office persuading Congress to ratify the Chemical Weapons Convention. It was the principle that underlay the unpalatable but necessary bargain with North Korea, in which the Clinton administration agreed to help Pyongyang obtain nuclear power plants to produce electricity in exchange for the North Koreans' abandoning their efforts to separate plutonium and build nuclear weapons. It was the reason why Clinton, in the State of the Union address that may have saved his presidency after the Monica Lewinsky episode, called for new efforts to protect Americans from the threat of chemical and biological weapons. And it was of course the reason for the administration's determination to isolate and cripple Iraq, which had defied orders from the U.N. Security Council to abandon its efforts to develop nuclear and chemical weapons.

In addition to cooperation on arms control and nuclear safety, the administration sought to advance relations with Russia by helping the Russians restructure and modernize the everyday workings of their government, a task assigned to a binational commission chaired on the U.S. side by Vice President Al Gore and on the Russian by the prime minister, originally Viktor Chernomyrdin. Gore and members of Clinton's cabinet, working with their Russian counterparts, involved themselves in an amazing range of activities in Russia: health, education, transportation, agriculture, public safety, and more. The idea was to help Russia build the machinery of modern governance and efficient public services, in place of the vacuum left by the fall of communism and the breakup of the Soviet Union.

As the Russian economy continued to disintegrate through the summer of 1998 despite the infusion of billions of dollars from the IMF, it became progressively harder for the administration to carry on business as usual with Moscow. Russia was by then in political chaos as well as economic turmoil.

On July 17, two days after the IMF and the World Bank had put together a $22.6 billion package of soft-loan assistance for Russia, the State Department's Stephen R. Sestanovich offered the first public signal that the administration was reevaluating its stay-the-course Russia policy.

Sestanovich, a former analyst at the Carnegie Endowment for International Peace, held the title of ambassador-at-large for the newly independent states. (Albright planned to create a new regional bureau in the department for East European and Eurasian affairs, separate from the bureau that deals with Great Britain and Germany, and put Sestanovich in charge of it as assistant secretary of state, but Senators Jesse Helms and Joseph Biden of the Foreign Relations Committee objected, saying that the new bureau would only contribute to the isolation of Russia from the rest of Europe.) Sestanovich was part of the inner circle of the administration's policymakers on Russia, along with Albright and Talbott at State; Gore and his national security adviser, Leon Fuerth; Carlos Pascual, the senior Russia director at the National Security Council; and Lawrence Summers, first as deputy treasury secretary and then in the top job.

In an appearance before the House International Relations Committee, Sestanovich noted that Clinton was due to travel to Moscow at the end of August for a summit meeting with Yeltsin. That trip would take place, Sestanovich said, at a time of "increased uncertainty" about Russia's future. He elaborated:

> The financial crisis in particular has highlighted the structural weaknesses of Russia's economy and led to concern about the country's political stability as well. These developments raise understandable questions about American policy toward Russia. . . . They have obliged the administration and members of Congress to take a hard look at our policy and the assumptions that underlie it.

After summarizing the immense stakes in Russia—its nuclear weapons, its abundant resources, its potential to either stabilize or disrupt much of Europe—Sestanovich restated the administration's goals:

> First, reduce the threat to the United States and international peace posed by weapons of mass destruction; second, support Russia's transition to a market economy; third, work with Russia's new generation of democrats as they build a society in which human rights, including religious freedom, are protected; and fourth, ensure that Russia deals cooperatively with its neighbors and is integrated into Euro-Atlantic and global institutions.

These goals would not be attainable unless Russia wanted to attain them as well, Sestanovich said, and even then they would not be easy to achieve. But Sestanovich confirmed that the Clinton administration's commitment remained unshaken and that Washington would continue to work with the Russian leadership as it had done "when it supported the Russian reformers in their successful battle against inflation or, frankly, when it stood with them against a communist insurgence."

Although acknowledging that the administration's Russia policy was under strain, Sestanovich did not announce a shift; on the contrary, he reaffirmed White House policy, even as he recognized the increasing difficulty of carrying it out. Still, his words foreshadowed a turnabout that Clinton was to unveil and Albright was to proclaim just a few weeks later. The administration was beginning to realize that Russia was going backward economically and politically; the vision of Russia as a fledgling eighth member of the G-7, the group of seven leading industrialized nations, which Clinton had proclaimed at the Denver G-7 meeting just a year earlier, was vaporizing. Around Washington, cynics joked that the administration used to think that Russia was becoming Canada, but really it had just become "Chad with nukes."

As late as August 14, administration officials were still stressing the positive as they talked about the upcoming summit. White House spokesman Mike McCurry and others portrayed the economic implosion as one element of a complex relationship that was otherwise making good progress on issues such as ensuring the security of nuclear weapons materials and enforcing the peace agreement in Bosnia. "From the beginning of this administration, we have identified a healthy Russian economy as something that was in the long-term strategic interests of the United States," a senior White House official said in the early summer of 1998, when that objective still seemed at least remotely achievable. He continued:

> We thought Russia had a once in a thousand year opportunity to change its own destiny—and with it, ours. We didn't know what the outcome would be. That is how we think about managing the economic crisis, among things that aren't of Russia's own doing, such as the fall in oil prices. We are being driven by a practical perception of our priorities: Get them through this crisis. That is the big strategic issue for us.

But on August 17, the Russian government, headed by Sergei Kiriyenko, a thirty-six-year-old advocate of free-market economic reform, devalued the ruble and effectively defaulted on Russia's domestic debt. These decisions precipitated an economic free fall. Yeltsin fired Kiriyenko, leaving Russia without a government virtually on the eve of Clinton's visit. A restive Parliament rejected Yeltsin's attempt to bring back Chernomyrdin, dismissed earlier in the year, as prime minister.

At the same time, public opinion polls in Russia were painting a picture of disenchantment with the economic reforms that had plunged the country into ruin, and of anger at the United States, which was perceived as their chief sponsor. According to one private analysis, "fifty-two percent of Russia's young people think that Western assistance is provided in order to increase Russian dependence on the west, and 57 percent think that the demise of the Soviet Union was a bad development."[25]

But the White House was reading a different set of opinion samplings, showing that whereas Russians over the age of thirty-five were disenchanted because they remembered the days of guaranteed employment and secure pensions, those under thirty-five tended to be more entrepreneurial in their outlook, supportive of capitalist economic programs and less gripped by nostalgia for the Soviet era. Those polling data were as much on Clinton's mind as the grim economic indicators when he set out for Moscow, White House officials told me afterward.

On his first day in Moscow, September 1, Clinton offered reassurance and encouragement to an audience of mostly young Russians, telling them that with courage and hard work they could forge a bright future. "We wanted to solidify the younger crowd's sentiments, to tell them 'You can do it,' to encourage a younger generation more inclined to support the reform movement," a member of Clinton's staff said.

The next day, however, Clinton delivered a much sterner message to a gathering of opposition politicians, leaders of rival political parties, and fractious members of the communist-dominated Russian legislature. He told them not to treat the economic crisis with prescriptions from the past, such as restrictions on currency flows or increased state management of the economy. But he also stressed that the choice was Russia's. By making that statement, he signaled for the first time that the administration was prepared to distance itself from Russia and adopt a strategy of damage control.

"By mid-August, it had become pretty clear that Russia faced dramatic and unpleasant policy choices with no good options," one senior official told me. "There is a stage in every crisis where you have this moment. It becomes very perilous to give advice because the game is already up. Do you want your fingerprints on something that is going to become very messy?"

The talk around Washington began to change. The "Who lost Russia?" question was on the table. People recalled the old joke about the pet food company that invested heavily in developing and marketing a new dog food, only to see sales decline. For weeks the company sought an explanation as its market share eroded and customers shunned the product. The answer, somebody finally explained, was simple: "Dogs don't like it." In Russia, the "dogs" were the unpaid soldiers and civil servants, unemployed miners and factory workers, ordinary citizens, struggling to stay alive in a barter economy while a new class of "oligarchs," or fat cats, profited from an economic system that seemed to have a "Made in USA" label on it.

Albright was beginning to recognize the accuracy of a diagnosis offered by Kim R. Holmes of the Heritage Foundation, who generally speaks for the Reagan wing of the Republican party. "The central flaw of the Clinton Administration's Russia policy," Holmes wrote, "has been in assuming that backing President Yeltsin personally was the same thing as backing reform and democracy in principle and in practice." It was not that Russia had tried democracy and reform and found them wanting, Holmes wrote; it was that Yeltsin had pretended to try democracy and reform without serious commitment, with the result that the concepts were discredited while the benefits they might have brought to Russia were unsighted. "As a result, Russians equate reform and democracy not only with President Yeltsin personally, but with failure and misery."[26]

It was finally necessary to recognize that in a democratic Russia, the "dogs" vote, and their opinions must be taken into account. It was no longer possible for Washington to believe or hope that Yeltsin's cadre of young, westernized free marketeers would regain control; the reformers were out of the government. Yevgeny Primakov, a former communist and former foreign minister with a reputation for being pro-Iraq, became prime minister—"the worst possible man," according to former U.S. defense secretary Caspar Weinberger.[27] As his chief deputy, Primakov installed Yuri Maslyukov, the former head of the Soviet central economic planning agency and a living antithesis of free-market economics.

Yeltsin was still president, and still sufficiently functional to receive Clinton for the summit conference in early September, but there was no way to disguise the scope of the setback for American aspirations. In the reformers' place were former Soviet apparatchiks and social conservatives who, although not trying to return to the communist system, were willing to consider currency controls, more government intervention in the economy, and restrictions on capital flows.

"It's over, it's not the same country," I was told by one regular visitor to Russia who had served in the State Department in Clinton's first term. "What are we trying to do in this summit conference, show continuity? There is no continuity, the reformers got eaten by the communists. The administration is playing a game of let's pretend: Let's pretend they still have a democratic country with a free-market economy."

In reality, Albright had decided to quit pretending that everything was going to be all right. Unlike Indonesia or South Korea, Russia was not unfamiliar territory to her; she had spent years studying it, and could speak the language. She knew Primakov, the foreign minister, who had emerged from the political rubble in Moscow to take over as prime minister and as de facto head of state because of Yeltsin's illnesses. It was time to reposition the United States, she concluded, to minimize the political and strategic damage that could result from the Russian implosion.

A senior administration official told me that there had been no official policy review on Russia that summer, no single meeting at which a decision had been made to modify the U.S. approach. He said that the new policy had evolved through "corridor conversations and car rides, and the fact that everyone was there in Moscow and saw a new situation that requires a new way of talking about it."

The "new way of talking about it," first hinted at by Clinton in his Moscow meetings, emerged formally in a speech Albright delivered in Chicago on October 2, a month after the Moscow summit, when it was apparent that the economic reforms demanded by the IMF in its bailout package would not be forthcoming. This was perhaps the most important policy address of her first two years. It received little media attention because she delivered it in Chicago at a time when the press was occupied by other matters. But the preparation she put into the speech indicated its significance to her and to the administration.

"In what many people thought was a fundamentally new environment, she wanted to get her views out about how we were going to conduct her policy," one of her senior aides said. "For her, the personal interest is very great, given her biography. I have heard no speech to which she has given more personal attention than this one. In Chicago, she was going over it line by line, changing individual words for tone and nuance. She used to be a Sovietologist, and it showed."

To firm up her thinking, she conferred over dinner two days before the Chicago event with Russia experts from universities and study centers such as the Carnegie Endowment for International Peace—people whose work she had read for years. Their consensus, according to participants, was that Washington had to acknowledge the changes that had overtaken Russia and step back a bit from a messy situation it could not control. Furthermore, the time had come for the administration to recognize that its espousal of Russian democracy could not be reconciled with its support for an economic reform program that most Russians had rejected. That became the most important new element in Albright's approach to

Russia: the explicit acknowledgment that if Russia is now a democracy, its people cannot and should not be expected to accept government policies that caused them relentless misery.

"Solutions to Russia's problems will not stick unless they have popular legitimacy within Russia," Albright said. "The policies we would like the Russian government to pursue have to be worked out democratically, with the support and understanding of the Russian people, or they are going to fail. This means we need to be patient with the workings of the democratic process in Russia."

In a way, this was stating the obvious. As Dimitri Simes put it a few months later, "To ask people to go through years of near-catastrophic deprivation and still support democracy and keep the regime in power was an extraordinary idea."[28]

But Albright's embrace of this perception was a major breakthrough in the administration's thinking about Russia. She put the administration on record as accepting, for the first time, the political legitimacy of Yeltsin's rivals and the finality of the country's rejection of unfettered capitalism. In place of the "Yeltsin or bust, free market or else" policy of the administration's first six years, Albright moved to a position of recognizing Russia as it is, not as she and Clinton and Talbott would like it to be. They stopped waiting for Chubais and the other reformers to be recalled to power by a Russian citizenry that had seen the light; it was not going to happen. My assessment at the time was that "[Albright's] vision of Russia as a full-fledged member of the Group of Eight industrialized democracies gave way to a damage-control effort with a limited agenda of bilateral cooperation and an interest in ensuring that Washington not take the blame for what went wrong."[29]

When television interviewer Charlie Rose asked Albright the "Who lost Russia?" question, she replied: "I think it was a huge issue, and I think we did not blow it. . . . I think that every country's responsible for itself, but the U.S.—I think our only fault is that we are optimists."[30]

Albright's Chicago speech unleashed a flood of rhetorical repositioning in the administration. Talbott, Summers, and Sestanovich all delivered public messages to Russia that could be summarized as: "We understand what's driving you, and we know you have to respond to the needs of your people. If you make the right choices and adhere to the path of reform, we will help you. But if you make the wrong choices, they are your choices, and there won't be much we can do for you."

To no one's surprise, administration officials now began saying that they had known all along that trouble was brewing in Russia. Once Albright laid down the new line, following Clinton's assessment while he was in Moscow, others went along, including Talbott himself, the original architect and implementer of the now discarded policy. "Nobody in our government is denying the proposition that a modern economy, by definition, means an economy that operates in a democratic political context," he told me. "Nobody in a responsible position in this administration has ever felt it was guaranteed that Russia was going to make it. The future has always been a matter of uncertainty and concern. What has happened is that it has become more of a concern." What had changed, he said, was not American policy toward Russia but Russia itself.

Talbott was speaking to me by telephone from Stanford University, where he had just delivered a strong criticism of the economic plan announced by Primakov a week earlier. "Since the numbers don't add up, the intended remedies only aggravate the disease," he said at Stanford. By monetizing its debt, a policy sure to stimulate inflation, Russia was driving away the external help it desperately needed, Talbott continued, leaving itself with "three disagreeable choices: one, crank the printing presses even faster; two, plunge deeper into default; or, three, stop paying wages and pensions and conducting basic government functions. Whatever combination of these measures the government adopts, Russia's economic situation is likely to deteriorate further," raising the possibility that "we may be in for some heightened tensions over security and diplomatic issues."[31]

This was harsh medicine for Talbott, who had worked tirelessly for more than five years to craft and implement the very policy that was now being jettisoned. Russian diplomats began commenting on Talbott's decreasing visibility on Russia policy, which they took to be a reflection of the administration's recognition that the policy had gone awry.

Within two months of Talbott's Stanford speech, bilateral relations were soured further by Russian unhappiness over American missile strikes against Iraq—in response to which the Russian state Duma, or Parliament, again postponed ratification of the second

Strategic Arms Reduction Treaty (START II)—and by Clinton's decision to close the American market and cut off American aid to three more Russian institutions suspected of supplying nuclear and missile technology to Iran.

The Iraq strikes, undertaken by the United States and Britain without a specific mandate from the U.N. Security Council, heightened Russian anxieties because the Security Council is virtually the only international forum in which Russia, a permanent member with veto power, retains important leverage. The Russians took the Iraq strikes as a deliberate U.S. move to circumvent the Security Council.

And with all these issues already on the table, defense secretary Cohen shocked the Russians by announcing that the administration was preparing to pump $6 billion over the coming five years into the development of a defense system that could intercept long-range ballistic missiles fired at the United States. Announcing the intention to develop such a system was not the same as deploying it, and in any case the Russians should not have been surprised by the announcement because Gore and Albright had told them in explanatory letters that it was coming and the White House had previously included the policy decision in public documents, but the response in Moscow was almost entirely negative. The Russians saw the announcement as a statement that the United States was planning to break out of an arms-control agreement that had defined the strategic balance between the two countries for a quarter century.

The Antiballistic Missile Treaty permits each country to have one—and only one—fixed site at which it may deploy a defense against intercontinental ballistic missile attack. Russia chose to defend Moscow, its capital. The United States chose to defend its ICBM launch silos in North Dakota, although that defense system has been inactive since 1976. The treaty prohibits sea-based or mobile defenses, and as interpreted by the Clinton administration it also bars space-based systems such as President Reagan had proposed with "Star Wars." In simplest terms, the treaty meant that neither side would attack the other, because neither would have the means to defend itself against the devastating retaliation that would surely follow.

In the arms-control fraternity, no cow is more sacred than the ABM Treaty. The mutual assurance it provided in the darkest days of the Cold War made possible the arms reduction agreements of the 1980s and 1990s. But Washington's defense hawks hated it. They believed that the United States needed a missile shield, not to defend against an attack by the Soviet Union but to protect the American mainland from a missile fired by some other country—China, perhaps, or a rogue state such as North Korea or Iraq—and they thought that it was irresponsible and pointless to cling to the letter of a treaty that was rooted in a bygone era.

These hawks, including influential Republican senators such as Jesse Helms, John Kyl of Arizona, and Thad Cochran of Mississippi, argued that the treaty was no longer valid because the country with which it had been negotiated, the Soviet Union, no longer existed. To them, it was like a treaty with the Ottoman Empire or the Venetian Republic, a historical artifact, irrelevant to contemporary policy.

The politics of arms control could fill a long book all by itself, and this is not the place to reconstruct the ABM Treaty controversy. It boiled down to this: The hawks wanted to scrap it as irrelevant and a hindrance to the development of a protective shield for the country. The doves, including Clinton and most of his national security team as well as senior Democrats in the Senate, valued it as a cornerstone of security against a Russia still armed with thousands of nuclear warheads. To them, the Republican clamor for a national missile defense evoked memories of "Star Wars," on which the country had spent billions to little apparent gain.

After Iraq fired SCUD missiles into Saudi Arabia and Israel during the Persian Gulf War of 1991, it was no longer possible to ignore the threat from rogue countries, a threat that was not even on the radar screen when the ABM Treaty was signed in 1972. Clinton and his defense advisers were guided by intelligence assessments reporting that midrange threats such as the SCUD were real but that long-range capabilities that would enable Iraq or North Korea to directly threaten U.S. territory were years in the future. On that assumption, the administration supported Pentagon efforts to develop defenses against intermediate-range, or "theater," missiles, with the intent of protecting American and allied troops in the Persian Gulf region, or South Korea, from missile attack.

The ABM Treaty did not specify the difference between theater missiles, against which interceptor defenses were permitted, and strategic or long-range missiles, against which defenses were essentially prohibited. At their Helsinki summit meeting in March 1997, Clinton and Yeltsin agreed on a definition, known as the demarcation agreement. This enabled Washington to pursue its intermediate-range missile defenses without breaching the ABM Treaty, while reassuring Moscow that it was not pursuing a strategic missile defense. The Helsinki demarcation agreement was an amendment to the ABM Treaty and therefore required Senate confirmation. The administration refrained from sending it to the Senate, however, for fear that Helms and his fellow hawks would use it as an instrument to attack the treaty itself. A few days before Albright left for Moscow in January 1999, Helms announced that he intended to do just that. He demanded that the administration submit the agreement for ratification by June 1, saying that he would block ratification of other agreements that the administration wanted approved until the Helsinki agreement and the Kyoto climate change treaty were sent to the Senate. He proclaimed: "The single most important item on the Senate's foreign policy agenda this year must be clearing the way for a national missile defense to protect the American people. And there is one thing standing in our way: the Clinton administration's stubborn adherence to the antiquated and defunct 1972 ABM Treaty."[32]

The administration refused to comply with Helms's deadline for submitting the amendments, taking the position that it would send them to the Senate only after the Russians ratified START II. In response, Helms let it be known—through a leak to me by members of his staff—that he would include in the ratification language of all future treaties a condition that they go into effect only upon submission of the ABM amendments.

In reality, events in 1997 and 1998 had already eroded the administration's position of absolute adherence to the ABM Treaty.

Pakistan tested a new intermediate-range missile. Intelligence reports indicated that Iran would soon be able to deploy missiles that could strike not only U.S. forces in the Persian Gulf region but also Israel and friendly countries in Europe. North Korea fired a missile that flew over Japan, demonstrating an incipient capability to attach a third-stage booster to its missiles that could eventually give Pyongyang the ability to hit targets in the United States. And there was no hiding from the alarming conclusions in what came to be known as the "Rumsfeld report."

On July 15, 1998, a bipartisan group of experienced and well-regarded national security experts, headed by former defense secretary Donald H. Rumsfeld and including G. Lee Butler, a retired four-star air force general who had headed the country's strategic nuclear forces, submitted to Congress an assessment of the growing missile threat. (Butler, despite his career record, is no defense hardliner with predictable views. In retirement, he spends his time crusading for the abolition of nuclear weapons.)

The members concluded unanimously that "concerted efforts by a number of overtly or potentially hostile nations to acquire ballistic missiles with biological or nuclear payloads pose a growing threat to the United States, its deployed forces and its friends and allies." Furthermore, they said, "the threat to the U.S. posed by these emerging capabilities is broader, more mature and evolving more rapidly than has been reported in estimates and reports by the Intelligence Community," and the ability of the spy agencies to monitor these threats is "eroding."[33]

The report triggered a reassessment of the missile defense issue within the administration. According to Jamie Rubin, Albright recognized that the time had come to reevaluate her "orthodox position in favor of the ABM Treaty," to think about amending or even scrapping it if necessary in order to protect the United States from these new threats—threats to which, in the American view, Russia was contributing by selling missile technology and nuclear equipment to Iran.

By itself, Cohen's announcement did not disrupt the Helsinki balance. One of Albright's arms-control advisers summarized the administration's position in these words: "Our program is not directed against Russia and it's not capable of countering or threatening Russia's strategic force," because Russia retained enough warheads and missiles to overwhelm any defense system Washington was contemplating. The adviser continued:

> The development program for this system is strictly in compliance with the ABM Treaty. No decision has been made on deployment. No decision will be made on deployment before the summer of 2000. We have set aside money to preserve an option for deployment if a decision is made. There's no deployment money for 1999. We are still committed to the ABM Treaty. The ABM Treaty is important to us. We understand how im-

portant the ABM Treaty is to the process of reductions and to further steps in strategic force reductions. If changes to the ABM Treaty are necessary for this program, we are committed to work with Russia on necessary amendments.

Cohen and Albright said that the United States wanted to negotiate with the Russians over modifications to the treaty to permit what Washington wanted to do, but they also mentioned that the treaty permitted either side to withdraw from it unilaterally if compelling national interest so required. Clinton said that he would never go that far, but if the administration had no intention of pulling out of the treaty, why raise the issue unbidden, as Albright and Cohen had done?

When the irrepressible Helen Thomas of United Press International asked Clinton how he could "justify chipping away at the ABM Treaty," he delivered a response so convoluted as to be almost indecipherable:

> Doing the research on a missile defense system, which is not a violation of ABM Treaty—it is theoretically possible that we could develop a missile defense system that, either by its nature or by where it was deployed, would be a violation of the ABM Treaty. I, personally, have told the Russians over and over again I have no intention of abrogating the ABM Treaty. Anything we do, we will do together.
>
> But the only threat we have—excuse me—the threat that the United States is likely to face 10 or 20 years from now from missiles coming in is by no means—not just from North Korea. It is a fact that many countries with whom we have serious differences now are making vigorous efforts either to build or to buy missiles with increasing ranges, that go distances far beyond anything that would be necessary to protect their own territory.
>
> General [Henry] Shelton [chairman of the Joint Chiefs of Staff] has said that this missile defense is tough, it's like trying to hit a bullet with a bullet. That's what missile defense is. I think if we believe that the technology might be there, we owe it to ourselves and to all of our allies—not just our old allies, but some of our post–Cold War allies—to try to develop that, along with an adequate warning system, to try to prevent countries that are desperately trying to get missiles—that they could not possibly need to defend their own territory—from ever taking offensive action against us or anyone else.

But I have no intention of supporting or initiating a unilateral abrogation of the ABM Treaty. I will not do that. We have been very candid with the Russians; we have talked to them about what we are doing. We have talked about what kinds of information we might share in the future. But I have never advocated, initiated, encouraged, sanctioned, or blinked at the possibility that we could unilaterally abrogate the ABM Treaty. I personally would be very opposed to that.[34]

This effort to proclaim allegiance to the treaty while signaling a desire to escape from its key provisions satisfied nobody. It alarmed arms-control advocates and supporters of the treaty, who feared that the administration was jeopardizing a crucial component of America's strategic understanding with Russia to pursue interceptor technologies that had failed every time the Pentagon tested them. It upset the Russians, who interpreted Cohen's announcement as a threat to the strategic balance. And it failed to placate congressional missile defense hawks, led by Helms and Cochran, who saw the announcement as a political ploy. Development of a national missile defense system had been a plank in the 1994 "Contract with America" campaign manifesto of House Republican conservatives. For Clinton to give it a lukewarm endorsement four years later looked like an effort to defuse a potential issue in the 2000 presidential campaign, not a sincere commitment to defend the American homeland.

Administration officials said that the timing of Cohen's announcement was a function of Washington's annual budget cycle and had no other significance. To the Russians, however, the announcement came while they were still smarting over the air strikes on Iraq, to which they had strongly objected, and contributed to a further erosion of bilateral relations.

That was the situation as Albright headed for Moscow in January 1999.

Chapter 8

WE WILL PREVAIL

I T WAS HARD to miss the symbolism of the plane Albright used for that long flight to Moscow: an air force E-4B, known as the "Doomsday Plane." The air force actually has four of these converted Boeing 747s, each equipped to be a flying presidential command center in case of a catastrophe, such as nuclear war, that would render the White House untenable. According to the air force, "In case of national emergency or destruction of ground command control centers, the aircraft provides a modern, highly survivable, command, control and communications center to direct U.S. forces, execute emergency war orders and coordinate actions by civil authorities." In other words, this is the plane from which the president could administer whatever was left of the United States after a Soviet nuclear strike. Hence the appellation, Doomsday Plane. It makes for depressing travel, because its bright fluorescent lights are on at all times, and it has no windows. It is outfitted for work, not for comfort.

The enemy the air force had in mind when the Doomsday Plane was built had ceased to exist. Albright was flying to Moscow at a time when a nuclear strike by an ICBM from the central Asian steppe was no longer a real threat. But in many ways relations with Moscow were more complicated than they had been in the era when doomsday seemed imminent.

Yeltsin was so enfeebled by illness—and perhaps by alcohol—that he seemed no longer able to run his country. At the time of Albright's visit, he was hospitalized with a bleeding ulcer. She spoke to him by phone but did not see him. The grim joke among

Russians was that Yeltsin could not govern, he could only block others from governing or simply fire people, as he had done the previous year, dismissing Prime Minister Viktor Chernomyrdin and then his successor, Sergei Kiriyenko. After Kiriyenko, Yeltsin appointed Yevgeny Primakov as prime minister, jettisoned him during the Kosovo war, named Sergei Stepashin to succeed him, and then dismissed Stepashin after less than three months. In a country less critical than Russia, such thrashing about would have been comical. Whereas when Chernomyrdin was prime minister the situation in Russia appeared to be serious but not hopeless, by 1999 it appeared hopeless but not serious.

With Yeltsin fading, Chernomyrdin out of the picture, and the young reformers whom Washington had supported discredited by Russia's dismal economic performance, Albright and her colleagues had to deal with a different group of Russian leaders, starting with Primakov and Deputy Prime Minister Yuri Maslyukov, who were considerably less compliant than their predecessors.

In her Chicago speech, Albright had recognized that in a democratic Russia, the voices of the people had to be heard. But she didn't like a lot of what those voices were saying. Some Russians were falling back on old conspiracy theories, blaming Jews, or Americans, or other outside forces for their plight. Others were calling for a retreat from the free market. On her agenda, in addition to the economic and security issues, was an effort to counter such thinking.

In her only appearance among members of the Russian public, Albright spoke to a gathering of intellectuals, religious-freedom activists, civil libertarians, and leaders of nongovernmental organizations in a book-lined hall at the State Library for Foreign Languages, a repository of works in French, German, and other languages to which Muscovites had had no access during the Soviet era. The library is known in Moscow as a gathering place for Russians committed to human rights and intellectual freedom.

Albright showed off a bit, prefacing her remarks with a few sentences in Russian and afterward responding to questions asked in Russian that were not translated for her. Predictably, Russian-speaking journalists said that her command of the language wasn't nearly as good as she liked to pretend, but the rest of the audience loved it.

"I want to tell you directly how much the American people want Russia to succeed in firmly establishing economic prosperity, the institutions of democracy, and respect for the law and human rights," she said. She respected and admired those in the audience, she said, because "you are courageously promoting a culture of tolerance where bigots are shunned and all are free to worship God in whatever way they choose. Every country, including my own, has room to improve in this respect." It was essential, she said, for Russians not to let hard times turn them away from the freedoms they had discovered after the fall of communism; it was essential not to look for scapegoats among those with different backgrounds or beliefs.[1]

It is hard to assess the impact of a speech delivered in a foreign language to a limited audience, even though it was videotaped for wider distribution later, but Russians in the audience said that the choice of venue would enhance the impact of her words. She reminded the Russians that great nations are built on diversity and intellectual daring, and they respect dissent. Her message reflected her belief that if Russia were to adopt such values, it would matter less what weapons it had. The belief that democracies do not attack other democracies is fundamental to the worldview of the Clinton administration.

The next night Albright went to Moscow's splendid old Bolshoi Theater to take in a sumptuous production of Verdi's *La Traviata*. Between acts, she met with Foreign Minister Igor Ivanov, searching for a common approach to the looming crisis over the Serbian province of Kosovo. That conflict, in which Albright was determined to unleash the military power of the NATO alliance if necessary to stop the killing of innocent civilians by Serb security forces, was only the most urgent of the many difficult issues she brought up in extensive and somewhat testy meetings with Primakov, Ivanov, and other officials, who got an earful. In an article I wrote during our flight from Moscow to Riyadh, Saudi Arabia, the next day, I summarized her statements to the Russians:

Your budget is unrealistic, and your revenue projections are phony. Until you get real, it will be hard for us and for the International Monetary Fund to help you.

The positions you have taken in negotiations on revising the Treaty on Conventional Forces in Europe, a keystone of future relations between Russia and NATO, are unacceptable.

Unless you stop selling missile technology to Iran, we will cut off your authority to launch high-orbit U.S. commercial satellites on your rockets—a lucrative business that you need to keep.

We don't like the recent outburst of anti-Semitic statements from prominent politicians in your country, or some of the trumped-up criminal cases that undercut personal freedom. We know times are hard in Russia, but blaming imaginary villains is not the answer.

We know you don't like our plan to develop and possibly deploy a defense against strategic missiles, because it seems to violate the spirit, if not the letter, of a treaty between us. But it's not directed at you—and anyway it's partly your fault, because you are the ones selling Iran the missile technology we're worried about.[2]

I later learned that Albright and her aides had found this summary useful as well as amusing because it disseminated her message in language much more blunt than she could use herself; but the important thing was that she seemed to have delivered these unpleasant messages without further antagonizing the Russians. Ivanov in particular emerged determined to put the best face on things. "It is fundamentally important," he said in a news conference at the conclusion of their talks, "that the adherence of Russia and the United States to the development of bilateral relations on the basis of equality, respect and due account of each other's interests was confirmed. . . . We believe that the non-coincidence of views on some matters should not serve as an obstacle to the development of our partnership relations."[3]

Of course, that could be read as boilerplate diplomatic language used to paper over real differences, and in some ways it was. But it was also a fact that Albright was able to go to Moscow at a time of serious strains in the relationship, when the Russians—bruised by their own problems and aggrieved by Washington's tactics on sensitive issues—could have emerged confrontational rather than conciliatory, and she had kept relations on a steady course. (Quite a few Russia experts in the Washington foreign policy establishment would dispute this assessment. They believe that the United States is inexorably and dangerously alienating a wounded Russia through policies such as the expansion of NATO. But the fact is that however much feelings in Moscow may have been wounded, Yeltsin—who had no political assets left other than his relationship with

Clinton—decided each time it came to the crunch to cooperate on crucial issues, such as the security of nuclear materials and the work of the U.S.-Russia binational commission, formerly known as Gore-Chernomyrdin, which Primakov did not dismantle. The war in Yugoslavia would put Yeltsin's commitment to its ultimate test, and the relationship survived; Yeltsin let ties to Washington fray but not snap.)

In addition to Ivanov's reaffirmation of the basic soundness of the bilateral relationship, Albright in Moscow obtained—or appeared to obtain—Russian cooperation on the Kosovo issue.

Americans can be forgiven if they cannot understand, or don't want to make the effort to understand, the confrontational politics of the Balkans. It is a region of tiny, mountainous countries, occupied by people with unfamiliar polysyllabic names who seem to have a propensity for appalling crimes. But Albright did not have the luxury of throwing up her hands. She was a senior member of the administration policymaking team that had thrashed about indecisively for three years over Bosnia, and she did not want to go through that again as the death toll among innocents mounted in another part of the former Yugoslavia.

Furthermore, aides explained, although Albright was resigned to the fact that in an unruly world she would always be fighting many fires simultaneously, she did not want to keep fighting the same ones over and over. This was a point on which she had expressed her frustration publicly just a few days earlier. "Like most Americans, I am goal-oriented, and I want to start a task and finish it and move on to the next one," she said. "But diplomacy today does not lend itself to that. Instead, it's like trying to fold one of those cardboard boxes. You get three corners in place, but they all start to come undone when you try to fold in the fourth one."[4]

This was why she wanted to end the thrust-and-parry game developed by Saddam Hussein in Iraq, and why she wanted to break the pattern established by Yugoslav president Slobodan Milosevic of pseudocompliance with United Nations resolutions followed by new rounds of provocation. Throughout the summer of 1998, Albright had been flogged by editorial writers for her supposed inaction after she had declared publicly that "we are not going to stand by and watch the Serbian authorities do in Kosovo what they can no longer get away with doing in Bosnia." One memorable blast, in the *Washington Post,* gives the tone of the commentary Albright was hearing and shows the kind of pressure she was under. Noting that more than five months had passed since Albright had drawn the rhetorical line over Kosovo, a *Post* editorial said:

> Now tens of thousands of Kosovo civilians are living like hunted animals in the woods, their homes bombed and burned out by Mr. Milosevic's troops, their livestock slaughtered, their crops destroyed. More than 300,000 civilians, some 15 percent of Kosovo's total population, have been forced from their homes. Ethnic cleansing—a "scorched-earth" policy, as U.N. secretary-general Kofi Annan put it—is in full swing. And the United States is . . . standing by and watching.

The editorial took note of a statement by Jamie Rubin that Albright had communicated to Milosevic her "shock and dismay" over what was happening and dismissed it with this sneer: "Shock and dismay? Please. The time is long past for sending messages and for feigning surprise at Mr. Milosevic's long-planned villainy. If President Clinton and the West are not prepared to act, they should at least have the decency to retreat into shamed silence."[5]

Albright is not the type to "retreat into shamed silence." She wanted to demonstrate that her words had not been hollow. She and all the senior members of her staff understood that the three years of dithering over Bosnia could not be repeated in Kosovo. Moreover, Albright believes that the chronic instability of southeastern Europe and the Balkans threatens the peace and good order of the entire continent, and therefore of the Atlantic alliance. Kosovo was not a narrow issue for her.

At the time of Albright's visit to Moscow, the Kosovo problem was being thrashed out in several arenas, on many levels. The stakes included European stability, the future of NATO, and the bilateral relationship between Russia and the United States. The challenge was daunting, but Albright brought many assets to the table: the administration's determination not to witness another Bosnia, her own extensive knowledge of Eastern European politics and history, her personal relationships with key figures in Europe, and the fact that nobody else had a better plan than the one she was promoting while in Moscow. By the time Albright arrived in Moscow, she had already persuaded Clinton to accept a plan she had devised to use NATO's military power not only to stop Milosevic's depredations in Kosovo—

the alliance had agreed to that the previous October—but also to en-
force a peace agreement she would insist he be forced to accept.
Backed by the threat of NATO action, she was going to dictate to
Milosevic the terms of his political capitulation.

The conflict in Kosovo and the story of Western efforts to halt it
are so complicated that they would require a separate book to sort
out. But in order to appreciate the package that Albright put together during her trip to Moscow—and to understand why, despite
her success at building support for it, it failed to settle the conflict—
it is necessary to review the basic situation.

Kosovo is a Connecticut-sized province of Serbia, the dominant
republic of what remains of Yugoslavia. The population was about
90 percent ethnic Albanian and mostly Muslim, different in language and religion from the dominant Serbs, but for historical reasons Kosovo is crucial to Serbia's national consciousness.

In 1998, chafing under repressive Serb control, the Albanians of
Kosovo began agitating for greater freedom from Belgrade's rule. At
the very least, they wanted restoration of the local self-government of
which Milosevic had stripped the province a decade earlier as part of
his political program of Serbian nationalism. Some relatively moderate Kosovo politicians were content to negotiate with Milosevic to
seek administrative autonomy and greater freedom for Albanian cultural institutions. But as Milosevic responded to these aspirations
with an increasingly violent crackdown by his troops and security police, a more aggressive Kosovar faction took up arms to demand full
independence. The United States and its major European allies did
not favor independence, which they believed would contribute to
the further fragmentation of the Balkans, but they were unwilling to
allow Milosevic to pursue his campaign of intimidation, which included the evacuation of entire communities and savage attacks on
the civilian population. Albright and other American officials believed that Milosevic was intent on purging the province of most of
its Albanian population, and on doing so in increments sufficiently
small as to limit international outrage. As NATO secretary-general
Javier Solana often expressed it months later during NATO's air war
against Yugoslavia, Milosevic apparently believed that "a village a day
keeps NATO away."

In October 1998, as tens of thousands of uprooted civilians faced
a looming Balkan winter, NATO—following the precedent established in Bosnia—threatened Milosevic with military action unless

he came to an accommodation with the Kosovars. The alliance had prepared itself to the point where Solana could have ordered planes into the air, but at the last minute Milosevic accepted a deal negotiated by Richard Holbrooke. It called for substantial withdrawals of Serb security forces from Kosovo, coupled with a start of good-faith negotiations on autonomy for the province.

Most of the refugees went back to their villages, but the respite was short-lived. The independence-minded rebels, collectively known as the Kosovo Liberation Army (KLA), were not under the control of the Kosovar civilian politicians who had assented to the Holbrooke-Milosevic deal, and they continued their attacks on Serb forces. Milosevic responded by halting the pullout of his security forces and turning them loose to strike with mounting ferocity. Reports of massacres proliferated. Neither side could prevail militarily, but escalation and prolongation of the conflict threatened to draw in several neighboring countries, adding to the instability of much of southeastern Europe.

Through an informal agreement that went back to the Bosnia war, responsibility for seeking a negotiated settlement in Kosovo fell to a loose grouping of six nations known as the "Contact Group." Its members were the United States, Germany, France, Great Britain, Italy—all NATO allies—and Russia. The participation of Russia was valuable because the Russians have historic ties to, and influence over, the Serbs. But Russia was also a complicating factor because Moscow was resolutely opposed to the use of force, especially because Kosovo is after all a province of Serbia and to some extent the Serb struggle against secession is legitimate. Given their own brutal response to the separatist rebellion in Chechnya, the Russians would not endorse the principle of NATO military action to end an internal conflict in a sovereign country.

Albright was convinced that Milosevic was a bullheaded dictator who responded only to force, a view reinforced by the experience of Bosnia, where Milosevic had accepted the Dayton settlement only after Croatian troops and NATO planes had driven back the Bosnian Serb forces in the field.

The instrument through which the threat of force would be issued in Kosovo—and carried out, if necessary—was NATO. But the Russians would not assent to the use of force unless it was authorized by the U.N. Security Council, where they would kill any such resolution by using their veto. (This was the same problem the United States had faced over the bombing of Iraq.) Furthermore, the Russians were unhappy at the prospect of a NATO military action that would expand the alliance's mission beyond its traditional defensive role and augment its influence at Russia's expense. On the American side, Washington favored the very expansion of NATO's role that Russia feared and wanted the issue kept out of the Security Council because the United States would never accept the principle that the Security Council held a de facto veto over NATO decisionmaking.

According to the Americans, the Russians would agree to threaten to use force, but not to actually do so. Members of Albright's team acknowledged that they found Russia's position incomprehensible: How can you project a credible threat of force, they asked, if you are opposed to using force no matter what? But whatever the intellectual merits of the Russian position, Albright wanted to accommodate it to prevent a further deterioration in a bilateral relationship already alarmingly frayed.

A few days before she arrived in Moscow, the Serbs played into her hands by killing at least forty-five Albanian civilians at a village called Rakac. Accounts from the scene, including assessments by official observers sent by the Organization for Security and Cooperation in Europe, described the killings as a massacre. Even the Russians were disgusted. It was an opportune moment for Albright, Solana, and British foreign secretary Robin Cook to orchestrate a quick sequence of events aimed at forcing the Kosovo factions to accept a settlement. There was no longer any hope that Milosevic would abide by the deal he had accepted in October.

By the time she left Washington, Albright had forged a unified administration position in favor of imposing a package deal that would stop the killing and give the people of Kosovo control over their own affairs—but not independence. The administration opposed independence because it feared that the creation of an economically nonviable, ethnically based state in the Balkans would inevitably destabilize the entire region, and would undermine the Bosnia peace agreement by ratifying ethnic separation.

On January 26, 1999, Albright and Ivanov issued a joint statement in Moscow condemning the Rakac massacre and insisting that the Serbs comply with their previous commitments and with demands laid down earlier by the Security Council. "The United States and Russia reiterate their indignation at the massacre of Kosovar Albanians at Rakac, which cannot be justified," their statement said. "Those responsible must be brought to justice." The statement also deplored "provocations" by the rebel forces, demanding that they end "immediately."

This statement was, as Jamie Rubin is fond of saying, a "necessary but not sufficient" part of the diplomatic three-cushion shot Albright was putting together with the aim of forcing the issue to a conclusion. The statement said nothing about the possible use of force, which the Russians still opposed, but as part of the Contact Group the Russians were committed to taking a firm stand against the Serb campaign of oppression.

While she was in Moscow, and the next day during a side trip to Saudi Arabia to discuss Iraq, Albright was repeatedly on the phone to NATO members, working with Cook and Solana to put together a complicated sequence that would force the Kosovo combatants to come to terms. Two days after Albright and Ivanov issued their statement, Solana announced that NATO also demanded an end to the conflict—"All parties must end violence and pursue their goals by peaceful means only," his statement said. If the fighting continued, "NATO stands ready to act and rules out no option to ensure full respect by both sides of the demands of the international community, and in particular observance of all relevant Security Council resolutions." That was the "credible threat of force" that Albright and Cook wanted to back up the political demands they were about to make.[6]

The key sentence in Solana's statement was this: "The appropriate authorities in Belgrade and representatives of the Kosovo Albanian leadership must agree to the proposals to be issued by the Contact Group for completing an interim political settlement within the timeframe to be established."

How could NATO demand that the Kosovo rivals agree to Contact Group proposals that had not yet been delivered? It could do so because NATO diplomats in Brussels knew what the Contact Group was going to decide when the six members convened in London the following day, January 29. We in the traveling press corps knew, too, because Jamie Rubin had told us what the deal would be.

Albright wanted to force the issue; she wanted to bring matters to a decisive moment and end the cycle of provocation and retaliation.

All that week, she pressed her counterparts in the Contact Group for clear-cut action. She refused to commit herself to attending a Contact Group meeting until she knew she would be satisfied with the outcome. She did not want to have a meeting for the sake of having a meeting. With Ivanov on board, Cook firmly in her camp, and NATO finally committed to action, she was able to get the Contact Group to issue the orders that would change the game.

The Contact Group would demand that the Belgrade authorities and the Kosovar Albanians not only open negotiations but commit themselves to accepting a framework solution imposed by the group. The previous October, Milosevic had promised to withdraw most of his security forces and open political negotiations; now he was being told that opening free-form negotiations with no predictable outcome was insufficient. He was ordered, under threat of NATO action, to show up prepared to accept an agreement that would give the Kosovar Albanians nearly complete autonomy, with control over their own security, taxes, police, and education.

And that was exactly what happened when the six Contact Group foreign ministers met in London. Albright, Cook, Ivanov, and their counterparts from France, Italy, and Germany directed both sides to appear at Rambouillet, France, within a week. They would then have two weeks at most to accept the precooked agreement imposed on them. The Serbs were also ordered to cooperate with international monitors, assist returning refugees, allow volunteer relief agencies to operate unimpeded, and investigate the Rakac massacre, bringing those responsible to justice.

The language of the Contact Group statement was uncompromising; it left the two sides no alternatives. It did not specifically threaten to use force, because Ivanov and the Russians opposed military action, but that omission was only a diplomatic artifice meant to placate Moscow. NATO had already declared that it would use force to back up whatever plan the Contact Group agreed upon.

Cook and Albright announced the Contact Group's decision in consecutive news conferences at the Foreign and Commonwealth Office in London. Albright said that the six had "sent the parties an unmistakable message: Get serious. Showing up is not going to be good enough." While she was speaking, I slipped out to a separate room where French foreign minister Hubert Vedrine was having his own briefing. I was looking for dissent, some hint of disagreement, any distance between the French position and that proclaimed by Cook and Albright, but there was none. Without visible discord, the six countries had banded together to force a sovereign country, Yugoslavia, to accommodate the demands of a secessionist province—demands that could lead to eventual independence for Kosovo, although that was not the Contact Group's stated goal.

"If [Milosevic] is once again subject to air strikes, the purpose will not be to dismember Yugoslavia, the purpose will be to force him back into compliance with his obligations," Strobe Talbott said during the Rambouillet meetings. "If Yugoslavia faces dismemberment, it's largely because of the policies of Milosevic. We believe that the territorial integrity and sovereignty of Yugoslavia should remain intact," meaning that Milosevic would be allowed to keep troops in Kosovo to patrol the international borders, not to repress the populace. This was the argument the administration hoped would persuade Milosevic to rationalize his acceptance of an otherwise unpalatable deal: It ensured Serbian sovereignty over Kosovo, which otherwise might be threatened by a spreading rebellion.[7]

Once the Contact Group issued its ultimatum, the U.N. Security Council endorsed it—an unnecessary gesture, from the American point of view, but useful anyway because it made the Russians feel better. Exactly a week later, Vedrine and Cook played host when representatives of the two sides showed up at Rambouillet as ordered to begin their negotiations, using the Contact Group plan as their text.

I was not at Rambouillet, but journalists who did try to follow the talks from outside the chateau's fence said it was apparent that Albright and her advisers, along with Cook, made at least one serious miscalculation: Their plan assumed that the Kosovar rebels would accept the agreement that was being offered to them, which the Americans repeatedly said was the best deal they were going to get. But the Kosovar Albanians balked. They were not part of NATO, not part of the Contact Group, and not members of the Security Council; agreements forged in those arenas were not binding on them. Despite NATO's commitment to send troops, the rebels were dubious about the West's ability and determination to protect them from Milosevic—especially because Milosevic rejected that part of the deal calling for the deployment of international troops, and the allies did not immediately do what they had promised to do if Milosevic balked: bomb Serbia. The Kosovar

Albanians had had a whiff of independence, a goal that had already been achieved by other parts of what had been Yugoslavia. Why should they settle for less? They could see that Milosevic, despite all the tough talk and all the ultimatums, not only rejected the "take it or leave it" settlement he had been ordered to accept, but was not even complying with the deal he had agreed to in his negotiations with Holbrooke three months earlier, and yet nothing was happening to him. The Kosovars were weak, politically divided, and marginally trained and equipped, but as Holbrooke observed, "It doesn't take more than a handful of people with a couple of grenades to provoke a crisis."[8]

It was easy, after Rambouillet, to conclude that Albright had again drawn a rhetorical line in the sand that she and Clinton were not prepared to defend. But in reality, the opposite had happened. They were prepared to back it up, once every possible alternative had failed. Albright told the Kosovars that NATO would not bomb to enforce its ultimatum unless the Albanians themselves accepted the Rambouillet package, and this argument had the desired effect. Two weeks after Rambouillet, the Kosovars signed. The day of decision had come; for the United States and for NATO, there was no more room to maneuver.

Sherlock Holmes said that in criminal investigations, when all other hypotheses have been eliminated, the one that remains, however improbable, must be the truth. There was a similar argument about the air war against Yugoslavia: When all other options, including that of doing nothing, had been eliminated, the one that remained had to be pursued, whether the Russians liked it or not.

On March 23, when Primakov, heading for Washington, ordered his plane to turn around over the Atlantic and return to Moscow, we knew that bombing was imminent. He had called Gore from a refueling stop in Shannon, Ireland, to see if there was any hope that Holbrooke's final mission would produce a breakthrough and forestall the bombing. Gore said it didn't look good and suggested that Primakov wait at Shannon until the outcome was definite. But Primakov took off, saying he would turn back if he got final word that there was no hope, and three hours later he did just that.

With this turn of events, Washington entered a full-scale crisis mode that had not been seen since Operation Desert Storm in 1991. The United States and its allies were undertaking a military campaign against a country that had not attacked any of them, they were doing it with a politically dictated strategy that compounded the operational difficulty, and they were doing it over the strong objections of an angry nuclear superpower. The next eleven weeks offered the sternest test of Clinton's commitment and Albright's diplomatic skill.

The strength of Albright's convictions, which has served her well in times of stress, was on daily display during the air war against Yugoslavia. Tension and tempers were high. The political and strategic stakes in the conflict were immense: the credibility and future role of NATO, the place in history of Clinton and his entire team, U.S. relations with Russia, and the stability of the Balkans and possibly all of Europe. The American military viewed the missions devised by the civilian officials as strategically dubious and tactically ill conceived. In addition, the air war had the entirely unpredictable side effect of undermining relations with China after NATO missiles hit the Chinese embassy in Belgrade by mistake.

As could be expected in the world capital of finger-pointing and second-guessing, the Washington columnists, armchair strategists, and retired officers reincarnated as television talking heads immediately began roasting the administration for doing too little, or too much, or for waiting too long, or not having waited long enough.

The message coming from NATO and from its most prominent national leaders, including Clinton, Albright, and Blair, was straightforward and apparently unequivocal: This is what we are going to do and this is how we are going to do it, and we will go on doing it as long as necessary.

In Washington's culture of cynicism, there was no political or journalistic payoff for accepting that message at face value, so few did. Informed by the history of Vietnam, the Iran-Contra affair, and the White House sex scandal, editorial writers, columnists, and television commentators had a field day: Airpower alone can't subdue Milosevic; Clinton will cut some deal; the Europeans will get the vapors; NATO is going over a cliff. But anyone who listened to what was being said at the NATO summit could sense that this was not politics as usual. We heard not only Clinton and Albright but British prime minister Tony Blair, foreign minister Robin Cook, and defense secretary George Robertson; French president Jacques Chirac; German chancellor Gerhard Schroeder; Italian foreign minister

Lamberto Dini; and virtually all the other participants saying the same thing: Milosevic had to be stopped, NATO had to prevail, the refugees had to go home. If Milosevic's campaign of repression and expulsion in Kosovo was allowed to succeed, it would leave a stain of shame on all of democratic Europe, destabilize much of the continent, emasculate NATO, and validate violence. Facing such outcomes, they said, NATO had no choice but to act and to succeed. In the face of the chronic incredulity of the media and the self-appointed experts, it was apparent to me that they meant what they said. Maybe Clinton was a feckless deceiver, but not all these others were too.

With lives on the line, the administration could not be seen to publicly waver in its commitment to the air war, no matter how high the anxiety level. In private, senior State Department and White House officials acknowledged that they were uncomfortable with what they were doing and the way they were doing it—and surprised by the stiffness of Belgrade's resistance—but said they would have been more uncomfortable with any other course. Senior officials said that they had considered all arguments and proposed alternatives raised by the critics and rejected them in advance as unworkable militarily or out of reach politically. In an alliance of nineteen democratic countries, the United States simply did not have carte blanche to make all the decisions about a war in Europe.

Naturally, people in the administration were exhausted and tense. Who wouldn't be, in such an environment? A month into the bombing campaign, I saw firsthand how much on edge they were when I was subjected to over-the-top, personal denunciations from senior officials who objected to my interpretation of one day's events. (One of them accused me of having my own "agenda," although he did not say what he thought that was.)

Through all this, Albright maintained a public posture of impressive self-confidence, sustained by her conviction that Milosevic's actions in Kosovo represented a profound evil that had to be confronted. Her aides told me that she was distressed by some press coverage, including an article by me, suggesting that the administration had miscalculated Milosevic's likely response to the bombing—which it clearly had. But she stayed—there is no better word for it—cool. She gave no ground to the second-guessers: The air war was justified, it would succeed, and the world would be better for it. The

Albright we saw during the air war was the Albright we had seen nearly two years earlier shoring up the sagging NATO-led peace implementation force in Bosnia by the sheer force of her commitment and will, persuading Clinton to keep U.S. troops there indefinitely and excoriating regional leaders for their multiple failures to live up to their commitments.

On April 15, three weeks into the bombing, when it was apparent that Milosevic was not going to cave in quickly, Albright appeared before a House Appropriations subcommittee. The members were nominally considering the State Department's budget request, but they naturally wanted to hear from her about Kosovo and the war.

"I am very proud of what this administration is doing," she told them, "because I think we are standing up for American values, [for] the necessity of dealing with it when there is a barbaric attempt to cleanse ethnically a whole group of people, and when we see the plight of the refugees."

Members worried about the cost of the war, the need for it, the duration, the possibility that it would fail to meet NATO's objectives and that ground combat troops would have to be sent in. Albright yielded nothing. "I would much prefer to be questioned by the press or questioned by all of you about what we are doing than to be sitting here and have all of you say, 'Why aren't you doing this? Why are you standing by while this great horror is carried on?'"

For a year, Albright had taken heat from critics who chastised her for failing to back up her words about Kosovo. She was reminded constantly that she and Clinton had pledged not to allow Milosevic to do in Kosovo what he had finally been stopped from doing in Bosnia. Now that her pledge was being fulfilled, she brooked no doubt about its justification. "America cannot stand by while people are slaughtered or raped and ethnically cleansed, and watch as that is taking place and creating a great sense of instability," she said. "I also happen to believe that the Balkan peninsula is very important to European stability and security, and since European stability and security is important to the United States, making sure that ultimately that peninsula is integrated into a Europe where there is democracy and prosperity is important to the United States."[9]

A few days later I saw her twice, at a White House briefing and at an appearance before the Senate Foreign Relations Committee. Both events were televised, increasing the pressure on her to perform well. To me she appeared totally confident, almost serene, about the choices the administration had made. "We will prevail," she told the senators.

Five weeks into the air war, the *Wall Street Journal* published a scathing commentary by Peter Krogh, a professor at Georgetown University and former dean of its School of Foreign Service, who had been one of Albright's mentors and a big booster at the time of her appointment. "I can recall no time in the past 30 years when American foreign policy was in worse shape," Krogh wrote. "This is not surprising because I cannot recall a time when our foreign policy was in less competent hands."[10] Coming from someone she regarded as a friend, these words were painful to Albright, but Krogh told me two weeks after the article was published that she had not said a word to him about it.

Krogh, at least, based his criticism on policy. Two months to the day after the bombing started, no less a personage than Norman Mailer weighed in with a furious denunciation of the war in which he went after Albright personally. He wrote that the collective lack of combat experience of Clinton, Cohen, and Albright had plunged the nation into "catastrophe." According to Mailer, "Milosevic has to be one of the wiliest, toughest, most treacherous, canny, tricky, ruthless and resourceful human beings Albright had ever encountered. She, too, had climbed a greasy pole, but it was as a hostess charming up the Beltway's A-list. . . . We must face it. She is no match for him."[11]

This was preposterous. Readers of these critical commentaries would never guess that Milosevic was in fact a woodenheaded loser whose repeated strategic blunders over the course of a decade had brought about the fragmentation and ruin of his country. Criticism of NATO's military tactics was legitimate, but it was absurd to portray Milosevic as a master strategist who had outwitted everyone.

In the early weeks of the air campaign, the pressures on NATO were compounded by the need to display total unity at the alliance's fiftieth anniversary summit, a major event that was scheduled to begin in Washington just as the air war entered its second month. In ways never anticipated when the summit was scheduled, the alliance was on the spot. Envisioned largely as a celebration of the alliance's achievement in facing down Soviet power during the Cold War, the summit evolved into a Kosovo war council. The alliance, which never fired a shot in its first fifty years, was now conducting a destructive military campaign against a country that had not attacked any alliance member.

Albright was, of course, committed to expanding the alliance and to redefining its mission in post–Cold War Europe. Created as a mutual defense organization, NATO was being transformed by the war in Kosovo into a European regional police force, a role that had been discussed in theoretical terms but that was now a reality without ever having been formally embraced by NATO's members. National Security Adviser Sandy Berger and Albright knew that the summit would attract hundreds of journalists, all of whom would want to know what would happen if the air war failed to subdue Milosevic. Would the alliance consider sending in ground troops to take over Kosovo by force? The official answer was no, no, no: The air war will succeed, we have no plans to send troops into a "nonpermissive environment," there is no consensus for that within the alliance.

Still, there was no way to duck the question. It was possible that Milosevic would never yield to the aerial bombardment. Defense secretary Cohen had raised that possibility in public, suggesting that if Milosevic refused to assent to an international military force in Kosovo, the vacuum left by his defeated forces would be filled by the Kosovo Liberation Army, an outcome neither Washington nor Belgrade wanted. Given Clinton's unequivocal commitment to sending the refugees home into a safe environment under NATO protection, it would have been foolish not to begin the political preparation for sending ground troops. The White House wanted the idea of ground troops to circulate but did not want to appear to originate it, since that would be perceived as a violation of Clinton's promise to the country and an admission of miscalculation. The vehicle for opening this door was an "assessment" that NATO had done the previous year of what it would take to send troops into Kosovo.

Albright brought this up at her April 15 House appearance. Asked by Representative John Edward Porter, an Illinois Republican, about whether such troops might be needed, she replied:

I do think it's important for people to know that NATO has done detailed planning for ground troops as part of an international security presence if an agreement is reached. And also, last fall NATO completed an assessment of options to introduce ground troops in a nonpermissive environment. And both of these plans could be updated very quickly if it were necessary to do so.

And so the question became, Will Javier Solana, the secretary-general of NATO, instruct the alliance's military commanders to update that assessment? If the answer was no, then ground troops really were out of the question. If the answer was yes, the door was open.

On the eve of the NATO summit, I was writing the Kosovo story that would appear on the *Washington Post*'s front page the next day, wrapping in all the day's developments about the air war, the diplomacy, and the refugees. Shortly before deadline, I got a call from an official of the National Security Council asking if I had spoken recently with my colleague Nora Boustany, who writes the paper's "Diplomatic Dispatches" column.

"Not since lunchtime," I said.

"Go talk to her," the official said. "She got an interview with Solana and we think he made news."

I walked over to Nora's desk and asked her about it. She had indeed talked to Solana and was astonished that the White House knew about it because she had just finished the interview and hadn't told anyone. The conversation had been arranged days earlier, she said, and was mostly fluff about the NATO summit. She didn't think he had made news but allowed me to read her notes to see if she had missed anything.

After looking them over, I called the White House official back. Yes, I said, Solana had talked to Nora Boustany, but neither she nor I saw anything newsworthy about his comments. "Stay by your phone," the official said. It was now less than an hour before deadline and I didn't have time for games, but it was clear that something was up.

Half an hour later, the phone rang again. The caller was none other than Sandy Vershbow, the U.S. ambassador to NATO, calling from Brussels, where it was nearly midnight. "Read me those notes," he said.

Normally of course I wouldn't do that—read a colleague's notes from an exclusive interview to a U.S. government official who had no right to demand them. But this was Washington; it was obvious that the White House wanted some important information to come out, and it was supposed to come from Solana, although it wasn't clear why they required this surreptitious channel to the *Washington Post*. If Solana had something to announce, why didn't he just announce it?

With my deadline looming, I had no time for ethical rumination. I read Vershbow the notes.

"Don't you see what Solana was trying to tell you?" Vershbow asked. "He has already ordered the reassessment of the ground troop plans. Here's his home number, give him a call."

"Wait a minute," I said. "Are you telling me that Solana is up at this hour, the night before he's supposed to fly here for the summit, waiting for me to call him?"

"Yes," Vershbow said, and sure enough, Solana took my call right away. Yes, Solana said, the revised planning was already under way. "Did I make news?" he asked, with what can only be described as a giggle.

He certainly did. His comments were the lead story in our paper the next morning and were picked up by news agencies and radio stations worldwide. Thus the idea of ground troop planning was already an accepted fact by the time the summit began, and it appeared to have been generated in Brussels, not Washington, since the source of the information was Solana. In fairness to readers, I wrote into the story that the White House had "helped to arrange" the conversation, a clue to people in Washington, at least, that the White House had engineered this scoop.[12]

I later learned that the same White House officials who would shortly be denouncing me for having my own "agenda" had chosen me as the conduit for this information because they thought I was generally a fair journalist, and they wanted the high impact of a story in the *Washington Post* on the day NATO leaders and the world's press were gathering for the summit. They asked Solana to talk to me. Their problem was that Solana, having chatted with Nora Boustany, thought that he had fulfilled his promise to talk to a *Washington Post* reporter. The White House officials, not knowing that he had talked to Boustany or that she was saving her account of that conversation for her column a day later, waited all afternoon for me to call them and ask them about the conversation they expected Solana to have had with me. Hence the last-minute scramble to arrange the call to his home.

This sort of maneuvering must seem ridiculous to people outside the Beltway, and it is. But the incident provides a useful illustration of the atmosphere in which Albright, Berger, and Cohen were operating at the time: high stakes, exhausted people, life-or-death decisions to be made on short notice, and unrelenting journalistic scrutiny that exaggerated the impact of every nuance.

Three weeks after the NATO summit, in the eighth week of the air war, I attended a dinner party given by a veteran ambassador from an Arab country. There were two dozen people at the table—ambassadors and other diplomats, Washington political activists, a few journalists. Nobody predicted a positive outcome to the air war. All the guests agreed that the terrible things that were happening, such as the mistaken bombing of the Chinese embassy in Belgrade and the mounting incidence of civilian casualties, combined with the political crisis in Russia, made it inevitable that the alliance would rupture and seek compromise before Milosevic did.

That same weekend, Albright and her British counterpart, Robin Cook, published an op-ed article in the *Washington Post* predicting just the opposite result. "The refugees must go home to a Kosovo made safe by an international security presence, with NATO at its core," they wrote. "On that point, there is no room for negotiation. We will carry on attacking Milosevic's military machine until he yields." Despite the missed targets and intelligence blunders, the air campaign was having its intended effect, they wrote, adding: "We have the shared resolve to see it through. That does not just mean keeping our nerve when things go well. It also means standing firm when our will is tested."[13]

Of course, political leaders always say such things to their constituents in times of conflict. In the case of Madeleine Albright, though, what we saw was what we got. When she said, "I feel that we did the right thing, and I am proud of the role I played in it," there was no reason to doubt her.[14]

As the air campaign wore on through the late spring with no sign that success was imminent, Albright held firm. It became almost a ritual of the war: Bombs and missiles fell, some civilians were killed by mistake, refugees were relentlessly forced out of Kosovo, critics in

Washington and in Europe griped, Albright and Cook emerged with reassuring words of confidence and commitment. After one tumultuous week, featuring an open disagreement between Britain and Germany on the ground troops issue, Albright appeared on television with Cook to proclaim once again that everything was under control.

"We believe that we will prevail, that the air campaign is working and will work," she said in a network television interview. Of course, in an alliance of nineteen vigorous democracies there would be differences of opinion about how best to proceed, she said, "but the goals are firm, the conditions are clear, and we will prevail."[15] Albright said that the effort required "patience and perseverance," qualities that were difficult to project in a nation accustomed to sound bites, with journalists demanding instant gratification. Journalists were by now depicting Albright and Cook as political leaders desperately defending a flawed policy in defiance of the evidence. A day or so later, however, the commander of NATO's airborne strike force said that their confidence was justified.

Lieutenant General Michael C. Short of the U.S. Air Force said that the escalating campaign was grinding down the Yugoslav forces in Kosovo and predicted that they would be defeated or chased out within two months. "If you are getting pounded by B-1s and B-52s, and A-10s are chasing you every day, and if you know that every time you move you are liable to be hit, at some point your spirit will break, particularly if you are not getting any help from Belgrade," he said. That was the reality confronting the Serb forces in Kosovo.[16]

This sounded suspiciously like those briefings of thirty years earlier in which Pentagon big shots explained how the United States was winning the war in Vietnam, especially because the Pentagon brass had made clear their reservations about the ability of airpower to drive the Serbs out of Kosovo, but Short's assessment was reinforced by messages from Milo Djukanovic, the elected president of the Republic of Montenegro, Serbia's junior partner in what was left of Yugoslavia. Djukanovic, a pro-Western moderate who wanted to link his little republic with Europe and wanted nothing to do with Milosevic's policies, told State Department officials that the air campaign was having its desired effect and urged the United States not to cut any deals with Milosevic. In the first days of the bombing, Albright and other American officials had expressed fears that Milosevic would stage a coup in Montenegro to get rid of Djukanovic, whose position was weakened by NATO air strikes against some facilities inside Montenegro. That he was still in power and still supportive two months later was a comforting development.

When the bombing began, Albright's role changed. Winning unanimous NATO support for the air strikes and keeping the issue out of the Security Council had been accomplished. Now her mission was to hold the alliance together, to preserve consensus, and to ensure that no one, however well intentioned, open any parallel or competing channels of negotiation with Milosevic that the Serb leader might exploit to his advantage. The U.S. position was that NATO was in charge, and although Russian participation in persuading Milosevic to yield was welcome, no diplomatic freelancing would be tolerated. Neither the Russians nor anyone else could be allowed to offer Milosevic any terms but the ones dictated by NATO.

Holding the alliance firm was not easy. Several members, including Greece, Italy, and Hungary, faced domestic opposition to the air campaign. Others were eager to bring the United Nations back into the game. Since Milosevic was clearly banking on weak-kneed NATO members creating a split in the alliance, any diversion from the unified line could have been disastrous. Albright was on the telephone night and day, stiffening spines and battling what aides called "envoy envy," as U.N. secretary-general Kofi Annan, the Greek government, the Czechs, and others sought to open separate channels to Belgrade.

For the Czech-born Albright, who had beamed with joy as her native country formally joined the NATO alliance just a few months earlier, the prospect of her longtime friend, President Vaclav Havel, failing the first test was especially troubling. "She read the Czechs the riot act," one of her inner circle said. "She told them they can't deviate from NATO's position, and that if they did they would undermine support for further NATO expansion."

On June 3, 1999, Milosevic capitulated. Yeltsin's decision a few days earlier to work with NATO rather than against it gave the Serb leader no choice. Yeltsin's envoy, Viktor Chernomyrdin, and the president of Finland, Marti Ahtisaari, flew to Belgrade to make clear to Milosevic that his position was untenable. NATO air strikes were destroying his country, an intensification of the air campaign was beginning to take a terrible toll on his troops, and he had no diplomatic allies. Milosevic could not dismiss these gentlemen as agents of the enemy NATO: Russia's hostility to the air campaign was well known, and Finland is not a member of NATO. Albright had proposed the Finn as a suitable partner for Chernomyrdin because he was a skillful, respected diplomat, knew the Balkans, and led a country that was about to assume the six-month rotating presidency of the European Union. When he and Chernomyrdin jointly presented Milosevic with a settlement plan that reiterated every one of NATO's demands and informed him that it was not negotiable, the game was over.

Still, when Chernomyrdin and Ahtisaari reported to Washington and to the NATO allies in Brussels that Milosevic had accepted, the news came so suddenly that it took Albright and the rest of the administration team several hours to convince themselves it was not a trick. The outcome was sweet vindication for Albright, who had been battered for weeks by the most vocal and scornful criticism she had ever faced, but she resisted the temptation to say so.

At a staff meeting that morning attended by Jamie Rubin, Elaine Shocas, Tom Pickering, Kosovo coordinator James Dobbins, and others, Albright cut off one participant who talked of the war in the past tense. "I don't want to hear any talk that we have achieved our objective," she said. "We have a lot of humanitarian work to do."

She was scheduled to fly to Mexico that evening but put off the trip to deliver that same message to her counterparts in other NATO countries and begin consultations about the immediate postwar work of taking control of the province and tending to the refugees. "I would have been going nuts in Mexico," she told me.

That afternoon, she met reporters at the State Department to assess the day's events. "The acceptance by Belgrade of these terms is a vital first step, but the confrontation cannot end until these terms are complied with and implemented. As a result, caution is the word of the day," she said.

When Barry Schweid of the Associated Press, dean of the diplomatic press corps, asked if she wanted to respond to the critics who had been accusing her of blunders and miscalculations, she did not rise to the bait. "There will be plenty of time to draw the lessons from this," she said—but she could not prevent a little smile from breaking out.[17]

When I talked to her by telephone the next day, she made no reference to one of the critical articles that had angered her the most early in the bombing campaign, which I had written. Anyone would be tempted to score some points at such a moment, but she refrained. We talked as if she had never been angry.

Of course, the apparent success of the air campaign was good news, she said. So was the cohesion of the NATO alliance under the most stress it had ever endured. In talks with her counterparts in other NATO countries that day, she said, "There was a sense of appropriate pride that NATO has stayed together, but everybody is very realistic about how much we have accomplished and how much we need to do. The reason that none of us are out there pounding our chests is that this is the beginning of a process that has to be implemented."[18]

Two weeks later she finally allowed herself to appear jubilant. An Associated Press photographer snapped her picture as she raised both arms skyward, a huge grin on her face, during a visit to a Kosovo refugee camp in Macedonia. *Newsweek* ran the photo with an essay by that old geostrategist Henry Kissinger, in which he tipped his cap. "Those of us who questioned the wisdom of the diplomacy preceding the war over Kosovo owe it to the Clinton administration to express our respect for the fortitude with which it persevered, and the skill with which it buttressed Allied unity and achieved Russian acquiescence," he commented.[19]

Years after the Dayton agreement, Bosnia is still a fragile and fragmented country. It will take even longer to stabilize Kosovo and Serbia, if the task can be accomplished at all. Jesse Helms and other conservative critics denounced the cease-fire agreement that ended the air war, even though that agreement met all of NATO's conditions for halting the bombing, because it left Milosevic in power in Belgrade and stipulated that Kosovo was to remain under Serbian sovereignty. In effect, this made NATO—and the U.N. Security Council, which had approved the agreement—guarantors of Serbian rule over a province whose inhabitants the Serbs had brutalized and expelled.

The Kosovo war exposed once again the ad hoc nature of American diplomacy in Bill Clinton's presidency. The ultimatum to the Serbs may well have been appropriate and principled. But there was no theoretical framework to explain why the Serbs were forced to accommodate rather than suppress the rebellion when no such pressure had been put on, say, the Russians over Chechnya, or India over Kashmir.

Nevertheless, Albright was vindicated by the outcome. Just as she had promised fourteen months earlier, she and Clinton, together with the allies, did not allow Milosevic to get away with what he could no longer get away with in Bosnia. It was hard to argue with the self-congratulatory assessment of British defense secretary George Robertson:

> However you look at the events of this past year, a defining moment has been reached in Europe's history. The generation like mine which found its initial entry into politics motivated by resistance to the Vietnam War suddenly found ourselves on the banks of a historic Rubicon. That Rubicon has now been crossed and our continent will never be the same again. We have taken a stand and prevailed. We have seen a horror and have stood up to it. Out of diplomatic options, we had to turn an Alliance created for the Cold War against an entirely different threat. Faced with the ultimately tough and stomach-churning dilemma, an Alliance of free nations, configured for collective defense, did not hesitate to act in the name of humanity. With all the formidable challenges we face, I still contend that the world is a better and a safer place because of what we did over Kosovo. We refused to stand back and let crimes against humanity prevail, and I am proud of what we did.[20]

The air war halted a brutal conflict that was threatening to spiral out of control and engulf much of central Europe. It demonstrated that the United States and Great Britain, America's closest ally, really had learned the lessons of Bosnia and were determined to act rather than dither. It engaged the Russians, angry and resentful as they may have been about other issues, in a venture they might well have chosen to torpedo, and by extension allowed Washington and Moscow to continue portraying themselves as cooperative powers rather than rivals. It established a principle, which Albright was eager to promote, that NATO would take on new missions, including assignments outside NATO territory, as the alliance evolved from a purely defensive grouping into something different, perhaps a Europe-wide security force.

Moreover, the relationship with Russia, attenuated though it was, survived a test even sterner than that posed by the economic crisis. The Russians were deeply opposed to the air war, to NATO's intervention in the internal affairs of a sovereign, nonmember country, and to the alliance's decision to undertake military action without the approval of the Security Council. Just a week before Chernomyrdin accompanied Ahtisaari to Belgrade for the final showdown, the Russian envoy had a published an angry op-ed article in the *Washington Post* arguing that diplomacy could not succeed as long as the bombing continued and threatening to recommend to Yeltsin that he end all cooperation with Washington—including nuclear disarmament cooperation—unless the air strikes ceased. The article shocked the Clinton administration because the Americans trusted Chernomyrdin and had welcomed his assignment as a Kosovo peace envoy when Yeltsin suggested it to Clinton in a telephone call during the NATO summit. The designation of Chernomyrdin and the dismissal of Primakov as prime minister had been read in Washington as signals of a conciliatory posture by Russia.

As Albright hoped, nuts-and-bolts cooperation with Russia on matters other than the Balkans continued despite the strains over the bombing. Four weeks into the air war, for example, the Energy Department's Rose Gottemoeller remarked at a Washington conference that Kosovo had not ended cooperation on the nuclear safety and material storage initiative. "We have been very pleased," she said, "with the way MINATOM [the Russian nuclear energy ministry] said please, let's just keep a quiet work schedule going. We don't need to get into the newspapers right now, nor do we need to be talking about what we are doing, but let's just keep working."[21]

In the end, Yeltsin, as feeble as he was physically and politically, was not ready to go as far as Chernomyrdin had threatened. Three days after the envoy's manifesto was published, Yeltsin ordered his new prime minister, Sergei Stepashin, Chernomyrdin, Ivanov, and other officials to draft a new position that would lead to an agreement.

Albright and other officials said that Yeltsin's intervention showed once again that he did not want to take Russia back to the days of confrontation with Europe and the United States. He was due to participate two weeks later in the annual summit of the Group of Seven industrialized nations, or G-7, which Clinton had expanded informally into the G-8 by including Yeltsin, even though Russia's economy did not warrant membership. The Russian leader did not want to miss that event, or show up as the perceived obstacle to peace in Kosovo.

Before the month was out, despite arguments between Russia and NATO over the future role of Russian troops in Kosovo, Clinton and Yeltsin were back to business as usual, almost as if the war had never happened. Meeting on the margins of the G-7 summit in Cologne, Germany, the two presidents agreed to a new round of arms-control negotiations, "confirming their dedication to the cause of strengthening strategic stability and international security."

Clinton backed off from American insistence that the Russians ratify START II before negotiations on a third treaty could begin; the Russians dropped their objections to renegotiating the Antiballistic Missile Treaty to accommodate the U.S. position on theater missile defenses. Stepashin reaffirmed these agreements when he visited Washington in July.

By the fall of 1999, serious negotiations between Washington and Moscow were under way, as the United States offered to help the Russians complete a large missile-tracking radar station in Siberia in exchange for an agreement to modify the treaty to accommodate American missile defense plans. Republican senators such as Mitch McConnell and John McCain said the offer showed that Ronald Reagan had been right all along.

Stepashin, however, was not the recipient of the offer. A few weeks after his visit to Washington, Yeltsin fired him, too, nudging Russia across the thin line between tragedy and farce. Russia's political leaders, embarrassed, threw up their hands. But the sacking of Stepashin had nothing to do with the United States; it was all about domestic politics in Russia. Managing this intricate relationship never got easier. Yeltsin's abrupt resignation in late 1999, in the midst of another brutal military campaign in Chechnya, opened a new period of uncertainty. By January 2000, after he had held the Russia portfolio for seven years, Talbott was describing the relationship as one of "mutual strategic mistrust." Still, bilateral relations did not unravel, and Yeltsin's handpicked successor, Vladimir Putin, told Albright that he thought of the United States as a partner. The answer to Charlie Rose's question was that nobody lost Russia, or at least nobody in Washington. Russia is a weak and fragmented country with a declining population, but it is not necessarily destined to remain so, and indeed as the Clinton administration entered its last year, many Russia experts were reporting signs of an economic turnaround. In the end, the Russians will determine their own fate.

Chapter 9

THIS IS WHAT PEOPLE CARE ABOUT

A FEW MINUTES AFTER James F. Collins was sworn in as ambassador to the Russian Federation on September 2, 1997, he stepped to the microphone in the State Department's ceremonial Ben Franklin room to tell colleagues, friends, and family members how he intended to approach the job.

He said he planned to concentrate on four areas of special concern in the bilateral relationship: preventing the proliferation of weapons of mass destruction, restructuring the post-Soviet economy, reinforcing democracy, and focusing on what he called "the issues of the future, not the issues of the past," such as combating international organized crime and protecting the environment. "These are problems we cannot solve on our own," Collins said.

When a career diplomat such as Collins, embarking on the ambassadorship to a country that had been America's preeminent security threat for half a century, included crime and the environment on his agenda, it was a sign that Albright was beginning to succeed in imposing the Clinton administration's hierarchy of global concerns on a recalcitrant State Department bureaucracy. Over time, this could be her most durable legacy.

To Bill and Hillary Clinton, Al Gore, Madeleine Albright, and their closest advisers, it is an article of faith that the fall of the Berlin Wall, the breakup of the Soviet Union, and the end of the Cold War required a corresponding restructuring of the purposes and objectives of American diplomacy. They believe that the old security threat—expansionist communism backed by Soviet nuclear power—has been replaced by a host of new security threats that must be confronted in new ways. These are the so-called global or transnational issues—terrorism, the spread of infectious disease, degradation of the environment, organized crime and corruption, and the devaluing of groups or classes of people—women in some societies, religious or ethnic minorities in others—that foster poverty, political unrest, and illegal immigration. Because these issues know no boundaries, they do not lend themselves to resolution through traditional bilateral diplomacy.

Proclaimed in many forums right from the beginning of Clinton's first term, this assessment became the cornerstone of administration thinking about the world, reflected in the State Department's "Strategic Plan" for future operations and in the White House's official statement of American security policy:

> Globalization—the process of accelerating economic, technological, cultural, and political integration—means that more and more we as a nation are affected by events beyond our borders. Outlaw states and ethnic conflict threaten regional stability and economic progress in many important areas of the world. Weapons of mass destruction, terrorism, drug trafficking, and organized crime are global concerns that transcend national borders. Other problems that once seemed quite distant—such as resource depletion, rapid population growth, environmental damage, new infectious diseases, and uncontrolled refugee migration—have important implications for American security. Our workers and businesses will suffer if foreign markets collapse or lock us out, and the highest domestic environmental standards will not protect us if we cannot get others to achieve similar standards. In short, our citizens have a direct stake in the prosperity and stability of other nations, in their support for international norms and human rights, in their ability to combat international crime, in their open markets, and in their efforts to protect the environment.[1]

Accordingly, foreign aid spending was no longer to be motivated by the desire to keep Country X aligned with Washington instead of with Moscow. Instead, it was to be motivated by the belief that an improved quality of life gives people in poor countries a stake in political stability: Give them clean water and access to school and credit, help their babies survive and their crops grow, and you will reduce their incentive to take up arms, embrace fanaticism, cut down rain forests, or migrate.

This is not altogether a new concept. George W. Ball, who was undersecretary of state in the Johnson administration in the 1960s, advanced it in the mid-1970s, arguing that the real threat to U.S. security was posed not by an enfeebled Soviet Union but by unrest in an overpopulated Third World. "With burgeoning populations, poor countries will require vast food imports that exceed their financial means," Ball wrote. "Unemployment and urbanization will threaten the continued authority of governments, drive more and more activist young people into outlaw gangs, terrorism and other illegal activity, and impel migrations that will threaten neighboring states."[2]

Even an old cold warrior like Zbigniew Brzezinski, Albright's former professor and White House boss, came around to the view that social disorder abroad, spurred by a shortage of resources, could threaten the United States. Predicting "a general degradation of the human condition," he wrote:

> Particularly in the poorer countries of the world, the demographic explosion and the simultaneous urbanization of these populations are rapidly generating a congestion not only of the disadvantaged but especially of the hundreds of millions of unemployed and increasingly restless young, whose level of frustration is growing at an exponential rate. Modern communications intensify their rupture with traditional authority, while making them increasingly conscious—and resentful—of global inequality and thus more susceptible to extremist mobilization.[3]

Even before Clinton's election, the State Department—at the direction of Congress—was issuing annual reports on human rights in every country, on terrorism, and on narcotics trafficking, demonstrating that concern for these issues did not suddenly spring up in 1993 with the return of the Democrats to the White House. The difference is that these issues, along with control of weapons of mass destruction, are moving toward the top of the diplomatic agenda; no longer are they frills or minor considerations to be dealt with as time permits. Relations with a country such as, for example, Chile, are now assessed according to the progress of democracy there, the opening of its markets, and its participation in international peacekeeping missions, not according to whether Chile's leader is aligned with Moscow.

For years after the fall of the Berlin Wall, Defense Department doctrine held that the United States had no substantial security or strategic interests in sub-Saharan Africa. Now, according to Susan Rice, the assistant secretary of state for African affairs, Africa presents a "panoply of transnational security threats" that pose direct danger to Americans: Networks of terrorists, the unrestrained proliferation of weapons, crime, and drug trafficking are flourishing on a continent of weak governments, deforestation, and AIDS and other diseases. Clinton, Warren Christopher, and Albright all went to Africa, Rice said, because they recognized that the long-term interests of the United States lie in helping Africa overcome these problems. "These are security problems that threaten us directly and indirectly, and we ignore them at our peril," Rice said.[4]

The difference lies not in Africa but in Washington's perception of Africa, in Washington's redefinition of national security. To traditional defense planners, Africa was more important twenty-five years ago, when Cuban troops were fighting in Angola and the Soviet Union was building a naval base in Somalia, than it is today. Not so to Clinton and Albright.

To the Clinton administration, the challenge of staving off the cataclysms foreseen by Brzezinski and other gloomy forecasters and building a more benign world involved much more than the reallocation of foreign aid. The administration's basic tenet has been that it is legitimate, indeed essential, for the United States to try to persuade other countries and other societies to conduct themselves like Americans, to embrace American political, legal, social, and economic ideals as the best avenue to a stable and prosperous future.

Albright articulated this ambition many times, most definitively in an article in *Foreign Affairs* as she neared the end of her second year in office. "To protect our interests," she wrote,

> we must take actions, forge agreements, create institutions and provide an example that will help bring the world closer together around the basic principles of democracy, open markets, law and a commitment to peace. If we succeed, the American people will benefit from a world economy that has regained its footing and resumed broad-based growth. We will find it safer, easier and more rewarding to trade, travel, invest, and study

abroad. And our armed forces will be called upon less often to respond to urgent and deadly threats. In such a world, more people in more nations will recognize their stake in abiding by the international rules of the road and seeing that others follow suit. Nations will be more likely to work together to respond to new dangers, prevent conflicts and solve global problems.[5]

These are not just gauzy themes dreamed up by liberals in Washington. Many foreign policy leaders in other countries hold similar views. Japan, for example, has joined the United States in developing an ambitious "common agenda" to "work together on global issues to improve the future of the world." This includes joint efforts to eradicate polio, educate girls in Guatemala, protect national parks in Indonesia, conserve coral reefs, and improve road-building technology. Bulgaria's foreign minister, Nadezhda Mihailova, on her first official visit to Washington, said that her country had completed its political transition from communist dictatorship to stable democracy and was well along on economic reform as well. "The real threats to our security now," she said, "are organized crime, narcoterrorism, and drugs," the same sorts of security challenges defined by the White House.[6]

The lofty vision expressed in the White House security document and Albright's article has had extensive—but still mostly symbolic—impact on actual policy, primarily in the new importance attributed to issues not previously recognized as foreign policy priorities, such as religious freedom and the fight against AIDS. In a statement on World AIDS Day in 1997, the State Department proclaimed that "reducing the threat of infectious diseases, including HIV/AIDS, is a major goal of U.S. foreign policy" and that the administration had committed more than $800 million to AIDS projects in forty-two countries—not a trifling amount at a time when Albright was struggling to find money for conventional diplomacy. This vision has also had some serious real-life impact on the practice of diplomacy. It underlay, for example, the administration's insistence that any countries seeking admission to NATO first resolve peacefully and finally any lingering ethnic or territorial disputes with their neighbors.

At the working levels of the State Department, however, the effort to translate the administration's new definition of security into specific initiatives and concrete outcomes has been hampered by a shortage of money and by a culture that has traditionally rewarded prescient political reporting and the fostering of bilateral relationships. Rank-and-file foreign service officers and their supervisors were not conditioned to put issues such as child labor or species protection at the top of their list of interests.

Most working-level diplomats at the State Department are organized by, and assigned to, bureaus that deal with specific regions or subjects. Regional bureaus develop expertise about various parts of the world: African Affairs, South Asian Affairs. Functional bureaus address issues that are not defined by geography: Population, Migration, and Refugees; Democracy, Human Rights, and Labor; International Narcotics and Law Enforcement, otherwise known as "Drugs and Thugs."

At least since World War II, the department's internal culture has placed a higher value on the work of the regional bureaus than on that of the functional bureaus. It is in the regional bureaus that diplomats develop the foreign language skills and knowledge about the political workings of specific countries that have been rewarded by advancement in the foreign service.

The functional bureaus, working on issues regarded as less relevant to vital national security interests, have often been marginalized in decisionmaking and the allocation of resources. Career diplomat Monteagle Stearns wrote that these bureaus "have traditionally been less powerful than the geographic bureaus" because the issues for which they are responsible are "the department's stepchildren."[7] The department has had an environmental affairs bureau since 1973, but many foreign service officers think of an assignment there as an exile to career Siberia. One reason is that the work of the functional bureaus, other than disaster relief and aid to refugees, hardly ever has an immediate, visible payoff. When a war ends, troops redeploy, refugees go home, and schools reopen, outcomes that can be seen on the nightly news; but a long-term international pact to limit agricultural runoff into rivers, for example, may never produce filmable results.

Strobe Talbott, who before taking up diplomacy was a writer at *Time* specializing in Soviet affairs and arms control, said that this attitude was understandable, given the history of the past sixty years, but outdated. "For the professionals working the issues, it's a question of mindset, of worldview, and of personal experience. Most of us who got into the business of understanding and trying to have an impact on the world during the Cold War, myself included, concentrated on the classic syllabus of international relations. Primarily, that meant the power politics of nation-states." Although nation-state rivalries and alliances will continue to matter, Talbott said, "we are beginning to understand, perhaps for the first time, the sometimes devastating, sometimes promising, always complicating interaction between human history and natural history."[8]

At the beginning of Clinton's first term, the president and Secretary of State Christopher persuaded Congress to create a new position at State to coordinate the implementation of their new vision of foreign policy: undersecretary of state for global affairs. (At the same time, the administration created a new high-ranking job at the Defense Department to incorporate environmental issues into military operations such as base closings.)

The State Department job went to Timothy E. Wirth, a former Democratic senator from Colorado and a committed environmentalist. He soon found himself frustrated by the pervasive attitude Talbott had described, which Wirth summarized as "real men don't do environment." He complained that he constantly had to struggle to get his issues, which included drug trafficking as well as the environment, added into the secretary's speeches and travel itineraries and onto the agendas of high-level bilateral meetings. He said publicly that the department was structurally ill equipped to deal with emerging transnational security issues and would remain so until it modified its promotion policy to encourage its officers to work on such matters.

Other than creating Wirth's job, the State Department did little in Clinton's first three years as president to address this internal structural question or emphasize the importance of the issues heaped on Wirth's agenda. According to Elizabeth Drew, the reason was that "by Christopher's own admission, he wasn't very interested in the new global issues of the environment, population and the like."[9] One of Christopher's confidants, however, gave me another reason: It took three years for the secretary to demonstrate what his confidant called "basic competence" before he felt sufficiently comfortable to begin the internal organizational work needed to alter the department's value structure. The crises in Bosnia, Haiti, and

Somalia, combined with Christopher's dogged determination to broker a Middle East peace agreement no matter how much time the effort took, left little room in his schedule for addressing Wirth's portfolio.

The U.S. intervention in Haiti, however, had the unexpected side effect of increasing the administration's sensitivity to the importance of the environment as a security issue. Talbott and others have re-counted many times the deep impression made on President Clinton by what he saw when he looked out the window of Air Force One as it crossed the border between the Dominican Republic and Haiti.

"What most struck him was that you could tell which country was which from high in the air," Talbott said. "The Dominican side was canopied with forests, while on the Haitian side there were mostly bare mountains. The president had been to Haiti in the seventies, with Mrs. Clinton, and he remembered it as a lush, green land." Now, with 98 percent of its forests and half of its topsoil gone and its population growing rapidly, Haiti faced a grim struggle for survival, let alone progress.[10]

Contrary to Drew's assessment, Christopher was indeed interested in the environmental component of diplomacy. He had seen the impact of environmental degradation firsthand as a boy in North Dakota during the Depression, when dust storms ravaged the crop-lands and his father, a small-town banker, drove around foreclosing on the neighbors' farms. As a trustee of Stanford University, Christopher had been influenced by the university's president, Donald Kennedy, a prominent biologist and environmental activist. As secretary of state, Christopher said, he was inspired by Vice President Gore to think of issues such as global warming as foreign policy concerns, since they could be addressed only through international cooperation.

Kennedy's input was crucial because he strongly believed that environmental degradation and competition for scarce resources such as water can provoke civil wars and regional conflicts. He was the principal author of an influential study that projected a grim future in which impoverished masses driven by disease, thirst, infant mortality, and failing crops challenge the security of industrialized nations trying to preserve their privileged status.[11]

Kennedy's view is not universally accepted—many economists, for example, think that mineral and agricultural commodities are more readily available today than in decades past, as reflected by their inflation-adjusted lower prices—but Christopher signed on with the more pessimistic projection.[12] Within the U.S. government, Christopher noted, "environmental matters had long been considered primarily the domain of such domestic agencies as the Environmental Protection Agency and the Department of the Interior. The State Department had an Oceans, Environment, and Sciences Bureau, but it was a kind of organizational orphan, seemingly lost in the bureaucracy."[13] Only after three tumultuous years in office did Christopher turn serious attention to this "orphan."

He issued an internal memorandum entitled "Integrating Environmental Issues into the Department's Core Foreign Policy Goals." It declared that "America's national interests are inextricably linked with the quality of the earth's environment" and instructed all assistant secretaries to submit detailed proposals for integrating environmental concerns into their operations. He ordered that the itinerary for every trip he made overseas include at least one environment-related event and that either Wirth's office or the environment bureau be represented in planning sessions for every bilateral meeting and international conference on the department's schedule. He further directed that every embassy's "Mission Program Plan" include environmental concerns. And he instructed the department's budget officers to come up with the money to do this work.[14]

Then Christopher went to Stanford and—with Kennedy as his host—made his commitment public with a landmark speech, the first ever given by a secretary of state devoted entirely to environmental matters. He said:

> In carrying out America's foreign policy, we will, of course, use our diplomacy backed by strong military forces to meet traditional and continuing threats to our security, as well as to meet new threats such as terrorism, weapons proliferation, drug trafficking, and international crime. But we must also contend with the vast new dangers posed to our national interests by damage to the environment and resulting global and regional instability. As the flagship institution of American foreign policy, the State Department must spearhead a government-wide effort to meet these environmental challenges.[15]

Albright embraced Christopher's commitment. In one public appearance after another, in the United States and abroad, she stated her views in blunt and uncomplicated terms. The language of her commencement address at the University of Minnesota in 1998 was typical:

> We are about to enter a century when there will be far more of us around the world, living closer together, consuming more, demanding more, using more and throwing more away. Isn't it only common sense that we take reasonable steps to restrain population growth and safeguard the health of our air and the cleanliness of our rivers, lakes and coasts? For if we fail to do that, we will deny our children and our children's children the legacy of abundance we ourselves inherited. That would be a felony against the future. And it is not acceptable—to you, or to me.[16]

Nevertheless, as Christopher predicted, it has been difficult to reorganize the State Department and get the money to translate this policy into action. Albright scrapped, for example, the issuance of annual reports on the status of the global environment, along the lines of the annual appraisal of human rights, after only one report because of a shortage of funds. But she pressed ahead with Christopher's challenge to the department's bureaucracy to change the way it thinks about the practice of diplomacy in this new era.

In her first year, she summoned all the undersecretaries, assistant secretaries, and their deputies to a brainstorming session about the diplomatic agenda. The discussion was organized not around specific countries but around issues that cross national boundaries such as water and energy. "She told people she wants them to plan their work around these issues," a senior aide said. A similar session at the beginning of her third year addressed the question of what the United States could do to encourage and sustain the spread of democracy.

Albright instructed Edward "Skip" Gnehm, a career diplomat and director general of the foreign service, to revamp personnel policies to reward officers who took up the transnational issues. "She said, 'Skip, I'm completely convinced that if the United States is going to remain powerful, we have to convince other countries to see it our way on narcotics, the environment, crime and terrorism. But your people don't like doing these jobs. They don't like doing multilateral diplomacy,'" Gnehm recalled. The promotion and assignment system must reward those who heed this call, she told him.[17]

Albright reorganized the so-called D Committee, which selects candidates for the department's most prized senior positions, to include representatives from the global affairs office and the economic bureau, enhancing the prospects for career advancement. She directed the Foreign Service Institute, the department's diplomatic training center, to expand the portion of its curriculum devoted to environmental and other transnational issues.

In her third month in office, she went to the institute to convey these instructions personally. "There are still some who refuse to accept that confronting these new threats is real, serious foreign policy," she said.

> Like Bismarck, they want to play geopolitical chess, but don't realize the board is not two-dimensional anymore. The players today are not only nations, but a host of nonstate actors. The issues are often not separable, but interconnected. The rules change with every scientific breakthrough. And the outcome is not zero-sum: In the long run, either we will all do better, or none of us will. To function successfully in this diverse, fast-paced and rapidly changing environment, we will need women and men trained to deal with the world not as it was but as it is and as it will become.

She said that the department needed "people who can think and act globally" rather than bilaterally, and would consider such capabilities in "our recruiting, our training, our promotions, our operations and our performance."[18]

The State Department regularly announces developments relating to environmental issues, migration, women's rights, public health cooperation, and religious freedom but these announcements attract little public attention, partly because most of my colleagues in the press corps share the foreign service officers' bias about their relative importance. I once mentioned to Albright that my friends in the pressroom made fun of me because I occasionally wrote about environmental issues, which they routinely ignored.

"Hang in there with me, Tom," she said, "because this is what people care about. This is the reason to care about foreign policy. The nuclear priesthood that wrote about nuclear weapons, they're going out of business."

To make this claim is not to say that "power politics doesn't exist," she added. "I'm not naive in terms of understanding that power politics between nations goes on." But in the next century, she said, the "global issues" will be of paramount importance. "We have an opportunity to get some understanding about these now and integrate them into our way of thinking so that when they are even more front and center, we're more capable of dealing with them." She said that she would not tolerate the attitude that "these are soft issues that you do when you don't have anything better to do" because it was clear that environmental matters in particular are "intrinsic to the basis of how many countries operate, in terms of whether their economies function because their forests are being burned for charcoal or whether their water is undrinkable or whether the pollution is such that they can't breathe."[19]

That was the significance of Collins's remarks a few months later: They showed that the message was getting through, that the ambassadorial in-box was expanding to accommodate the so-called soft issues, which their boss had instructed them to take seriously. Since Collins has been in Moscow, of course, the political and economic turmoil there has limited what he can accomplish on the environmental front, but the Russians have generally recognized that they must address the ecological disasters inflicted on them by the policies of the Soviet Union, and environmental work has emerged as an important area of cooperation in the bilateral relationship, as it has in China.

Collins was reflecting the gist of Christopher's Stanford remarks. "There can be no doubt," Christopher said,

> that building stable market democracies in the former Soviet Union and Central Europe will reinforce our own security. However, for these new nations to succeed, we must help them overcome the poisonous factories, soot-filled skies and ruined rivers that are one of the bitter legacies of communism. The experience of this region demonstrates that governments that abuse their citizens all too often have a similar contempt for the environment.

This is not to say that everyone in the department has accepted, or even heard, Albright's message, or that the incremental changes begun under Christopher will necessarily survive her departure. As Talbott observed, "The susceptibility of an institution to reform is inversely proportional to its venerability, and the State Department is no exception."[20]

Nor is the environment the only "global issue" to meet institutional resistance. In May 1999, as the air war against Yugoslavia was intensifying, the administration's Advisory Committee on Religious Freedom Abroad, which was based in the State Department's human rights bureau, described the same mind-set in its final report to the secretary of state and to the president.

The committee, made up of theologians, members of the clergy, and scholars of many faiths, noted with satisfaction that the administration was receptive to the religious freedom issue, but said that that was not enough.

> Secretary Albright, in one of her first statements after taking office, announced clearly and publicly that religious freedom must be treated as a foreign policy priority. Through a series of worldwide cables, Secretaries Christopher and Albright instructed all U.S. diplomatic posts to give greater attention to religious freedom both in their reporting and in their advocacy, emphasizing the need for State Department employees and foreign governments alike to treat religious liberty as a priority in U.S. foreign policy. Despite a positive trend and several constructive new initiatives, however, the State Department and U.S. Embassies often approach religious freedom issues in an ad hoc and reactive manner. Responses to particular problems have often been shaped by factors such as U.S. Ambassadors' attitudes on intervention in human rights cases, media or congressional interest, and U.S. Embassy staffing levels. The result is an approach that varies somewhat from case to case and country to country. This pattern is attributable, in part, to lingering institutional uncertainty in the State Department about the role of human rights in U.S. foreign policy and about the relative importance of religious freedom when weighed against other foreign policy priorities.[21]

That report came out at a time when the State Department was fighting several major diplomatic fires at once, not just in Kosovo, where the bombing had strained relations with Russia and China, but on the Korean peninsula, in central and East Africa, and in Southeast Asia. There was no way the fate of the Bahais in Iran, for example, or of independent churches in Vietnam could command front-burner attention in such a time of stress. In this sense, diplomats in the foreign service are like journalists: They want to be where the action is, a natural response that makes it difficult to channel their energies elsewhere.

Just a day or two after Albright's remarks at the Foreign Service Institute about changing this culture, I saw what she was up against when a midlevel official flagged me down in a State Department hallway to ridicule her comments. He said that he wanted me to be aware of his concerns, which he said many colleagues shared.

He described the global issues agenda as "hyperactivity," which he said rendered the United States unable or unwilling to differentiate the vital from the merely desirable. He scorned Albright's commitment to women's rights, a matter about which he said, "We can't do anything," and said that elevating issues such as AIDS prevention and religious freedom to prominence in foreign policy reduces the significance of what he said are the serious national security issues. "When everything is important, nothing is important," the official said. Rather than trying to restore order in Africa, which in his view is beyond American competence and beyond America's real need, the department should be worrying about "suitcase nukes," small nuclear weapons smuggled out of Russia for sale to terrorists. As for the underlying notion that fostering democracy overseas promotes American national security because democratic countries do not start wars with each other, he called that "an expression of hope" rather than a workable policy.

This gentleman was not alone in his views; indeed, his opinions are shared by many foreign policy specialists in Washington, in the government as well as in private institutions. But the fact is that Clinton and his team, with Albright's vigorous support and commitment, steered the focus and practice of foreign policy in new directions.

Frank E. Loy, who succeeded Wirth in the fall of 1998, said he found that the effort to restructure the department and reshape the attitude of its professional employees had advanced sufficiently that "there is absolutely no possibility that it will blow over" after Albright's departure.

I don't mean to suggest that it's even across the board. Some recognize this much more fully than others, but I think there is no going back. And that's true, I believe, both because there is an increasing intellectual understanding of the proposition that these issues increasingly shape what we try to do, what we try to accomplish in the way of foreign policy, and also because I think there is increasingly a habit of thinking on the part of foreign policy professionals that recognizes that these are not sideline issues but central issues.

Loy served in the department during the administrations of Lyndon Johnson and Jimmy Carter, so he had a basis for comparison. Despite Carter's personal commitment to the human rights issue, Loy said, the department's human rights bureau "was viewed as a very special exotic animal that constantly tried to introduce subject matter that didn't belong here."

Now, he said, he has no difficulty in getting global issues such as the environment or human rights onto the agenda for any conference or overseas trip by the secretary of state, or included in the talking points for Clinton's or Albright's meetings with foreign leaders. "There's hardly a head of state who emerges from the Oval Office who did not end up discussing climate change with the president. Sometimes that's true even if it's not in the talking points because by now some of these issues are so imbedded in our sense of priorities," Loy said.[22]

Any doubt about this evolution of priorities should have been dispelled by the proceedings at the second Summit of the Americas in 1998, a gathering in Santiago, Chile, of the leaders of every Western Hemisphere country except Cuba. The Cubans were excluded because their government was still communist, and Fidel Castro could not be admitted into a gathering promoted by Washington to celebrate the triumph of democracy in the Americas.

The Summit of the Americas represented nothing less than an ambitious effort by the United States to enlist the support and cooperation of the Western Hemisphere nations in a mutually supportive joint effort to advance the cause of democracy. It was made possible by the startling transformation that had swept through Latin America in the late 1980s and early 1990s: The long civil wars in Central America came to an end, and the military dictatorships in

Argentina, Chile, Venezuela, Brazil, Bolivia, and Paraguay were replaced by more or less democratic civilian governments.

The theme of the Santiago gathering, promulgated by Clinton and endorsed by the host, Chilean president Eduardo Frei, was that democracy is not necessarily self-sustaining. Especially in countries with scant democratic tradition, it had to be reinforced by a so-called second generation of social and economic reform that would prove to ordinary people that democracy pays off. It was one thing for elected leaders to adopt resolutions; it was another for the new political systems to deliver health care, education, land reform, jobs, economic opportunity, and an equitable criminal justice system.

The final communiqué issued by that hemispheric summit was an astonishing document. The leaders pledged that their countries would achieve a state of political, economic, social, and environmental elevation never attained by any society in history. They approved a thirty-four-page "Plan of Action" intended to put an end to discrimination and injustice, guarantee access to education for everyone, eliminate infectious diseases, protect the environment, respect the cultures of "indigenous peoples," expand economic opportunity and access to credit, combat drug trafficking, and in general "continue reforms designed to improve the living conditions of the peoples of the Americas and to achieve a mutually supportive community."

So grand and sweeping were the objectives laid out in this communiqué that the document lent itself to ridicule. Journalists attending the event joked that if its commitments were carried out, they would lose their jobs because there would never be any bad news to write about. It was much easier to envision a prosperous, healthy future in resource-rich, relatively stable countries such as Chile and Argentina than in Haiti, say, or Nicaragua, or some of the tiny island states of the Caribbean.

In fairness, many elements of the "Plan of Action" were more than just self-congratulatory hot air; they contained specific ideas and commitments that, if carried out, would offer millions of people a better shot at a decent, peaceful life. For Madeleine Albright and Hillary Clinton, the objective was to ensure that the beneficiaries included women.

During the summit, Josefina Bilbao, minister-director of the Chilean National Women's Service, convened a "colloquy" on the opportunities and challenges facing women in public life. Albright, who as secretary of state was required to attend the summit's formal sessions with President Clinton, could not participate in the event but sent this message:

> Make no mistake. Defending and strengthening the status of women and girls in the Americas is essential to ensuring that the democracy and growing prosperity that we celebrate here in Santiago is equitable and durable. Women are more than fifty percent of the voters, the consumers, the heads of household, and the educators of our children, from the first moments of a child's life throughout the many phases of a child's life. Women have roles and responsibilities that form the very fabric of society. We shape lives and are determinants of history, the history of our families, our communities and our countries. However, many of our contributions are frequently undervalued or taken for granted.
>
> In the Americas today, the reality is that women are not able to fully participate in the political, economic and social lives of our countries because legal, economic and societal barriers prevent us from doing so. Actions necessary to eliminate the formal barriers that are enshrined in law, as well as the informal barriers that are imbued in the attitudes and in customs, limiting women's full contribution to political and economic life, are addressed in the language of the Plan of Action our leaders will sign tomorrow. The goal of legal equality between women and men, with focus on gender equity, by the year 2002 lays a challenge before us that we can and must meet.[23]

Albright was certainly right about what the summit participants would say on this subject. "The strength and meaning of representative democracy lie in the active participation of individuals at all levels of civic life. The democratic culture must encompass the entire population," said the final document issued by the national leaders, almost all of them men. "We will combat all forms of discrimination in the hemisphere. Equal rights and opportunities between men and women and the objective of ensuring active participation of women in all areas of national endeavor are priority tasks."

Holding no official position, Hillary Clinton did not take part in the formal summit deliberations, but that was not a handicap for her in pressing the women's agenda; it liberated her to take the message to the people. While the summit participants deliberated in Santiago, she flew 500 miles south to the city of Temuco for a day of missionary work among the indigenous Mepuche people. Her message: Summit resolutions and high-minded statements of governmental policy are useful, but the real work of building a community and establishing social equity must be done at the local level, at the grass roots. She agreed to take a few reporters with her, and I was happy to turn the formal summit proceedings over to the *Post*'s resident correspondent in South America and hit the road with Mrs. Clinton.

"In Santiago," she said in a ceremony I observed at a Mepuche school and cultural center, where the local people would be able to study their own language,

> the leaders will be talking about how to protect democracy, how to create a justice system that works for all people, how to fight poverty and protect human rights, how to make sure every boy and girl is educated and every person has health care, how to protect the rights of indigenous people to be able to use their own language and follow their own customs, and how to create respect among all people throughout our entire hemisphere.

All that is laudable, Mrs. Clinton said, but "the real work of making what the leaders say real in our lives will be up to people like us. What goes on in Temuco will determine whether what the leaders like my husband, President Clinton, and your president, Eduardo Frei, decide is actually put into practice in our everyday lives."

This concern for "everyday lives," especially those of women, is the single most distinguishing feature that has set the Clinton administration's foreign policy apart from those of preceding administrations. It had not been much in evidence, of course, during three years of appalling war and atrocities in Bosnia, or during the 1994 spasm of mass death in Rwanda, when the administration refused to utter the word "genocide" lest it incur an obligation to intervene. But by the time Clinton was well into his second term and Albright was established as his chief foreign policy officer, the administration had developed a collective belief that the key to avoiding such calamities in the future was to help rebuild damaged societies from the ground up, through education, economic opportunity, and political freedom. That was what Albright was saying when she got down on her hands and knees in an open courtyard to embrace Afghan children in a refugee camp; it was what she was doing when she went to a community center in a black township on the outskirts of Cape Town, South Africa, where three young black men had killed a white woman from California who had devoted herself to their community's cause, to attend a reconciliation ceremony with the woman's parents; and it was what Mrs. Clinton was doing as she spread the gospel in Temuco.

Nobody could object to these aspirations, although there was obvious irony in seeing Hillary Clinton stumping for universal health care in Chile when she had bungled the task of bringing it to Americans at home. The point she was making in her tour of Temuco, however, was that the aspirations would remain unfulfilled, regardless of summit declarations, unless local people joined forces in their own communities to do the "real work" of social and economic development. Here was a clear display of the Clinton administration's foreign policy at work: expanding the traditional definition of national security to emphasize economic opportunity and political and social equity for ordinary people—people who might otherwise resort to violence, or cut down their trees, or spread diseases, or become refugees, in ways threatening to American citizens. This was another version of the message Albright and Mrs. Clinton had delivered on their travels in Africa: The long-term security interests of the United States are measured as much in stability and justice in remote corners of the world as they are in submarines and missiles and strategic alliances.

"During the time of military dictatorships [in Latin America]," Mrs. Clinton said as we flew down to Temuco aboard her air force plane, "civil society was largely destroyed. There was no way for people to claim or enforce any of their rights. Now it's necessary to rebuild civil society," an effort that she said had to start at the grass roots with programs such as "microcredit."

This term, which appears to have originated in the pioneering program developed by the Grameen Bank in Bangladesh, refers to the provision of small amounts of credit—sometimes as little as $50—to aspiring village entrepreneurs to enable them to start small businesses. These businesses are extremely modest—perhaps involving the construction of a vending stand to sell snacks made in a home kitchen, or, as in Temuco, the formation of a sales cooperative among women who grow flowers in their backyards. The vast majority of these loans in Asia, Africa, and Latin America are made to women, enabling them to contribute to their families' support, establish their own dignity, and in many cases have fewer children because they have other things to do.

Mrs. Clinton, Albright, and J. Brian Atwood, director of USAID until 1999, are all microcredit enthusiasts. Just a few days after the Santiago event, Albright, back in Washington, met with Milo Djukanovic, the elected president of the Yugoslav republic of Montenegro. The topics of discussion, she said, included expansion of American economic assistance "in such areas as independent media, privatization, agriculture, bank reform and the availability of microcredit." This was the same theme she and Mrs. Clinton promoted all around the Third World: The availability of small amounts of money could provide economic opportunity that would improve the lives of people in troubled countries and shore up their support for a fledgling democratic system because they would perceive it to be working for them. Whether the system to be replaced was old-style eastern European communism, as in Yugoslavia, or Latin American–style oligarchy, as in much of South America, the objective and the tools to reach that objective were the same.

One country represented at the Santiago summit was Paraguay, a fragile democracy emerging from decades of military dictatorship, which had already received a firsthand tutorial in the Clinton administration's new theory of diplomacy.

President Juan Carlos Wasmosy came to the United States in April 1997, just three months after Albright became secretary, on one of the most unusual visits ever arranged by the State Department for a visiting leader. Wasmosy never got anywhere near Washington; he went only to South Florida and the Mississippi Delta. He was on an Earth Day tour arranged and led by Wirth, who wanted Wasmosy to see the ecological damage that could be caused by well-intentioned flood control and swamp drainage projects.

Wasmosy was a strong supporter of the planned five-nation Hidrovia, a massive aquatic engineering project that would give Paraguay and Bolivia access to the sea by straightening and dredging the Paraguay and Parana Rivers from their headwaters in Brazil to the Atlantic coast in Argentina. Wirth's message was, If you build that project, don't make the same mistakes we made in the Everglades and on the Mississippi. Think especially about the harm that could come to the Pantanal, a watery 54,000-square-mile ecosystem rich in wildlife.

Environmental groups throughout the Americas have expressed alarm about Hidrovia's projected impact on the Pantanal, and Wirth wanted to be sure Wasmosy understood what they were concerned about. He said that the idea was to show Wasmosy, an engineer by training, how the Everglades had shrunk and how its wildlife had dwindled because of flood control and water supply work done there by the U.S. Army Corps of Engineers. He and Wasmosy also flew over the Kissimmee River project, which Wirth described as "a massive channelization project that destroyed a whole valley in Central Florida."

After their aerial tour, Wirth called me to tell me about it, and then he put Wasmosy on the phone. "I think the American experience is going to be very valuable," the Paraguayan president said, without committing himself to anything.

~

More and more, these global issues such as the environment have come to infuse the administration's diplomatic agenda. They tend to pass with little notice because the media naturally focus on crises such as Kosovo and Iraq. Of course, crisis management will always command time and resources, but the administration has embraced the proposition that if the global issues are managed creatively, there will be fewer crises to manage. Yes, Talbott cleared his calendar and flew to South Asia on a high-profile emergency trip after India tested nuclear weapons; but he also went to Asia on another occasion to seek international cooperation to preserve coral reefs. ("Strobe got the environmental religion on that trip," a senior colleague said.)

Dan Geisler, president of the American Foreign Service Association, a professional organization for diplomats, is among the many who are skeptical about the sincerity of the administration's commitment to the global issues agenda. "The secretary interrupted her South Asia trip to deal with Iraq," he said. "Can you imagine her interrupting the trip to deal with global warming? A town meeting on Iraq? Sure, but not on the drug issue."[24]

But Geisler was mixing apples and oranges. Saddam Hussein's defiance of the United Nations required an immediate response; climate change and the other global issues do not.

Loy said it was true that at Talbott's regular morning meetings with the assistant secretaries, the representatives of the regional bureaus got more time than those from the functional bureaus, but he emphasized that that was not a valid indicator of the relative priorities on the department's agenda. "We just don't have all that many overnight breaking events that have to be dealt with," he said. "The war in Kosovo plays out every day, elections here, assassinations there, earthquakes, Hurricane Mitch, you have events that change the tenor of a country just like that, and they get a lot of attention," he continued. By contrast, Loy's staff was working on issues that may not be resolved for months or years and may never have immediate, observable impacts—one example he cited was an effort to forge an international agreement on trade in genetically engineered food products, which would drag on for another eight months before negotiators reached agreement—and therefore there was no reason to demand an equal share of Talbott's time at the morning meetings.

"I don't worry about that," Loy said. "I think what matters is whether people can keep their eye on the important things, and I think generally we do pretty well at that. If I said to the secretary, 'Look, we're in the middle of a crucial negotiation, and it's likely to go better if you come in,' she probably would, but how many times am I going to do that?"

Geisler might have been less dubious if he had watched Albright on a brief trip to Guatemala in the spring of 1997, where her agenda was neatly symbolic of the transition from the diplomatic issues of the past to those of the present and future.

The first stop was a cluster of plywood huts known as Tululche, in a remote corner of northwestern Guatemala. The place was a camp for former leftist guerrillas who had turned in their weapons after a thirty-four-year-long civil war against a right-wing military government originally installed by the CIA and who were now being trained for life as civilians—"the living end of the Cold War," as one of Albright's staff members described it. The United States put up $260 million for the demobilization program.

The camp had electricity from a solar-powered generator and a well that provided safe drinking water, but few other amenities and no shops or paved streets. The arrival of Albright's helicopter, kicking up clouds of red dust from the arid earth, brought out a legion of healthy-looking but undersized children to see what was going on.

"As I look at all the young children here," the secretary said, "you need to know that the peace is for you. Some of you may wonder why in heaven's name the Secretary of State is here. Why would she and the United States care about what is happening here? The reason is that we are all one family, and when one part of our family is not happy or suffers, we all suffer."[25]

It is hard to imagine Henry Kissinger saying such things, or almost any previous secretary of state. Albright's predecessors were mostly educated in the school of thought that teaches that the purpose of American diplomacy is to advance the security and prosperity of the United States, a goal to which the political future of illiterate villagers in the Guatemalan highlands could be seen as irrelevant, just like the childbearing practices of Africans or the timber management policies of Cambodians. To the Clintons, Gore, Albright, and their team, this is outdated thinking. To them, the best guarantee of security for the United States is the development of democracy, prosperity, the rule of law, and environmental responsibility abroad, not sealed borders or superior firepower.

From the guerrilla retraining camp, Albright flew down to the capital, Guatemala City, for the other main event on the day's schedule, completion of a bilateral treaty aimed at curbing a menace that strikes Americans more directly than the threat of communism in Central America ever did: car theft. This agreement commits each side to return to their rightful owners any stolen cars or unreturned rental cars seized by law enforcement authorities, and details the procedures to be followed right down to who pays storage and towing costs. However useful such an agreement might be, it seemed like an odd use of Albright's valuable time to get so personally involved, even trumpeting the event at a joint news conference with her Guatemalan counterpart, Eduardo Stein.

Not so, she said. Such agreements are part of an effort to enshrine the "rule of law" in Latin America, just like the hemisphere-wide agreement brokered through the Organization of American States to outlaw commercial bribery. She said that cross-border car theft is "a problem of quite large proportions for us, and it shows the kind of cooperation where nothing is too small and nothing is too big to talk about with our friends."

The same jet aircraft and instant communications that enable Americans to travel, study, and do business all over the world have also made it easier for criminals and terrorists to operate internationally. Thousands of Americans, for example, have been victimized by Nigerian scam artists who offer attractive—but phony—business propositions by fax and e-mail. In Russia, Albania, Ukraine, South Africa, Hungary, Mexico, and other countries where open government is a novelty, corruption and crime have eroded the stability and credibility of the state. Drug traffickers have overrun some of the small island states of the Caribbean.

This reality helps explain why the FBI, which has traditionally been responsible for domestic criminal investigations, unveiled in 1996 a plan to spend $80 million in Clinton's second term to double its presence overseas, stationing agents in twenty-three new foreign capitals in addition to the twenty-three where it was already represented.

The FBI's job is to catch criminals and develop evidence that can be used in court. As practiced by Clinton and Albright, however, American foreign policy aims to head off crime before it occurs by attacking the conditions that breed it. This is the basis for treating such nontraditional concerns as depleted fishing grounds, illegal logging, infant mortality, inadequate education, and the rights of women as legitimate foreign policy issues—so much so, in fact, that Talbott wrote of "the end of foreign policy" in an article explaining how globalization has changed the aims, and the practice, of diplomacy. "In the context of the many global problems facing the United States today, and also in the context of their solution, the very word 'foreign' is becoming obsolete," Talbott wrote. "From the floor of the stock exchange in Singapore to the roof of the world over Patagonia where there is a hole in the ozone layer, what happens there matters here—and vice versa."[26]

"These issues are the twenty-first century writ large," another senior official said. She continued:

> If you cut down your trees and plant palm oil plantations that will be played out in twelve years, you're going to have problems. The Malaysians used hardwood forest revenue to finance industrial growth. Now they recognize they have to have a balance. In the short run, it's very hard to talk about bombing Iraq and stabilizing water quality at the same time. But for

the long term, we're trying to persuade people that if they don't have a healthy population, they won't be competitive. Look at the Soviet industrial cities: childhood respiratory diseases, asthma, spontaneous abortions, high lead levels, stunted growth. And in China, you have high levels of heavy metal exposure, poor air and water quality. And we can't insulate our own society.

Albright and Gore, in fact, seized upon China's environmental problems as a tool for building a constructive relationship with Beijing even as the Chinese remained truculent on human rights and security issues and even as evidence mounted that China had stolen nuclear weapons secrets from U.S. laboratories.

China's leaders are amenable to cooperation, Albright said, because they understand their country's grim environmental predicament.

China's demand for energy will more than double in the next decade. It is already the second-largest emitter of greenhouse gases, the leading producer of ozone-depleting substances and home to five of the world's ten most polluted cities. . . . Since the United States is the world's leader in environmental technology, it is both smart and right for us to work with China on behalf of a healthy global environment.[27]

To translate her vision of environmental diplomacy into action, Albright designated the U.S. embassies in Jordan, Costa Rica, Ethiopia, Thailand, Denmark, Nepal, and Uzbekistan as "regional environmental hubs," where a foreign service officer is assigned specifically to address environmental issues on a regional, rather than bilateral, basis. This move was controversial in the department because Congress refused to provide extra money for the hubs, which meant they had to be staffed and funded out of existing resources. It also stirred resentment at USAID, where Director Atwood argued in vain that USAID country directors would have more access to status-conscious host-government officials than any midlevel diplomat dispatched by the State Department. One ambassador whose country was tentatively listed as a hub rejected the designation, arguing that a USAID officer was already doing useful environmental work on a regional basis and that there was no need to duplicate the effort. In a time of tight budgets, Albright's decision to devote scarce resources to the creation of the hubs signaled her determination to elevate the environmental agenda.

Public State Department documents describe the assignment of each of the regional hubs and the issues the environmental officer has been directed to address. At the hub in Bangkok, for example:

> Of particular concern is the Mekong River which flows from the Tibetan Himalayas southward through China, Laos, Thailand, Cambodia and Vietnam to the South China Sea. The annual flooding of the Mekong supports one of the most biologically diverse river systems in the world, habitat for over 1,000 species of fish. As the primary economic base for millions of people, plans to build cascades of dams on the Mekong for hydropower could have profound social and economic effects in the riparian states. . . . Many inhabitants of the region directly depend on forests and the vast array of plants and animals housed in them for their livelihood and survival. The consequences of some subsistence farming practices, uncontrolled logging, and unsustainable forest management have impacted and will continue to affect the overall economies of several nations in the region.
>
> Land-Based Sources of Marine Pollution: Given high rates of regional economic growth and increased trade both within and outside of the region, experts fear environmental degradation from land-based sources of marine pollution will grow exponentially. The seas of southeast Asia are the habitat for over 2,500 species of fish and invertebrates, and provide over 11 percent of the world's total marine catch. Overfishing and management of highly migratory fish stocks such as tuna are complex issues in the region, which are aggravated by destructive practices such as the use of cyanide and dynamite to capture coral reef fishes.

Meantime, in Jordan,

> The Amman Hub will promote, develop, and support regional water and environment activities, particularly those arising from the Middle East Peace Process. The Hub will work through existing regional mechanisms and institutions, and with national governments, environmental nongovernmental organizations, donor organizations, and the business communities within the region. Key areas on which the Hub will focus initially include: water; desertification; the Gulf of Aqaba.

The idea that environmental and natural resource issues can be dealt with most effectively on a regional basis is neither new nor uniquely American. Egyptians, for example, have long understood the need to cooperate with Sudan and Ethiopia in the allocation of the Nile's water. The creation of the hubs was merely an administrative novelty, which may or may not turn out to have been a good idea. Their significance so far lies less in what they have achieved than in their creation and existence as bureaucratic symbols of the importance attached to global issues. "I'm not going to tell you that all the hubs are equally effective, because they're not," Loy admitted.

The Clinton administration's best-known and most controversial international agreement on the environment was the Kyoto Protocol on Climate Change, negotiated in Kyoto, Japan, in December 1997. The United States committed itself to reducing its emissions of the greenhouse gases believed to be responsible for global warming down to 7 percent below the 1990 level. The European Union and Japan accepted similar limits, to be achieved over a five-year period beginning in 2008. But the administration refrained from submitting the agreement to the Senate for ratification because it faced certain rejection in the absence of a commitment from developing countries such as China and India to accept comparable restraints. Many senators complained that the Kyoto limits would put the United States at an economic disadvantage, without achieving the promised environmental gains, if polluting factories in fast-growing countries such as China were not subject to the same limitations. The Kyoto protocol, however, is not a valid indicator of the rise of global issues on the foreign policy agenda because concerns about global warming, and arguments about how to restrain it without undermining the nation's economy, preceded the Clinton administration, and the issue involves a wide range of nongovernmental participants.

With considerably less fanfare and controversy, the State Department and USAID have concluded a wide range of international environmental agreements that may be less ambitious than Kyoto but could nevertheless have significant long-term effects on air and water quality and protection of marine life. Among them:

- A "prior informed consent" treaty, in which the United States and ninety-four other countries agreed to require exporters of twenty-seven dangerous pesticides and industrial chemicals to demonstrate that the destination countries know what they are receiving and what the risks are. This pact was aimed at preventing the dumping of toxic chemicals on unsuspecting or economically desperate Third World countries.

- An agreement with five Latin American countries, Japan, the European Union, and the tiny Pacific island nation of Vanuatu on measures to protect dolphins from being trapped in nets during tuna fishing operations, a pact that Albright called "one of the strongest agreements ever negotiated to conserve marine life."
- Assistance to Egypt to end the use of leaded gasoline and convert Cairo's taxi fleet to run on natural gas.
- Adoption of a "Protocol on Persistent Organic Pollutants" requiring most countries in North America, western and central Europe, and the former Soviet Union to ban the production of eight toxic organic compounds such as DDT, phase out others, and limit emissions of those that are unavoidably discharged as industrial by-products. The United States and the European Union agreed to lead an effort to extend this agreement worldwide.
- An agreement with the other members of the Group of Seven industrialized nations and Russia—announced at the height of the air war against Yugoslavia, which Russia opposed—to establish coordinated forest preservation programs, including the provision of spy satellite data to nongovernmental environment groups.

Although these may not seem to be dramatic or glamorous accomplishments, they are real agreements that could have a genuine impact on people. It is much harder to quantify specific accomplishments in the other "Global Issues" agenda item to which Albright has devoted the most time and energy, advancing the rights of women.

Championing women's rights is much different from espousing protection of the environment, much harder to achieve, and much more dubious as a security issue for Americans. After all, there is no culture that endorses fouling its drinking water or turning arable land into desert; people in other countries may welcome American help on such matters. But there are many cultures and societies committed to the belief that women should remain in their traditional roles and that when resources are scarce, men should have priority in access to them. Observing the scale of domestic violence, divorce, and family dissolution in the United States, these other cultures resist exhortations to modify their societies to emulate America's. And whereas Americans may feel threatened by drug traffickers or the spread of AIDS, they do not feel threatened by female genital mutilation in Africa, say, or the denial of schooling to girls in Afghanistan. Horrified, perhaps, but not threatened.

These considerations did not deter the Clintons or Albright from raising the women's rights issue all over the world (except in Saudi Arabia, where it would be truly inconvenient) and from grafting it onto the policymaking apparatus of the U.S. government. Albright was not content to lead by example; she chaired the President's Interagency Council on Women, which operates out of the State Department and is responsible for coordinating the work of USAID, the Justice Department, the Labor Department, and other agencies in promoting women's health and education, improving women's economic status, combating violence against women, and trying to halt international trafficking in women for purposes of prostitution or indentured servitude. In Clinton's second term, with women heading the Departments of State, Justice, Labor, and Health and Human Services, as well as the Immigration and Naturalization Service, the Environmental Protection Agency, and the Office of the U.S. Trade Representative, the president's endorsement of the advancement of women as a foreign policy goal was welcomed at the top of the international affairs bureaucracy, if not by the rank and file.

As stated many times by both Clintons and by Albright, the rationale for establishing women's rights as a foreign policy pillar is simple: Developing countries cannot afford to squander the creative energy of half their populations, and augmenting the education and economic status of women will enhance democracy and contribute to the development of a stable middle class. Moreover, it is the right thing to do.

Clinton enshrined this view as a foreign policy commitment in public remarks as he signed a proclamation marking International Human Rights Day on December 10, 1996. He endorsed the

"Platform for Action" adopted the year before at the U.N. Fourth World Conference on Women in Beijing, which both Hillary Clinton and Albright attended. The president said:

> Beijing's message was as clear as it was compelling. We cannot advance our ideals and interests unless we focus more attention on the fundamental human rights and basic needs of women and girls. We must recognize that it is a violation of human rights when girls and women are sold into prostitution, when rape becomes a weapon of war, when women are denied the right to plan their own families, including through forced abortions, when young girls are brutalized by genital mutilation, when women around the world are unsafe even in their own homes. If women are free from violence, if they're healthy and educated, if they can live and work as full and equal partners in any society, then families will flourish. And when they do, communities and nations will thrive.
>
> We are putting our efforts to protect and advance women's rights where they belong—in the mainstream of American foreign policy. During the last four years, we have worked to steer more of our assistance to women and girls, to help protect their legal rights and to give them a greater voice in their political and economic futures.

Hillary Clinton and Madeleine Albright have preached this gospel all over the world, sometimes directly challenging local customs and traditions. On a trip to Africa, Mrs. Clinton saluted the leaders of Ghana for enacting a law barring the genital cutting of females and called on neighboring countries to do the same, and announced a grant of $1 million to help African and American women share ideas over the Internet. In Argentina, a mostly Roman Catholic country with restrictive abortion laws and three times the rate of anorexia and bulimia of the United States, she called for open access to "family planning and reproductive health services" and criticized attitudes that value women's appearances over their ideas and accomplishments.

Albright rejected in particular any suggestion that the role of women was a cultural issue and an inappropriate subject for diplomacy. Halting violence against women, she said in a message to the foreign service, "is a goal of American foreign policy around the world, where abuses range from domestic violence to dowry murders to mutilation and to forcing young girls into prostitution. Some say all this is cultural, and there's nothing we can do about it. I say it's criminal, and we each have a responsibility to stop it."[28] Just six weeks after taking office, she presided at an International Women's Day ceremony and proclaimed that "advancing the status of women is not only a moral imperative, it is being actively integrated into the foreign policy of the United States. It is our mission. It is the right thing to do, and frankly it is the smart thing to do."[29]

Albright demonstrated the importance she attached to this cause during her trip to India and Pakistan in November 1997. This was the ill-fated trip during which her schedule was disrupted by the crisis in Iraq. Several long-planned events were jettisoned, but Albright insisted on going ahead with one event: a visit to a school for girls at a camp for Afghan refugees near the Khyber Pass in Pakistan. Albright wanted to deliver two messages. One was that the Taliban, the reactionary Muslim militia that rules most of Afghanistan and has barred women from the workplace and closed schools for girls, would never gain diplomatic recognition or acceptance by the United States or other Western countries so long as this abuse of women continued. The other was that the United States recognized the special vulnerability of women in refugee populations anywhere; they are exposed to rape, and they often have to care for children as well as for themselves.

With Albright's support, the State Department's Bureau of Population, Migration, and Refugees—headed by a woman, Julia V. Taft—worked with the office of the U.N. high commissioner for refugees to set standards for refugee camps on how far women's toilet and shower facilities should be located from their sleeping quarters. The objective was to reduce the women's exposure to violence, a chronic problem in refugee camps. This is a small detail in the scope of the world's problems, but administration officials cited it as an example of the real-world gains for women that can be achieved with minimal investment. Another example is the $1.5 million from the State Department's modest discretionary funds that Albright contributed to buy firewood for Somali women at a refugee camp in Kenya. Women leaving the camp to forage for firewood were frequently raped by armed bandits. The availability of bundled firewood at the camp reduced the number of reported rapes from seventy-two in the first quarter of 1998 to sixteen in the same quarter of 1999.[30]

At the camp in Pakistan, Albright spoke to women and girls whose lives are so different from hers that they could be from another planet. Afghanistan is a poor and backward country that offered few opportunities for women even before the Soviet invasion of December 31, 1979—an event that precipitated nearly two decades of war, first against the Soviets, then between Afghan factions vying to control the country. Some of the women in the Nasir Bagh camp had been there for years, and their children had been born there. The Taliban had stabilized much of the country and the shooting had mostly stopped, but the new government's social policies made it all but impossible for the refugee women to go home. Albright told them that she had been a refugee herself, but she had never faced what they faced—she was never destitute, illiterate, or separated from her parents. Arriving by helicopter from a world that the Afghan women could hardly imagine and free to leave whenever she wanted, she had nothing in common with the refugees other than her femaleness. It was not even clear that the Afghan women quite understood who Albright was.

Nevertheless, words and symbols are useful tools in diplomacy, conveying messages and reinforcing policies. In talking to the refugee women, Albright was addressing many audiences, including the Taliban. "No society can prosper and do well if it does not modernize, and it is impossible to modernize if half the population or more is left behind," she said. All factions in Afghanistan were guilty of human rights abuses, she said, but the Taliban had been "especially backward and harsh in denying women adequate health care. And they deny them the opportunity to work and [deny] girls the opportunity to attend school."[31] These comments signaled to the Afghan public what the State Department had told a Taliban delegation back in Washington: Even if you consolidate your control over the entire country, the United States will not recognize you, give you aid, or let you claim your country's seat at the United Nations if you persist in your unacceptable social policies.

By keeping her appointment at the camp while canceling a planned visit to the Taj Mahal and other events, Albright was sending a message back home, too: This issue matters.

Within the department, that message has been conveyed in many ways. One woman who has had a close-up view of Albright's efforts to promote the women's rights agenda told me with delight about the time the secretary, on her way to the Middle East, read a newspaper article about how women from Russia and Ukraine are duped into prostitution in Israel. Albright decided on the spot to bring up the matter with Natan Sharansky, the former Soviet dissident who was then Israel's trade minister and the government's frequent point of contact with Moscow. Her staff asked the Bureau of Near Eastern Affairs to help prepare the talking points. The bureau objected, arguing that this was not an appropriate topic for the secretary to bring up while she was trying to engage the Israelis on the subject of peace with the Palestinians. She went ahead anyway, Sharansky was responsive, and the eventual result was an agreement among Israel, Russia, Ukraine, and the United States to cooperate in combating the racket described in the newspaper account.

Frank Loy and other department officials have said that such negative responses from the regional bureaus became less frequent as they absorbed the message that women's rights and abuse of women are to have a prominent place on the diplomatic agenda.

On International Women's Day, March 11, 1998, Albright; Hillary Clinton; Bonnie Campbell, director of the Justice Department's Office of Violence Against Women; and Theresa Loar, the State Department's senior coordinator for international women's issues, met with a group of reporters to offer a progress report on the subject and outline the agenda for the coming year. I asked Albright how she was doing in overcoming the kind of institutional resistance she had encountered on the Israel trip.

"Well, we do it here on a daily basis by making very clear that women's issues are national security issues because they are the basis of how societies operate," Albright said, asking Loar to provide more details.

"I can tell you that with Secretary Albright at the head of this department, her example sends very strong signals," Loar said. "When assistant secretaries go out to the region, they come and ask me for a briefing: What are the issues, who are the people I should be working with, what of your points can I incorporate on this trip? This is not the way it was a few years back at the State Department. This is a sea change." When Albright herself travels, Loar added, her own office is always alerted to advise the secretary of issues to be brought up in the countries on her itinerary.

"I think you have to view it, as I do, as a kind of historical process," Hillary Clinton said. "You move from the theoretical to the rhetorical to the practical and policy implications." The theoretical breakthrough on women's rights occurred thirty years ago, Mrs. Clinton added. Now the Clinton administration was moving bureaucratically and institutionally toward practical results.[32]

That same afternoon, President Clinton signed an order to Albright, Attorney General Janet Reno, the administrator of USAID, and the director of the U.S. Information Agency to "continue and expand [your] work to combat violence against women here in the United States and around the world." The order included nine specific steps to develop legal, economic, and diplomatic weapons against international trafficking in women and girls. Reno, for example, was directed to find ways to allow victims of trafficking, or witnesses to such commerce, to remain in the United States even if they were brought here illegally.[33]

Trafficking in women for purposes of prostitution or sweatshop labor is not a new phenomenon, of course, but it is only now beginning to be recognized as an international problem of staggering dimensions. According to Anita Botti, senior adviser on the trafficking of women in Theresa Loar's office on international women's issues at the State Department, at least 700,000 women and girls were bought and sold around the world in 1998, the largest number from the former Soviet Union. Some are kidnapped from vulnerable sites such as refugee camps and war-stricken villages, but most are apparently duped with false promises of employment or education. This is largely a law-enforcement problem that the State Department cannot do much about by itself, but with State Department prodding the issue has worked its way onto the agendas of the Organization for Security and Cooperation in Europe and other international groupings that can work together to address it.

The Clinton administration's efforts did not immediately produce any ambitious global agreements on women's rights comparable to the Kyoto climate change agreement. Most of what was done was modest and symbolic, such as the sponsorship of "Vital Voices" conferences to provide forums for women in other countries to make their views heard. USAID, which was directed by Congress as long ago as 1974 to address women's concerns in planning development assistance programs overseas, has handed out modest grants to aid refugee women, promote the education of girls, and enable women to start small businesses. In Nepal, USAID provided the resources enabling 260,000 rural women to learn how to read. In Bangladesh, it provided secondary school scholarships to 6,000 girls. In the Gorazde area of Bosnia, USAID organized a "cow bank," which gave a pregnant cow to each of forty women. The women were allowed to consume or sell the milk and cheese; the only requirement was that the cow's first calf be given back to the bank to be passed on to others. In Rwanda, the United States provided small grants to teach home construction techniques to women. These are modest programs; no direct U.S. economic assistance or advice from Washington on modernizing legal codes is intended by itself to rectify inequality or end violence over a broad horizon. Much of the work that has been done has been attitudinal rather than material, such as the administration's sponsorship of activism against sex-based violence in Kenya. And some of Albright's efforts have amounted to nothing more than old-fashioned jawboning, trying to persuade people in other societies that they would be better off if women there had full social, economic, and political parity.

One example of such inducement was a brief statement issued on May 17, 1999, welcoming an announcement by the ruler of Kuwait that women would be permitted to vote, and run for office, in elections beginning in 2000. "Support for wider political participation, including the vital role of women in the political process, has long been a pillar of U.S. policy. This decree represents a significant advance for women's rights and democratization in Kuwait," the statement said. The emir of Kuwait did not issue his decree to please Washington; rather, he was responding to the halting but perceptible social changes that modernization and education are bringing to the conservative Arab sheikhdoms of the Persian Gulf region, as was the ruler of Qatar, who had made a similar move a year earlier. In a tradition-bound Muslim society such as Kuwait, it is unclear whether many women will actually vote, much less run for office. Parliament defied the ruler, refusing to ratify his degree and effectively continuing the ban on female participation. Certainly a comment from the State Department would not produce any immediate results or actions, but it would be reported in the press throughout the region, where words from Washington are taken seriously.

The belief that societies benefit from fuller participation by women may be gaining traction, for reasons that go well beyond anything Madeleine Albright and Hillary Clinton have done. According to Jane S. Jaquette, a feminist diplomatic historian at Occidental College,

> The rise of women's movements worldwide has heightened women's awareness of their political potential and developed new issues for which women are ready to mobilize. . . . [A]s social issues supplant security concerns in the post–Cold War political environment, opportunities have opened for a new style of leadership and have reordered political priorities.[34]

The always provocative scholar Francis Fukuyama examined the feminist component of foreign policy and found it valuable. "The core of the feminist agenda for international politics seems fundamentally correct: the violent and aggressive tendencies of men have to be controlled, not simply by redirecting them to external aggression but by constraining those impulses through a web of norms, laws, agreements, contracts, and the like," he wrote. "In addition, more women need to be brought into the domain of international politics as leaders, officials, soldiers, and voters. Only by participating fully in global politics can women both defend their own interests and shift the underlying male agenda."[35]

Albright's view is different. She does not believe that the reason women should be educated, protected from violence, and offered economic opportunity is that they behave better than men; she believes that societies in general are enhanced by the full participation of everyone who has something to contribute. "I am not among those who believe that if the world were run solely by women, war would disappear. The human capacity for folly and miscalculation is widely shared," she said. "But the history of this century tells us that democracy is a parent to peace. And common sense tells us that true democracy is not possible without the full participation of women."[36] This is part of what she described as "helping friends to assemble the nuts and bolts of freedom."[37] It was both a strength and a weakness of the administration's practice of diplomacy in an unruly and imperfect world: a strength because it builds on and promotes the bedrock ideals of the United States; a weakness because it diverts attention and resources to idealized outcomes essentially unrelated to the imminent security threats of the present.

Chapter 10

FREEDOM IS
AMERICA'S PURPOSE

B ILL CLINTON CAMPAIGNED for the presidency in 1992 stressing domestic issues and the economy. When he focused on international affairs, it was mostly to criticize the actions of his incum-
bent rival, President George Bush, whom he accused of "eagerness to
befriend potentates and dictators." Clinton's favorite target was
Bush's decision to send envoys to Beijing to shore up the relationship with China after the Tiananmen Square massacre of 1989. In
truth, Bush and his secretary of state, James Baker, had a creditable
record in foreign policy; they steered the nation through the tumultuous period following the breakup of the Soviet Union, forged the
improbable coalition that drove Iraq out of Kuwait in the 1991 Gulf
War, and laid the groundwork for negotiations that would produce
Middle East peace agreements. Their humanitarian intervention in
Somalia seemed like a reasonable thing to do; few foresaw at the
time the disaster it would become under Bush's successor. It is true
that Bush and Baker did nothing to head off the Balkan wars that followed the dissolution of Yugoslavia, but even in the campaign summer of 1992, the conflict in Bosnia had not yet metastasized into the
nightmare it would become. Bush was not vulnerable on Bosnia in
1992; many Americans agreed with Baker's premise that it was primarily a European problem, that "we don't have a dog in that fight."
Only later would the flaws in that assessment become manifest.[1]

As Elizabeth Drew wrote in her study of the Clinton administration's first year, "the campaign strategy of maneuvering Clinton

slightly to the 'right' of Bush, of having him appear more the activist in some areas (such as aid to Russia, which Clinton managed to call for about an hour before Bush did), led him to say some things that he would later regret."[2] Once in office, Clinton figured out that perhaps Bush's policies were not as objectionable as he had portrayed them—in fact, Clinton adopted most of them himself, exposing himself almost immediately upon taking office to charges that he was vacillating or switching positions, that he failed to understand the realities of international security issues, and that he put expediency ahead of principle.

Within weeks of his inauguration, Clinton backed away from his campaign positions on China, Bosnia, and Haiti. These switches—combined with the widespread assessment that his foreign policy team, with the possible exception of Madeleine Albright at the United Nations, was flabby and indecisive—put Clinton on a foreign policy defensive from which he did not fully recover for three years. The moment when a U.S. Navy ship, the USS *Harlan County*, turned away from Haiti rather than confront a handful of pistol-waving thugs on the pier may have been the nadir.

"After the new president retreated from his more bellicose campaign rhetoric on Bosnia and Haiti," Drew noted, "Warren Christopher, his Secretary of State, observed on *Meet the Press* in late February, 'I don't suppose you'd want anybody to keep a campaign promise if it was a very unsound policy.'"[3] That was not exactly a forceful statement reflecting a comprehensive, clearheaded grasp of the world situation, but Christopher got little help from his boss. As the historian Douglas Brinkley noted, "Clinton made just four major foreign policy speeches during his first eight months in office, and all of them stressed continuity with his predecessor's policies."[4]

Clinton's indecisiveness and his penchant for hedging his foreign policy bets to avoid political damage at home were only the most obvious causes of the administration's early foreign policy distress. Another was that it had inherited some very difficult problems: Bosnia, Haiti, Somalia, Iraq, a truculent North Korea, and a fragile, unstable Russia. Moreover, Clinton and his advisers initially had no theoretical or conceptual framework for managing post–Cold War world affairs. Not until September 1993 did they lay out a comprehensive policy framework, and by that time events in Bosnia and Somalia had fostered a widespread impression of ineptitude.

Another problem was the personnel lineup. The senior members of Clinton's first-term team—Christopher, Anthony Lake, CIA director James Woolsey, the irrepressible defense secretary Les Aspin, and deputy secretary of state Clifton Wharton, who was totally out of his depth—were competitive with each other, held divergent views on key issues, and were generally ineffective in presenting the administration's case on television. Because the White House press secretary, DeeDee Myers, did not have access to decisionmaking meetings, no one was able to control and unify the administration's public statements on important issues—a fact that every reporter was able to discern and take advantage of, sowing further confusion. Christopher, although an experienced and effective negotiator, was widely criticized as inept, but much of this criticism was misplaced. His real problem was that he was a lawyer with a bad client, a client who kept changing his mind, giving conflicting signals and injecting domestic politics into security considerations.

In one memorable moment that dramatized the disarray, reporters traveling with Christopher to Budapest and Moscow—who had been told that there would be no briefings on the plane during the transatlantic flight—were roused from their sleep about two hours out of Budapest for a briefing by Stephen Oxman, then assistant secretary of state for European affairs. Speaking on "background," meaning that he could be identified only as a "senior official," Oxman delivered important news: Christopher, looking for a mechanism to stabilize the security of central Europe without antagonizing Moscow, would propose a major initiative known as the "Partnership for Peace," a loose security agreement in which former Soviet republics and former Warsaw Pact states could share information, communications, and military training with NATO.

The reporters, myself included, were furious. Why would they tell us there would be no briefing, then send Oxman out on background to reveal this important initiative knowing that we would arrive in Budapest too late to file it for that night's television news or the next morning's newspapers? The answer, it turned out, was that Aspin had held his own unauthorized news conference in Germany that same afternoon, while we were airborne, and had revealed the Partnership for Peace initiative—despite what Christopher thought was an understanding that nothing would be said publicly until after he had briefed the Hungarians. When wire-service accounts of

Aspin's comments were relayed to Christopher's airborne party, the traveling State Department team was forced to improvise in an effort to reclaim the policy initiative.

This episode had multiple negative consequences: It demonstrated confusion within the administration, diluted Christopher's message, eroded the morale of the midlevel staff members who had worked on the substance of the proposal and the plans for presenting it, and whetted the appetite of the press corps for more stories about disarray and competing agendas. Moreover, Christopher's aides compounded the error by insisting that Oxman speak only on background, rather than for attribution. Our editors back home were not about to use after-deadline stories from anonymous State Department officials when they had obtained the same information from Aspin on the record several hours earlier. As a result, readers and viewers got the impression that the initiative originated at the Pentagon.

Christopher's spokesman at the time, Mike McCurry, was competent and well liked, but he had no control over Aspin, Woolsey, or energy secretary Hazel O'Leary, who was cutting deals with the Russians on nuclear issues on her own initiative. Only when McCurry left the State Department to become White House press secretary halfway through Clinton's first term did the administration develop foreign policy message discipline. The only beneficiary of the early confusion was Albright, who came across as level headed and forthright as she represented American interests at the United Nations.

Clinton became president at a time of global uncertainty and shifting priorities; many of these priorities had not been sorted out by the beginning of his second term, when Albright became his chief foreign policy adviser. The two made an odd couple: Clinton, who had opposed the Vietnam War and is by nature a temporizer and compromiser, and Albright, a person of straight-ahead instincts and forceful views, who has often been frustrated by her boss's desire to reconcile and placate competing constituencies.

For most of Albright's life, the world has been an arena of two great struggles in which the forces of good and evil seemed clearly distinguishable: the confrontation between the free world and dictatorship, first fascist, then communist; and the quest of the peoples of Asia and Africa to put an end to colonialism and establish their independence. By the mid-1990s, these contests had disappeared, and so had the comfortable certainties they had provided to decisionmakers in Washington. Questions that might have been easy to answer in the 1970s—how to respond, say, to Russia's sale of 300 ground-to-air missiles to Cyprus—were much less so two decades later, when Washington was trying to build strong relations with a postcommunist Russia that needs export sales to support its economy. The old Washington lineup of "hawks versus doves" still emerges in arguments about China policy and missile defense, but otherwise there is less clarity in foreign policy thinking today than at any time since the late 1930s.

In late 1997, Moises Naim, editor of *Foreign Policy*, asked international affairs pundits in several countries to assess Clinton's foreign policy record and how it was perceived in their part of the world. "We did not anticipate much of a convergence of views," Naim wrote. "We were wrong." Although each commentator saw the United States through a different regional filter, Naim continued, "a common theme emerges: Clinton's lack of a coherent, long-term strategy or vision." The contributors found what Naim called a "strategic void" in the administration, based largely on the perception that domestic politics came first.

> Accusing any president of being too political is like criticizing a ballerina for being too skinny. It comes with the job, the training and, perhaps, the genes. But just as ballerinas can become dangerously thin, presidents can take the political nature of their jobs too far. Clinton's political reluctance to tackle tough issues—another theme of our contributors—until the last minute (whether Bosnia or the Chemical Weapons Convention) usually followed by a heroic *Sturm und Drang* that is then spun by the White House into an epic triumph, has allowed problems with allies and friends to fester, fueled public cynicism, and wasted time and energy on needless come-from-behind victories.[5]

Naim wrote that before the war in Kosovo, the biggest come-from-behind victory of Clinton's second term.

The appearance of political motivation sometimes subjected the administration to unwarranted criticism, most notably in the spurious accusation that Clinton had dreamed up NATO expansion in a quest for ethnic voting support in Chicago and Cleveland. But there were other issues on which the criticism was valid, as on the Helms-Burton cave-in or the reluctance to stand up to Israeli prime minister Benjamin Netanyahu, as James Baker had done with the previous Likud government in the early 1990s.

In the same *Foreign Policy* essay, Naim cited multiple reasons why any president would today have difficulty playing the "leader of the free world" role against which Clinton is measured: shortage of financial resources, multiplicity of players both domestically and internationally, confusion in strategic thinking fostered by the end of the Soviet threat, the worldwide process of decentralizing authority.

This is not to say that Clinton and his advisers have not struggled mightily to develop and articulate a coherent theoretical framework for foreign policy decisionmaking. Right at the beginning of Clinton's first term, in March 1993, Christopher gave a speech in Chicago that laid out the administration's plan to do exactly that. "Like the last generation's great leaders who met the challenges of the Cold War, we need a new strategy for protecting and promoting American interests in this new era," he said. "President Clinton has responded to these challenges by laying out an American foreign policy based upon three pillars: first, building American prosperity; second, modernizing America's armed services; and third, promoting democracy and human rights abroad."[6]

Obviously, it is debatable whether the administration has indeed modernized and strengthened the armed forces; pro-defense members of Congress such as John Kyl and Floyd Spence believe just the opposite. But despite what Naim's international correspondents wrote in *Foreign Policy,* it cannot be argued that the administration has failed to present a clear articulation of its objectives and strategy. Christopher's early speech had little impact, and the administration was soon overwhelmed by the crises in Bosnia, Somalia, and Haiti; but beginning with Clinton's address to the U.N. General Assembly that September, the president, Christopher, Anthony Lake, Sandy Berger, and especially Albright laid out in clear language, in many forums, over several years, their assessment of the post–Cold War world, the difficulties looming in an uncertain future in which the technology of mass death is readily available, and their sense of what the United States can or should do about it.

Innumerable critics of the administration's foreign policy have scored many points over individual issues, such as the failure to respond to the genocide in Rwanda or the surreptitious policy reversal on Iraq. But it is simply wrongheaded to assert that the administration has had no "strategic vision," no overall formulation of what it wants to achieve in world affairs. That formulation may be flawed or even at times naive, but at least it has been clearly expressed.

Anyone seeking information about Madeleine Albright's strategic vision need look no further than the article she published in *Foreign Affairs* as she neared the end of her second year as secretary of state. If I had to pick one paragraph that summarizes her approach, it would be this:

> To protect our interests, we must take action, forge agreements, create in-stitutions and provide an example that will help bring the world closer to-gether around the basic principles of democracy, open markets, law, and a commitment to peace. If we succeed, the American people will benefit from a world economy that has regained its footing and resumed broad-based growth. We will find it safer, easier and more rewarding to trade, travel, invest and study abroad. And our armed forces will be called upon less often to respond to urgent and deadly threats.[7]

Those who had watched Albright's performance in office found little new in the *Foreign Affairs* article, but that is exactly the point: She, like Clinton, articulated this vision and these themes so often, and so consistently, that there was little new to say. It's entirely reasonable to quarrel with the administration's decisions on any particular issue; it may even turn out in twenty or fifty years that the administration's most fundamental and far-reaching strategic initiative, the expansion of NATO, was the historic blunder that some critics said it was. But it cannot reasonably be argued that the administration has acted in the absence of a clear sense of what it was trying to accomplish.

What Clinton and his advisers have failed to do is find a short, catchy phrase to describe their overall foreign policy, a phrase that would resonate with the public. Cold War, Domino Theory, Iron Curtain, Evil Empire, Mutual Assured Destruction, Containment of Communism—none of these was relevant any longer, and Clinton's team had no simple notions with which to replace them. The world had become quite confusing since the end of the Cold War, and so were the attempts to describe Clinton's view of it.

Clinton and his advisers eventually settled on the buzzword "enlargement," as in the enlargement of free markets and of the circle of democratic nations. Clinton and Lake used it in speeches in September 1993—in a weeklong foreign policy speechmaking blitz that represented the administration's first serious effort to articulate a comprehensive overseas program—and the administration published a global review of its foreign policy and national security objectives under the title "A National Security Strategy of Engagement and Enlargement." The public, however, never picked up on the expression.

"Unfortunately for the administration, 'enlargement' proved to be a public relations dud; few liked it or even took a passing interest. The foreign policy community greeted the Clinton and Lake speeches with indifference and even derision," Douglas Brinkley wrote in a study of how the term was adopted.[8]

"This is no strategy at all, in terms of laying out goals and describing how the country achieves them, but rather a vague set of slogans intended to justify existing policies," Kim Holmes, foreign policy director of the conservative Heritage Foundation, wrote in early 1998. "Although it remains the official U.S. strategy, the theme of 'engagement and enlargement' has been quietly dropped and is seldom used by Administration officials. It has proved to be embarrassingly inadequate to explain the purpose and direction of U.S. foreign policy"—both of which Holmes said the administration lacked.[9] Indeed, a revised version of the administration's policy document, issued in October 1998, dropped the terms; it was titled "A National Security Strategy for a New Century."

"Trying to get the bumper sticker term for our foreign policy is a waste of time," said Robert Zoellick, a former senior State Department official, long after the administration had given up its quest for any such catchphrase. "But you can have a foreign policy with priority values, rather than one that is case-by-case, reactive and designed to immunize political threats at home."[10]

Zoellick is not a disinterested commentator; he worked for President Bush. Nevertheless, his observation went to the heart of the foreign policy conundrum that has lasted through Clinton's entire presidency: the inability or reluctance to relate specific events in the international arena to America's core interests and values. Within the overall framework of supporting democracy and free markets, specific issues have been pursued on a case-by-case basis, exposing the administration to charges of inconsistency, lack of principle, and failure of will.

In fact, Albright herself proclaimed, during that speechmaking week of September 1993, that the administration would follow a "case-by-case" approach in deciding whether and where to intervene in conflicts abroad. Addressing the National War College, she said that the United States under Clinton would assess such conflicts "on a case-by-case basis, relying on diplomacy wherever possible, on force where absolutely necessary."[11] Five years later, her views had not changed. "Obviously we do not use the same approach with an established modern power that we use with a government whose authority is weak and institutions wobbly. We consider the domestic pressures that may be affecting a government along with the proclivities and capacities of its leaders," she wrote. "For example, there has been much debate about whether we are more likely to influence the actions of ornery foreign governments by using the carrot of engagement or the stick of sanctions. The answer, of course, is that it depends."[12]

Of course, on one level it only states the obvious to say that the administration would address international problems on a case-by-case basis. It would be foolish to establish a rigid set of guidelines to control decisionmaking. That was the premise that underlay Albright's one-liner, "We have consistent principles but flexible tactics." On another level, however, such an approach often exposes the administration to the influences of lobbying, emotion-laden television images, ethnic-group interests, and congressional grandstanding, without having the tools to resist such pressures. The best-known examples are Cuba and Taiwan.

Four years after her 1993 "case-by-case" remarks, I asked Albright what such an approach meant in practice, now that she was secretary of state. She replied,

> The U.S. cannot deal with all issues and we are a superpower but that doesn't mean we can do everything alone. I believe that what we need to do is to find the right tool for the right circumstance. And in certain cases the use of force is the right circumstance and then it has to be subdivided in terms of what kind of use of force. This is what we have learned a great deal about in the last seven or eight years. . . . I think you decide what is

doable, where you can make a difference and whether your injection of force at a given moment can tip the balance one way or another, or whether there's somebody else that can do the job.[13]

Naturally, this approach is never going to satisfy those with a different sense of what is or ought to be "doable." When Albright appeared before a House subcommittee on April 15, 1999, three weeks into the air war against Yugoslavia, Representative Michael Forbes of New York asked her why the administration would risk so much over Kosovo while it was unwilling to make a comparable investment anywhere among Africa's endless conflicts. "This is one of those damned-if-you-do, damned-if-you-don't [situations]," she replied. "If I came here and asked you for money for every conflict in the world, you would say the U.S. is trying to solve everything. And if I don't, then you say we're not paying attention to them. So there's no cookie-cutter approach to this. We are trying different methods in different places."

No matter how many times she answered this question, however, it kept coming up because it was always valid. A few weeks after her exchange with Forbes, *Time*'s Walter Isaacson, who had written a biography of Henry Kissinger, asked her to explain again the rationale for committing so much to Kosovo when the administration had been reluctant to commit anything to halt the far worse atrocities in Rwanda. And she responded:

> We get involved where the crime is huge, where it's a region that affects our stability—the stability of Europe is something that's been essential to the U.S. for the last 200 years—or where there is an organization capable of dealing with it. Just because you can't be everywhere doesn't mean you don't act anywhere. We're evolving these rules. There's not a doctrine that really sets this forth in an organized way yet.[14]

She had been secretary of state for more than two years, and Clinton had been president for more than six, when she made that comment.

To a great extent, this is an "inside the Beltway" discussion. For all the carping among columnists, in the universities, and in Washington's think tanks, there is scant evidence that the American public believes the administration's foreign policy record to be seriously flawed, at least not since its performance bottomed out in the summer of 1993. During Albright's tenure as secretary, Americans have felt prosperous and secure; old fears of Soviet nuclear aggression and Japanese economic domination have receded, and although American troops were conducting dangerous operations in many unpleasant places, few of them were dying. As Christopher said,

> Not very many people at the beginning of the administration would have thought that foreign policy would turn out to be an asset for the president. Yet when he ran in 1996, it was an asset for him; it certainly was not a hindrance. So judged by the test of that reality, which is one of the few tests we had, I think that the way we handled matters was judged to be appropriate.[15]

According to the comprehensive quadrennial survey of public attitudes about foreign policy prepared by the Chicago Council on Foreign Relations, Clinton at the end of 1998 had the highest "very successful" rating of any of the ten post–World War II presidents. "The results show that by any measure, Bill Clinton has substantially improved his performance on foreign policy in the minds of the public since 1994. . . . The public appears to associate the perceived absence of international crises affecting them with the successful handling of foreign policy," the survey reported. "Some credit is perhaps also due to Secretary of State Madeleine Albright," who received "highly favorable" ratings.[16]

The survey was taken before the onset of the air war over Kosovo. Assuming that the public is satisfied with Clinton's leadership in that conflict, the findings indicated that Republicans would not have much to work with in terms of foreign policy issues as they entered the 2000 election campaign, and indeed the major GOP presidential contenders made little effort to go after Clinton and Gore on this front as they campaigned in the early primaries. Clinton's ability to co-opt Republican positions on domestic issues served him equally well in international affairs, as demonstrated by his reversal on missile defenses, his acceptance of the Helms-Burton law, and his decision to jettison Boutros Boutros-Ghali at the United Nations.

Perhaps the most comprehensive criticism of the Clinton administration's foreign and national security policies was an early broadside entitled "Security and Insecurity: A Critique of Clinton Policy at Mid-Term," published in 1994 by Empower America, a conservative advocacy group in Washington. The group's leadership could mostly be described as right of center but within the Republican mainstream: Steve Forbes, Lamar Alexander, and Jack Kemp, all of whom would be active in the 1996 presidential campaign; Trent Lott and Newt Gingrich, leaders of the GOP-controlled Congress elected in 1994; and Donald Rumsfeld and Jeane Kirkpatrick.

A sampling of the chapter headings gives the flavor of this volume: "The Haitian Mess"; "Clinton's Japan Policy: Bluff and Bluster"; "President Clinton's Economic Diplomacy: A Litany of Lost Opportunities"; "Clinton's North Korea Policy: Raising the Risk of War."

Despite predictions that the end of the Cold War would begin a new era of economic rather than strategic competition, Kirkpatrick and coeditor Jeane Tillman wrote in their foreword:

> Proliferation of horribly destructive weapons and ballistic missile delivery systems are on the rise and Americans have no defense against this danger; ethnic cleansing and aggression are about to be rewarded in Bosnia-Herzegovina; neo-communists are replacing the new democrats that had produced so many hopes for a better, more peaceful, freer world; our closest allies are becoming remote and the institutions which bound us together are weakening. The Clinton Administration's well-intentioned foreign policy team is making too many miscalculations.[17]

Written just after the distressing first two years of Clinton's presidency, when the administration's indecisive management of foreign policy had been on all-too-visible display, this volume made many valid points. But they were mostly about the management of U.S. foreign policy, not the objectives. Most of the goals Kirkpatrick and her fellow critics said the United States should espouse were the ones the administration did in fact espouse—eventually even including missile defenses. Among the objectives endorsed by the report:

> Democracy. The United States needs a democratic world. That means helping move the world toward free societies, free governments and free markets. We need a productive and prosperous economy and a civilized

world in which people can live in freedom. . . . Democracies do not start
aggressive wars. Democracy is the best guarantor of human rights, the best
peace process, the best arms control program and the best framework for
economic development.

Albright could have written that herself, as could Christopher.

Open markets. The U.S. needs open markets and free trade. We think
everyone does. Freer trade with our global partners means more exports
and more American jobs. We want to increase access to foreign markets,
not by triggering trade wars but by promoting free and fair trade around
the globe.

Again, this sounds very much like Clinton and Albright, who promoted open economic systems and argued for restoration of "fast
track" trade negotiating authority and against any return to protec-
tionism in countries facing economic hardship.

Similar arguments can be made with regard to most of the other
objectives sought by the Empower America analysts: "Judicious use
of force," "Peaceful resolution of conflict," "Defending against proliferation."[18] Who could argue with those? Certainly not Bill Clinton
or Madeleine Albright.

What this collection of essays illustrated is that for many of the administration's critics—on the left as well as on the right—the question was not what the United States wanted to accomplish in the
world but how to accomplish it. If the United States wants to promote democracy and human rights as well as free trade, does that
add up to shunning China because of its repressive internal policies
or engaging with China on the premise that economic expansion
will advance individual freedoms there? If the United States wants to
shore up fragile democracies, discourage the "neo-communists" of
central Europe, and strengthen the existing institutions of stability,
are those goals best met by taking new members into NATO or not?
If the United States seeks to discourage Iran from developing nuclear weapons, is that objective best advanced by imposing trade
sanctions that infuriate America's European allies and close a major
market to American business, or by seeking an accommodation with
Tehran in the hope of moderating its policies? If the United States
wants to curb the drug traffic in Mexico that is spewing death and

addiction across the border, should the president decertify Mexico as an ally in the war against drugs or not?

These are fair questions, and for many of them there may not be any single correct answer—or, as in Bosnia, the right answer may become apparent only over time, and at some risk. This illustrates the advantages as well as the weaknesses of Albright's case-by-case approach to the issues. Flexibility seems desirable, but to the extent that decisions about these matters are usually made while Congress is in session, or as an election is approaching, the case-by-case method of analysis subjects the decisionmaking process to the desire to score political debating points, or save money, or keep a particular shipyard in business to save its jobs.

Clinton gave a good example of this in his first campaign, savaging George Bush for "coddling dictators" in China. His attacks sounded good on the campaign trail but did not provide a sound basis for making policy. Had Bush known that the foremost among those same dictators would be the guest of honor at a state dinner in Bill Clinton's White House a few years later—while Chinese dissidents still languished in prison—he might have been better able to defend himself.

And Clinton himself was pushed by anti-Chinese sentiment in Congress (sentiment sparked by the same Tiananmen massacre that he had criticized in the campaign) to give a U.S. visa to the president of Taiwan—a decision that infuriated the Chinese leadership and created a dangerous breach with Beijing that took two years of diplomacy to repair.

So it is true enough that the "enlargement" slogan was a flop, but that is not the same as saying that the policy it sought to describe was a flop. That is like saying that a product is only as good as its most recent advertising campaign.

In many speeches and papers going back to her confirmation hearing, Albright has separated the nations of the world into four categories: first, the "good citizens of the international community," with democratic governments and responsible economic policies, who can be counted upon to observe the rule of law and honor treaty commitments; second, "societies in transition," trying to become members of the first group; third, countries that are too poor or disorganized to determine their own fate or make rational choices; and fourth, the rogue or terrorist nations, which "deliberately want to destroy the system because they have no stake in it."[19]

This formulation may be useful in explaining the world to audiences of limited sophistication, but it fails to account for countries that do not fit into any of the four categories, such as Iran, Afghanistan, Belarus, or Singapore. Still, according to Albright, the administration's goal has been to move as many of the countries in the three lower tiers as possible up toward the first tier. This effort has taken many forms—expand NATO, isolate the regime in Sudan, encourage U.S. investment in Kazakhstan, embrace President Andres Pastrana in Colombia—but it has been consistent. Even signing the Helms-Burton law, which was an act of political cowardice, can be seen as fitting into this overall set of objectives, because it is nominally consistent with support for a democratic transition in Cuba.

One of the clearest examples of what this framework has meant in practice was the administration's successful effort in April 1996 to prevent a military coup against the president of Paraguay, Juan Carlos Wasmosy. Fearing a military takeover, Wasmosy—the first democratically elected president of Paraguay in half a century—took refuge in the U.S. embassy in Asunción, a development that in the past might have presaged a quick departure into exile. In this case, however, the United States, in the person of Strobe Talbott, joined with Brazil, Argentina, Uruguay, and the Organization of American States for a collective show of diplomatic clout to head off the coup. The days of easy coups are over, they told the military dissidents; if you do this, we will see that you regret it. Within three days, the threat evaporated and Wasmosy returned to his office to serve out the rest of his term. In the short run, it makes little difference to anyone in the United States who runs Paraguay; during the decades it was ruled by Alfredo Stroessner, a military dictator, nobody in Washington cared. But Albright and Talbott saw the threat to Wasmosy as an important test case for democracy in all of Latin America. If the military had retaken control of Paraguay, who was to say that Chile or Brazil would not be next? The South American countries that joined with the United States to oppose the threatened coup in Paraguay had all had their own experiences with military dictators; by joining forces with Washington, they reinforced the message that South Americans do not want to go back down that road.

In the Paraguay case, the threat was imminent, the choices clear-cut, the stakes easy to explain, and the risks minimal. Failure to act would have exposed the administration's commitment to worldwide democracy as a sham. But more often than not in today's world, murky situations and competing objectives make the choices more difficult, and consequently more difficult to explain and defend. The most notable examples are the administration's commitment to maintaining a constructive relationship with China no matter how provocative Chinese behavior, and the decision to bet the future of NATO and of relations with Russia on the use of airpower over Kosovo; in both cases, there were credible arguments to support policies opposed to those the administration pursued.

The other clear and sustained line of foreign policy in Clinton's presidency has been to promote free trade and open capital markets as the keys to global economic expansion. This is a global "rising tide lifts all boats" theory, in which economic development is seen as the path not only to encouraging the growth of democracy but also to overcoming the transnational problems of overpopulation, environmental degradation, and drug trafficking. According to this argument, people living in democratic societies where economic opportunity is at hand are less likely to have ten children or to engage in illegal ivory trafficking, bootleg nuclear materials, or cultivate opium poppies. A thriving middle class is a natural constituency for open government, stable international relations, and the rational use of natural resources. These were the fundamental tenets endorsed by the collective leadership of the Western Hemisphere at the Santiago Summit of the Americas in 1998.

Viewing the world through this prism can provide a useful framework for analyzing relations with Russia (does the proposal promote democracy within Russia and help the Russian economy so that Moscow does not have to sell nuclear equipment to Iran?); or with China (does it contribute to the economic revolution within China, which in turn will lead to economic liberalization and environmentally sound choices on energy and water use?); or with the Democratic Republic of Congo (is Laurent Kabila putting the country on a path toward political stability and economic recovery or is he turning out to be just another African "big man"?).

For Clinton and Albright, the problem has not been in the lack of a policy but rather in the inconsistency of application. Why would the administration bestow political and economic favor upon Vietnam while continuing to shun Cuba, which never fired a shot in anger against the United States? Why would the administration apply tight economic sanctions against Burma for its human rights violations but shelve the same sanctions against China? Why would the administration provide political and material aid to Sudan's neighbors in an effort to bring down the government there while maintaining warm relations with Saudi Arabia, an oppressive society characterized by arbitrary justice and religious bigotry? Why would President Clinton, during his precedent-setting trip to Africa, put in a call from his airplane to President Charles Taylor of Liberia, a sham democrat who fomented a civil war and ruined his country in order to seize power, while shunning President Sani Abacha of Nigeria, a military ruler who seized power by force but never approached the scale of carnage inflicted by Taylor?

Albright's glib responses—we have consistent principles and flexible tactics, we can't have a cookie-cutter foreign policy—were in the end not satisfactory. They explained but did not persuade; they did not insulate any decision from attack.

The administration never did an adequate job of explaining to critics at home and to frustrated allies abroad the realities of dealing with a Congress that has become increasingly assertive on foreign policy issues. Secretary Christopher and several other administration officials, for example, said that the president had signed the Helms-Burton bill even though he and his advisers hated it because Congress had passed it by a veto-proof margin and was certain to override a veto. That being the case, the president—then running for reelection—decided not to take the political risk of vetoing the bill for the sole purpose of making a statement. Perhaps he ought to have made that statement—he should have stood up for what he believed in—but it is futile to expect any president to filter out all political considerations. The same could be said about the visa issued to Lee Teng-Hui, the president of Taiwan. That visa, and the way Lee conducted himself during his American visit, infuriated Beijing and sent U.S. relations with China into a tailspin. But the president's decision to grant the visa was virtually dictated by Congress—only one member of either house voted against the resolution calling for it. The president could have taken an isolated position as a matter of principle and defied that sentiment; in acceding to the wishes of Congress, however, Clinton sought to avoid a political backlash without retreating from his policy of constructive engagement with Beijing. The outcome was entirely negative: Relations with China soured, China-bashers in Congress got a boost, and the president's reputation for putting politics ahead of principle was reinforced.

Thus the administration's overall stated policy, although generally useful in explaining what the president was trying to achieve on a global basis, did not provide sufficiently disciplined guidance for specific situations, leaving Clinton and his team open to the very problem Albright had pointed out in her September 1993 speech— the necessity of making ad hoc choices—exposing them to charges of inconsistency and lack of strategy.

Espousing democracy and advocating free markets are strategies that provide little guidance in making decisions about countries that are backsliding, moving down through Albright's four categories rather than up, such as Belarus and Angola. Since it had no specific meaning, the slogan "enlargement" was easy to set aside when it was inconvenient, most notably in relations with Saudi Arabia, which has neither democracy nor a free market.

Throughout Clinton's presidency and specifically Albright's tenure as secretary of state, issues arose and decisions had to be made that could not be based on the foundation of "enlargement": How to coax or coerce Benjamin Netanyahu into complying with Oslo without rupturing the U.S. bond with Israel? What to do if evidence revealed Iranian complicity in the Khobar Towers bombing but no American allies endorsed a military strike? How to keep Colombia from falling entirely into the hands of the drug traffickers and their Marxist guerrilla allies without getting dragged into the war? How to adhere to the principle that NATO membership is open to all European democracies without alienating Russia by taking in the Baltic states? How to prevent all-out war between Eritrea and Ethiopia without sacrificing the help of either in confronting Sudan? In each of these and scores of other real-time foreign policy conundrums, absent the Cold War framework, the administration by necessity had to balance strategic, economic, and political objectives with a calculation of what was actually achievable—the clearest

example being the decision to de-link human rights and trade policy with China. China was not going to bend on human rights;
therefore there was no point in sacrificing promising economic relations and risking strategic conflict for an issue of principle. Albright
acknowledged as much at her confirmation hearing, telling senators
that she used to believe in linking trade and human rights but gave
it up because it did not produce the desired results.

To Albright and her colleagues, this was reasonable, practical, and
flexible; they rejected all charges of inconsistency. In the *Foreign
Affairs* article Albright published near the end of her second year on
the job, she took some pains to explain the difference between the
administration's response to China and its policy toward Burma.

Burma has resisted all change, rejected all overtures, and tolerated wide-scale production and export of heroin, Albright argued.
The Burmese opposition has supported the American policy of os-
tracizing the regime. China, by contrast, "is changing rapidly. The
government is committed to economic reform" and has shown new
willingness to cooperate on weapons proliferation issues.[20]

To critics, this determination to engage with China even as the evidence mounted of Chinese misbehavior—including spying in
American nuclear weapons laboratories—demonstrated inconsistency, incoherence, and an unseemly willingness to jettison principle for political expediency. Capitol Hill suffers periodic bouts of
China-bashing fever, but China is an emerging great power that
commands respect and cannot be bullied. Even the conservative analysts at the Heritage Foundation, no left-wingers, recognized as
much. It is easy to sit in a congressional office or at a university or
think tank and snipe at decisions taken by a president and secretary
of state, but dealing with China is hard. The same applies to the
drubbing the administration took for its failure to solve the Saddam
Hussein problem; for weeks, Washington resonated with calls from
pundits and members of Congress for a campaign to bring down
the Iraqi dictator. None of those commentaries offered a credible
formula for achieving that goal.

Henry Kissinger, for example, wrote that Saddam Hussein had
emerged from the inspections confrontation of late 1997 and early
1998 strengthened politically and diplomatically because he had accomplished, or nearly accomplished, his four major objectives.
According to Kissinger, these were: "(1) to focus the world's atten-

tion on Iraq's grievances, (2) to force into the open the latent split between the permanent members of the Security Council, (3) to involve the secretary general as mediator, thus putting Saddam Hussein on the same level as his adversaries and (4) to shift the focus of the debate from inspections to lifting the sanctions."[21]

The outcomes Kissinger listed turned out to be spurious—the Security Council did not split, and Saddam Hussein remained isolated; he did not emerge "on the same level as his adversaries." But even if Kissinger's diagnosis had been correct, what was his prescription? "It is therefore imperative to develop a long-range policy for the gulf—especially toward Iraq." That does not advance the cause. What it does is illustrate the difficulty of formulating effective policies for achieving objectives that everyone agrees are desirable, such as getting rid of Saddam Hussein, ending drug corruption in Mexico and Colombia, promoting democracy in Nigeria, advancing human rights and individual freedoms in China, or stabilizing the Balkans. President Clinton and his advisers, including Albright, had greater success in some of these quests than in others, but with the exception of the war in Bosnia it would be difficult to cite a country or a crisis where opponents or critics of the administration's course of action (or inaction) were able to offer a coherent alternative around which a consensus could form.

The end of the air war against Yugoslavia marked the start of a new interval of relative stability in American foreign relations as Albright entered her last eighteen months in office. Relations with China, which bottomed out with the accidental bombing of the Chinese embassy in Belgrade, remained touchy because of loose talk of independence from Taiwan and Chinese threats to use force in response. But Russian troops were deployed alongside NATO peacekeepers in Kosovo as the United Nations began the task of reconstruction with the dissipation of tensions. Israel's new prime minister, Ehud Barak, announced a commitment to set his country back on a course toward peace with its Arab neighbors and let it be known that he wanted to deal directly with the Palestinians, relying less on the United States. Asian nations began to recover from their collective economic meltdown. Even in Africa, tentative peace agreements offered hope for the end of several conflicts that had been dragging the entire continent backward.

These encouraging developments made it possible for Albright and her advisers to step back, survey the state of the world, and consider what they wanted to accomplish before the end of Clinton's presidency. Talk of "legacy" was in the air.

Albright authorized her director of policy planning, Morton Halperin, to proceed with what came to be known as the Community of Democracies project. Halperin, a veteran of the Washington policy wars whose background included a tour as president of the American Civil Liberties Union, believes even more energetically than Albright or Clinton that American-style democracy is the best organizing principle for society and that the United States not only can but should encourage or cajole other countries to adopt it. Long after the word "enlargement" had vanished from the administration's policy lexicon, Halperin was still promoting it.

A decade after the fall of the Berlin Wall, the world is full of countries that were formerly dictatorships of one kind or another and are now democracies, or at least claim to be democracies. A partial list would include Benin, Mongolia, Paraguay, Yemen, Nicaragua, Bulgaria, Mali, and of course Russia. In some relatively recent democracies, such as Poland and Argentina, the idea of democracy—political power granted and controlled by the voters, free press, independent judiciary, rule of law, free choice in work and travel—seems firmly entrenched and unthreatened. In others, notably Liberia and Cambodia, democracy is a veneer adopted by autocratic rulers seeking to legitimize their power. In a third category are important countries such as Nigeria and Indonesia that have just begun a transition to democracy and where the commitment is untested. Albright herself listed Nigeria, Ukraine, Indonesia, and Colombia as "priority countries" to which the United States should channel resources to support their transitions.

But what does it mean to support and encourage democracy? The question confronting Albright and Halperin was, what more could the United States and other established democracies actually do to help the new converts, encourage the democratic trends, and fight off the forces of regression—and how could they do it without fostering resentment of American meddling? Already, as Albright herself noted, "from Asia to Africa to the Andes, U.S. agencies and nongovernmental organizations are training judges, drafting commercial law codes, teaching the rules of parliamentary procedure, supporting efforts to protect children and empower women, fostering the development of independent media and otherwise helping friends to assemble the nuts and bolts of freedom."[22] What else is there?

The first person who told me what Albright and her aides were thinking about had been a guest at one of the secretary's policy dinners, a forum she has used frequently to sound out expert opinion about issues and countries. These dinners are supposed to be off the record; participants are asked not to talk to the press about the discussions because, by definition, they represent policies in formulation that are not yet ready to be presented to the public. The reality, of course, is that word of these dinners travels around town quickly, and reporters can usually find a guest or two willing to talk.

My first source professed incredulity about what she had heard at the dinner she attended. She described an ambitious plan to build a permanent institution, a "club" of democratic nations, admission by invitation only, that would become Albright's legacy.

This is what journalists jokingly call "a story that's too good to check"—that is, it sounds like a real scoop, a wave-making story, so go with it; don't check it out because it might turn out not to be accurate. (Of course, responsible reporters always check, and check again. Frequently, as in this case, no printed article results because the original account does not withstand the scrutiny.)

As I called around to people who had attended the dinner or been consulted by Halperin in other settings, I found that if he and Albright had ever contemplated the establishment of a freestanding organization, they had backed off because nobody else had thought it a good idea. One of the secretary's other senior aides assured me that she had never envisioned the creation of any "legacy" institution and had told Halperin not to present any such proposal. Everyone favored modest steps to encourage the trend toward democracy, but all thought the goal would be ill served by the creation of a "members only" grouping sponsored by Washington. Some argued that many countries that have embraced democracy, such as South Africa, would reject any initiative that carried a "Made in USA" label. Others said that any government-sponsored institution created by Albright or bearing her name would wither and die as soon as a Republican became president. Still others argued that any organization that tried to be selective in its membership would fragment over the definitional question: Which countries qualify? How about Iran, for example, which has a popularly elected president and a spunky, outspoken press? How about Taiwan, which now has a democratic government but which the United States does not recognize as a separate country? The group asking these questions included Zbigniew Brzezinski, Albright's former professor and mentor, who said that creating such an organization would either alienate friends such as Saudi Arabia by excluding them or water down the definition of democracy by bringing them in, rendering the effort meaningless. Several specialists argued that the most effective way to advance the goal of democracy was through regional groupings such as the Organization of American States, whose members have made democratic governance a condition of participation and committed themselves to joining forces to head off any threatened coups or takeovers.

By the time I talked to Halperin, he had evidently been persuaded. "We do not see the need for a new permanent institution," he said. Instead, he was contemplating a onetime gathering, to be held outside the United States under the sponsorship of several countries, at which participants would be expected to commit themselves to the principles of democracy and to provide transitional societies with whatever help they might need: funding for rural elections, for example, or assistance in drafting legal codes, or training for judges. Many private and governmental institutions already do such work; Halperin was looking to expand the circle of countries that would welcome this kind of assistance. He favored issuing blanket invitations: Any country could attend if it stated its commitment to democratic principles. Even if that commitment were phony, the professed adherence would open a door for the United States and other established democracies to demand compliance, as had happened in Europe when a still-communist Soviet Union nominally accepted the human rights obligations of the Helsinki Final Act.

Albright eventually settled on a "Community of Democracies" gathering in Poland in June 2000, in which Chile, the Czech Republic, South Korea, India, and Mali joined as "co-conveners." The purpose, she said, was to "explore ways that we can cooperate more effectively in strengthening democratic societies and values."

The real problem with this democracy initiative, however, is not one of procedure; it is one of overoptimism about the workings of the world and about America's ability to influence events. In Russia, Iran, Ukraine, Indonesia, Nigeria, Haiti, and Venezuela, regression is as likely as progress, no matter what the United States does. The administration's collective belief that global betterment is possible and that it can be expedited by American example and American inputs simply strikes many thoughtful analysts as flawed and naive, and the public is dubious as well.

The same Chicago Council on Foreign Relations survey that gave Clinton high marks overall for his foreign policy performance contained hints of more serious and sustainable criticism of the administration's approach to world affairs as practiced not just by Clinton and Albright but also by Vice President Gore and Hillary Rodham Clinton. The survey found very little support for "goals that might be associated with altruistic internationalism, or goals that would primarily benefit others. For example, helping to improve the standard of living of less developed countries is seen as a very important goal by only 29% of the public; it shares the very bottom of the list with the aim of helping to bring a democratic form of government to other nations." Moreover, Americans are committed to engagement in world affairs to protect their own interests "rather than to foster change around the world according to an American model."[23]

This finding validates to some extent the criticism of such academics as Michael Mandelbaum, who famously skewered the administration for practicing "Foreign Policy as Social Work," and Walter McDougall, who trashed the administration's policy as "Global Meliorism," from *melior,* the Latin word for "better." McDougall wrote:

> Global Meliorism is simply the socio-economic and politico-cultural expression of an American mission to make the world a better place. It is based on the assumption that the United States can, should and must reach out to help other nations share in the American dream. The modal verbs "can, should, and must" in return imply the assumptions that the American model is universally valid, that morality enjoins the United States to help others emulate it, and that the success of the American experiment itself ultimately depends on other nations escaping from dearth and oppression.[24]

Like the anonymous citizens surveyed in the Chicago Council's poll, many foreign policy specialists and practitioners are wary of, and even hostile to, global meliorism. They believe that it dilutes American influence, expends money and energy that should be conserved, and ignores the harsh realities of the human condition to sally around the globe trying to bring democracy to failed states in Africa or peace to brutalized but marginal countries or dignity to women in tradition-bound societies. They don't buy Albright's argument that marginal improvements in the lives of village women in the Andes, for example, are important or even relevant to the advancement of America's fundamental interests. To them, the Clintons and Albright are to foreign policy what Ramsey Clark was to law enforcement.

Mandelbaum described Clinton's team as "a group of people who, during the Carter administration, had been uncomfortable with and unsuccessful at waging the global conflict with the Soviet Union, but who believed they could take the political capital the public had furnished for 40 years to oppose the Soviets and put it to uses they deemed more virtuous. In this they were wrong."[25] Albright seemed especially annoyed by Mandelbaum's comments and rejected his "social work" analogy. "These policies are not some kind of international social work," she said. "They respond to the reality that pollution, disease and despair respect no national borders."[26] But Mandelbaum, a professor at Johns Hopkins University's School of Advanced International Studies, is hardly alone in his convictions.

"The persistence of geopolitics, or realpolitik, has come as a rude and distressing shock to the neo-Wilsonians who took office under Clinton," wrote another prominent commentator, Harvey Sicherman.

Many were veterans of the only administration that genuinely attempted to transcend the geopolitical approach to world affairs—Jimmy Carter's. They believed that the collapse of Soviet power had made the "enlargement" of democracy and free markets possible and, indeed, inevitable. In their view, the era of the meat-eaters was over and that of the plant-eaters at hand. American power should therefore be harnessed to various projects the Cold War had precluded, such as the enforcement of human rights, economic cooperation, arms control and reinvigoration of the

United Nations—with nation-building a sideline to hurry along any Third Worlders too dim to recognize the dawning of the new day. . . . What has happened to U.S. foreign policy over the past several years, therefore, is this: the more the Clintonians pressed their plant-eater agenda, the more room they made for the meat-eaters, with the perverse result that geopolitics, far from becoming obsolete, returned with a vengeance.

Citing events in the Persian Gulf, Haiti, Bosnia, China, and Russia as examples, Sicherman added: "All that sorely perplexed and distressed the Clintonians, whose high-minded excursions into the realm of strategy under such slogans as 'enlargement' and 'assertive multilateralism' had been routed by incorrigible events."[27]

Harvard's Samuel Huntington, one of the most provocative contemporary thinkers about the state of the world, wrote:

The argument is frequently made that American "leadership" is needed to deal with world problems. Often it is. The call for leadership, however, begs the question of leadership to do what, and rests on the assumption that the world's problems are America's problems. Often they are not. The fact that things are going wrong in many places in the world is unfortunate, but it does not mean that the United States has either an interest in or the responsibility for correcting them.[28]

Similarly, the economic columnist Robert J. Samuelson disputed the administration's thesis that "prosperous and democratic electorates" are the key to global stability. "What's wrong with this vision is that it's neither inevitable nor self-fulfilling," Samuelson wrote. "The lesson of Kosovo is that many conflicts—big and small—exist outside its reassuring framework. Hatreds endure, nationalism survives and poverty rules. We have overestimated our ability to export the U.S. economic model and its associated political virtues. Russia, of course, is the obvious example."[29]

This is, of course, an argument that cannot be settled. As long as human society has existed, philosophers and scholars have contemplated whether it can be perfected and harmonized, or whether it will always be under assault somewhere from greed, violence, or ambition. Albright struggled throughout her tenure to reconcile her proud image as a tough-talking, straight-shooting "doer" with the administration's *Candide*-like belief in human improvement—that is, with its embrace of global meliorism. Still, she seemed surprised when I asked her about Sicherman's "plant-eater" assessment. She responded:

> When I was brought into campaigns, such as the [Michael] Dukakis campaign, I was always the hard-liner. There were those who talked about my anticommunist credentials or whatever. There were doves who kind of automatically said, "Well, Madeleine was born in Czechoslovakia, she's anticommunist, that explains what her problems are." I was discounted for a long time in Democratic politics for being too hard line. So I have always been pretty hard line, very hard line. I don't think you can say that I always choose the toughest option [when preparing options for the president], I always choose what I think is the best option. I consider myself very pragmatic. What I find interesting—I don't want you to think I'm nuts, and that I'm overstating things, but I have been reading the [Dean] Acheson biography—but I describe myself as a pragmatic idealist, and I was very interested that that's the way they described him, somebody who had a goal and tried to sort out what the best method was to get it.[30]

Despite its ultimately successful outcome, the 1999 air war against Yugoslavia demonstrated the mismatch between the objectives of American foreign policy and the tools available to bring them about. When the overriding objective was to deter Soviet aggression and avoid nuclear war, the development of the NATO alliance and the maintenance of strategic superiority, or at least parity, were—and were seen to be—the appropriate instruments. When the objective is to promote democracy or end ethnic conflict in countries of dubious importance to American interests, the choices are murkier. This was a chronic problem for the Clinton administration and will remain a chronic problem for the next several administrations, Republican or Democratic. In small countries, such as Bosnia and Haiti, the United States may have the power to impose its vision by sending in troops. But does it have the right to do so? Or the obligation? Or the money? Except in the rare cases where stark and clear-cut choices are presented and everyone can understand the stakes—as in Iraq's invasion of Kuwait—every action or inaction will be debatable, and some of the choices made will turn out to be wrong.

Even during the Cold War, presidents and secretaries of state made near-catastrophic choices. With the possible exception of Gerald Ford, who watched helplessly as Saigon fell to the North Vietnamese but who was clearly not to blame, every president since Dwight Eisenhower has at least one major blot on his foreign policy copybook. For John F. Kennedy, it was the Bay of Pigs. For Lyndon Johnson, it was the Vietnam War—to which he sent half a million troops even though, as we now know, he believed from the start that the effort was doomed to failure. For Richard Nixon, that great strategic thinker, it was the secret bombing of Cambodia, which facilitated the rise of the Khmer Rouge, and the coup against Salvador Allende in Chile. For Jimmy Carter, it was the Iranian revolution and the seizure of the American embassy in Tehran. For Ronald Reagan, it was the Iran-Contra scandal. And for George Bush, it was inaction in the face of Serb aggression in Bosnia.

Saying that other leaders blundered, too, is not meant as a defense of Clinton and Albright. It is to point out that foreign policy decisions are difficult to make and often have unintended consequences that may not become evident for years. I believe, for example, that it was a good thing that the helicopter-borne mission ordered by Carter in an attempt to free the hostages at the embassy in Tehran was aborted before arriving in the capital; had the mission reached Tehran, the rescuers and the hostages would have been killed. But what if the mission had somehow succeeded, like Israel's raid at Entebbe? Carter would have emerged as a decisive, perhaps heroic leader and saved his presidency. With lives at stake and the security of the country on the line, such choices are made in a crucible, and are always easy to second-guess.

Albright has been secretary of state in a time when the American people are prosperous and at peace. Nobody on her watch has sent nearly 60,000 Americans to die in a faraway country for a futile cause. Some of the decisions she made and some of the advice she gave the president will turn out to have been wrong. But if secretaries of state were chosen by election, Albright could go to the voters with a creditable record. If things had turned out differently in Kosovo, she might have been remembered as the woman who had forced the issue only to face disaster, but with Milosevic's capitulation she emerged as the pillar of principle who stiffened the spines of the waverers. She forged the alliance that finally faced down Serb aggression in the Balkans and held it together during the war—and she did it without a total rupture with Moscow. At the same time, she kept the Israeli-Palestinian peace negotiations from falling apart completely while Benjamin Netanyahu was prime minister, so that Netanyahu's successor, Ehud Barak, could build on a foundation that was still intact. She nursed the relationship with China and opened the door to better relations with Iran. That is not an inconsequential list of accomplishments.

It is still too early to determine how Madeleine Albright's policies will affect the hard choices that lie ahead for the most critical countries: China, Russia, Iran, Indonesia, Brazil, Congo. She has never resolved the tensions that have been inherent in Bill Clinton's administration between pragmatism and "global meliorism," and between commonsense diplomacy and domestic political considerations. But there can be no doubt what Madeleine Albright, as an American, has stood for. As she herself wrote:

> Freedom is America's purpose. Like other profound human aspirations, it can never fully be achieved. Liberty is not a possession; it is a pursuit. And it is the star by which American foreign policy must continue to navigate during the remaining years of this century and throughout the next. ... The success or failure of the American people's foreign policy remains the single greatest factor in shaping our own history and the future of the world.[31]

If that vision makes her a plant-eater in a world of meat-eaters, she will live with it proudly.

NOTES

CHAPTER 1

1. *Wall Street Journal*, February 13, 1997, A19.

2. *Vanity Fair*, November 1998, 177.

3. *USA Weekend*, cover story, February 26, 1999.

4. *Bay Window* (Hudson's Bay High School, Vancouver, Wash.), November 24, 1998, 10.

5. Madeleine Albright, remarks at induction ceremony, National Women's Hall of Fame (Seneca Falls, N.Y., July 11, 1998).

6. Madeleine Albright, address to Women's Foreign Policy Group (Washington, D.C., November 19, 1996).

7. For details on the support of women's groups for Albright's candidacy, see Ann Blackman, *Seasons of Her Life* (New York: Scribner, 1998), 255–265.

8. Warren Christopher, remarks at Madeleine Albright's confirmation hearing, U.S. Senate (Washington, D.C., January 8, 1997).

9. Madeleine Albright, interview by Ed Bradley, *60 Minutes*, CBS, February 9, 1997.

10. Blackman, *Seasons of Her Life*, 153–158; see also *Vogue*, September 1997, 641–642.

11. For a full account of Albright's life before her appointment as secretary of state and the development of her network of political connections, see Michael Dobbs, *Madeleine Albright: A Twentieth-Century Odyssey* (New York: Henry Holt, 1999).

12. Molly Sinclair, "Woman on Top of the World," *Washington Post*, January 6, 1991, F1.

13. *Washington Post*, April 27, 1994, 13.

14. Ibid.

15. Ibid.

16. Philip Gourevitch, *We Wish to Inform You That Tomorrow We Will Be Killed with Our Families: Stories from Rwanda* (New York: Farrar, Straus, and Giroux, 1998), 150–151.

17. Compiled by the United States Information Agency; available: [www.usia.gov/admin/005/wwwh1213.html].

18. Blackman, *Seasons of Her Life,* 268–270.

19. Amre Moussa, conversation with *Washington Post* reporters, March 7, 1997.

20. Eduard Balladur, conversation with author, January 19, 1997.

21. Conversation with author, February 21, 1997.

22. Sonny Callahan, remarks at hearing of House Appropriations Subcommittee on Foreign Operations (Washington, D.C., February 12, 1997).

23. John Kerry, remarks at Madeleine Albright's confirmation hearing, U.S. Senate (Washington, D.C., January 8, 1997).

24. *Vogue,* September 1997.

25. Madeleine Albright, interview by author, June 3, 1997.

26. Richard M. Mills Jr., "Tales of the Transition," *State Magazine,* May 1997, 14.

27. Warren Christopher, *In the Stream of History: Shaping Foreign Policy for a New Era* (Stanford: Stanford University Press, 1998), 330–331.

28. Ibid., 332.

29. Ibid.

30. *Washington Post,* December 27, 1993, D1.

31. This account is based on interviews with administration officials and diplomats at the United Nations conducted by the author and by John M. Goshko of the *Washington Post.* For a more extensive account in which the deposed secretary-general seeks revenge with a negative and angry view of Albright's role, see Boutros Boutros-Ghali, *Unvanquished: A U.S.-U.N. Saga* (New York: Random House, 1999), 253–334.

32. *New York Times,* June 22, 1996, A1.

33. Albright, interview, June 3, 1997.

34. Madeleine Albright, remarks to social gathering of military wives (Washington, D.C., November 12, 1997).

35. David Cannadine, *History in Our Time* (New Haven: Yale University Press, 1998), 296.

CHAPTER 2

1. Madeleine Albright, interview by author, June 3, 1997.

2. Casimir A. Yost and Mary Locke, *U.S. Foreign Affairs Resources: Budget Cuts and Consequences* (Washington, D.C.: Institute for the Study of Diplomacy, Georgetown University, 1996), 13.

3. *Washington Post,* January 14, 1997, A13.

4. Bill Clinton, letter to Richard Lugar, January 7, 1997.

5. White House, Fiscal Year 1998 International Affairs (Function 150) Budget Request, supplementary fact sheet. Italics in original.

6. Madeleine Albright, Jesse Helms Lecture (Wingate University, Wingate, N.C., March 25, 1997).

7. Jesse Helms, statement to U.S. Senate, March 25, 1998.

8. Madeleine Albright, interview by author, October 30, 1998.

9. Madeleine Albright, address at Henry L. Stimson Center (Washington, D.C., June 10, 1998).

10. Benjamin Gilman, opening statement, hearing of House International Relations Committee (Washington, D.C., October 8, 1998).

11. Madeleine Albright, remarks at Spina Bifida Association dinner (Washington, D.C., October 1, 1998).

12. Richard Valeriani, *Travels with Henry* (Boston: Houghton Mifflin, 1979), 3–4.

13. Albright, interview, June 3, 1997.

14. Valeriani, *Travels with Henry*, 13.

15. Madeleine Albright, remarks at Bronx High School of Science (New York, October 1, 1997).

16. *Washington Post,* May 31, 1997, A20.

17. Albright, interview, June 3, 1997.

18. Madeleine Albright, remarks in tribute to Gerald Ford (Grand Rapids, Mich., April 16, 1997).

19. Statement by the spokesman, February 13, 1997.

20. *Economist,* February 15, 1997, 21–23.

21. Madeleine Albright, interview by author, April 19, 1997.

22. Madeleine Albright, interview by author, October 29, 1998. See also Ann Blackman, *Seasons of Her Life* (New York: Scribner, 1998), 195–196.

23. George W. Ball, *Diplomacy for a Crowded World: An American Foreign Policy* (Boston: Little, Brown, 1976), 200–201.

24. *New York Times,* March 1, 1997, 6.

25. Valeriani, *Travels with Henry*, 19.

26. Ibid., 344–345.

27. Eric Alterman, *Who Speaks for America? Why Democracy Matters in Foreign Policy* (Ithaca: Cornell University Press, 1998), 7.

28. Ibid., 15.

29. Richard Burt et al., *Reinventing Diplomacy in the Information Age* (Washington, D.C.: Center for Strategic and International Studies, 1998), 76.

30. *New York Times,* September 21, 1998, A23.

31. Bill Clinton, veto message to the House of Representatives, October 21, 1998.

32. Kofi Annan, interview by *Washington Post* reporters, October 16, 1998.

33. Albright, interview, October 30, 1998.

34. Christopher Smith, public statement, October 22, 1998.

35. Ted Stevens, remarks at hearing of Senate Appropriations Committee (Washington, D.C., June 17, 1998).

36. White House, "International Affairs Summary and Highlights," Fiscal Year 2000 budget documents.

37. Mitch McConnell, remarks at hearing of Senate Appropriations Subcommittee on Foreign Operations (Washington, D.C., May 22, 1997).

38. John E. Reilly, ed., *American Public Opinion and U.S. Foreign Policy 1999* (Chicago: Chicago Council on Foreign Relations, 1999), 8–9.

39. Madeleine Albright, address to Business Council on the United Nations (New York, September 28, 1998).

CHAPTER 3

1. Madeleine Albright, address at U.S. Coast Guard Academy (New London, Conn., May 20, 1998).

2. *New York Times*, April 5, 1999, A23.

3. *New York Times*, February 26, 1997, A29. See also Ann Blackman, *Seasons of Her Life* (New York: Scribner, 1998), 281–293.

4. Madeline Albright, remarks at Jewish Museum (Prague, July 13, 1997).

5. Madeleine Albright, address to State Department Holocaust Conference (Washington, D.C., December 1, 1998).

6. Richard A. Melanson, *American Foreign Policy Since the Vietnam War: The Search for Consensus from Nixon to Clinton*, 2d ed. (Armonk, N.Y.: M. E. Sharpe, 1996), 113.

7. George W. Ball, *Diplomacy for a Crowded World: An American Foreign Policy* (Boston: Little, Brown, 1976), 330.

8. Madeleine Albright, remarks at State Department news conference (Washington, D.C., March 25, 1999).

9. Colin Powell, *My American Journey* (New York: Random House, 1995), 576.

10. *Defense Business*, August 1998, 13.

11. James F. Dobbins, "Haiti: A Case Study in Post–Cold War Peacekeeping," *Institute for the Study of Diplomacy Reports* (Georgetown University, Edward A. Walsh School of Foreign Service), vol. 2, no. 1 (October 1995): 6.

12. Madeleine Albright, address to American Legion (New Orleans, September 9, 1998).

13. Madeleine Albright, remarks at State Department ceremony (Washington, D.C., February 9, 1999).

14. Madeleine Albright, remarks at hearing of House International Relations Committee (Washington, D.C., February 25, 1999).

15. Maureen Steinbrunner, remarks at Center for National Policy (Washington, D.C., January 13, 1998).

16. *Economist*, August 15, 1997, 17.

17. Elizabeth Drew, *On the Edge* (New York: Touchstone Books, 1995), 320.

18. *New York Times*, August 10, 1993, A19.

19. Richard Holbrooke, remarks at Global Economic Forum (Washington, D.C., January 12, 1998).

20. Douglas Brinkley, "Democratic Enlargement: The Clinton Doctrine," *Foreign Policy*, no. 106 (Spring 1997): 119.

21. *Washington Post*, June 13, 1993, A33.

22. Madeleine Albright, address at George Mason University (Fairfax, Va., March 19, 1998).

CHAPTER 4

1. *Washington Post*, February 1, 1998, C9.

2. Madeleine Albright, interview by John F. Kennedy Jr., *George*, February 1998, 78.

3. Richard Holbrooke, remarks at Global Economic Forum (Washington, D.C., January 12, 1998).

4. Madeleine Albright, remarks at news conference, National Press Club (Washington, D.C., May 12, 1998).

5. Madeleine Albright, address at U.S. Coast Guard Academy (New London, Conn., May 20, 1998).

6. Strobe Talbott, remarks at press briefing (Washington, D.C., May 28, 1998).

7. Ibid.

8. Jesse Helms, remarks at hearing of Senate Foreign Relations Committee (Washington, D.C., May 13, 1998).

9. Madeleine Albright, address at Henry L. Stimson Center (Washington, D.C., June 10, 1998).

10. James Rubin, State Department daily press briefing (Washington, D.C., May 29, 1998).

11. Atal Bihari Vajpayee, address to Indian Parliament (New Delhi, May 27, 1998), item 10.

12. Madeleine Albright, remarks at news conference (Geneva, June 4, 1998).

13. Naresh Chandra, interview by author, June 15, 1998.

14. Albright, remarks (Geneva, June 4, 1998).

15. Sandy Berger, conversation with *Washington Post* reporters, June 17, 1998.

16. Strobe Talbott, press briefing (Washington, D.C., June 18, 1998).

17. Jaswant Singh, "Against Nuclear Apartheid," *Foreign Affairs*, vol. 77, no. 5 (September–October 1998): 44–46.

18. Strobe Talbott, "Dealing with the Bomb in South Asia," *Foreign Affairs*, vol. 78, no. 2 (March–April 1999): 110–122.

19. *Washington Post*, June 21, 1998, C7.

20. Leonel Jospin, conversation with reporters, June 19, 1998.

21. Madeleine Albright, remarks at "town meeting," Ohio State University (Columbus, Ohio, February 18, 1998), transcript recorded by Legi-Slate, Inc.

The transcript of this event posted on the State Department's web site omits many of the notations about shouting and hecklers.

22. *New York Times,* August 17, 1998, 15.

23. *Washington Post,* August 27, 1998, A1.

24. Madeleine Albright, telephone interview by author, August 28, 1998.

25. Madeleine Albright, interview by Larry King, *Larry King Live,* Cable News Network, July 6, 1998.

26. *International Herald Tribune,* March 28, 1998.

27. Robert Zoellick, quoted in the *Baltimore Sun,* July 20, 1998.

28. Robert Novak, syndicated column, July 16, 1998.

29. *New Republic,* September 7, 1998, 12.

30. *Economist,* August 15–21, 1998, 25.

31. Ibid.

32. Albright, interview, August 28, 1998.

33. Madeleine Albright, interview by Wolf Blitzer, Cable News Network, September 1, 1998.

34. Tom Pickering, interview by author, August 28, 1998.

35. *Washington Post,* January 13, 1999, A11.

CHAPTER 5

1. Charles Kurzman, "Soft on Satan: Challenges for Iranian-U.S. Relations," *Middle East Policy* (June 1998): 64–65.

2. Warren Christopher, interview by author, July 16, 1998.

3. Madeleine Albright, conversation with *Washington Post* reporters, October 28, 1997.

4. See Graham Fuller, "Repairing U.S.-Iranian Relations," *Middle East Policy* (October 1998): 140–144.

5. James P. Foley, statement, August 18, 1998. Foley was the State Department's deputy spokesman.

6. Madeleine Albright, address to Asia Society (New York, June 18, 1998).

7. Kamal Kharrazi, address to Asia Society (New York); printed in *Middle East Insight* (November–December 1998): 9–10.

8. "Patterns of Global Terrorism 1998," State Department report, available: [www.state.gov].

9. Martin Indyk, remarks at hearing of House International Relations Committee (Washington, D.C., June 8, 1999).

CHAPTER 6

1. See, for example, the text of the pretrip background briefing for the press by a "Senior State Department official" on September 8, 1997. By State Department rules, the briefer could be quoted but not named. To anyone fol-

lowing the issue closely, this cover was so thin as to be transparent. It was Dennis Ross.

2. Madeleine Albright, remarks at breakfast meeting with *Washington Post* reporters (Washington, D.C., October 28, 1997).

3. Madeleine Albright, interview by student reporters, Hudson's Bay High School, Vancouver, Wash., October 30, 1998.

4. Arab American Institute, statement, October 2, 1998; and James Zogby, interview by author, October 2, 1998.

5. Hillary Rodham Clinton, remarks at United States Information Agency (USIA) Worldnet discussion with Israeli and Arab students (May 5, 1998), as recorded by USIA.

6. Amre Moussa, conversation with reporters, Egyptian ambassador's luncheon, October 3, 1997.

7. Hanan Ashrawi, remarks at Center for Strategic and International Studies (Washington, D.C., October 9, 1997).

8. Madeleine Albright, interview by author, October 30, 1998.

9. Madeleine Albright, conversation with reporters, October 7, 1998.

10. Albright, interview, October 30, 1998.

11. *Washington Post,* October 24, 1998, A1.

12. Sandy Berger, remarks at White House briefing (Washington, D.C., October 23, 1998).

CHAPTER 7

1. Monteagle Stearns, *Talking to Strangers: Improving American Diplomacy at Home and Abroad* (Princeton: Princeton University Press, 1996), 3.

2. John Gerard Ruggie, *Winning the Peace: America and World Order in the New Era* (New York: Columbia University Press, 1996), 6.

3. Madeleine Albright, address to American Legion convention (New Orleans, September 9, 1998).

4. Madeleine Albright, "The Testing of American Foreign Policy," *Foreign Affairs,* vol. 77, no. 6 (November–December 1998): 64.

5. Albright, address (New Orleans, September 9, 1998).

6. Sandy Berger, address to Center for Strategic and International Studies (Washington, D.C., March 27, 1997).

7. "America's National Interests" (John F. Kennedy School of Government, Harvard University, Cambridge, July 1996), 11.

8. George Kennan, "Diplomacy Without Diplomats?" *Foreign Affairs,* vol. 76, no. 5 (September–October 1997): 206.

9. Richard A. Melanson, *American Foreign Policy Since the Vietnam War: The Search for Consensus from Nixon to Clinton,* 2d ed. (Armonk, N.Y.: M. E. Sharpe, 1996), 255.

10. Stuart Eizenstat, interview by author, March 23, 1999.

11. Albright, "Testing of American Foreign Policy," 56.

12. Eizenstat, interview, March 23, 1999.

13. Alan Larson, remarks at Institute of World Affairs (Milwaukee, February 16, 1999).

14. Jeffrey E. Garten, "Lessons for the Next Financial Crisis," *Foreign Affairs,* vol. 78, no. 2 (March–April 1999): 80–81.

15. *Washington Post,* November 1, 1998, A10.

16. Madeleine Albright, interview by author, October 30, 1998.

17. Warren Christopher, address to Chicago Council on Foreign Relations (Chicago, March 22, 1993).

18. Warren Christopher, *In the Stream of History: Shaping Foreign Policy for a New Era* (Stanford: Stanford University Press, 1998), 36–37.

19. George Kennan, "America and the Russian Future," *Foreign Affairs,* vol. 29, no. 3 (April 1951): 352.

20. Melanson, *American Foreign Policy,* 270.

21. *National Interest* (Winter 1998–1999): 12.

22. Michael Dobbs, *Down with Big Brother* (New York: Knopf, 1997), 317–318.

23. Madeleine Albright, remarks during joint news conference with Yevgeny Primakov (Moscow, February 21, 1997).

24. U.S. Department of Energy, Office of Nonproliferation and National Security, "MPC&A Program Strategic Plan," 1998.

25. Cited in unpublished paper for private clients.

26. Kim R. Holmes, Heritage Foundation, Heritage Lectures no. 629, January 8, 1999, 4.

27. Ibid., 50.

28. Dimitri K. Simes, remarks at Nixon Center (Washington, D.C., January 8, 1999).

29. *Washington Post,* November 22, 1998, A33.

30. Madeleine Albright, interview by Charlie Rose, November 11, 1998.

31. Strobe Talbott, address at Stanford University (Stanford, Calif., November 6, 1998).

32. Jesse Helms, remarks to Conservative Political Action Conference (Washington, D.C., January 22, 1999).

33. Commission to Assess the Ballistic Missile Threat to the United States, *Final Report* (Washington, D.C.: U.S. Government Printing Office, July 1998).

34. Bill Clinton, remarks at news conference (March 5, 1999).

CHAPTER 8

1. Madeleine Albright, remarks at State Library for Foreign Languages (Moscow, January 25, 1999).

2. *Washington Post,* January 28, 1999, A20.

3. Igor Ivanov, remarks at news conference (Moscow, January 26, 1999), State Department translation.

4. Madeleine Albright, remarks at Center for National Policy (Washington, D.C., January 21, 1999).

5. *Washington Post,* August 13, 1998, A20.

6. North Atlantic Treaty Organization, press release (99)11, NATO press and media service (Brussels, January 28, 1999).

7. Strobe Talbott, conversation with reporters, Washington, D.C., February 10, 1999.

8. *New Perspectives Quarterly* (Winter 1999): 45.

9. Madeleine Albright, remarks at hearing of House Appropriations Subcommittee on Foreign Operations (Washington, D.C., April 15, 1999).

10. *Wall Street Journal,* April 28, 1999, A18.

11. *Washington Post,* May 24, 1999, A25.

12. *Washington Post,* April 22, 1999, A1.

13. *Washington Post,* April 16, 1999, B7.

14. *Time,* May 17, 1999, 35.

15. Madeleine Albright, remarks on *Good Morning America,* ABC-TV, May 21, 1999.

16. *Washington Post,* May 24, 1999, A1.

17. Madeleine Albright, remarks at news conference (Washington, D.C., June 3, 1999).

18. Madeleine Albright, interview by author, June 4, 1999.

19. *Newsweek,* June 21, 1999, 48.

20. George Robertson, remarks to the Royal United Services Institute (London, June 30, 1990).

21. Rose Gottemoeller, remarks at Carnegie Endowment for International Peace (Washington, D.C., April 20, 1999).

Chapter 9

1. White House, "A National Security Strategy for a New Century" (October 1998), 1; available: [www.whitehouse.gov].

2. George W. Ball, *Diplomacy for a Crowded World: An American Foreign Policy* (Boston: Little, Brown, 1976), 319.

3. Zbigniew Brzezinski, *The Grand Chessboard: American Primacy and Its Geostrategic Imperatives* (New York: Basic Books, 1997), 196.

4. Susan Rice, conversation with reporters, May 15, 1999.

5. Madeleine Albright, "The Testing of American Foreign Policy," *Foreign Affairs,* vol. 77, no. 6 (November–December 1998): 53–54.

6. Nadezhda Mihailova, interview by *Washington Post* reporters, June 17, 1997.

7. Monteagle Stearns, *Talking to Strangers: Improving American Diplomacy at Home and Abroad* (Princeton: Princeton University Press, 1996), 157.

8. Strobe Talbott, remarks at Foreign Service Institute (Arlington, Va., September 10, 1996).

9. Elizabeth Drew, *On the Edge* (New York: Touchstone Books, 1995), 140.

10. Talbott, remarks (Arlington, Va., September 10, 1996).

11. See Donald Kennedy et al., *Environmental Quality and Regional Conflict* (New York: Carnegie Corporation, 1998).

12. See, for example, *Strategic Forum Newsletter* (Institute for National Strategic Studies, National Defense University, Washington, D.C.), no. 7 (September 1994).

13. Warren Christopher, *In the Stream of History: Shaping Foreign Policy for a New Era* (Stanford: Stanford University Press, 1998), 413.

14. Warren Christopher, undated memorandum circulated within the State Department (early 1996).

15. Warren Christopher, address at Stanford University (Stanford, Calif., April 9, 1996).

16. Madeleine Albright, address at University of Minnesota (Minneapolis, June 14, 1998).

17. Edward Gnehm, interview by author, April 12, 1998.

18. Madeleine Albright, remarks at Foreign Service Institute (Arlington, Va., April 9, 1997).

19. Madeleine Albright, interview with author, June 3, 1997.

20. Strobe Talbott, "Globalization and Diplomacy: A Practitioner's Perspective," *Foreign Policy,* no. 108 (Fall 1997): 72–74.

21. State Department, Advisory Committee on Religious Freedom Abroad, "Final Report of the Advisory Committee to the Secretary of State and to the President of the United States" (May 17, 1999).

22. Frank E. Loy, interview by author, May 24, 1999.

23. Madeleine Albright, "The Rights of Women: A Challenge for the Americas," statement to the Summit of the Americas (Santiago, Chile, April 18, 1998).

24. Dan Geisler, interview by author, March 24, 1998.

25. See account of this visit, *Washington Post,* May 5, 1997.

26. Talbott, "Globalization and Democracy": 81.

27. These and related documents on environmental policy are posted on the State Department's World Wide Web site at [www.state.gov].

28. *State Magazine,* September–October 1997, 2.

29. Madeleine Albright, remarks at International Women's Day (March 12, 1997).

30. *Washington Post,* June 3, 1999, A19.

31. Madeleine Albright, remarks to Afghan refugees (Nasir Bagh camp, Pakistan, November 18, 1997).

32. Madeleine Albright, Theresa Loar, and Hillary Clinton, remarks at media roundtable (Washington, D.C., March 11, 1998).

33. White House, presidential memorandum, March 11, 1998.

34. Jane S. Jaquette, "Women in Power: From Tokenism to Critical Mass," *Foreign Policy*, no. 108 (Fall 1997): 27.

35. Francis Fukuyama, "Women and the Evolution of World Politics," *Foreign Affairs*, vol. 77, no. 5 (September–October 1998): 34.

36. Madeleine Albright, remarks at International Women's Day (Washington, D.C., March 11, 1998).

37. Albright, "Testing of American Foreign Policy": 63.

CHAPTER 10

1. Richard Holbrooke, *To End a War* (New York: Random House, 1998), 22–23.

2. Elizabeth Drew, *On the Edge* (New York: Touchstone Books, 1995), 138.

3. Ibid., 139.

4. Douglas Brinkley, "Democratic Enlargement: The Clinton Doctrine," *Foreign Policy*, no. 106 (Spring 1997): 112.

5. Moises Naim, "Clinton's Foreign Policy: A Victim of Globalization?" *Foreign Policy*, no. 109 (Winter 1997–1998): 34–35.

6. Warren Christopher, address to Chicago Council on Foreign Relations (Chicago, March 2, 1993).

7. Madeleine Albright, "The Testing of American Foreign Policy," *Foreign Affairs*, vol. 77, no. 6 (November–December 1998): 53.

8. Douglas Brinkley, "Democratic Enlargement: The Clinton Doctrine," *Foreign Policy*, no. 106 (Spring 1997): 119.

9. Kim R. Holmes, "The Foreign Policy Challenge: A Conservative Agenda," Heritage Foundation, Washington, D.C., 1998, 8.

10. *New York Times*, March 7, 1999, sec. 4, 3.

11. *Washington Post*, September 29, 1993, A10.

12. Albright, "Testing of American Foreign Policy": 57.

13. Madeleine Albright, interview by author, June 3, 1997.

14. *Time*, May 17, 1999, 35.

15. Warren Christopher, interview by author, July 16, 1998.

16. John E. Reilly (ed.), *American Public Opinion and U.S. Foreign Policy 1999* (Chicago: Chicago Council on Foreign Relations, 1999), 36–37.

17. Jeane Kirkpatrick et al., "Security and Insecurity: A Critique of Clinton Policy at Mid-Term," Empower America, Washington, D.C., 1994, vi.

18. Ibid., 5–7.

19. See, for example, Madeleine Albright, remarks to Hugh O'Brian Youth Leadership Group (July 23, 1998); see also Madeleine Albright, interview by John F. Kennedy Jr., *George*, February 1998, 78.

20. Albright, "Testing of American Foreign Policy": 57.

21. *Washington Post,* March 23, 1998, A10.

22. Madeleine Albright, remarks at hearing of Senate Finance Committee (Washington, D.C., July 9, 1998).

23. Reilly, *American Public Opinion,* 22.

24. Walter A. McDougall, *Promised Land, Crusader State: The American Encounter with the World Since 1776* (Boston: Houghton Mifflin, 1997), 173–174.

25. Michael Mandelbaum, "Foreign Policy as Social Work," *Foreign Affairs,* vol. 75, no. 1 (January–February 1996): 19.

26. Madeleine Albright, address to Silicon Valley Forum (San Jose, Calif., October 29, 1998).

27. Harvey Sicherman, "The Revenge of Geopolitics," *Orbis,* vol. 41, no. 1 (Winter 1997): 8.

28. Samuel Huntington, "The Erosion of American National Interests," *Foreign Affairs,* vol. 76, no. 5 (September–October 1997): 36.

29. *Washington Post,* May 26, 1999, A29.

30. Madeleine Albright, interview by author, October 30, 1998.

31. Albright, "Testing of American Foreign Policy": 29.

BIBLIOGRAPHY

Alterman, Eric. *Who Speaks for America? Why Democracy Matters in Foreign Policy.* Ithaca: Cornell University Press, 1998.

Ball, George W. *Diplomacy for a Crowded World: An American Foreign Policy.* Boston: Little, Brown, 1976.

Blackman, Ann. *Seasons of Her Life.* New York: Scribner, 1998.

Boutros-Ghali, Boutros. *Unvanquished: A U.S.-U.N. Saga.* New York: Random House, 1999.

Brzezinski, Zbigniew. *The Grand Chessboard: American Primacy and Its Geostrategic Imperatives.* New York: Basic Books, 1997.

Christopher, Warren. *In the Stream of History: Shaping Foreign Policy for a New Era.* Stanford: Stanford University Press, 1998.

Dobbs, Michael. *Madeleine Albright: A Twentieth-Century Odyssey.* New York: Henry Holt, 1999.

Drew, Elizabeth. *On the Edge.* New York: Touchstone Books, 1995.

Holbrooke, Richard. *To End a War.* New York: Random House, 1998.

Isaacson, Walter. *Kissinger: A Biography.* New York: Simon and Schuster, 1992.

McDougall, Walter A. *Promised Land, Crusader State: The American Encounter with the World Since 1776.* Boston: Houghton Mifflin, 1997.

Melanson, Richard A. *American Foreign Policy Since the Vietnam War: The Search for Consensus from Nixon to Clinton.* 2d ed. Armonk, N.Y.: M. E. Sharpe, 1996.

Ruggie, John Gerard. *Winning the Peace: America and World Order in the New Era.* New York: Columbia University Press, 1996.

Stearns, Monteagle. *Talking to Strangers: Improving American Diplomacy at Home and Abroad.* Princeton: Princeton University Press, 1996.

Valeriani, Richard. *Travels with Henry.* Boston: Houghton Mifflin, 1979.

INDEX